MACHIAVELLI'S GOSPEL

MACHIAVELLI'S GOSPEL

The Critique of Christianity in *The Prince*

William B. Parsons

UNIVERSITY OF ROCHESTER PRESS

First published 2016

University of Rochester Press
668 Mt. Hope Avenue, Rochester, NY 14620, USA
www.urpress.com
and Boydell & Brewer Limited
PO Box 9, Woodbridge, Suffolk IP12 3DF, UK
www.boydellandbrewer.com

ISBN-13: 978-1-58046-491-8

Parts of chapter 3 were published in "'La Carità Propria' and the Uncertain Foundations of Unarmed Principalities," in *In Search of Humanity: Essays in Honor of
Clifford Orwin*, edited by Andrea Radasanu (Lanham, MA: Rowman & Littlefield,
2015), 165–76, and are reprinted with permission.

Library of Congress Cataloging-in-Publication Data

Names: Parsons, William B., 1976– author.
Title: Machiavelli's gospel : the critique of Christianity in The prince / William B.
    Parsons.
Description: Rochester, NY : University of Rochester Press, 2016. | Includes biblio-
    graphical references and index.
Identifiers: LCCN 2016004045 | ISBN 9781580464918 (hardcover : alk. paper)
Subjects: LCSH: Machiavelli, Niccolò, 1469–1527. Principe. | Christianity and
    politics. | Jesus Christ—In literature.
Classification: LCC JC143.M3946 P37 2016 | DDC 322/.101—dc23 LC record
    available at http://lccn.loc.gov/2016004045

A catalogue record for this title is available from the British Library.

This publication is printed on acid-free paper.
Printed and bound by CPI Group (UK) Ltd, Croydon, CR0 4YY

For Heather, with whom all things appear truly possible

No one . . . should be terrified that he cannot carry out what has been carried out by others, for . . . men are born, live, and die always in one and the same order.

—Discourses I.11.5

CONTENTS

ACKNOWLEDGMENTS

Many people helped me complete this book. First among these is my wife, Heather Barnes. Without her, I would not have an academic career. Moreover, she patiently indulged my penchant for writing in the early mornings and much of the weekends these last five years. Second is my editor, Ryan Peterson, who knew this was a book before I did, and generously loaned maximum support and his keen critical eye. I would not have been in a position to write a book on Machiavelli without the outstanding instruction of Michael Palmer and Clifford Orwin, both of whom are also superior Machiavelli scholars. Their lectures and scholarship, which attend closely to Machiavelli's problematic relationship to Christianity, were the true starting point for my inquiry. I am also grateful to the broad community of Machiavelli scholars who have welcomed me into their ranks, despite my astonishing lack of credentials: chief among these are Vickie B. Sullivan, Nathan Tarcov, and Erica Benner, each of whom generously reviewed portions of this work. I thank Alexander Duff and Lorraine Smith Pangle for encouraging my early attempts to examine this subject. I am also grateful to Diego Von Vacano, Thomas L. Pangle, and Guillaume Bogiaris for facilitating my attendance at a Machiavelli workshop at Texas A&M University in February 2014. Many others have reviewed portions of the book: I hope I have profited adequately from the suggestions of Alexandra Hoerl, Benjamin Mitchell, Paul Ulrich, Steven Kelts, Erik Pratt, Jeffrey Metzger, Alexander Orwin, George Crowder, and several anonymous reviewers—including especially the reviewers obtained by the University of Rochester Press. Like most who study Machiavelli, I am indebted to the translations by Harvey C. Mansfield and Nathan Tarcov, who also accomplish herculean interpretive work in their revealing footnotes. Several individuals at my institution helped me: the staff of the Office of the Vice President of Academic Affairs, especially Paula McNutt; Vicki Kirk; Heather Navratil and Kathy Martin at the Corette Library; the Faculty Development Committee; and the members of the Department of Political Science and International Relations supported me in every possible way. Brian Matz and Gerardo Rodriguez charitably fielded my naive questions about the Bible and Christian history. Elvira Roncalli graciously intervened to resolve my most troublesome confusions about Machiavelli's Italian; Donald Jacques displayed his characteristic generosity when fielding myriad questions about Latin and Greek. Henry Jorden, Elizabeth Rabishaw, and Heather Barnes helped to prepare the manuscript, which Robert Fullilove improved with his skillful copyediting and informed judgment. It was my good fortune to work with a copy editor familiar with the New Testament. I also thank the editorial and publicity staff at the University of Rochester Press for their efficient and meticulously professional work. Finally, I wish to thank my daughter, Eudora Rose Barnes, who has recently made my burden especially light. As a comfort to all to whom I owe so much, I remind the reader that any errors, misinterpretations, or mistranslations are mine alone.

INTRODUCTION

Christianity, Christ, and Machiavelli's *The Prince*

Niccolò Machiavelli's *The Prince* serves as a critique of Jesus Christ and his teachings. In particular, *The Prince* instructs readers to abandon Christ as a model for human life and adumbrates a vision of political life that rejects Christian politics as hostile to progress and human flourishing. Crucial to this project is Machiavelli's exhortation to wage war against the Catholic Church: while he comments in the *Discourses* that "its ruin or its scourging is near," he encourages its ruin in *The Prince*.[1] His desire to hasten the ruin of the Church leads Machiavelli to endorse the conquest of Italy and its subjection to princely rule as the surest means to accomplish this goal. Machiavelli's judgment of what might become of Christianity itself, however, is more equivocal. He surely contemplates its ruin, but also imagines that it might be scourged successfully. The requirements of this scourged Christianity, however, appear paradoxical: so damaging are the consequences of Christ's teachings that any politically salutary version of Christianity must abandon the commandment to imitate the life of Christ.[2] Machiavelli's anti-Christian understanding of politics, human nature, and morality inform this plan, but it is his call for an anti-Christian prince that reveals most clearly his revolutionary vision of the future of Italy, Europe, and the broader world. Hence, *The Prince* indicates that Machiavelli's plan entails a rejection—rather than a renewal or renovation—of Christ's teachings and example.[3] Machiavelli is a radical critic of the Church, the teachings it propagates, and its founder.

Attention to Machiavelli's critique of Christ in *The Prince* clarifies his intention in writing the book, which I maintain is largely defined—and limited—by his goals regarding the Church and Christianity. Most of the existing scholarship concerning Machiavelli's view of Christianity limits its analysis to the *Discourses on Livy*, problematically focuses on Machiavelli's presumed private attitudes toward religion, attributes Machiavelli's most cynical statements about religion to the influence of his intellectual milieu, or excuses Machiavelli's troubling statements regarding Christianity with demonstrations of his ardent patriotism: this study will correct these defects.[4] I, instead, seek to make explicit a minor theme of the current scholarship, which recognizes Machiavelli as a teacher of evil, and in opposition to Christ's teaching.[5] *The Prince* communicates this opposition most clearly. By attending to this infamous book, I hope to clarify Machiavelli's broadest vision for modern politics, which consists in the abandonment of Christ as a model for human life and the reformation of European politics along Machiavellian lines, and in accordance with Machiavellian goals of material prosperity, human flourishing, and eventually, liberty.

Machiavelli's Life and Works

Born in Florence in 1469, Machiavelli was, in part, a creature of the Renaissance. Nonetheless, he would seek to transcend that movement in his greatest works. He enjoyed a long and varied career—as a poet, comedian, historian, diplomat, and civil servant—but by his own admission, his life was most clearly marked by a sustained dialogue with the ancient works that the Renaissance made accessible to fifteenth-century Italians: Lucretius, Xenophon, Polybius, Herodian, Livy, and Plutarch are among the authors with whom Machiavelli communed during his philosophical ruminations.[6] While other Renaissance thinkers evince a strong attraction to ancient history and wisdom, Machiavelli appears especially impressed by the contrast he observed between the pre-Christian world described in these ancient books and the world in which he lived: indeed, his greatest works are inspired by this disjuncture. It is true that Machiavelli sometimes advances this contrast between the ancient and modern worlds rather crudely. In particular, he frequently exaggerates the evils of the latter and the virtues of the former. He reinterprets—and even alters—the history of each in order to promote his own plan, which "departs from the orders of others."[7] According to the crudest rendering of this contrast—but one that Machiavelli generally encourages—one world produced an impressive, although sometimes imperiled, host of thinkers and writers, while the other claimed a long, although recently diminished, history of persecution of these men; one practiced a religion made subordinate to civil authority, while the other espoused a universal religion that was indifferent to or dismissive of the claims of earthly powers; one praised a martial virtue supportive of liberty, while the other encouraged a meekness productive of servitude; in sum, one conduced to success, and the other to failure. Thus, Machiavelli's "continuous reading of ancient" (*P* DL) texts led him to argue that the modern world was decidedly inferior to the ancient world. His most important books, *The Prince* and the *Discourses on Livy*, were written to elaborate this critique and to teach modern men how to transform their world. This project led Machiavelli to confront directly the Church and Christianity, which stood as the most decisive impediments to the change he sought to engender.

Machiavelli's relationship to Christianity is both complex and hotly contested. He lived during a period (1469–1527) of profound corruption within the Catholic Church, and his writings are replete with condemnatory accounts of the Church and its prelates.[8] His experience with the iniquity of the Renaissance Church led him, like many of the humanists of his day, to criticize its political influence in Italy and Europe. Like many Italian humanists, Machiavelli sometimes criticizes the Church in language that might have earned him excommunication fifty years later, during the Counter-Reformation: indeed, *The Prince* would appear on the first index of books banned by the Catholic Church.

Nonetheless, I do not judge that Machiavelli's critique of Christianity is conventional. I argue instead that Machiavelli distinguishes himself by offering a radical critique of Christianity: in *The Prince*, Machiavelli blames Jesus Christ and his teachings—rather than contemporary Christians—for the depredations visited upon contemporary Christendom. This critique leads him to reject what is most essential to Christianity: the commandment to imitate the life of Christ. As an alternative to Christ and his teachings, Machiavelli offers new, unchristian models for imitation. He also sketches a new political order, aimed at increasing material security, expanding human power, and creating the preconditions for liberty: this new political order requires, among other things, a radical revision of virtue. To accomplish this revision, Machiavelli teaches his readers that the knowledge and practice of evil is a necessary precondition to the creation of a genuine and tangible common good. His critique of Christ most clearly discloses this knowledge of evil.

Machiavelli died in 1527, uncertain whether his project would ever be accomplished. Painfully aware of his own inability to execute his orders, he left his greatest works to "show the path to someone who with more virtue, more discourse and judgment, will be able to fulfill this intention" (*D* I.P.1). Early modern thinkers like Francis Bacon acknowledge their debt to Machiavelli, and identify a fundamentally new teaching on morality—and a subtle, but important critique of Christ—as among the Florentine's most important legacies.

> We are much beholden to Machiavel and others, that write what men do, and not what they ought to do. For it is not possible to join serpentine wisdom with the columbine innocency, except men know exactly all the conditions of the serpent; his baseness and going upon his belly, his volubility and lubricity, his envy and sting, and the rest—that is, all forms and natures of evil. For without this, virtue lieth open and unfenced. Nay, an honest man can do no good upon those that are wicked, to reclaim them, without the help of

the knowledge of evil. For men of corrupted minds presuppose that honesty groweth out of simplicity of manners, and believing of preachers, schoolmasters, and men's exterior language. So as, except you can make them perceive that you know the utmost reaches of their own corrupt opinions, they despise all morality. *Non recipit stultus verba prudentiæ, nisi ea dixeris quæ, versantur in corde ejus* [Fools find no pleasure in understanding, but delight in airing their own opinions].[9]

Bacon, himself deeply engaged in a project to hasten the arrival of modernity, with all of its worldly charms, sees in Machiavelli's works a rumination on the problem attendant on combining the dovelike innocence of Christ with the worldly wisdom of the serpent, and concludes that "knowledge of evil" is necessary for "honest men" to defend virtue.[10] Yet if knowledge of evil is most necessary to virtue, what is the value of Christlike innocence? Can the two be combined, or must the latter be relegated to mere folly? This is perhaps the most pressing question attendant on Machiavelli's revision of virtue and elaborated critique of Jesus Christ in *The Prince*. It is this question that I seek to answer.

Recent Approaches to Machiavelli's Thought

In the twentieth century, scholars began to give new attention to Machiavelli's intentions. In an early example of this renewed attention, J. H. Whitfield observed that Machiavelli, as a witness to the dismal politics of late-fifteenth-century Italy, "may be, as they say, pitiless in his analysis of what is: he is nevertheless untiringly optimistic with regard to what might be. When Florence falls, and his life-work might seem wasted, the real life-work of Machiavelli begins."[11] But what is the work of Machiavelli's life? What are his goals? Is he an Italian patriot or an unprincipled opportunist? Is he a civic humanist in the tradition of the Renaissance or the proponent of modern realism?[12] Are his seemingly immoral prescriptions excused by his devotion to republican liberty, or are they the hallmarks of villainy? And most important to this study, what does he intend for Christianity? A cursory examination of the scholarship reveals that modern scholars do not agree.

Any review of the literature on Machiavelli ought to begin by sketching the debate between Leo Strauss and the Straussians, on the one hand, and the Cambridge school, established by J. G. A. Pocock and Quentin Skinner, on the other, which centers on a profound disagreement about Machiavelli's intentions and teachings.[13] The debate between the Straussians and representatives of the Cambridge school of Machiavelli scholarship has generated a vast amount of literature: any reader who enters the world of Machiavelli scholarship confronts a slew of interpretations claiming a debt to one or the other tradition. This debate has important implications for the study of the history of political philosophy—and is particularly germane to the question of how one should approach the important texts of the Western tradition.

Both approaches begin with a careful study of Machiavelli's texts, but Straussian scholars—who, despite this monolithic designation, often disagree—tend to hew more closely to what Machiavelli writes in his major works. While their interpretations remain acutely aware of Machiavelli's historical circumstances—especially insofar as Machiavelli alerts the reader to those circumstances—they generally tend to subordinate considerations of Machiavelli's historical circumstances to textual exegesis. While Strauss is the progenitor of this scholarly tradition, Mansfield offers perhaps its most vigorous exposition.[14] What are the reasons for adopting this interpretational method? Judging Machiavelli as a strikingly original and profound thinker, engaged in a dialogue with thinkers of the classical and Christian tradition, the Straussians consider him capable of communicating his full thought in the texts he left behind. If problems arise within the text—for example, if one of Machiavelli's positions is difficult to understand, appears to contradict the historical record, or is too shocking to consider true—these problems ought to be resolved by reference to Machiavelli's text and the historical and philosophical texts to which he refers explicitly (or, as is more frequently the case, those he appears to have used): together, these provide historical information sufficient to understand Machiavelli's intent. Reading his minor works and private correspondence can help to inform or confirm one's understanding of Machiavelli, but they are not crucial to understanding his thought, as communicated in *The Prince* and the *Discourses*.

In their diverse studies, scholars of the Cambridge school generally seek to understand Machiavelli by examining his texts in historical context. If problems arise within the text, they judge that these problems are most soundly answered by referring to Machiavelli's political, cultural, social, intellectual, or religious milieu: his current employment status, his private correspondence, and most importantly, his placement in the political world of Renaissance Italy, the influence of which, these scholars argue, explains much—if not all—of his thought.[15] If the Straussians view Machiavelli as a thinker in a dialogue with the classical and Christian world, those of the Cambridge school generally maintain that Machiavelli is writing with reference to his fellow Italians, living and dead: Lorenzo de Medici, Guicciardini, Petrarch, and others. Considering Machiavelli's service to the Florentine republic and his many positive judgments of republican politics, more generally, they conclude that Machiavelli's chief goal is the restoration of republicanism in Italy.[16]

These competing interpretational schools have bred very disparate presentations of Machiavelli's thought—especially concerning his intention in writing *The Prince* and his critique of Christianity. Yet no scholar has offered a sustained treatment of Machiavelli's critique of Christianity or Christ in *The Prince*. Straussians nonetheless view *The Prince* as crucial to Machiavelli's plan to subvert (or transform) the established moral, political, and religious order, and identify the book as the herald of modernity, with all of its problematic implications.[17] For representatives of the Cambridge school, however, *The Prince* represents a thorny problem: the book's apparent endorsement of tyranny challenges their view of Machiavelli as an ardent republican patriot. Consequently, they seek either to minimize its importance, stressing the necessity that led Machiavelli to write it, or to treat the book as a work of subtle irony.[18]

The Prince and Machiavelli's Judgment of Christianity

Reflective of this division within the scholarly community, the scholarship on Machiavelli's views of Christ and Christianity may be divided roughly into three categories.[19] The first group of scholars argues that Machiavelli's writings are diametrically opposed to Christian teachings, and that his long-term project is the destruction of the Church and the transformation of political life as defined by Christianity. Many of these scholars also elaborate Machiavelli's implied critique of Christ himself, especially as it emerges in chapter 6 of *The Prince*.[20] Elements of this first approach may be found within Strauss's works on Machiavelli, but Harvey Mansfield, Nathan Tarcov, and Leo Paul de Alvarez elaborate this position most fully.[21]

The second group of scholars maintains that while Machiavelli is indeed hostile to many features of Christianity and Christian politics, his plan is to reform Christianity by appropriating its language—and its name—for the sake of his broader project. This reform entails a considerable corruption of Church teachings, to which, according to this interpretation, the unchristian Machiavelli remains indifferent. While elements of this presentation may be found in Strauss's interpretation, Vickie Sullivan is the leading exponent of this thesis, which Mark Hulliung advances less strongly.[22] Distinguishing this interpretation from the first can be difficult. Because both locate in Machiavelli's thought an abiding hostility toward Christianity, the difference between "Machiavelli the destroyer" and "Machiavelli the reformer" can appear obscure.

The third group of scholars—which is the largest, and features much of the Cambridge school—maintains that Machiavelli's opinions on religion are basically conventional. Some of these scholars—most notably, Pocock and Skinner—maintain that Machiavelli's critique of the Church is consistent with late-Renaissance opinion and that his departures from Church teachings are reflective of the Italian humanism of his day.[23] According to Alison Brown, Machiavelli ought to be understood as a member of a distinguished line of religious skeptics created by the intellectual ferment of the period—and especially the recovery of Lucretius's *On the Nature of Things*.[24] Other scholars within this group, however, argue that Machiavelli is a Christian, simply. Thus, they judge that his apparent departures from Church teachings, while problematic from an orthodox Christian perspective, are nonetheless consistent with the particular form of Christianity that could be found in the Italy of his time. Sebastian de Grazia and Cary Nederman advance versions of this thesis, but Maurizio Viroli, who maintains that Machiavelli endorses Christianity as crucial support for civic virtue, is the leading exponent of this position.[25]

Methodology

My attempt to interpret Machiavelli's thoughts on Christ is informed by five judgments. These judgments originate in a reflection on the voluminous scholarship on Machiavelli's political and religious thought. They concern the proper evaluation of context, the relationship between the actions and the thoughts of the most profound thinkers, my assessment of textual evidence, a reflection on Machiavelli's approach to reading history and the Bible, and a consideration of the ways in which Machiavelli critiques the New Testament.

The Problem of Context

While context surely "matters," it is rarely decisive: while readers of Plato's *Republic* can undoubtedly benefit from the knowledge that political innovation was occurring in Athens at the time the dialogue allegedly took place, such knowledge is not necessary to interpret the dialogue's central meaning. To explain Machiavelli's most problematic and unchristian statements by reference to his historical context gives too little credit to Machiavelli, and too much credit to twentieth-century historians of political thought. It limits Machiavelli's thought to that which we imagine a fifteenth-century Florentine might conceive. This approach diminishes Machiavelli's boldness and deproblematizes his wickedness. Context is too often employed to offer an apology for statements for which Machiavelli appears unapologetic.

Reconciling Action and Contemplation

That Machiavelli was a man of both action and contemplation is important, and deserving of serious consideration. Yet while it might be necessary to consider Machiavelli's active life, it does not strike me as decisive in a consideration of his thought in *The Prince* and the *Discourses*, both of which confess his life of action. For example, is it necessary to understand the minutiae of Thucydides's and Xenophon's political and military careers to understand their thoughts, or do their books reveal sufficiently the degree to which practical political events informed their judgments? Consider the following example from *The Prince*. In addition to a general profession of his long experience in politics, in *The Prince* Machiavelli elects to relate two conversations from his diplomatic career. In the first, he reports that a French cardinal, reflecting on Italy's dismal martial record, had informed Machiavelli that Italians do not understand war. Machiavelli tells us that he responded by saying "that the French do not understand the state, because if they had understood they would not have let the Church come to such greatness" (*P* 3). In the second, he listens (in apparent silence) as the "sick to death" (*P* 7) Cesare Borgia justifies his decision to consent to the elevation of an enemy to the papacy. Then, in his eulogy of Cesare, Machiavelli warns the reader that Cesare's belief in reconciliation with the pope was fatal, because it was based on the belief that "new benefits will make old injuries be forgotten" (*P* 7). I judge it significant that Machiavelli, who could choose from a lifetime of diplomatic and military experiences to which he was a party, elects to relate these—and only these—particular stories in *The Prince*. As I shall argue below, his responses to the cardinal and Cesare reflect the theme of the book as a whole, and inform his judgment of Christ as a defective model for human beings. Scholars who scrutinize Machiavelli's political career to explain problems in the text risk obscuring his meaning, which I submit he conveys sufficiently through his text.[26]

Textual Evidence

Given my judgment of these methods, I conclude that there is simply too much evidence within Machiavelli's texts suggesting he was engaged in a more audacious project than scholars of the Cambridge school generally maintain. I shall seek to demonstrate that he explicitly addresses a grander tradition than they tend to identify, and that attention to Machiavelli's text reveals that he seeks an audience beyond Florence, Italy, and even Europe: whereas they tend to cast Machiavelli as an innovative temporizer, I judge him as a destructive founder, intent on securing a new world for his unchristian disciples. His attack on Christianity, Christian politics, and Jesus Christ himself, I argue, is the most important part of this plan.

Machiavelli's Reading of the Bible as History

As support for my argument, I shall consider Christ's lessons in the Gospels, which, as I maintain, Machiavelli opposes throughout *The Prince*. While some may doubt the wisdom of a project that seeks to compare Machiavelli's words to those of the Gospels, without reference to the rich tradition of medieval and Renaissance Christian theology, I judge there to be good reasons for adopting this strategy.[27] First, my method mirrors Machiavelli's own. While his works are scattered with references to Old Testament figures, he never explicitly engages the voluminous theological literature when he discusses events in the Bible, preferring instead to consider Moses's and David's exploits as "the actions of excellent men" (*P* 14). Machiavelli's major works contain no explicit references to the New Testament, and even the oblique references evince no concern with theological debates that might lead a Machiavelli scholar to plunge into their murky depths. For example, during his famous discussion of free will in chapter 25, Machiavelli eschews mention of the intellectual luminaries who contributed to this debate, with whom he was surely familiar. While he treats the Christian figures Savonarola, Saint Gregory, Saint Francis, and Saint Dominic, and quotes from Dante and Petrarch, his treatment of these men is resolutely untheological and, moreover, betrays his anti-Christian animus. He criticizes Savonarola for his lack of arms, rather than the content of his sermons; he writes exclusively and critically about the political implications of the saints' religious power; he misattributes a religious quote of Dante's to a political work, and obscures its meaning; he closes *The Prince* by quoting the pious Petrarch so as to reverse his meaning.[28] As the remainder of the book shall demonstrate, Machiavelli's use of Christian texts and figures is consistently and radically subversive.

Some might claim that my reliance on the text of the New Testament leads to an anachronistic reading of Christianity, and that one should filter his reading of that text through the scholastic intermediaries who dominated Renaissance theology. I believe this is an inapt method for understanding Machiavelli. When Machiavelli writes that he has gained "knowledge of the actions of great men, learned by me from long experience with modern things and continuous reading of ancient ones" (*P* DL), I take him at his word. I judge that Machiavelli's thought consists of his own peculiar commentary on ancient history, rather than a distillation or reflection of modern commentary on that history. Thus, it makes sense to apply this critical approach to understanding Machiavelli's opinion of the New Testament, which is, according to his own curious bifurcation of history, the most ancient of modern texts.[29] This critical approach is a particularly apt tool for understanding Machiavelli's judgment of the Gospels, which purport to be the clearest record of Jesus's "knowledge and actions" (*P* DL).

Indeed, as numerous scholars have noted, Machiavelli's approach to history may be described as skeptical, or even deceptive. He repeatedly alters the Old Testament and Livy to teach the reader distinctly Machiavellian lessons. When it serves his purposes, he omits references to God, ascribes different motivations to historical figures, and obscures the outcome of certain events.[30] As innumerable scholars have noted, Machiavelli distorts the lone direct quotation from the New Testament to appear in either the *Discourses* or *The Prince*: he attributes to the Old Testament's David what Mary attributes to God during the Magnificat (*D* I.26.1). Machiavelli's skeptical approach to history leads him to recommend that one consider (as much as possible) the histories of men without recourse to philosophical or theological intermediaries.[31] The histories of excellent men are puzzling—and often present significant challenges to the modern reader; indeed, their value to modern men depends on retaining their puzzling character, which is too often obscured by justificatory accounts of later philosophers and theologians. To avoid these perils, I have compared Machiavelli's lessons to those of the Gospels, generally without recourse to philosophical commentaries or theological discourses. To those who might claim that I am privileging my own reading over the variously interpreted Gospels, I reply only that I have attempted to conduct a Machiavellian reading of those texts. This means that I have endeavored to read them as Machiavelli read the Old Testament and Livy—with mulish skepticism of the miraculous claims contained therein and especial attention to the broadly political lessons that may be derived from Jesus's life and teachings.[32] The fact that the Gospels do not always agree complicates this attempt; this difficulty is especially acute when Machiavelli alludes to the Gospel of John, which differs significantly from the synoptic Gospels. To overcome this difficulty, I have given all accounts equal weight and have endeavored to indicate significant differences among the accounts in the notes.

The Character of Machiavelli's Critique of the New Testament

Because Machiavelli refers explicitly to Christ only once in his two most important books—and that reference appears in the *Discourses*—it is sensible to ask: how can *The Prince* be a critique of Christ?[33] I argue that Machiavelli discloses his opposition to Christ and his teachings in three ways in *The Prince*. First, many of Machiavelli's teachings simply contradict Christ's, while making no direct allusion to passages from the Gospels. He assumes that his reader possesses an understanding of the Gospels and the rest of the New Testament; by propounding teachings that are diametrically opposed to Christian teachings, he silently refutes the New Testament. This is especially true of his teachings on friendship, acquisition, violence, warfare, and worldly glory.[34] More rarely, however, Machiavelli makes more direct allusions to Christ and his teachings. This is true of Machiavelli's problematic revision of charity, his critique of mercy, his unchristian conception of redemption, and especially his condemnation of unarmed prophets, among whom Christ is the most important example in history—although Machiavelli scrupulously avoids his name.[35] Taken together, these contradictions and critical allusions constitute compelling evidence of Machiavelli's anti-Christian animus. To preserve clarity, I shall endeavor to distinguish carefully between teachings that merely contradict those of the Gospels and teachings that allude to specific biblical passages or characters. A third way in which Machiavelli discloses his anti-Christian animus is by commending or criticizing historical figures to whom he discreetly invites a comparison with Christ: this is true of his praise of Moses and David, but this tactic is particularly evident in chapter 14 of *The Prince*, in which Machiavelli praises Philopoemen as a consummate prince of war and introduces Scipio, whom he later criticizes for the corruption wrought by his extraordinary mercy.[36]

While my interpretation is grounded chiefly in a reading of *The Prince*, I shall also turn to Machiavelli's critical account of Christianity in the *Discourses*. Because Machiavelli asserts that each book conveys his comprehensive understanding, it is helpful to read one with reference to the other.[37] Nonetheless, it is *The Prince* that provides the clearest evidence of Machiavelli's anti-Christian orders.

Plan of the Work

Each subsequent chapter is animated by a question regarding Machiavelli's treatment of Christianity and the political problems and corruption of spirit it engenders. Chapter 1 (chapters 1–5 of *The Prince*) begins to elaborate Machiavelli's opposition to Jesus Christ by examining how Machiavelli's teachings contradict Christ's. Crucial to this critique is Machiavelli's account of the failed invasion of Italy undertaken by Louis XII of France, which demonstrated the ways in which the Church—and Christianity—confound Christians' attempts to make progress in the world by enervating their ambition and exploiting their faith for the benefit of Christianity's corrupt earthly institutions. Moreover, it is in these early chapters that Machiavelli unveils the first of his unchristian teachings—concerning acquisition, friendship, and the proper bonds of communities—that prepare the reader for the radical revision of virtue that occurs in the middle of the work.

In chapter 2, I consider Machiavelli's most unmistakable critique of Christ, especially as it appears in chapter 6 of *The Prince*. There, by condemning unarmed prophets, he illuminates the failures of Jesus Christ in comparison to superior prophet-founders; while Christ attempted to refound a religion armed only with words from God, Machiavelli insists upon the necessity of arms to any successful founding.[38] Hence, Machiavelli invites us to compare Christ unfavorably to Moses. He exhorts men to question the value of meekness and forbearance—too often expressed by Christians as a devotion to pacifism, or extreme ambivalence concerning violence—yet also discloses how Christianity succeeded, despite the manifest defects of its founder.

The critique of Christ's deficient arms is closely related to Machiavelli's critique of Christian politics (chapters 7–13 of *The Prince*), which I treat in chapter 3 of this work. Cesare Borgia, the Church, and the defective arms of Italian republics are the principal subjects of these chapters, but in chapter 10, Machiavelli also offers a "destructive analysis" of the political psychology that allows unarmed princes to survive.[39] That discussion discloses the theoretical core of Machiavelli's plan to subvert Jesus's power over men. This section of the book culminates in Machiavelli's explicit endorsement of the "Prince of War" in chapter 14. His example replaces the deficient model proffered by Christ, the "Prince of Peace." Chapter 14 is the subject of chapter 4 of this work, in which I discuss Machiavelli's most heretical—and most surreptitious—critique of Christ.

I examine Machiavelli's attack on Christian virtue (chapters 15–18 of *The Prince*) in chapter 5. This attack is well defined in the current scholarship, but I nonetheless offer an account of the ways in which Machiavelli's revision of virtue constitutes a rejection of crucial Christian teachings, especially charity, mercy, spiritual firmness, and faithfulness. As an alternative, he encourages his model prince to imitate qualities that will enable him to attack the Christian flock mercilessly.

In chapter 6, I consider chapters 19 through 23 of *The Prince*. Having demonstrated the failures of Christianity and Christ in Europe, Machiavelli begins to offer his plan for the future in these extremely dense and complicated chapters. In chapters 19 and 20, he exposes the radical limits of the papacy, identifying its defect with those of its founder and model. In chapters 20 and 21, he condemns Christianity's most popular military and political strategy—the building of fortresses—and adumbrates the limits of the most successful Christian prince, Ferdinand of Aragon. By disclosing the radical limits of a Christian politics, he exposes Christian political institutions—and, indeed, the religion itself—to acute danger.

Chapter 7 examines *The Prince*'s final rhetorical arc (chapters 24–26). Having established the inability of the preeminent Christian prince to accomplish progress, Machiavelli suggests a way forward in chapters 24 and 25: to reject divine providence, eschew indolence, and wage war against the forces that militate against human endeavors: fortune, God-bred indolence, and the fixity of human nature. As a coda for the book as a whole,

The Prince culminates in a call for a new, armed prophet—and not the return of Christ—to acquire for Italy land, bread, and security. I consider the radical implications of this prophetic and bloody vision of politics, which necessitates the "decapitation" of Italy and the purgative slaughter of its defective arms. I conclude the book by reflecting on what Machiavelli's vision was for Christendom and what are the most important implications of his deliberate rejection of Jesus Christ and his teachings.

CHAPTER ONE

Christianity's Siren Song

In early chapters of *The Prince*, Machiavelli is critical of the Church's delete-rious effect on Italian politics. The scholarship demonstrates this amply.[1] It devotes less attention, however, to the explicitly anti-Christian teachings of these chapters.[2] This book attends especially to those anti-Christian teach-ings. While scholars universally identify Machiavelli's critique of European princes and their ill-advised subservience to the pope, they direct less attention to Machiavelli's critique of several of Christ's most important directives in the first part of *The Prince*. There, he begins to disclose his dis-agreements with Christ—which are far more radical than most of the cur-rent scholarship suggests, and which outstrip his concern with the political influence of the papacy that informs, but is not identical to, his broadest politico-philosophical project: the rejection of Jesus Christ as a model for human beings.

Among the questions Machiavelli addresses are: Should human life be consumed with acquisition? Should men act expeditiously to secure their interests or be confident in providence? Is Christlike friendship possible for human beings? What can faith accomplish? As I shall argue, Machia-velli's response to each of these questions reveals the radically unchristian ground on which he will construct the argument of *The Prince*. Indeed, his efforts in the early chapters of *The Prince* may be understood as a rejec-tion of the Apostle Paul's advice in 1 Corinthians. In his famous ode to Christian love, Paul identifies "faith, hope and love" (13:13) as most cru-cial to Christianity. Machiavelli explicitly rejects the first and last of these dispositions in these early chapters, while problematically appropriating the second. While Christ enjoins men to exhibit faith in their fellow man, Machiavelli will encourage doubt and suspicion; while Christ recommends that men trust in hope, Machiavelli will praise skepticism, preemption, and calculation; while Christ commands men to exhibit love and mercy, Machi-avelli will cite hatred and revenge as superior bonds for communities. This largely implicit critique of crucial Christian teachings prepares the reader for Machiavelli's rejection of Jesus Christ as a founder.[3]

Machiavelli dedicates *The Prince* to Lorenzo de Medici, a hereditary prince who owes his position to a fellow Medici, Pope Leo X. Machiavelli presents himself as an office-seeker, and engages in flattery, referring to Lorenzo throughout as "your Magnificence" (*P* DL).[4] This flattery is, however, rather insulting. "Magnificent" was the epithet given to Lorenzo's illustrious grandfather, who had the same name, but a very different career. The elder Lorenzo was a lauded Italian diplomat and patron of the Renaissance; his grandson could claim rather pedestrian accomplishments; having been placed in his office by the pope, he would die at the age of twenty-seven, leaving no magnificent legacy. By calling young Lorenzo by the name of his illustrious grandfather, Machiavelli invites one to consider the inadequacy of the younger Lorenzo.

As a republican sympathizer who was recently tortured by the Medici, Machiavelli is impertinent to offer princely wisdom—so he offers an image to justify his proffered knowledge. The image places princes on mountaintops and the people (and Machiavelli) on the plains. Machiavelli's unique perspective allegedly excuses his cheek: he can best survey the actions of princes from his low position. While the image suggests that princes are best able to understand the people, Machiavelli never asks Lorenzo for any advice. In fact, the last line of the letter suggests that Lorenzo has squandered even his opportunity to learn about the people, insofar as he appears to be gazing idly at the surrounding mountaintops: "And if your Magnificence will at some time turn your eyes from the summit of your height to these low places, you will learn how undeservedly I endure a great and continuous malignity of fortune."

When contrasted with the knowledge that Machiavelli has secured "with so many hardships and dangers," Lorenzo's indifference to knowledge marks him as unreflective and self-satisfied—and uninterested in the plight of his people, including Machiavelli. Hence, we ought to be skeptical of Machiavelli's stated hope that should Lorenzo read the book, "you will learn from it my extreme desire that you arrive at the greatness that fortune and your other qualities promise you." Fortune is a dubious quality, and Machiavelli has not indicated what Lorenzo's "other qualities" might be. Moreover, insofar as fortune is Lorenzo's only evident quality, Machiavelli's persistence under a "great and continuous malignity of fortune" marks an important difference between the two: Lorenzo's greatest benefactor is Machiavelli's greatest scourge. Does this not make them enemies? A cursory consideration of Lorenzo's career reveals that papal support is arguably the clearest earthly manifestation of Lorenzo's good "fortune." Machiavelli thus begins to disclose his hostility to the Church by slyly indicating his contempt for one of its princely clients.

This hostility toward Lorenzo is confirmed by a reading of Machiavelli's explicit teaching concerning hereditary principalities. That teaching begins in chapter 2, where Machiavelli initiates his formal treatment of principalities with a discussion of princes like Lorenzo. Chapter 2 suggests that hereditary principalities are easy to maintain: the people love their hereditary prince so much that even if some "extraordinary and excessive force" (*P* 2) should cast him out, he will be invited to return by his sheepish people. The first several lines of chapter 3, however, shatter this reassuring image of the hereditary principality. Machiavelli announces that "men willingly change their lords" and that any principality can be secured if the conqueror first murders the extended family of the defeated prince and then maintains the existing laws and tax codes. These pronouncements ought to disconcert the hereditary prince.[5]

Based on the first pages of *The Prince*, it is clear that Lorenzo de Medici— and the hereditary princes he typifies—will not benefit from this book. The dedicatory letter prepares the reader for Machiavelli's rhetorical strategy in *The Prince*: if read quickly, it appears as a polite dedication to a potential political patron. When read with more care and in light of the book as a whole, it impresses the reader as an insolent—and rather sinister—critique of the princes whose failures prompt Machiavelli to write *The Prince*. As the rest of the book makes plain, the dismal record of these princes cannot be extricated from their devotion to Christianity, which prevents them from imitating "the actions of great men" (*P* DL).[6]

Acquisition and Machiavelli's Amoral Classification of Principalities

In the first chapter of *The Prince*, Machiavelli distinguishes among various principalities. His classificatory system is novel, and reflects the amoral character of his political science: he classifies all principalities according to how they were acquired, rather than according to any independent moral standard.[7] By proceeding in this way, he departs from the long tradition of political philosophy. First, he rejects Plato's distinction between just and unjust regimes and Aristotle's classification of regimes according to whether they aim at the common advantage; second, and more importantly, Machiavelli rejects the distinction most common in his own day, which Christians observed between Christendom and the rest of the world.[8] Italians were growing more acutely aware of the presence of non-Christian civilizations during this period. Exploration increased contact with the broader world. The Ottoman Empire, which was approaching the height of its power during the fifteenth century, was becoming increasingly involved in Italian affairs. Machiavelli writes of the Turk and the Sultan of Egypt, yet here, he is indifferent to this crucially important religious distinction, just as he is indifferent to any classificatory principle that orders regimes according to whether they aim at some morally salutary end.[9] Placed in Renaissance Italy—a world dominated by religious divisions and influenced heavily by the resurgence of classical philosophy—Machiavelli views the world as a twentieth-century realist might: the acquisition and application of political power is decisive to his political science.

How did Christ view political regimes? This question is important, because while it is true that Machiavelli's contemporaries generally judged regimes by their devotion to Christianity, Christ seems relatively indifferent to the ends—and, certainly, the acquisition—of earthly government. His famous response to the Pharisees' insistent questions about the taxes owed to Caesar—in which he denigrates, while acquiescing to, the Roman Empire's power—is among his most famous statements on governmental power.[10] The Apostle Paul offers a more extreme version of this teaching in his letter to the Romans, where he recommends submission to governing authorities for two reasons: their placement is ordained by God, and, in any case, the salvation of believers is near.[11] The principal lesson of Romans is that Christ's appearance on earth binds his believers to a law that transcends any claim earthly powers might make; the good Christian thus submits to earthly government, while awaiting patiently the hour of redemption.[12] While Christians' indifferent obedience to civil authority and deference to a higher moral power might be construed as quiet defiance of the former, Romans does not promote earthly revolution. Why bother, when "our salvation is nearer now than when we first believed"?[13] This alerts us to a crucial disagreement between Machiavelli and Christ. While Christ enjoins his followers to "seek first his kingdom and his righteousness, and all these things will be given to you as well," Machiavelli stresses the primacy—and sufficiency—of earthly acquisition.[14]

While the book as a whole may be understood to provide instruction about how to acquire and maintain a principality, Machiavelli also offers an explicit theoretical teaching on acquisition in chapter 3. It is perhaps the most stridently anti-Christian teaching of *The Prince*. While discussing Louis XII's failed invasion of Italy, Machiavelli writes that "truly it is a very natural and ordinary thing to desire to acquire, and always, when men do it who can, they will be praised or not blamed; but when they cannot, and wish to do it anyway, here lie the error and the blame" (*P* 3). Machiavelli concedes that all who acquire may not be praised, but denies emphatically that they will be blamed. Only failures will be blamed.[15]

Importantly, this is not Christ's position. When the Apostle Paul warns Timothy that "the love of money is a root of all kinds of evil," he is conforming to Christ's unequivocal and emphatic condemnation of acquisition.[16] When confronted by a man who wanted his brother to divide an inheritance, Christ responds with reproach: "Watch out! Be on your guard against all kinds of greed; life does not consist in an abundance of possessions."[17] Men who acquire are "fools" (Luke 12:20) who overestimate their ability to provide for themselves and display insufficient faith in God. Consequently, Christ advises his disciples to "sell your possessions and give to the poor. Provide purses for yourselves that will not wear out, a treasure in heaven that will never fail, where no thief comes near and no moth destroys" (12:33). Christ repeats this condemnation of acquisition throughout the Gospels.[18] From his perspective, the problem of acquisition is twofold. First, a devotion to acquisition suggests a lack of faith in God's providence. Second, a preoccupation with acquisition—of money, and the commodities of life—enervates our devotion to God.[19] He judges, "For where your treasure is there your heart will be also"; the danger of corruption is so great that he recommends that his disciples divest themselves of all of their wealth.[20] Indeed, Jesus employs physical violence only once in the Gospels, overturning "the tables of the money changers and the benches of those selling doves, and [he] would not allow anyone to carry merchandise through the temple courts."[21]

Machiavelli conspicuously rejects the Christian teaching concerning acquisition. Acquisition will be the foundation of his new political science—as it applies to principalities, republics, and men.[22] Unlike Christ, he does not blame those who attempt to acquire. His amoral teaching on acquisition presumes avarice among men; rather than discourage it, he seeks to clarify its limits and thereby enable it. In so doing, he claims to be adhering to common opinion, which holds as blameworthy only those who fail. Yet if the desire to acquire is "very natural and ordinary" (P 3), would Machiavelli blame men for their failures? Or will he, departing from common opinion that these men should be blamed, simply judge them to be in error? In this book, Machiavelli displays his unchristian humanity by teaching men how better to acquire the world.

Machiavelli's Problematic Revision of Friendship

Machiavelli's rumination on friendship—arguably, the first positive moral teaching of the book—marks another important departure from Christ's teaching. The discussion of friendship arises in Machiavelli's consideration of the perils of acquiring a mixed principality.[23] Foremost among these is the fact that "you have as enemies all those whom you have offended in seizing that principality, and you cannot keep as friends those who have put you there because you cannot satisfy them in the mode they had presumed and because you cannot use strong medicines against them, since you are obligated to them" (P 3). This is the first mention of "friends" (amici) in the book.[24] Friendship is a crucially important theme of the Gospels. In John, Christ teaches, "My command is this: Love each other as I have loved you. Greater love has no one than this: to lay down one's life for one's friends."[25] This teaching corresponds to Jesus's injunction in the Gospel of Matthew to "do to others what you would have them do to you, for this sums up the Law and the Prophets."[26] Yet Christ discloses most clearly the limitlessness of a Christian's duty to his fellow man in the Sermon on the Mount.

> "You have heard that it was said, 'Love your neighbor and hate your enemy.' But I tell you, love your enemies and pray for those who persecute you, that you may be children of your Father in heaven. He causes his sun to rise on the evil and the good, and sends rain on the righteous and the unrighteous. If you love those who love you, what reward will you get? Are not even the tax collectors doing that? And if you greet only your own people, what are you doing more than others? Do not even pagans do that? Be perfect, therefore, as your heavenly Father is perfect."[27]

Christ thus exhorts us to a godly, universal, and perfect love of man. If we love only our friends, we are not imitating godly love.

Machiavelli's definition of a friend is much narrower than Christ's. In chapter 3, friends are those who have helped you, and expect to gain something for their troubles; their friendship depends on a calculation of benefit. In this particular case, they want to "fare better" (*P* 3) under a new prince's rule; they expect, somehow, that a new ruler will change fundamentally their situation.[28] Machiavelli, however, dismisses their hopes as groundless. When your friends realize—as they must—that you cannot possibly benefit them in the way they expected, they will become your enemies. Machiavelli's friend does not ask, "What have you done for me lately?" but "What will you do for me soon?" If the answer is "nothing," then the friendship is over, logically.[29] Indeed, insofar as Machiavelli suggests that no prince will be able to benefit his friends in the way that is expected, all friendships depend ultimately on a *mis*calculation of benefit—a mistaken belief that other men are solicitous of our interests. Friendship is thus a species of self-deception. Prudent princes can encourage this error in others.

The only thing that prevents a prince from "using strong medicines" (*P* 3) against his former friend, and now enemy, is an obligation (*obligato*): he ought not to be the first to betray the other, even though, as Machiavelli's ironclad reasoning establishes, he inevitably will be betrayed.[30] What is a prince to do? A good Christian, lamenting the evil to which men are prone, might patiently await the dreadful moment of betrayal. Yet those already corrupted (or inclined thereunto) will begin sharpening their daggers and concocting the necessary "medicines." Machiavelli targets the latter group with this teaching on friendship: he encourages them to see clearly that by perpetuating the facade of friendship with men who are truly enemies, a prince is preparing to lay down his own life for his "friends." The unchristian implications of this teaching are clear enough: Machiavelli speaks subtly and conspiratorially to those who doubt their own ability to love their enemies, and the wisdom of doing so.

By presenting betrayal as an inevitable feature of friendship, Machiavelli seeks to arouse in his readers a desire to act preemptively. His endorsement of preemption among men who are nominally friends has important implications. Insofar as friendship is often considered a foundation for justice in political life, Machiavelli undermines our hopes for justice—in principalities, and perhaps in political communities in general.[31] And if we compare Machiavelli's teaching to the Gospels, we can see that he also presents a model contrary to that which Christ exhibits in his relationship to Judas Iscariot. Christ possesses foreknowledge of Judas's betrayal, and yet moves resolutely to his own destruction. When confronted by Judas in Gethsemane, he remarks, "Do what you came for, friend," and instructs his disciples to forgo a violent defense of their savior.[32] Christ's self-sacrifice is a model for his followers, almost all of whom would martyr themselves for their love of him.

Clearly, the Gospels exhort men to risk death for the sake of friendship. In one of the first anti-Christian teachings of *The Prince*, Machiavelli does not. Importantly, both *The Prince* and the Gospels recognize man's capacity for betrayal. Confronted with this feature of human nature, the Gospels exhort men to self-sacrificial love. Machiavelli's unwholesome instruction encourages men to reason coldly about the best means to their own preservation. To explain it bluntly: both acknowledge that betrayals like Judas's will be a regular feature of human life; Christ urges us to show forbearance and to repent, while Machiavelli subtly recommends violent preemptive action. Even more problematically, and as a necessary accompaniment to this unchristian argument, Machiavelli's teaching on friendship seeks to divest the Judases of the world of their guilty consciences.[33]

Machiavelli clarifies his sinister teaching on friendship when he considers the subject of how a prince should be "with subjects and with friends" (*P* 15) in chapters 15–18. He emphasizes the crucial importance of maintaining false appearances: a prince ought never to allow a friend (or a subject) to see his true disposition. Machiavelli's advice contradicts Christ's. Addressing his disciples, Christ says: "I no longer call you servants, because a servant does not know his master's business. Instead, I have called you friends, for everything that I learned from my Father I have made known to you."[34] Machiavelli rejects Christ's ingenuousness as fatally naive. While the appearance of honesty and conventional virtue can enable a prince to "get around men's brains" (*P* 18), Machiavelli concludes that unflinching devotion to those same virtues will ruin a prince, since "human conditions do not permit" (*P* 15) their regular observance.

The wickedness of men requires that the prince engender fear, rather than love, among his friends.[35]

Summarizing what he believes to be Christ's teaching on the subject of love and fear among friends, John teaches, "There is no fear in love. But perfect love drives out fear, because fear has to do with punishment. The one who fears is not made perfect in love."[36] Machiavelli, who denies both the power and the possibility of perfect love, recommends fear as a surer bond of political communities—and friendships. In so recommending, Machiavelli reveals more of the unchristian ground on which he builds his political science.

Some might object that Machiavelli's teaching on friendship applies to the wicked world of politics rather than to human beings, generally speaking. There is much weight to this objection. Although Machiavelli routinely casts men as self-interested power-seekers, his numerous friend-ships—especially those with fellow men of letters—would seem to testify to the existence of friendships that do not end in bloody daggers, spilled wine goblets, and mutual betrayal. He sometimes praises friendship expansively, and it appears to constitute one of the great joys of his life.[37] Nonethe-less, here in *The Prince* Machiavelli urges one to consider the limits of any friendship: can one "lay down one's life for one's friends," or must friend-ships crumble in the face of the pressing necessity of self-preservation?[38] The political friendships that he describes in *The Prince* are perhaps only the most susceptible to this necessity.

Christian Virtue in the Laboratory of European Politics: Louis XII's Failed Invasion of Italy

While chapter 3 begins with Machiavelli's advice about how to add heredi-tary principalities to one's own, he then turns to a more general topic: how to acquire principalities "disparate in language, customs, and orders."[39] His examples of this sort of acquisition are Louis XII's failed conquest of Italy, ancient Rome's successful conquest of Greece, and the modern Turk's conquest of the same province. The clear-sighted Romans refused to defer necessary wars, practiced preemption by crushing forcibly even the smallest sign of revolt, speedily created colonies, and steadily extended their empire; the modern Turk, whom Machiavelli mentions as a success, but does not examine fully, lived in Greece so as to maintain that conquest; Louis's abortive imperial venture would end in a tangle of broken alliances and a French defeat.[40] Machiavelli's extended comparison of ancient Rome and modern France thus reveals the superiority of the Romans to the French king, and prepares the reader for a general lesson of the book: ancient princes succeed, while modern princes fail.[41] His fleeting acknowledgment of the successful Turk reveals, however, that not all modern princes are failures. Why did Louis XII fail? I shall argue that Machiavelli teaches that Louis's reliance on—and residual belief in—Christianity best explains his failure to seize and hold Italy. To consider Louis's example fully, however, we must first consider the details of his attempted conquest, which Machiavelli relates in chapter 3.

Louis XII wanted to invade Italy. He did not, however, possess the friends necessary to facilitate this invasion. He could not gain "a foothold" (*P* 3) within the country. Thus he entered into an alliance with Venice, a powerful commercial republic in northeastern Italy. The Venetians coveted the northern Italian province of Lombardy but did not believe they could conquer it alone. In 1499, Venice and France began a joint venture to subdue and divide Lombardy. This alliance constituted no error: Machiavelli has already insisted that any conqueror must rely on friends to enter a province (*P* 3). After this was successful, however, the Venetians realized they had committed a grave blunder: Louis was greeted by a slew of weak and fearful Italian city-states that were anxious to escape the domination of the two hegemonic powers of north-central Italy: Venice and the Church. As Machiavelli writes, "To acquire two lands in Lombardy, [the Venetians] made the king lord of two-thirds of Italy" (*P* 3). Machiavelli ruminates on the security and promise of Louis's initial position:

> One may now consider with how little difficulty the king could have maintained his reputation in Italy if he had observed the rules written above and had held secure and defended all of those friends of his, who ... [due to their fears of Venice and the Church] were always under a necessity to stay with him; and by their means he could always have secured himself easily against whoever remained great among us. (*P* 3)

Louis squandered this position. While Machiavelli will eventually cite six errors committed by Louis, his most egregious error was his decision to loan an army to Pope Alexander VI so that the latter "might seize the Romagna" (*P* 3). In doing so, he alienated many of his weak allies and increased the temporal power of the Church. Louis realized too late that the ambitions of Alexander VI were fatal to his own interests in Italy.[42] He was later compelled to invade Italy to thwart Alexander but was in a much weaker position than before he made his arrangement with the pope. By 1511, following a series of strategic blunders, Louis would be driven from Italy by the Holy League, led by the Church and aided by Spain.

While subsequent errors certainly worsened Louis's predicament, most of these errors result from his momentous decision to provide Alexander VI with an army. Why did he do this? Summoning imaginary objectors to his account, Machiavelli considers two possibilities. First, he considers whether Louis ought to have conceded the Romagna to the Church and half of Naples to Spain in order to avoid a war with those powers. Repeating the lesson derived from the history of Rome, Machiavelli tersely states "that a disorder should never be allowed to continue to avoid a war, because that is not to avoid it but to defer it to your disadvantage" (*P* 3). The implications of this brief statement are striking. As a temporal power, the Church represents an obstacle to Louis's conquest of Italy.[43] Eventually, France would have needed to declare war against the "Bride of Christ." Machiavelli's analysis ignores the impiety of this act. Instead, he notes merely the error of arming the very power that you will need to defeat in battle.

Machiavelli presents the second possible explanation for Louis's decision to arm the Church as follows: "And if some others should cite the faith [*la fede*] the king had pledged to the pope, to undertake that enterprise for him in return for dissolving his marriage and for the [cardinal's] hat of Rouen, I reply with what I will say below on the faith of princes and how it should be observed" (*P* 3).[44] Machiavelli is referring to chapter 18 of *The Prince*, titled "In What Mode Faith Should Be Kept by Princes." There he instructs a prince to combine the appearance of faithfulness with actual faithlessness: since men do not observe faith with you, you cannot safely observe faith with them. Importantly, Machiavelli names Alexander VI as a model of duplicity: he "never did anything, nor ever thought of anything, but how to deceive men, and he always found a subject to whom he could do it. And there never was a man with greater efficacy in asserting a thing, and in affirming it with greater oaths, who observed it less; nonetheless, his deceits succeeded at his will, because he well knew this aspect of the world" (*P* 18).

Clearly, then, Louis should not have placed faith in Alexander VI. Why did he do so? Louis was not a fool. As Machiavelli's later analysis of France makes clear, being king of France was not an easy task: the king needed to guard himself constantly against the ambitious plots of the barons and lords who populated his country (*P* 4). If Louis had realized that the pope's ambitions would be fatal to his own, it is doubtful that he would have endangered his interests in this way. What prevented Louis from perceiving the threat posed by an armed Church? Machiavelli's imaginary objector suggests that he was constrained by necessity to arm the Church: he needed the cardinalate to consolidate religious control within his country and an annulment to pursue a politically advantageous marriage. Without the pope's support, he could gain neither. Yet Machiavelli categorically rejects this reasoning in a most auspicious way: he departs from his usual third-person narrative to relate a story from his own diplomatic career.

The Political Problem Posed by "the Faith"

Machiavelli had a long career as a public servant and diplomat in Florence. His correspondence reveals that he was directly involved in scores of important political and military events. Yet while his experiences inform his judgment and supply many of his examples, he generally refrains from recounting his own role in these events. Indeed, in *The Prince* and the *Discourses*, he relates only three such examples. Each of these circumstances involves the exercise of papal power; in each, Machiavelli recommends a strategy for opposing or diminishing the power of the Church.[45] Chapter 3 contains one of the two firsthand reports of his diplomatic activity to appear in *The Prince*—a conversation with the cardinal who had gained the "hat of Rouen" as a result of Louis's agreement with Alexander VI. Machiavelli reports that "when the cardinal of Rouen said to me that the Italians do not understand war, I replied to him that the French do not understand the state, because if they understood they would not have let the Church come to such greatness" (*P* 3).

If the greatness of the state is indeed undermined by the ascendancy of the Church, this lesson may be understood in three ways. First, as discussed above, the Church's greatness in Italy is an impediment to the state in a conventional sense: its territorial ambitions thwart those of the French king. Second, and more importantly, the Church's greatness *within France* constitutes an impediment to the greatness of the French state. Louis, as a Christian king of a Christian people, is constrained to defer to this greatness in two decisive respects: the appointment of a religious figure and the granting of his annulment. His desire to secure two favorable religious decisions leads him to give the pope an army—a gift no prince would grant to a hostile temporal power. Constrained to display obeisance to a foreign religious power that claims authority within his own state, Louis finds himself at the mercy of that institution. Third, and perhaps most decisively, however, Machiavelli reveals that the greatness of the Church constitutes a subtler, psychological impediment to Louis's—or any Christian's—ambitions: its teachings imperil men by exhorting them to exhibit a misguided faith in their fellow man.

Machiavelli's critique thus invites a fuller discussion of "the faith" (*la fede*) Louis had pledged to Alexander VI. This marks the first appearance of this term in *The Prince*.[46] While it could be read as one Italian noun among many, it is important to note that *la fede* is also among the most common epithets of Christianity. Insofar as "the faith" is described as crucial support for Louis's decision to trust the leader of the Church, Machiavelli's usage appears particularly pregnant. Most literally, "the faith" Louis pledged consisted in a promise to provide arms in exchange for these religious determinations. Clearly, however, another sort of faith minimized the perceived dangers of this pledge: Louis had faith that Alexander VI would be an honest partner in this exchange. He did not believe that the pope would betray him. The earlier discussion of the requirements of Christian friendship, and the commandment that one ought to "do to others what you would have them do to you," is relevant to this discussion, because Louis—a king whose kingdom demanded canny management of ambitious barons and lords—evidently believed that Alexander VI would display more faith than the "malcontent" (*P* 4) and innovating barons of France.[47] So while Alexander VI's lack of faith is striking, Louis's credulity in this story is also surprising. This would-be conqueror displays an ill-founded faith in the leader of "the faith." Machiavelli encourages us to conclude that the religious authority of the pope is crucial to this deception, and is ultimately responsible for the failure of the most promising attempt to unite Italy by means of external conquest that would occur in Machiavelli's lifetime.

Overcoming the Problem of Mixed Principalities

Machiavelli rejects categorically Louis's decision to aid the Church. But faced with the need to annul his marriage to Jeanne de Valois so as to marry Anne of Brittany and keep that province united with France, and secure the appointment of a cardinal, what ought he to have done?[48] As de Alvarez implies, Machiavelli's reasoning suggests a solution akin to that employed later by Henry VIII of England, when faced with very similar circumstances.[49] Desiring an annulment of his marriage to Catherine of Aragon and finding the pope disinclined to grant his request, Henry VIII convinced the archbishop of Canterbury to dissolve the marriage. When the Church responded by excommunicating the English king and the archbishop, Henry VIII united political and religious power within England. By way of a series of parliamentary acts, Henry was declared head of the Church of England and responsible for all ecclesiastical appointments. Obedience to the pope, rather than the king, would henceforth constitute an act of treason.[50] Henry's acts marked an important step in the Protestant Reformation, and in the gradual decline of papal power in Europe. Importantly, Louis might have avoided the errors that Machiavelli catalogs had he pursued a similar strategy by granting the religious authority to Rouen on his own authority, declaring himself head of the Church of France, and beginning a war against the Roman Church—a war that Machiavelli has already judged inevitable and necessary.[51]

Yet Louis proved himself incapable of this bold strategy. One can discern the cause of his incapacity by considering the juxtaposition of his example with that of ancient Rome—which, at the time of the conquests Machiavelli describes in chapter 3, was still a republic. Both regimes sought to create mixed principalities by conquest. Rome succeeded, largely because it refused to defer wars to its disadvantage and relied entirely on its own power. Louis did not. He was less clear-sighted, and more reckless, making and breaking alliances and enlarging his possessions haphazardly. "The faith" that Louis placed in Alexander contrasts sharply with Rome's consistently clear-sighted and suspicious view of human beings. Rome trusted no one, and trusted in no other power but its own. Its judgment was uncorrupted by the Christian siren song that commands men to love even their enemies, a commandment that Machiavelli has indicated is fatal to its adherents.

Yet in the circumstances surrounding Louis's expulsion from Italy, a particularly salient difference between Louis and Rome emerges. Louis relied on a foreign power (the Church) for political legitimacy. The Romans, who exhibited "virtue" and behaved as "wise princes should," did not (*P* 3). As Vickie Sullivan and Harvey Mansfield observe, Louis's failure reminds us that Rome—with its civil religion—was not constrained by a foreign religious power.[52] Indeed, when directed by prudent captains, Rome's religion provided crucial support for military exploits. Rome succeeded in acquiring mixed principalities because, in part, by surreptitious means it rendered everything it touched "Roman."[53] In this respect, Rome was fundamentally different from France—and all other European countries. As chapter 3 reveals, modern Christian nations are constrained profoundly by the Church's temporal and spiritual powers. In this way, France, like all European countries, is a "mixed principality." This admixture of domestic civil power and foreign religious power enervates the power and will of the state and is the best evidence that "the French do not understand the state" (*P* 3). Louis's failure also shows how the faith lays claim on the souls of believers, whose power and will are thus enervated.

With this comparison of ancient pagan Rome and modern Christian France, we are reminded that a crucial change has occurred in world politics since the ascendancy of the Roman Republic. The Roman Empire eventually dominated world affairs. In its wake, the Church of Rome, with its calls for love of one's fellow man, has risen as both a moral and a political power: it is able to convince otherwise prudent men to have faith in their fellows and can steer the course of world events with wholly spiritual powers—the powers to appoint bishops and dissolve "holy" unions. Its universal and absolute character, in contrast to the particular and flexible character of the Roman civil religion, hinders successful international conquest.[54] More than any other cause, it is Louis XII's inability to understand or defy these powers that leads to his failure.

Italian Political Geography 101

Chapter 4 contextualizes Louis's failure by revealing more fully the snares into which he fell after invading Lombardy. Machiavelli accomplishes this by elaborating (albeit indirectly) the political geography of Italy. By disclosing the complex political structures of Italy, and especially the crucial role of the Church in Italian politics, Machiavelli arms a potential conqueror with important knowledge—knowledge that may be directed against the "Bride of Christ," among other Italian powers.

The title of chapter 4 refers to several ancient pagans, and contains no examples of contemporary Italy.[55] Given the ostensible aim of the book, the absence of such examples should strike the reader as odd.[56] The question of this chapter is: why did Asia, which Alexander the Great conquered just before his death, fail to rebel from Alexander's successors? Before he answers this question, Machiavelli engages in a long digression that purports to classify all principalities "of which memory remains" (*P* 4). It is this digression that is of interest here, because by Machiavelli's own admission, it communicates the key to understanding Italy, as well as all other principalities. By comparing Machiavelli's practical account of Italy in chapter 3 to the theoretical account of principalities in chapter 4, one can gain a better understanding of how to conquer—and thereby unify—Italy.

Machiavelli begins his digression by explaining that all principalities have governments like that of the Turk or that of the king of France. Under the monarchy of the Turk, one prince directs several servants, who act as his ministers (sanjaks) and serve at his discretion. They hold the prince in great authority, but do not bear him any particular love. Under the French monarchy, one prince manages "an ancient multitude of lords" (*P* 4), each of whom owes his position to hereditary right. These subordinate lords are held in affection by their peoples, and so the French king cannot harm them with impunity. "Turkish" kingdoms are more difficult to attack, because "one cannot be called in by the princes in that kingdom, and one cannot hope to facilitate the enterprise through rebellion of those around him": even if one persuades a few ministers of the Turk to betray their king, those traitors will not be able to "bring their peoples with them," and so any conqueror "must necessarily assume that he will find [the Turk] entirely united, and he better put his hope more in his own force than the disorders of others." "French" kingdoms are easier to attack, since "malcontents and those who desire to innovate can always be found," and as hereditary princes, these malcontents can deliver the support of their peoples.

While "French" kingdoms may be easier to attack, Machiavelli judges that they are difficult to hold. The conquering prince finds himself surrounded by several unmanageable princes, each with a distinct and legitimate base of power. Typically, these men also aspire to kingly rule. As the reasoning of chapter 3 suggests, the conquering prince cannot satisfy these lords in the way that they hope—and so the conqueror of a "French" kingdom is surrounded by those who will inevitably betray him. Once conquered, the "Turkish" kingdom, however, is relatively easy to hold. One must only eliminate the "bloodline of the prince," and then "there remains no one whom one would have to fear, since others do not have credit with the people; and just as the victor could put no hope in them before his victory, he should not fear them after it" (*P* 4). Conquering a "Turkish" principality thus requires a total war, rather than a clever conspiracy. The conqueror must place his faith in his own arms, and eliminate all remnants of the "Turkish" dynasty. The people, accustomed to servitude, will easily slip under the new conqueror's yoke.[57]

The successful and lasting conquest of a "French" kingdom constitutes a thornier—but not insoluble—problem. Of the ancient lords who populate France, Machiavelli writes that "since you can neither content them nor eliminate them, you lose that state whenever their opportunity comes" (*P* 4). The would-be conqueror should not, however, lose hope. In the previous chapter, Machiavelli offered advice about how to conquer and hold these principalities: eliminate the bloodline of the "ancient prince" and refrain from changing laws or raising taxes (*P* 3). This project, applied to an "ancient multitude of [hereditary] lords" (*P* 4), would entail much bloodshed. So, while the conquest of a "French" kingdom is an exceedingly difficult, complex, and bloody undertaking, it is nonetheless possible.

How do these theoretical models of principalities help us understand the complex Italian political landscape, as adumbrated in chapter 3? In one respect, Italy appears to be a highly decentralized version of a "French" kingdom. It is populated by a multiplicity of hereditary princes, but lacks a single "king" who might serve as a centralizing and stabilizing force. The complexity of Italy is increased by the fact that the country—as Machiavelli will disclose in chapter 5—also features a handful of independent republics. In order to conquer Italy, then, one must be prepared to eliminate all of the hereditary bloodlines of the Italian principalities *and* to extirpate the memory of the few spirited republics that persisted to Machiavelli's day.[58] A grim undertaking, this would require the murder of scores of families and the destruction of the last bastions of liberty within Italy.

Yet these bloody measures would be insufficient to accomplish the lasting conquest of Italy, because they do not account for the principal obstacle to such a conquest, as established in chapter 3: the Church, and more specifically, the pope. A few brief reflections confirm that the pope is no mere "French king" of Italy. First, the pontiff lacks the hereditary bloodline of the French king. The Church does not establish the pope's successor until after he dies. Insofar as he claims a bloodline, it is transmitted through the college of cardinals, which may choose any male who is baptized Catholic as the next pontiff—but usually elects the successor from the higher ranks of the ecclesiastical order. As Machiavelli argues in chapter 11, this fact helps explain why the Church has typically struggled to assert temporal power. Although Machiavelli does not indicate this here (he will do so in chapter 19), the Church resembles the kingdom of the Turk in its succession practices. During Machiavelli's day, Turkish rulers did not name their successors during their lifetime.[59] Typically, they would scatter their sons among various provincial governorships; after the death of the ruler, these potential heirs would battle for the throne—this process, codified in the mid-fifteenth century—was subject to the influence of court intrigue and often resulted in fratricide.[60] In Machiavelli's time, papal succession was also subject to court intrigue; he claims that the factional conflict of the Orsini and Colonna families best explains the erratic succession practices of the papacy and the weakness of that institution (*P* 11). As in the kingdom of the Turk the new pope might hail from any region of Christendom, although proximity to the capital city was among the most auspicious attributes a candidate could possess.[61] The pope could also claim more extensive authority than the French king: with cardinals, bishops, and priests established at his discretion throughout Italy (and Christendom), the pope possessed an administrative structure that resembled that of the Turk who could make and unmake sanjaks at his pleasure. The ecclesiastical order generally lacked the temporal power of Turkish sanjaks, but as Louis's desire to influence the appointment of the cardinal of Rouen makes clear, they nonetheless possessed important political influence.[62]

If the pope's position resembles that of the Turkish "king," the rules for a successful conquest are clear enough. A prince ought to eschew conspiracies that require the involvement of the ecclesiastical order, since they are "slaves" who are "bound by obligation" to the pope (*P* 4). Even if he were to corrupt a wayward cardinal, that cardinal could not bring the people to the conqueror's side: excommunication would deprive the former of his authority. Instead, the prince must defeat the Church in an open battle and, once victorious, eliminate the "bloodline" of the pope. Given the succession practices of the Church, this would require ecclesiasticide: the murder of cardinals, archbishops, bishops, and priests—or, indeed, any man who might plausibly claim the right to inherit the throne of Peter. Machiavelli suggests that if this were accomplished, most Christians would slip easily under the yoke of the conqueror, as they are accustomed to the servitude inculcated by Christianity.

By inviting its comparison with the kingdom of the Turk, Machiavelli reveals the Church's relative weakness. Anyone attacking the Turk will find him armed and united; anyone attacking the Church will find it united and unarmed.[63] This difference between the Church and the Turks results directly from the teachings and examples provided by their religious founders; while Muhammad's rule was predicated on the combination of worldly and spiritual power, Christ's eschewal of worldly power and violence employed in furtherance thereof leaves those who inherit his ministry relatively unprotected.[64]

Thus, if we apply the theoretical models of chapter 4 to the Italy of Machiavelli's day, it appears as though Italy is a highly decentralized version of the French kingdom, but with a Turkish monarchical-administrative structure grafted upon it. The successful conquest of Italy requires much bloodshed—and the exercise of precisely those qualities that Christ instructs us to avoid. Indeed, the task of conquering and unifying Italy seems so great that one might wonder whether Machiavelli actually intends to show its *impossibility*. Yet two stories from Machiavelli's other works suggest otherwise.

The Spiritual Snares Attendant on Conquest of the Papacy: The Cases of Baglioni and Porcari

In the *Discourses* (I.27), Machiavelli relates his wonder at the notion that Giovampagolo Baglioni, an incestuous parricide, balked at killing the impetuous Pope Julius II, who had arrived unarmed to arrest Baglioni. Machiavelli discloses that "the rashness of the pope and the cowardice of Giovampagolo were noted by the prudent men who were with the pope, and they were unable to guess whence it came that he [Baglioni] did not, to his perpetual fame, crush his enemy at a stroke and enrich himself with booty, since with the pope were all the cardinals with all their delights" (I.27.1). Baglioni proved himself incapable of the destruction of the Church hierarchy that might have facilitated its eventual conquest. According to Machiavelli, the men assembled concluded that Baglioni's reticence "arose from men's not knowing how to be honorably wicked or perfectly good; and when malice has greatness in itself or is generous in some part, they do not know how to enter into it" (I.27.1). Yet Machiavelli corrects this judgment in the very next sentence, opining that Baglioni

> did not know how—or to say better, did not dare, when he had just the opportunity for it—to engage in an enterprise in which everyone would have admired his spirit and that would have left an eternal memory of himself as being the first who had demonstrated to the prelates how little is to be esteemed whoever lives and reigns as they do; and he would have done a thing whose greatness would have surpassed all infamy, every danger, that could have proceeded from it. (I.27.2)

Baglioni, whose audacity is evidenced by his many crimes, does not dare to assassinate the pope and the college of cardinals, even though the act would have filled his coffers and burnished his reputation. This inability attests to the power the Church holds in the hearts of men. In Christendom, even the inveterately sinful tyrant is possessed by a residual piety that prevents him from acting reasonably to pursue his interests. Baglioni's daring—which enabled him to flout familial, religious, and civil laws—evaporates when confronted by the Holy Father.[65]

The tale of Messer Stefano Porcari communicates a different potential obstacle to a Christian's attempt to conquer the papacy. In the *Florentine Histories*, Machiavelli informs us that Porcari wished "to be called the new founder and second father" of Rome, and conceived that he ought to conspire to "take his fatherland from the hands of the prelates."[66] His hopes were buoyed by the "evil customs" (*FH* VI.29) of the ecclesiastical order and his belief in the prophetic quality of a *canzone* of Petrarch's, which seemed to foreshadow the ascendancy of a noble man who would redeem Rome. Convinced that he was this redeemer, "he was unable to conduct himself in a mode cautious enough not to reveal himself" (VI.29). The pope banished him to Bologna, whence he directed his conspiracy from afar. Under suspicion by ecclesiastical authorities, he nonetheless attracted a number of coconspirators, whom he invited to a dinner in Rome. He appeared among them ostentatiously at the end of the meal, instructing them to "steady their spirits" (VI.29) and disclosing his plan to execute a putsch against the Vatican. Before Porcari could execute his plan, however, the pope learned of the plot—either because Porcari made his presence in Rome manifest or because of the "little faith" (*poca fede*) of some of his friends.[67] Porcari and most his of coconspirators were arrested and executed. Machiavelli concludes: "And truly the intentions of this man could be praised by anyone, but his judgment will always be blamed by everyone because such undertakings, if there is some shadow of glory in them, have almost always very certain loss in their execution" (VI.29).[68]

Yet given the peculiar nature of Porcari's defects, one ought to question Machiavelli's qualified judgment that such plans will "almost always" fail (VI.29). Porcari's belief in the divinely ordained nature of his mission certainly endowed him with requisite daring, but it also engendered in him a fatal combination of recklessness and ostentation. Could a more sober—and less credulous—man succeed where Porcari failed?

Arrested after a dinner with his followers, in the city from which he was estranged, and at the end of which he discloses fully his plan for "so glorious an undertaking" (VI.29), Machiavelli's account of Porcari's last evening of freedom constitutes a crude allusion to Christ's.[69] Like Christ, it is unclear whether he is doomed by the watchfulness of hostile authorities or by friends who demonstrated "little faith" (VI.29). This allusion is not accidental: convinced of the prophetic quality of Petrarch's poetry, Machiavelli portrays Porcari as a Christian believer. He is not, to be sure, a typical Christian: Machiavelli praises the "excellence of his spirit" that impelled his ambition and convinced him of his superiority "to every other Roman" (VI.29). Thus, while his proud excellence renders him similar to the successful ancient Romans, the faith he evinces in his own divine purpose renders him similar to Christ. By inviting a comparison of Porcari's and Christ's careers, Machiavelli warns readers of the snares that await believers who attempt to conquer the papacy. In particular, the conviction that one might serve a divine purpose by scourging the papacy is extremely dangerous. A Christian who believes he is a redeemer will fare poorly when confronted by the cruelty of the papacy, which exceeds Pilate's. While the latter reluctantly executes only Christ, the former executes Porcari and "the greater part of his partners" (VI.29).[70]

While Porcari and Baglioni failed to accomplish their undertakings, taken together, their examples suggest what sort of spirit is needed for successful conquest of the Church. In particular, Machiavelli suggests that the successful conqueror must blend extreme circumspection with audacity. As the example of Porcari suggests, it might be helpful to claim that yours is a divinely inspired mission—provided that you do not actually believe that your purpose is divine. Machiavelli thus teaches that the conquest of the Church is possible—provided that the plan is carefully conceived, discreetly commanded, and boldly executed. In chapter 4 of *The Prince*, Machiavelli aids this project by revealing a crucial weakness of the Church, which is an unarmed "Turkish" monarchy situated amid a multitude of inferior "French" lords. Whether any Christian actually possesses the spirit necessary to accomplish this undertaking, however, remains uncertain.

The Superior Utility of Hatred and Revenge: Machiavelli's Paean to the Anti-Christian Elements of Republican Virtue

At the end of chapter 4, Machiavelli comments that conquests vary in difficulty, according to "the disparity [of virtue] in the subject." The Church's regime, which resembles the Turk's, appears to be among the principalities that are difficult to conquer but easy to hold. It is predicated on the servitude of its members; moreover, because it is unarmed, it ought to be easier to conquer than the Turk's. Hence, in at least one way, the conquest of Italy would be relatively easy to accomplish.[71] Machiavelli's treatment of republics in chapter 5 of *The Prince* complicates this assertion, with its suggestion that republics may doom any attempt to conquer Italy. Most importantly to this study, Machiavelli teaches that they pose an obstacle to conquest precisely because they tend to perpetuate and enflame the anti-Christian passions of hatred and revenge as a means to preserve their political liberty.[72] In republics, the impassioned love of liberty overthrows the love of man taught by Christ. Because this love of liberty manifests itself primarily as hatred and revenge, healthy republicanism is in tension with the demands of Christianity.

Presented amid a great mass of slavish Christians and princely subjects, republicans are the only stubbornly free men to appear in the book. Machiavelli's praise of republican regimes thus directs the reader to the work that reveals his highest aspirations for political life—the *Discourses*. Chapter 5 of *The Prince* ostensibly teaches princes how to acquire republics, which are described as "states . . . accustomed to living by their own laws and in liberty." After some equivocation, Machiavelli resolves: "There is no secure mode to possess them other than to ruin them" (*P* 5). French and Turkish kingdoms may be conquered with a combination of victory on the battlefield and acts of violence directed against ruling families, but the successful conquest of republics requires their utter destruction—or the relocation of the prince to the conquered territory.

> And whoever becomes patron of a city accustomed to living free and does not destroy it, should be expected to be destroyed by it; for it always has as a refuge in rebellion the name of liberty and its own ancient orders which are never forgotten either through length of time or because of benefits received. Whatever one does or provides for, unless the inhabitants are broken up and dispersed, they will not forget that name and those orders, and will immediately recur to them upon any accident . . . so that the most secure path is to eliminate them or live in them. (*P* 5)

Machiavelli is well known for his high praise of republics—both here and in the *Discourses*—yet his praise here is not particularly friendly. Republics may stubbornly resist conquest, but sufficient violence can secure even them.[73] Unsurprisingly, Machiavelli cites Rome as eventually successful in its attempts to conquer them.[74]

Republican obstinacy contrasts sharply with the weakness and servility of the peoples Machiavelli describes in the early chapters of the book. Once acquired, both the hereditary principalities of Christendom and the kingdom of the Turk can be held with relative ease. The Church, insofar as it appears to be an unarmed version of the Turkish kingdom, can also be defeated—so long as one does not fall into the snares laid by "the faith." Republics alone appear capable of retaining political agency in the absence of their leaders, and defending their sovereignty. It is not sufficient to defeat them on the battlefield; nor can one reduce the people to obedience by assassinating their "ruling" classes. What explains the resiliency of republics?

Machiavelli's general analysis suggests two answers. First, republics are strong because they, unlike principalities, can claim a supply of "infinite virtuous princes" (*D* I.20.1) to whom they might turn in a time of emergency. If a conqueror eliminates the bloodline of the hereditary prince, none will be left alive to challenge his rule; the inequality inherent to principalities produces a "slight aptitude for free life" (*D* I.17.3) that is difficult to overcome.[75] The relative equality within republics, however, means that every citizen is a potential threat; any might pick up the standard of republican liberty and resist a conquering army.

In addition to their structural superiority, Machiavelli also suggests that republics enjoy a spiritual advantage over principalities. It is their spiritual superiority that most directly pertains to this study, because Machiavelli's praise of the republican spirit provides definitive evidence of his dim opinion of the political utility of Christian teachings—and the impossibility of combining Christ's lessons with a free way of life. In the *Discourses*, Machiavelli discloses that republicans love their liberty because it offers them wealth, security, prosperous children, and for some, the ability to command (*D* I.16; II.2.1–3). In chapter 5 of *The Prince*, Machiavelli attributes republics' resilience to certain crucial passions—or characteristics of the soul—including "greater life, greater hatred, [and] more desire for revenge." Due to the presence of these passions, republicans' "memory of their ancient liberty does not and cannot let them rest" (*P* 5). Thus, the "life" of republics is sustained and reanimated by hatred and revenge, two passions that constitute sinful behavior, according to Christianity.[76]

Obviously, the New Testament teaches that the life of a Christian ought to be motivated by love and mercy, rather than hatred and revenge. The beatitudes of the Gospel of Matthew are perhaps the quintessential statement on the superior virtue or righteousness of the meek, the merciful, and the persecuted; in this passage, Christ enjoins his followers to be peacemakers who strive for pureness of heart.[77] He amplifies this teaching on hatred and revenge later in Matthew, when he clarifies his injunction to "love your enemies and pray for those who persecute you."[78]

> "You have heard that it was said, 'Eye for eye, and tooth for tooth.' But I tell you, do not resist an evil person. If anyone slaps you on the right cheek, turn to them the other cheek also. And if anyone wants to sue you and take your shirt, hand over your coat as well. If anyone forces you to go one mile, go with them two miles. Give to the one who asks you, and do not turn away from the one who wants to borrow from you."[79]

Christ's commandment to love and derogation of hatred is inextricably linked to his rejection of revenge: "For if you forgive other people when they sin against you, your heavenly Father will also forgive you. But if you do not forgive others their sins, your Father will not forgive your sins."[80]

Christ is unequivocal in his condemnation of revenge and his exhortation to love, yet his followers portray these teachings in perhaps even starker terms. Although the Apostle Paul concedes that Christians ought to "hate what is evil," he also suggests that this hatred ought to strengthen their devotion to good—and indeed, help them to "overcome evil with good."[81] He instructs believers: "Do not repay anyone evil for evil. . . . If it is possible, as far as it depends on you, live at peace with everyone. Do not take revenge, my dear friends, but leave room for God's wrath."[82] By displaying robust hospitality toward his enemy, Paul suggests that the Christian gains a victory over the persecutor, in which the Christian's imitation of Jesus Christ constitutes a spiritual rebellion, through which he defers to God for ultimate retribution—while modeling Christ's love, forbearance, and patient suffering on the cross.[83] The good Christian is unconcerned with securing an earthly victory—although Paul's preoccupation with God's punishment of sinners indicates that he still thirsts for revenge. In his first epistle, Peter renders the implications of Christ's teachings and example thus:

> Submit yourselves for the Lord's sake to every human authority: whether to the emperor, as the supreme authority, or to governors, who are sent by him to punish those who do wrong and to commend those who do right. For it is God's will that by doing good you should silence the ignorant talk of foolish people. Live as free people, but do not use your freedom as a cover-up for evil; live as God's slaves. Show proper respect to everyone, love the family of believers, fear God, honor the emperor. Slaves, in reverent fear of God submit yourselves to your masters, not only to those who are good and considerate, but also to those who are harsh. For it is commendable if someone bears up under the pain of unjust suffering because they are conscious of God. But how is it to your credit if you receive a beating for doing wrong and endure it? But if you suffer for doing good and you endure it, this is commendable before God. To this you were called, because Christ suffered for you, leaving you an example, that you should follow in his steps.[84]

As Peter insists, patient suffering, rather than a forward defense of earthly liberty, ought to animate the good Christian.

Readers of Machiavelli will recognize that Peter's injunction to "receive a beating" in order to be "commendable before God" is almost identical to the language Machiavelli uses to criticize Christianity in the *Discourses*, where he opines that "this mode of life thus seems to have rendered the world weak and given it in prey to criminal men, who can manage it securely, seeing that the collectivity of men, so as to go to paradise, think more of enduring their beatings than of avenging them" (*D* II.2.2).[85] In this famous passage, which is the root of much of the controversy regarding Machiavelli's opinion of Christianity, Machiavelli vacillates in assigning blame for the weakness of the modern world.[86] He begins by blaming modern education, which is grounded in modern religion. After criticizing several crucial Christian teachings and practices, he concludes that the Christian sacrifices make modern men less ferocious than their ancient counterparts, and prepare them for the subjugation he describes in the passage quoted above. Yet immediately after uttering this condemnation of Christianity, Machiavelli redirects blame to cowardly men "who have interpreted our religion according to idleness and not according to virtue. For if they considered how it permits us the exaltation and defense of the fatherland, they would see that it wishes us to love and honor it and prepare ourselves to such that we can defend it" (D II.2.2).[87]

Thus, while the analysis here has suggested that Christ's teachings are fatal to any hope for earthly liberty, Machiavelli balks at blaming Christ directly. So who disarmed heaven: Christ or his disciples? Machiavelli's allusion to 1 Peter suggests a provocative answer to this question. Exhibiting his characteristic irony, Machiavelli's refusal to blame Christ leads him to blame Peter, the one apostle in whom Jesus chooses to place his full authority: "And I tell you that you are Peter, and on this rock I will build my church, and the gates of Hades will not overcome it. I will give you the keys of the kingdom of heaven; whatever you bind on earth will be bound in heaven, and whatever you loose on earth will be loosed in heaven."[88] Indeed, one ought to remember that Peter was the first Church father, the first bishop of Rome, and the first—and the only directly appointed—"Vicar of Christ."[89] Thus, Machiavelli's more direct blame of Peter constitutes indirect criticism of Christ. Quite ridiculously, then, does Machiavelli accuse Peter of promulgating a "false interpretation" of Christianity, the ascendancy of which helps explain the decline of republics: "the world appears to be made effeminate and heaven disarmed" because of the "cowardice" (D II.2.2) of Peter, the man identified by Jesus Christ as the "rock" on which his Church will be built.[90] So can one really blame Peter and his fellow apostles for the "weakness into which the present religion has led the world" (D I.P.2), while excusing Christ? Machiavelli's text, when considered alongside these New Testament passages, suggests that the answer is no. Instead, we must conclude—following Harvey Mansfield—that Machiavelli's equivocations in this chapter are designed to provide "false comfort" to Christianity's disillusioned supporters.[91]

Yet Machiavelli's account in *Discourses* II.2 also offers a more direct—and much more devastating—critique of Jesus Christ. Machiavelli identifies the example provided by Christ's crucifixion as an especially problematic educative model. His critique of the crucifixion, and the practice of Holy Communion that seeks to remind us of Christ's sacrifice, occurs in the context of his praise of ancient religious practices. He complains that the humble sacrifices of Christianity compare poorly to the magnificent sacrifices of the Gentiles, which were "full of blood and ferocity . . . with a multitude of animals being killed there. This sight, being terrible, rendered men similar to itself" (D II.2.2).[92] According to Machiavelli, the Gentiles encouraged men to slaughter a multitude of inferior beings, which prepared them well for a violent defense of their fatherland. Christians, however, are told to imitate Christ, who placed himself on the sacrificial altar, to be butchered as the "Lamb of God."[93] Machiavelli suggests that this model of sacrifice, which is central to Christianity, educates men to weakness and servility. It assigns to them the position held by mere domesticated animals within the Gentile religions, and instructs them to submit piously to earthly indignities for the sake of future reward.

Some scholars have suggested that Machiavelli presents Christ's crucifixion as a helpful example for founders of principalities and republics, who might either sanctify their foundings or chasten their noble youths with well-timed human sacrifices.[94] While I concede the value of public executions of partisans and noble youths to Machiavellian political practice, the evidence in the Discourses and The Prince suggests that Christ is a poor model for such executions. The very bloodiness of Christ's sacrifice, which might have provided a helpful political education, is obscured by later Christian tradition, which—again, following Christ's explicit directive—substitutes for the body and blood of Christ mere bread and wine.[95] The passive reception of the Eucharist replaces the active and politically cathartic public execution of men. Rather than leaving its adherents "satisfied and stupefied" (P 7), the Christian Mass encourages "humble and contemplative" (D II.2.2) reflection on torturous physical suffering—often, while listening to the dulcet tones of an Agnus Dei. By offering this model of sacrifice, Machiavelli suggests that Christianity prepares men for their enslavement and slaughter. Peter, who cites the example of Christ's suffering when he instructs Christians to patiently "receive a beating," is following his savior's example precisely.[96] Machiavelli rejects this example.

Yet one need not limit an assessment of Machiavelli's opinion of Christ to an examination of his direct and indirect criticisms of Jesus's followers. In the only explicit reference to Christ to appear in either The Prince or the Discourses, Machiavelli most directly associates Christ with the depredations that have visited Christendom. Writing of the necessity to renew religions periodically, he opines that Christianity too would have been "eliminated if it had not been drawn back toward its beginnings by Saint Francis and Saint Dominic" (D III.1.4). These humble and impoverished saints followed "the example of the life of Christ," generating a renewal that "has maintained and maintains this religion" (III.1.4). Machiavelli thus casually discloses an important—and heretical—judgment: Christ is subject to the same limitations imposed on pagan founders, since his founding is insufficient to guarantee a perpetual sect. Yet the damaging consequences of this renewal are most pertinent to the present argument.

> Their new orders were so powerful that they are the cause that the dishonesty of the prelates and of the heads of the religion do not ruin it. Living still in poverty and having so much credit with the people in confessions and sermons, they give them to understand that it is evil to say evil of evil, and that it is good to live under obedience to them and, if they make an error, to leave them for God to punish. So they do the worst they can because they do not fear the punishment that they do not see and do not believe. (III.1.4)

Resolving any lingering ambiguity concerning the relationship of Christ to certain damaging Christian teachings, Machiavelli here suggests that Christ is the ultimate source of the Christian teaching that gives the world as "prey" (D II.2.2) to the petty criminals that populate modern Europe.[97] Indeed, Machiavelli's language suggests that during the time between the life of Christ and the appearance of these saints, Christianity may have existed under different, less abject, orders: he writes that the saints instituted "new orders" (*ordini loro nuovi*), but also maintains that they drew the Christian religion "back to its beginning" by emulating the "life of Christ" (D III.1.4).[98] Thus, Machiavelli suggests that a more worldly, and less slavish, interpretation of Christianity might have prevailed in those intervening centuries. Elsewhere, Machiavelli writes,

> whoever reads of the modes taken by Saint Gregory and by the other heads of the Christian religion will see with how much obstinacy they persecuted all the ancient memories, burning the works of the poets and the historians, ruining images, and spoiling every other thing that might convey some sign of antiquity. So if they had added a new language to this persecution, in a very brief time everything would have been forgotten. (D II.5.1)

These "persecutions" are surely the "malignity of the times" (D I.P.2) that Machiavelli laments in the *Discourses*. By acting thus, Saint Gregory and the Church fathers espoused an interpretation of Christianity that sought to make its intellectual enemies suffer.[99] Only their reliance on Latin (and, perhaps, Greek) prevented their success. If, however, such a version of Christianity existed, the examples of Francis and Dominic suggest that it must have assiduously avoided imitating Christ, whose example constitutes a thorny obstacle to worldly success.

Yet while the successful imitation of Christ encourages corruption, confirms servitude, and strengthens evil, one must also acknowledge the paradoxical character of Machiavelli's presentation of Christ in this passage: his critique of the effectual truth of Christian teachings also contains implicit praise of those teachings. After all, how could a religion with so little earthly good to recommend it continue to survive—and even thrive? The success of Christianity thus attests to its appealing power. What is the basis of this power?

Machiavelli suggests that Christianity succeeds because it appeals to the people, and in this passage from the *Discourses,* he identifies the rite of confession and the sermons delivered by priests as among Christianity's most powerful tools in this effort. The latter allow the people to gather together to hear stories that confirm the ultimate glory that awaits the impoverished, the meek, and the enslaved; the former represents the crucial requirement of the baptized Catholic who wishes to gain eternal reward and otherworldly triumph over the merely earthly—and sinful—forces of wealth, power, and prestige. Taken together, they—along with baptism and the Eucharist—are Christianity's chief means to enflame and confirm the hope that Christ offers his followers. Nor should we be surprised by Christian priests' uncanny ability to engender fantastic hopes among those who have ostensibly the least reasonable cause to hope. As Machiavelli would have learned from his reading of ancient history and his experience with contemporary Italians, those with the least cause to hope are perhaps most prone to exorbitant hopes. Christianity thus appears to enjoy a symbiotic relationship with human misery: wherever humans suffer most egregiously, priests will find an audience and Christianity will find adherents. Moreover, Christianity's effort to sanctify and glorify that suffering will serve to intensify human misery, poverty, and servitude. This is the core of Machiavelli's objection to Christianity. Crucial to Machiavelli's successful rebellion against this way of life is his appropriation of hope, which he seeks to redirect to the unchristian ends of earthly security, prosperity, and liberty.[100]

According to Machiavelli's teaching in chapters 1 through 5, the pervasive influence of this Christlike behavior largely explains the weakness of Italy, the general servitude of Europeans, and the inability of any conqueror—foreign or domestic—to unify Italy. Republics appear to be an exception to the general rule of Christian politics, and they are able to maintain their liberty, prosperity, and security precisely because they engender the anti-Christian passions of hatred and revenge. Yet the requirement of Christianity that one "overcome evil with good" necessarily enervates the political ethos of republics.[101] This helps to explain why the modern republics mentioned in chapter 5 experience uneven results in defense of their liberty, and in efforts to conquer their neighbors: Pisa falls under the yoke of the Florentine principality for eighty-nine years, and the Florentine republic struggles to reacquire Pisa—eventually reverting to a principality after fourteen years as a republic. Their spotty record ought to be compared with Machiavelli's report of the Roman Republic's activities in chapter 5: it crushed the republics it acquired.[102] Machiavelli's analysis suggests that they succeeded largely because they were unencumbered by the requirements of Christian virtue, and were thus prepared to meet hatred and revenge with sufficient violence.

Conclusion: Resisting the Siren Song of Christian Virtue

As this chapter has demonstrated, Machiavelli engages in an extended—albeit largely indirect—critique of central Christian teachings in the early chapters of *The Prince*. He teaches men that acquisition is a natural necessity, rather than a sin. He teaches that friendship is always conditional, and must thus lead to either betrayal or preemption. He teaches that faith is an unreliable foundation for political judgment. He teaches that hope is a poor substitute for foresight. Of all of Christ's teachings, however, Machiavelli rejects the commandment to love most emphatically. In place of this central teaching of Christ, Machiavelli suggests that fear is a surer guarantor of obedience to a prince, and that hatred and revenge are the principal supports for a free way of life. In sum, Machiavelli teaches that Jesus Christ provides a poor model for political life. Indeed, Christ's influence on politics—seen most clearly in the spiritual power the Church holds over modern Europeans—is pernicious. Thus, while he refrains from confronting directly the model of Christ, his teachings nonetheless exhort men to regard Christian virtue as a siren song that imperils their earthly ambitions.

While Machiavelli shows in the early chapters of *The Prince* that several of Christ's teachings are deleterious to European political life, he will advance a far more radical critique of Christ in the middle chapters of the work. These chapters reveal the full extent of his profound dissatisfaction with the spiritual founder of Christianity, and the necessity of finding a new model for human life.

CHAPTER TWO

Christ's Defective Political Foundations

Chapter 6 of *The Prince* is titled "Of New Principalities That Are Acquired Through One's Arms and Virtue." Machiavelli presents these principalities, which are "altogether new both in prince and in state," as the "greatest examples" (*P* 6). Yet these men are not merely the greatest princes: the preeminent examples in chapter 6 are all religious and political innovators, or prophets—a fact Machiavelli casually discloses in the second half of the chapter.[1] By attributing the accomplishments of these prophets to their own virtue and arms, Machiavelli's title ignores the alleged intercession of divine power that is reputed to have aided each of these men.

Machiavelli names Moses, Cyrus, Romulus, and Theseus as the most excellent examples. They introduced "new orders" (*P* 6) that would result in great civilizations: Judaism, Persia, Rome, and Greece.[2] This list of seminal politico-religious figures of the West is, however, incomplete. Machiavelli neglects to consider two crucially important prophets: Jesus Christ and Muhammad. Why?[3] They founded the two most dominant religions of the day. As Machiavelli was writing *The Prince*, Italy was surrounded entirely by Christians and Muslims. Machiavelli lived within Christendom. Machiavelli's silence about these founders is rendered only stranger by his decision to discuss two inferior examples in chapter 6: Brother Girolamo Savonarola and Hiero of Syracuse. He contrasts these men with the excellent prophetic founders, citing Savonarola as a failure whose demise demonstrates the crucial requirements of successful prophecy and Hiero as a "lesser example" (*P* 6) of the four named above. The inclusion of these inferior examples highlights Machiavelli's silence about Christ and Muhammad, but especially Christ. How does the Prince of Peace compare to these "most excellent" (*P* 6) new princes?

In chapter 6, Machiavelli's implied critique of Christ emerges gradually. In sharp contrast to the last line of chapter 4, and consistent with Machiavelli's revised teaching in chapter 5, Machiavelli says that in altogether new principalities, one encounters more or less difficulty depending on the degree to which one possesses virtue. Some fortune—representing an initial opportunity—is necessary to even these men, but Machiavelli insists that "he who has relied less on fortune has maintained himself more" (*P* 6). Virtue, a term that Machiavelli has used sparingly thus far, appears here to be identical with self-reliance—or relative freedom from fortune.[4] Moses, Romulus, Theseus, and Cyrus each exhibited this quality, but Machiavelli briefly equivocates concerning the inclusion of Moses, opining that "although one should not reason about Moses, as he was a mere executor of things that had been ordered for him by God, nonetheless he should be admired if only for that grace which made him deserving of speaking with God" (*P* 6). Machiavelli grounds his apparent reticence in the claim that Moses—unlike Romulus, Theseus, and Cyrus—actually spoke with God.[5] Paradoxically, however, this divine connection renders Moses less impressive: Machiavelli opines that he may be a "mere executor" (*P* 6) of God's plan, rather than a daring innovator. While this brief equivocation suggests that divine providence might be crucial to the success of the Abrahamic prophets, Machiavelli abandons this reasoning in the very next sentence, obscuring the distinction between Moses (who presumably had divine help) and the others (who presumably pretended to have divine help): "But let us consider Cyrus and the others who have acquired or founded kingdoms: you will find them all admirable; and if their particular actions and orders are considered, they will appear no different from those of Moses, who had so great a teacher" (*P* 6). The pagans' accomplishments are identical to Moses's. It is therefore possible that all of these men—including Moses—founded their principalities without divine support.[6] Machiavelli encourages this conclusion in the next lines, in which he describes the opportunities that allowed the founders to demonstrate their virtue: Moses found the Israelites "enslaved and oppressed"; Romulus was exposed at birth and was not "received in Alba"; Cyrus encountered decadent rulers in Persia; Theseus "found the Athenians dispersed." Machiavelli's account omits any discussion of the divine inspiration that allegedly impelled each of these prophets.[7] Moreover, he locates their signal good fortune in political events rather than in divine intercession. This is an impious view of prophecy, for which Machiavelli—with his problematic equivocation concerning Moses's unique relationship to God—offers a meager apology.

Machiavelli's Blasphemous Classification of Prophets

Because they are compelled to introduce "new orders and modes . . . so as to found their state and their security" (*P* 6), founders invariably find themselves in a very perilous predicament. Machiavelli traces the peril of founders to two sources. First, a founder must confront members of the old order who are his enemies. Second, he cannot rely on his defenders. Their belief in him is lukewarm. Based on Machiavelli's teaching on friendship in chapter 3, the friendship of these defenders was probably granted conditionally, depending on the improvement of their own material states. Machiavelli's analysis thus suggests that their belief in the founder is inextricably linked with their calculation of self-interest, which explains its "lukewarm" (*P* 6) character. These defenders are attracted by the promise of a new order, but are not convinced that their security depends on the founder's success. Most importantly, they do not appear wholly persuaded by the founder's pretensions to divine authority.

Machiavelli writes that founders, in fighting against these forces, may be divided into two types: unarmed prophets and armed prophets. Unarmed prophets are those who "depend on others" and must "beg" or "pray" (*preghino*) for help; armed prophets "stand alone" and "can use force" (*P* 6).[8] Machiavelli stipulates that "in the first case they always come to ill and never accomplish anything; but when they depend on their own and are able to use force, then it is that they are rarely in peril. From this it arises that all the armed prophets conquered and the unarmed ones were ruined" (*P* 6). Machiavelli identifies Moses, Romulus, Theseus, and Cyrus as armed prophets, while furnishing Brother Girolamo Savonarola as the lone example of an unarmed prophet. Although arms help the founder wage war against the old order, Machiavelli reveals that they are most crucial to instituting order and belief among one's own followers.

> For, besides the things that have been said, the nature of peoples is variable; and it is easy to persuade them of something, but difficult to keep them in that persuasion. And thus things must be ordered in such a mode that when they no longer believe, one can make them believe by force. . . . Men such as these, therefore, find great difficulty in conducting their affairs; all their dangers are along the path, and they must overcome them with virtue. But once they have overcome them and they begin to be held in veneration, having eliminated those who had envied them for their quality, they remain powerful, secure, honored, and happy. (*P* 6)

Machiavelli thus identifies a prophet's virtue with the possession of arms. This claim ignores the traditional distinction between true and false prophets, which corresponded roughly to the distinction between pagan prophets and those of the Abrahamic tradition, excluding Muhammad. Instead, Machiavelli blasphemously classifies all prophets according to whether they can ensure their security and consolidate their earthly rule. Moses, Theseus, Cyrus, and Romulus used their own arms to compel belief and consolidate rule—and thus, were successful.[9] Savonarola did not, and failed. Despite his initial equivocation regarding the inclusion of Moses, Machiavelli's analysis is indifferent to the prophets' various pretensions to divine inspiration. Arms appear necessary to and sufficient for the prophets' earthly success; claims of divine support may benefit these men in important ways, but it is not necessary "to found their state and security" (*P* 6).

Machiavelli's juxtaposition of Savonarola—a charismatic Dominican priest who briefly led Florence in rebellion against papal authorities—and these founders is curious. Savonarola's excoriation of papal authorities, religious moralizing, and claims of divine inspiration propelled him to a position of political power in Florence, from which he predicted a scourging of the corrupt Church and the political rebirth of Italy. Eventually, however, Savonarola's inability to stem skepticism within Florence, combined with the growing annoyance of Pope Alexander, ruined him. After failing to demonstrate divine support in a public test of his claims, Savonarola was arrested by a mob within Florence. Tortured by papal authorities, he confessed that he was a false prophet, and was hanged in a city square. His body was burned, and his ashes were strewn in the Arno.[10] Thus, while Savonarola is the only Christian to appear in this chapter, he does not escape Machiavelli's blasphemous classificatory principle: his claims of divine support proved useless in the absence of arms to compel belief among his followers.

As the only Christian example in chapter 6, Savonarola's example is disproportionate to the four founders: rather than found a civilization, he failed to consolidate his rule of a city. His appearance reminds one that Machiavelli has scrupulously avoided a discussion of the most prominent unarmed prophet, and the source of Savonarola's inspiration: Jesus Christ. Indeed, Machiavelli's inclusion of Savonarola is evidence of the particular care with which he approaches the central, albeit implied, question of chapter 6: how should we judge Christ, the prophet whom Machiavelli does not dare to "reason about" explicitly?

Although Savonarola often compared himself to Moses, as a priest, he modeled his career on that of Jesus.[11] His appearance in chapter 6 represents Machiavelli's discreet attempt to discuss Christ's demerits as a prophet and founder. Like Christ, Savonarola preached directly to the people, condemning the status quo and insisting upon a piety that eschewed worldly goods.[12] Like Christ, his prophecies gained credit with the people, before eventually attracting the attention of hostile representatives of the old orders. Like Christ, his supporters eventually abandoned him: their belief dissipated as the religious establishment aligned against him and he failed to demonstrate a miracle.[13] Like Christ, he had no recourse to arms with which he might have made "them believe by force" (*P* 6). Like Christ, he suffered an excruciating death after being castigated as a false prophet.[14]

Nonetheless, Christ's example would seem to rebut Machiavelli's assertion that "the unarmed [prophets] were ruined" (*P* 6). Christ may have lacked an army, but unlike Savonarola, his appearance precipitated the institution of a new order in his name. How might Machiavelli explain his success? To answer this question, one must establish a better understanding of Christ's career as an unarmed prophet and—abandoning Machiavelli's caution—compare the careers of Christ and Moses, in light of Machiavelli's political understanding of prophecy.

Given Machiavelli's suggestion that fortune—in the form of a political opportunity—must precede any founding, neither the Annunciation, nor the baptism of Jesus by John the Baptist, nor the many miracles that Jesus performs constitutes a Machiavellian opportunity.[15] Instead, Jesus's opportunity appears to resemble Moses's. While Moses found the Israelites "enslaved and oppressed" (P 6), Jesus had the good fortune to be born under the reign of Caesar Augustus, whose regime that had "with its arms and greatness, eliminated all republics and all civil ways of life" (D II.2.2)—and had left Jesus's own people oppressed under the empire.[16] By the reign of Augustus, Rome itself had succumbed to political and economic inequality.[17] The Gospel of John suggests the degree to which Jewish religious authorities were subject to Rome. When Pilate asks, "Shall I crucify your king?" the chief priests respond by claiming, "We have no king but Caesar."[18] This remote province of the hegemonic Roman Empire was fertile ground for the liberating promise of heavenly equality that Christ sows in the New Testament.[19] While we might compare Jesus to any of the founders, the text thus recommends a comparison of Moses and Jesus, since they both originate in the Abrahamic tradition and their opportunities lay in the ascendancy of great empires: the Egyptian and the Roman. As further evidence, note Jesus's claim that he comes to "fulfill the law" and the prophets, including Moses.[20]

Yet while Moses and Jesus each seek to enflame the hopes of the meek and the persecuted, their ultimate aims and methods differ significantly. Chief among these differences is their attitude toward arms and their teachings on violence. While warlike Moses always used his own arms, Jesus's eventual success required the intercession of a foreign army: the Roman Empire would serve as Christianity's greatest auxiliary, guaranteeing the promulgation of Christ's orders, which would be perpetuated for centuries by the psychological power of hope, on which Christ relies.[21] A general comparison of Moses and Christ discloses the crucial requirements of founding, explains why Savonarola could not imitate both prophets, and reveals most precisely why Machiavelli considers Jesus Christ a defective political model.

Waging War against Old Orders and the Incredulity of Men: Moses and Christ

Both Moses and Jesus encounter incredulity. First, the representatives of the old orders—the Pharaoh, the Jewish priests, and Pontius

Pilate—reject their claims to divine support, and (in the case of Pharaoh and the Jewish priests) vigorously defend their own authority.[22] Yet their confrontations with the old orders also differ in ways that demonstrate their different teachings on violence. Moses's founding is born in violence, while Jesus's is not: Moses's first act against Pharaoh is to murder an Egyptian who is beating a Hebrew slave, while Jesus's first acts are miracles that save or support lives.[23] Moses is also more truculent than Christ. After his exile, Moses arrives in Pharaoh's court to demand boldly his people's freedom.[24] Jesus's initial strategy is much more indirect. He begins by preaching directly to the people; only as he nears his arrest does Jesus confront representatives of the established political and religious powers more directly.[25] Finally, with the help of incredible violence, Moses eventually escapes the old orders; Jesus, who eschews violence, is crucified by partisans of the old orders, who are unchecked by his unarmed supporters. The most prominent difference between the two founders, then, concerns the role of violence in their founding. Moses threatens or employs violence against the external and internal enemies of the Israelites at every stage of his career. Jesus does not, necessitating recourse to his indirect, and more popular, mode of founding. The laws that Moses delivers to the Israelites promise bloody punishments for a variety of offenses. Christ, whose teaching generally relies on love rather than fear, reminds his disciples, "if you forgive other people when they sin against you, your heavenly Father will also forgive you."[26]

Jesus's general teaching against violence is located in his most important speeches to his followers.[27] His instruction to turn "the other cheek" is the clearest statement of Jesus's departure from the modes of Moses.[28] At his arrest, when his disciples threaten violence on his behalf, Jesus chides them: "Put your sword back in its place . . . for all who draw the sword will die by the sword."[29] In the Gospel of John, Jesus explains that his followers do not defend him against the Jewish leaders because his "kingdom is not of this world," an understanding that the Gospels confirm when an angel appears to "strengthen" Jesus as he prays in the garden before his arrest.[30] Throughout the entire New Testament, Christ exercises force only once—against the money changers whose tables he overturns as he drives them from the temple.[31] Even in those famous and vaguely apocalyptic passages in which Jesus tells his disciples to take up a "sword" or predicts future conflict in his name, his endorsement of violence is ambiguous. Before his arrest, and in contradiction to his earlier instruction, Christ directs his disciples to sell his "garment and buy [a sword]."[32] This passage, however, constitutes thin evidence of Christ's intent to arm his followers in order to resist his impending arrest or accomplish an earthly founding: when his disciples report that they have located two swords, Christ instructs them "that's enough."[33] In his apocalyptic prophesying in Matthew, in which he warns, "Do not suppose that I have come to bring peace to the earth. I did not come to bring peace, but a sword," attention to the context suggests that the sword will be used to divide believers from non-believers, rather than compel belief among "lukewarm" supporters.[34] Indeed, while Christ may intend to turn "a man against his father," the text avers that the followers of Christ will suffer—rather than inflict—violence: taking "up their cross," they will find their lives in heaven by losing them on earth.[35] This direct allusion to the Passion of Christ confirms that Christians ought to submit to violence, rather than inflict it. By doing so, they shall be rewarded in heaven.

As the foregoing passage indicates, the great appeal of Christianity lies in the hope that it offers its adherents. Throughout the New Testament, Christ grounds the hope for otherworldly salvation in the experience of this-worldly suffering. His lack of arms and refusal to employ violence correspond to this teaching. Indeed, Christ explains that those who suffer most egregiously will receive the greatest reward in heaven, insofar as their suffering is a species of Christlike love.[36] Yet Machiavelli's analysis, which derogates radically the importance of prophets' divine pretensions—including their lofty promises of divine reward—suggests that Christ's teaching conduces to earthly ruin. It does so particularly because it deprives a prophet of the means to consolidate support among his followers, which becomes necessary when the prophet encounters situations that enervate his people's belief in him. At this point, Machiavelli suggests that no miracle will save the prophet. He must resort to violence. He who lives by the sword survives, rather than dies.

By offering this teaching on violence while encouraging men to imitate the exploits of the armed prophet-founders, Machiavelli casts hope and fear as the foundation of political life. Hope and fear thus replace the faith, hope, and love proffered by Christ. Faith, hope, and love may possess you with the belief that you can accomplish anything, but they ignore what is most crucial to earthly accomplishments: the judicious use of violence to inspire fear. According to Machiavelli, fear reminds followers of the world as it is, and while it is perhaps limiting to rely entirely on fear, it offers a more stable foundation for political progress than do faith, hope, and love. The ability to inspire fearful belief with palpable violence allows one to establish new modes and orders.

The most famous example of Moses's use of arms to induce fear and compel belief appears in Exodus.[37] There, the Israelites, whose faith in Moses had dwindled during his removal to Sinai, urge Aaron to make a new god for them to worship. This request is predictable, given the "incredulity of men, who do not truly believe in new things unless they come to have firm experience of them" (*P* 6). Aaron complies with their wishes, and their subsequent worship of the golden calf enrages God, who threatens to destroy them. In a private conversation, Moses pleads with God to reconsider his decision, citing the promises he had made to the descendants of Abraham. God relents, and Moses returns to the camp. His first act is to grind the calf into dust, mix it with water, and force the Israelites to drink it. Then, consistent with Machiavelli's analysis of the requirements of prophecy, he employs arms against the Israelites "to make them believe by force" (*P* 6).

> So he stood at the entrance to the camp and said, "Whoever is for the LORD, come to me." And all the Levites rallied to him. Then he said to them, "This is what the LORD, the God of Israel, says: 'Each man strap a sword to his side. Go back and forth through the camp from one end to the other, each killing his brother and friend and neighbor.'"[38]

Faced with lukewarm supporters, Moses has recourse to the arms of the Levites to compel belief. While he claims that he is carrying out the commandments of God, the text of Exodus 32 contradicts this claim. God intended to destroy the Israelites utterly; Moses elects to slaughter only three thousand of them. The benefit of this discriminating slaughter is clear enough. Since the Israelites' belief in Moses dwindled when he left their company, they needed "firm experience" of the "new things" introduced by the prophet (*P* 6). Exodus 32 suggests that there is no firmer experience of new orders than the sight of a nonbeliever's death.[39] The Israelites did not see a pillar of cloud or a burning bush. They saw a Levite's sword in their neighbor's gut. The plague that follows this slaughter merely confirms Moses's violent and earthly consolidation of rule, which he will maintain throughout the Israelites' violent wanderings through the desert, and which the skeptical modern reader might characterize as genocidal marauding of foreign peoples, punctuated with acts of violence against lukewarm supporters.[40] With this allusion to Exodus, Machiavelli discreetly reveals the extreme violence necessary to consolidate support among one's followers.

Jesus also confronted incredulity among his followers: "even after Jesus had performed so many signs in their presence, they still would not believe in him."[41] In this respect, his experience is similar to that of Moses, whose people doubt him even after he led them out of Egypt with the help of several prominent miracles. Jesus is denied by his chosen successor, Peter, but the most infamous unbeliever among his followers is Judas, whose betrayal is a subject of chapter 1 of this work.[42] Although the Gospels indicate that Satan influenced Judas, the desire for material benefit, combined with a lukewarm belief in Christ's capacity to deliver his promises, appear to be the prominent mundane motivations for betraying Christ.[43]

Machiavelli's reasoning about prophets suggests that Jesus's refusal to endorse the use of arms leaves him defenseless against the machinations of his lukewarm believers, who conspire with members of the old religious orders to arrest and crucify him. Peter, "the rock" on which he builds his Church, denies him.[44] In his final hours, he receives only supernatural or scant help: an angel strengthens him in the garden; Simon carries his cross on the way to Calvary Hill; a soldier gives him sour wine on the cross.[45] Compared to the last days of Moses, in which Joshua is chosen as his successor, Moses is able to give a lengthy final address to his people, and God reveals the promised land to him before he dies, Jesus's final days appear wretched.[46] Jesus's body was utterly broken before he expired; "Moses was a hundred and twenty years old when he died, yet his eyes were not weak nor his strength gone."[47]

While Moses transforms the Israelites into a marauding army that is impelled by the tantalizing vision of the God-given promised land and compelled by the point of Moses's ubiquitous blade, Jesus promises his followers a heavenly reward, provided that they "seek first [God's] kingdom and his righteousness."[48] While Moses repeatedly exhorts the Israelites to a violent prosecution of their divinely sanctioned earthly interests, Jesus generally forbids his followers to do the same. After leaving Egypt, Moses treats the Israelites as an armed camp, and explains precisely the extreme limits of the violence they ought to employ against the enemies of the Lord.[49] Jesus renounces violence. Despite, then, Jesus's insistence that he has not "come to abolish the Law or the Prophets . . . but to fulfill them," his revision of Moses's teaching on violence is thoroughgoing and radical.[50] From Machiavelli's perspective, this new teaching betrays the most important defect of Christ as prophet and founder. Like Savonarola, he misunderstands the necessity of arms to a founding; like Savonarola, he fails, dying a violent and horrifying death.

The Folly of Jesus's Middle Way

Despite numerous critical allusions to Christian teachings, Machiavelli quotes from the Gospels only once in *The Prince* and the *Discourses*. He conceals this fact by misattributing the object of the quotation. In I.26 of the *Discourses*, in a chapter entitled "A New Prince Should Make Everything New in a City or Province Taken by Him," Machiavelli writes,

> The best remedy whoever becomes prince of either a city or a state has for holding that principality is to make everything in that state anew, since he

is a new prince, and so much more when his foundations are weak and he may not turn to civil life by way either of kingdom or of republic; that is, to make in cities new governments with new names, new authorities, new men; to make the rich poor, the poor rich, as did David when he became king—"who filled the hungry with good things and sent the rich away empty."

As other scholars have noted, in Luke 1:53, Mary says this of God, and not David; she utters these words immediately after the Annunciation by the angel Gabriel.[51] She thus identifies the arrival of Jesus with the fulfillment of God's promise to the descendants of Abraham; according to Mary, the Annunciation is another instance in which God "has scattered those who are proud in their inmost thoughts. He has brought down rulers from their thrones but has lifted up the humble."[52] According to Machiavelli, these modes—which Luke attributes to God and identifies with the arrival of the Christ-child—are most necessary to those whose foundations are too weak to found a "civil life" (D I.26). Founding a kingdom or a republic is preferable to maintaining these modes, which Machiavelli describes as "very cruel, and enemies to every way of human life, not only Christian but human" (I.26). Those with "weak foundations" (I.26), however, must persist in the use of these inhuman modes: given the context of the quote, Machiavelli certainly includes David and God among the inhuman and anti-Christian rulers. Given the foregoing account of Moses's career, one may also include him among the enemies to human and Christian ways of life.[53]

Yet despite Mary's hopes, one may not include Jesus among these ranks. Unlike Moses and David, in his earthly life, Jesus does not endeavor "to build new cities, to take down those built, to exchange the inhabitants from one place to another" (D I.26). Nor does he remake the state "so that there is no rank, no order, no state, [and] no wealth there that" does not come from him, although his prophetic vision promises a radical reordering in heaven.[54] Instead, Jesus's attitude toward the temporal status quo is more ambivalent—and much more risky. On the one hand, his preoccupation with the "kingdom of heaven" renders him relatively indifferent to the temporal world.[55] On the other hand, his novel teachings signify his opposition to the political, economic, and religious status quo, thus heralding a new way of life. To exacerbate his peril, Jesus eschews the use of force. According to Machiavelli's analysis, this ambivalence—or "middle" way—is fatal to a new prince. Because he possessed "weak foundations" and could not imitate the inhuman and unchristian ways of God, it would have been more prudent for Jesus of Nazareth "to live in private rather than as a king" (D I.26). This is the implied teaching of the one passage in which Machiavelli quotes from the Gospels.

The Folly of Combating Envy with Goodness:
Savonarola, Christ, and Piero Soderini

Ultimately, Christ's error seems to originate in a misunderstanding of the stories of the Old Testament, in which he evinces an uncritical belief. Machiavelli recommends a more skeptical approach to the Old Testament. In the *Discourses*, he opines that "whoever reads the Bible judiciously will see that since he wished his laws and his orders to go forward, Moses was forced to kill an infinite number of men who, moved by nothing other than envy, were opposed to his plans" (*D* III.30.1).[56] This is Machiavelli's clearest judgment of the sacred texts of the Abrahamic tradition: a judicious reading of the Bible ascribes the principal innovations of the Old and New Testaments to human beings, rather than to God.

Machiavelli's claim that Moses killed an "infinite [*infiniti*] number of men" is significant, because it implicates Moses in Israelite deaths that the Pentateuch ascribes to divine punishment or natural disaster.[57] The three thousand killed at Sinai are the only Israelites sentenced to death by the agency of Moses, rather than God or divinely ordained natural forces; by claiming that Moses killed "infinite" envious men, Machiavelli departs from the explicit teaching of the Pentateuch. Machiavelli's account is brazenly impious: the violent acts of the Pentateuch are one man's efforts to combat the ordinary human inclination to envy, and to institute *his* laws and orders. Machiavelli's broad language about reading the Bible judiciously suggests that one should read the New Testament, which constitutes part of the Bible, similarly.

Importantly, Machiavelli juxtaposes this blasphemous but complimentary evaluation of Moses with a critique of Savonarola.[58] The Dominican priest, who appears as an imitative substitute for Christ in chapter 6 of *The Prince*, understood this lesson but "did not have the authority" (*D* III.30.1) to oppose the envious with deadly force.[59] Since Savonarola was incapable of inciting violence, he heaped scorn upon the envious who opposed him, whom he identified as the "wise of the world" (III.30.1). This strategy for overcoming envy—the excoriation and shaming of the envious—is insufficient to combat the problem of envy and led to his ruin.

By scorning the "wise of the world" (III.30.1), Savonarola was following a famous New Testament teaching. While Jesus critiques worldly powers, it is the Apostle Paul who originates Christian usage of the "wisdom of the world."[60] Thus, Machiavelli's critique of Savonarola is also a critique of Christian belief sanctioned by Paul, who denigrates the "wisdom of the world" in comparison to the sacred "foolishness" of the cross (1 Corinthians 1:18–31). Despite the apparent folly of Christlike sacrifice, Paul commends those who find hope, faith, and wisdom in the crucifixion of Christ.

> Jews demand signs and Greeks look for wisdom, but we preach Christ cru-
> cified: a stumbling block to Jews and foolishness to Gentiles, but to those
> whom God has called, both Jews and Greeks, Christ the power of God and
> the wisdom of God. For the foolishness of God is wiser than human wisdom,
> and the weakness of God is stronger than human strength. . . . God chose the
> foolish things of the world to shame the wise; God chose the weak things of
> the world to shame the strong. God chose the lowly things of this world and
> the despised things—and the things that are not—to nullify the things that
> are, so that no one may boast before him. It is because of him that you are
> in Christ Jesus, who has become for us wisdom from God—that is, our righ-
> teousness, holiness and redemption. Therefore, as it is written: "Let the one
> who boasts boast in the Lord."[61]

By recommending that one employ human strength and wisdom in violent
efforts against the envious, Machiavelli subscribes to the view of the Jews
and Gentiles whom Paul criticizes.

Despite his criticism of Savonarola, Machiavelli refrains from character-
izing the Dominican friar as a mere fool who failed to implement the lessons of Moses: instead, he suggests that Savonarola was aware of the need
to eliminate the envious—and used his sermons to exhort others to do
this—but "was not understood well by those who followed him, who would
have had authority for it" (D III.30.1). Savonarola's followers did not realize that their priestly leader secretly wished for them to kill his envious
opponents. What is to blame for the failure? Were they especially obtuse,
or is it unreasonable to expect believing Christians to be attuned to exhortations to violence that proceed from a man who imitates Jesus Christ?[62]
Savonarola's example demonstrates the difficulty of imitating Moses's militant modes within Christ's pacific orders.

Indeed, it seems that Machiavelli judges Savonarola as superior to Jesus
in this regard. The canny Dominican was more concerned with earthly
punishments, as reflected by the preponderance of Old Testament language in his sermons and his persistent rumination on the violent earthly
scourging that would visit his enemies.[63] Rather than turning the other
cheek or loving his enemies, he sought this-worldly punishment of those
who opposed him: this punishment might occur in the form of a foreign
invasion, a plague, or a political revolution. Machiavelli judges this as evidence of Savonarola's astuteness, identified here as sensitivity to Machiavellian political considerations—but could this desire also correspond to
doubts about whether God would intervene on his behalf?

Jesus, of course, is unusual precisely because he believed so ardently
that God would save him. Indeed, Jesus's trust in God and rejection of violence perpetrated on his behalf and against the envious renders him more
similar to Piero Soderini than to Savonarola. Writing of the gonfalonier in
the same passage, Machiavelli opines:

The other believed that with time, with goodness, with his fortune, with benefiting someone, he would eliminate this envy; seeing himself very young of age, and with so much new support that the mode of his proceeding brought him, he believed he could overcome as many as were opposed to him through envy without scandal, violence, or tumult. He did not know that one cannot wait for time, goodness is not enough, fortune varies, and malignity does not find a gift that appeases it. (*D* III.30.1)

While much of this critique applies to Soderini, given the context of this discussion, it more plausibly applies to Jesus.[64] Unlike Soderini, he was, in fact, of a "very young age" when the envious conspired to doom him. Soderini was fifty-two years old when elected gonfalonier and sixty-two years old when he committed the errors that forced him into exile; Jesus was thirty-three years old at the time of his betrayal and execution. Jesus believes that he enjoys the benefit of time and frequently alludes to a future resolution of all things; for example, before the Last Supper, he predicts fulfillment of his prophecy, but insists, "You do not know when that time will come."[65] He repeatedly exhorts his followers to goodness and trust in God, promising extravagant benefits to those who follow him.[66] With these claims, Jesus contravenes several important Machiavellian teachings. First, he evinces a lack of urgency. In Machiavelli's praise of the Roman Republic, he comments approvingly that "nor did that saying ever please them which is everyday in the mouths of wise men of our times— to enjoy the benefit of time—but rather, they enjoyed the benefit of their virtue and prudence. For time sweeps everything before it and can bring with it good as well as evil" (*P* 3). Jesus's presumed goodness did not inoculate him against changing fortune. Indeed, perhaps precisely because he believes the "kingdom of heaven," in which the good will be rewarded, is so "near," he acts imprudently.[67] Second, Jesus mistakenly believes that he can convert enemies by promising benefits, although Machiavelli teaches that "whoever believes that among great personages new benefits will make old injuries be forgotten deceives himself" (*P* 7). To compound his peril, Jesus preaches amid those who oppose him. This strategy, while successful in certain instances, eventually leads to his ruin, because it ignores the necessity that the malignancy of human nature imposes on a founder.

Christ's Misunderstanding of the Old Testament: David, Hiero, and the Full Significance of Auxiliary Arms

A Machiavellian reading of Jesus's final words confirms the judgment that Jesus failed to read the Bible "judiciously" (*D* III.30.1). Before he dies, Jesus shouts, "My God, my God, why have you forsaken me?"[68] This is a reference to Psalm 22, in which David is offering praise of God, who gives aid to his imperiled people: "In you our ancestors put their trust; they trusted and you delivered them. To you they cried out and were saved; in you they trusted and were not put to shame."[69] Jesus's exclamation suggests that he holds a similar hope, and indeed, his final hours mirror the tribulations described by David in Psalm 22. Jesus thus consciously identifies himself with the man who suffers, but is to be redeemed by the God of Israel, a teaching he implicitly attributes to David.

Jesus's implicit understanding of David differs significantly from Machiavelli's. In chapter 13, Machiavelli offers an account that questions the degree to which David relied on God. Machiavelli's readers will not err as Jesus and Savonarola did: if they read the Bible as Machiavelli does, they will learn that it is necessary to "stand alone" rather than "pray" for support (*P* 6). Machiavelli's discussion of David appears alongside his account of Hiero of Syracuse. Both David and Hiero, according to Machiavelli, rejected the use of auxiliary forces. They were "total owner[s]" (*intero possessore*) of their arms (*P* 13).[70] In chapter 6, Hiero was named as a "lesser example" of the founder-prophets who nonetheless retained "some proportion" with them. Machiavelli's association of David with Hiero in chapter 13 thus invites us to compare also David to the founders of chapter 6.

First, however, we must consider why Machiavelli considers Hiero comparable to the founders. Like them, he was capable of employing extraordinary violence to consolidate his power. Convinced that the mercenary soldiers of Syracuse were useless, "he had them all cut to pieces, and then made war with his arms and not alien arms" (*P* 13). Machiavelli praises Hiero for this decision.[71] Hiero's motive, like that of the founders, was to ensure his personal security and the foundation of his state. Since "he could neither keep [the mercenaries] nor let them go" (*P* 13), Machiavelli's analysis dictates that they be slaughtered. Hiero exhibited virtue sufficient to accomplish this bloody task, and Machiavelli praises him without compunction.

In the very next passage, Machiavelli cites David as an examplar "apt for this purpose": "When David offered to Saul to go and fight Goliath, the Philistine challenger, Saul, to give him spirit, armed him with his own arms—which David, as soon as he had them on, refused, saying that with them he could not give a good account of himself, and so he would rather meet the enemy with his sling and his knife." As numerous scholars have noted, Machiavelli's account departs from the biblical version in important ways.[72] In 1 Samuel (17:39–40), David refuses Saul's arms because he is "not used to them," and not because he wishes to "give a good account of himself"; he is armed with a staff, five stones, and a sling, rather than a knife; in order to behead Goliath, the biblical David must use Goliath's own sword.[73] Indeed, by placing a knife in David's hand, Machiavelli contradicts explicitly the biblical account: "So David triumphed over the Philistine with a sling and a stone; without a sword in his hand he struck down the Philistine and killed him" (17:50). Most importantly, however, Machiavelli's revision of the story omits mention of the principal cause of David's success, according to David himself. The young king-to-be repeatedly invokes the support of God, proclaiming that with his victory, "all those gathered here will know that it is not by sword or spear that the LORD saves; for the battle is the LORD's, and he will give all of you into our hands" (17:47). Machiavelli's revision of this story alerts us to the character of his "judicious" reading of the Bible. He reads the accounts therein as if they are human history, and seeks to explain its principal events in human, rather than divine, terms. In doing so, he subordinates the biblical history to his own understanding of human nature and the requirements of politics. Machiavelli renders the story of David thus: History teaches that only armed prophets succeed. David defeated Goliath. Therefore, David must have been armed sufficiently—even if the account in 1 Samuel does not teach this. Insofar as he understood this Machiavellian teaching, David is superior to Christ. This impious reading of divine texts is informed by Machiavelli's understanding of history, and is the truest source of his blasphemous understanding of prophecy.[74] His revision of 1 Samuel conforms to the central teaching of chapter 13: a prudent prince must avoid using auxiliary arms. Machiavelli's David stands alone, refusing the auxiliary arms offered by both Saul and God.

Although David's orders are not new—since he operates in the context of the Mosaic orders—his modes are identical to those of the founders, insofar as he seeks to imbue worldly violence with divine pretension. The juxtaposition of David and Hiero thus alerts us to the crucial difference between Hiero and the founders of chapter 6: while his career resembles theirs—and David's—in many ways, Hiero is not a prophet.[75] Like David, he knew better than to rely on external support—human or divine; unlike David, he never claimed to have divine support. Thus, while he did not "receive anything more from fortune than the opportunity," showed prudence in the maintenance of his arms, and committed a proportionate act of violence to secure his state, his neglect of prophecy apparently renders him a "lesser example" (P 6). Why? This question is important, because, while conceding that it may initially gain one credit among the people, Machiavelli argues that prophecy is insufficient to maintain belief. Eventually, your followers will require "firm experience" (P 6) of your new orders. To provide this, one must be armed. What, then, does prophecy contribute to a founding?

Machiavelli's puzzling inclusion of Hiero in the chapter titled "Of Auxiliary, Mixed, and One's Own Soldiers" suggests an answer to this question. Since Hiero famously led mercenary soldiers to their deaths, Machiavelli

might have praised him in chapter 12, which treats the defects of mercenary arms.[76] He does not, preferring instead to emphasize that he was the
"total owner" (*P* 13) of his own arms, and is comparable to David in his
clear-sighted understanding of the necessity of being armed—and stand-
ing alone, without God, while perpetrating a founding. Since Hiero is a
prince who refuses to claim divine support and attempts to found new
orders without claiming God as an auxiliary, a consideration of the limits
of his accomplishments helps to explain what, precisely, prophecy contrib-
utes to a founding—and how Christianity succeeded despite Jesus's failure
to secure his own arms.

The Crucial Importance of Prophecy: Christ, Hiero, and Rome

The predominant role of arms in founding might prompt one to ask: can
one found lasting new orders without claiming to talk to God? Are lasting
secular orders possible? We can discern Machiavelli's answer to this question by examining the careers of two Syracusans. The first is Hiero. The
second is criminal tyrant Agathocles, who despite his Machiavellian virtue,
cannot "be celebrated among the most excellent men" (*P* 8).

A consideration of their careers suggests that prophecy improves a
founding in two ways.[77] First, it can help burnish a founder's reputation
by providing divine justification for the bloody acts that are identical with
founding a new order. Without such justification, subsequent generations
will, at best, identify the prince as a merely temporal figure, intent on
securing political power. Hiero is an excellent example of this phenomenon because although he ruled Syracuse with such "mildness and magna-
nimity" that when he died the Syracusans felt "they had lost a father," his
destruction of the mercenaries is remembered merely as the action of a
capable and shrewd king—rather than the wrathful act of a just God intent
on founding a new people.[78] The example of Agathocles demonstrates the
justificatory value of prophecy more clearly. A career criminal, Agathocles
rose through the ranks of the Syracusan military. From the height of that
force, he "became king of Syracuse" (*P* 8) by murdering the entire Senate, along with the wealthiest class of citizens. Machiavelli initially identifies
Agathocles as virtuous, and readers of the first seven chapters of *The Prince*
might understand why: founding requires violence, and Agathocles, who
"decided to become prince and hold [his position] with violence and without obligation to anyone else" (*P* 8), certainly did not shrink from necessary violence. Yet Machiavelli conspicuously avoids this conclusion.

> Yet one cannot call it virtue to kill one's citizens, betray one's friends, to be
> without faith, without mercy, without religion; these modes can enable one

to acquire empire, but not glory. For, if one considers the virtue of Agathocles in entering into and escaping from dangers, and the greatness of his spirit in enduring and overcoming adversities, one does not see why he has to be judged inferior to any most excellent captain. Nonetheless, his savage cruelty and inhumanity, together with his infinite crimes, do not permit him to be celebrated among the most excellent men. (*P* 8)

Machiavelli, who pointedly identifies the tyrant Agathocles as a "king," and praises his "virtue of spirit," "greatness of spirit," and even his "virtue," nonetheless recognizes that his reputation for criminality diminishes his status (*P* 8). In particular, his failure to exhibit faith, mercy, and—perhaps, especially—religion, meant that his crimes were plain to the entire world.[79] This neglect of prophecy was not fatal to his earthly empire, but it does deny him glory.

The power of glory helps to explain the second benefit of prophecy. Glory can help to perpetuate political orders beyond the founder's death. Despite his largely beneficent rule, history's judgment of Hiero is ambivalent. Polybius describes him as a "king," and when he dies, Livy informs us that the Syracusans mourned as if they had been orphaned.[80] Yet while he had wished to establish Syracuse as a free state upon his death, he was unable to prevent his family from assuming monarchical powers. Their despotic rule eventually precipitated a popular revolt that ended in the massacre of the entire royal family. In the years after Hiero's death, Syracuse experienced war, confusion, and plots—many of which were fomented or manipulated by the Roman Republic as it battled Hannibal and the Carthaginians.[81]

Unlike the four prophets, Hiero fails to establish an order that survives his own lifetime. Since we have seen that his actions concerning arms appear no different from those of the founders, Machiavelli's account suggests that his neglect of prophecy explains his inability to perpetuate new orders. According to Xenophon, the religiously observant Cyrus dies at the height of his powers, and while his empire briefly fractures as his sons fight among themselves, Darius eventually rules over the empire.[82] Romulus gives Rome its laws only after receiving numerous auguries and after the claims of religion had been "duly acknowledged"; according to Livy, he disappears from Rome at the end of his career, prompting a belief in his divinity.[83] Theseus's career is similar to Romulus's, a point that Plutarch emphasizes in the opening lines of his account of the Athenian.[84] Moses cites God's authority in the selection of Joshua son of Nun as his successor; Joshua had distinguished himself in earthly military exploits and served as Moses's protégé.[85]

Had Hiero behaved like these founders, he might have been able to accomplish his goal. Instead, Livy confirms that he ruled his city in the shadow of Romulus's orders: though virtuous, he served as an auxiliary to the Roman Republic as "the one man whom Rome could fall back upon."[86] Without prophetic claims that might have established Hiero as the center of the Syracusans' universe, Hiero's city remained an auxiliary, captured in the orbit of the Roman Republic. His example teaches that the principal value of prophecy is its novelty and daring. Prophecy frees a founder from existing orders, giving him recourse to the extraordinary modes that allow him to found new and lasting orders. Hiero failed because he neglected to exploit the potential value of otherworldly claims. Had he pretended to talk to God, or exploited the semimythic account of his origins, he might have been able to escape from Rome's gravitational force and perpetuate his own orders.

Both in his particular failures and his relationship to Rome, Christ is the anti-Hiero of *The Prince*. Christ employed prophecy, while neglecting the worldly requirements of founding. He invests Peter with a heavenly mandate because Peter is the first disciple to declare his faith that Jesus is "the Messiah, the Son of the living God," and yet fails to provide him with the means to perpetuate that faith.[87] Nonetheless, Christ's orders infiltrated, usurped, and then eventually replaced the Roman Empire, while Hiero's orders became the plaything of the Roman Republic. Livy regards Hiero as Rome's most faithful auxiliary; Machiavelli regards Rome as Christ's most powerful auxiliary. Rome provided the arms necessary to accomplish Christ's founding: this explains how Christianity succeeded despite his defective modes and orders. Machiavelli's analysis suggests that without the intercession of the prudent, expansive, and armed Roman Empire, Christianity could not have thrived. Unlike Christ, "the Romans knew that war may not be avoided but is deferred to the advantage of others," and armed themselves appropriately. As "wise princes," they understood that arms are necessary to any founding (*P* 3). Without the intercession of Romulus's city, the fate of Christ's orders ought to have been similar to Savonarola's. Instead, by 380, Christianity became the official religion of the Roman Empire, a regime that had demonstrated its ability to subjugate far-flung peoples.[88]

Conclusion: Christianity's Political Problem

A reflection on the alleged defects of Christ helps to explain an important difference between Christian political thought and its antecedents. In particular, Christ attempts to refute, and thereby obscures, the ancient teaching that violence is necessary to found new politico-religious orders— a teaching for which the ancients nonetheless generally apologize. In the *Republic*, for example, the just "city in speech" is born in an act of unjust violence: the interlocutors "must cut off a piece of [their] neighbor's land," thus necessitating a war; immediately after the discussion of war, Socrates introduces a revision of Greek religion and an education of the guardians that culminates in a preposterous divine myth that deliberately obscures the city's unjust origins.[89] Plato's *Laws* begins with a discussion of the divine origin of laws, which, according to the three old men, must necessarily be concerned with victory in war.[90] We may add these accounts to the ancient tales of Romulus, Theseus, and Cyrus, whose violent founding acts, imbued with religious pretensions, are discussed above. In classical political philosophy, tyranny is often associated with impiety, but only because the unrestrained nature of tyrannical rule is reminiscent of the unbounded rule of the tyrant-king Zeus, who founded his rule by committing horrendous crimes—and who maintains his position with superior force.[91] Thucydides credits the initial development of Greece to the rule of tyrants, whose efforts against piracy made the development of Greek civilization possible. He praises especially the tyrant Minos, who suppressed piracy and founded numerous colonies.[92] Minos infamously demanded a gruesome Athenian tribute, but also claimed Zeus as his father.

As the classical preoccupation with tyranny suggests, Zeus was a tempting model for ambitious pagans.[93] As the foregoing has demonstrated, the most important figures from the Old Testament also routinely practice violence, as does the God of the Old Testament. Christ differs from these earlier models. He neither practices nor sanctions the violence of Moses, David, Romulus, Cyrus, Theseus, Minos or Zeus, and rejects unequivocally the practice of deception and violence to further earthly ends. Given the rigorous requirements of Christian piety, this restriction is not surprising. Christianity maintains—much more vigorously than either Greek and Roman paganism or Judaism—that one's eternal soul will be judged and disposed of according to one's actions on earth.[94] Moreover, the stakes are much higher, insofar as the Christian God is a much more scrupulous enforcer of justice than are the pagan gods—and is less tolerant of earthly violence than pagan gods, the God of the Jews—or, one may add, of the Muslims. This abhorrence of violence is due partly to Christ's more robust concern for the inward disposition of one's soul; the exercise of earthly violence indicates a preoccupation with the world that is a sign of little faith, and violates Christ's injunction that "whoever does not carry their cross and follow me cannot be my disciple."[95]

I do not suggest that belief in Christ renders men pacifists. For Christ, as for Machiavelli, human nature does not permit pacific human relations. While Christianity casts men as susceptible to sin, Machiavelli teaches that worldly affairs require violence, and human inclinations—which tend to be self-seeking or malignant—naturally conduce to violent interactions. Thus, while Christians will not abstain from violence, they will understand their inclinations to violence as sinful, and will tend to renounce the arms necessary to satisfy those inclinations.[96] Christianity thus undermines the importance of arms in three ways. First, the example of "Christ crucified" recommends self-sacrifice to his followers.[97] Second, it teaches men that their salvation may be imperiled by earthly violence; this makes them more hesitant, and less capable of perpetrating the stunning criminal violence required of founders. Third, it leads them to abandon the very possession of arms as dangerous to the state of their immortal souls. Machiavelli's account of contemporary Italy confirms that Christianity produces this defective and dangerous relationship to arms. The next chapter examines this damning account, and confirms that Machiavelli seeks to divest Christ of disciples by unapologetically declaiming ancient teachings on the necessity of violence to the creation of lasting political orders.

CHAPTER THREE

Hope Is Not Enough

As numerous scholars have noted, chapter 6 is a high point of *The Prince*.[1] Beginning in chapter 7, Machiavelli descends from a discussion of the "greatest examples" (*P* 6) to a discussion of "two examples that have occurred in days within our memory." Francesco Sforza became Duke of Milan through virtue, while Cesare Borgia relied on "others' arms and fortune" (*P* 7) in his exploits as Duke Valentino. The remainder of chapter 7 consists of an examination of Cesare's career, and it is tempting to conclude that Cesare was of sufficient virtue to consolidate a state founded by fortune.[2] Machiavelli opines that Cesare

> made use of every deed and did all those things that should be done by a prudent and virtuous man to put his roots in the state that the arms and fortune of others had given him [and] . . . he had laid for himself great foundations for future power, which I do not judge superfluous to discuss; for I do not know what better teaching I could give to a new prince than the example of his actions. And if his orders did not bring profit to him, it was not his fault, because this arose from an extraordinary and extreme malignity of fortune. (*P* 7)

With this allusion to the dedicatory letter, Machiavelli implies that he and Cesare are fellow sufferers, insofar as both labor under a "malignity of fortune." In the dedicatory letter, Machiavelli's malignant fortune was identical to Lorenzo de Medici's good fortune: the patronage of the Church assured the Medici's ascendancy in Florence, just as it ensured Machiavelli's exile.[3] In chapter 7, Cesare Borgia's relationship to the Church also constitutes his fortune, but his position is more ambiguous than either Lorenzo's or Machiavelli's: while the Church launches Cesare's career, it also limits his potential.

Machiavelli writes that princes like Cesare "come to be" (*P* 7) in one of three ways: buying a principality, being given a principality, or corrupting the soldiers in order to attain rank. Because they do not "depend on their own . . . and use force" (*P* 7), they find themselves at the head of very insecure principalities. They lack the knowledge of command and "do not have forces that can be friendly and faithful to them" (*P* 7). Thus, except in those rare cases in which extraordinarily good fortune visits an extraordinarily virtuous man, these principalities are short-lived. Importantly, Cesare lacked such extraordinary virtue: Machiavelli will recount that when Cesare's luck runs out, he meets his "ultimate ruin" (*P* 7). His efforts to conquer Italy falter when papal support evaporates. Yet since Machiavelli also suggests that an "extraordinary and extreme malignity of fortune" (*P* 7) afflicts Cesare, could he be the rare man whose exemplary virtue is overwhelmed by bad luck?

Machiavelli's ambivalent presentation of Cesare does not support this thesis. He reveals the "extraordinary" nature of Cesare's malignant fortune when he opines that "Alexander the VI had very many difficulties, both present and future, when he decided to make his son the duke great" (*P* 7). We thus learn two crucial facts about Cesare's career. First, he was the son of Pope Alexander VI—which is, indeed, an extraordinary instance of fortune. Second, Cesare's father planned his political career. In the praise of Cesare that follows, therefore, we cannot presume that Cesare's career is truly his own. Often, "the example of his actions" (*P*7) will actually demonstrate his father's virtue. When Alexander VI dies, Machiavelli reports that Cesare feared "that a new successor in the Church might not be friendly to him and might seek to take away what Alexander had given him" (*P* 7). When Cesare is compelled to stand alone, without the "fortune of his father" (*P*7), his empire crumbles. In chapter 11, Machiavelli obviates any lingering ambiguity concerning Cesare's autonomy by describing him as Alexander's "instrument."[4] Alexander's role in Cesare's career thus ought to diminish our estimation of his virtue; he is a "mere executor" (*P* 6) of the pope's wishes.

Alexander struggled to muster a loyal and effective army for Cesare. The Church, adhering to the pacific dictates of Christ, lacked an army, and the existing arms of Italy "were in the hands of those who had to fear the greatness of the pope" (*P* 7).[5] To "make himself lord securely" (*P* 7) of new states and equip himself with arms, Alexander needed to disrupt Italian affairs. He accomplished this by consenting to Louis XII's invasion of Italy. For this support—and the annulment and cardinalate discussed in chapter 3 of *The Prince*—Louis loaned Pope Alexander arms in the form of the Swiss mercenaries.[6] Cesare was able to acquire the Romagna with these borrowed arms, but did not trust them, so he tested their fidelity by attacking a city that Louis XII coveted. When the Orsini attacked "cooly" and Louis ordered him to desist, "the duke decided to depend no longer on the arms and fortune of others" (*P* 7). Yet, lest one conclude that Cesare had learned his lesson, Machiavelli almost immediately contradicts this unequivocal proclamation, when he informs us that when the suspicious Orsini fomented rebellion in the newly acquired Romagna, Cesare resorted to the aid of the French—even though he knew that Louis was hostile to his ambitions. This was a significant error, which exposed Cesare to considerable risk—had Louis XII been willing or able to betray the pope's son. Typical of Cesare's career, this error was accompanied by a praiseworthy and violent deceit that conduced to his security: he invited the leading men of opposing factions to a dinner, at which he had them all strangled. Would these men have attended a banquet held by an enemy who was *not* the son of the pope? Probably not. One of the doomed attendees, Liverotto da Fermo, had orchestrated an identical treachery against his own uncle one year before.[7] Cesare's paternity appears to have blinded these enemies, just as Alexander VI blinded Louis XII. In chapter 18, Machiavelli writes that Alexander VI "never did anything, nor ever thought of anything, but how to deceive men, and he always found a subject to whom he could do it," and Louis XII and the dinner guests at Sinigaglia appear to be among those deceived.[8] It was Cesare's good fortune to be the son of a man in whom Christian princes regularly misplaced their faith.

Yet we cannot attribute Cesare Borgia's brief success merely to suspect arms and a fortunate paternity. Machiavelli also directs the reader to consider Cesare's subsequent efforts in the Romagna, remarking, "Because this point is deserving of notice and of being imitated by others, I do not want to leave it out" (*P* 7). Due to the intrigues of the Orsini, Cesare found the Romagna governed by rapacious lords who created discontent and inspired rebellion. In order "to give it good government, if he wanted to reduce it to peace and obedience to a kingly arm," he empowered Remirro D'Orco, a "cruel and ready man," who "reduced it to peace and unity, with the very greatest reputation for himself" (*P* 7). D'Orco pacified the province by tremendous cruelty. In order to stem the hatred of the people—who might correctly have attributed D'Orco's cruelty to Cesare—the duke subjected D'Orco to a trial by kangaroo court: "and having seized this opportunity, he had him placed one morning in the piazza at Cesena in two pieces, with a piece of wood and a bloody knife beside him. The ferocity of this spectacle left the people at once satisfied and stupefied" (*P* 7). With this bloody sacrifice of his henchman, Cesare eliminates a potential rival for his power, secures the gratitude of those whom D'Orco terrorized, and impresses upon those same people his own capacity for stunning violence, executed without regard for the norms of due process.[9] In other words, this act transformed the Romagna into a faithful province, on which Cesare could rely for armed support. It is, indeed, reluctant to abandon Cesare after Alexander's death. Machiavelli encourages his readers to imitate this action.

A Province Unarmed

While Cesare eventually created his own arms, it took him five years to do so. The Borgias' inability to locate faithful and capable arms in Italy is not accidental. According to Machiavelli's analysis in chapter 12, the repulsion of the Holy Roman Empire accelerated the growing decadence of Italian arms. As Italy began to fracture, "the pope gained much reputation in temporal affairs" (*P* 12). In some cities, the Church supported the popular rebellions that arose against quisling Italian nobles; in others, citizens became princes of their cities without the Church's support. The Church did not act on patriotic motives: it sought "to give herself reputation" (*P* 12). Neither did it seek to nurture institutions that produce liberty; if it had, it might have directed the reconstitution of Italian republican orders, and with them, republican virtue. Instead, Machiavelli says that at the end of this political transformation, "Italy had almost fallen into the hands of the Church and a few republics" (*P* 12).

Yet even in these republics, one could not detect the virtue of ancient Rome. Even if modern republics had been capable of the hatred and revenge that sustain and defend republics, they lacked the knowledge of arms that might empower those passions. Italy's long subjection to empire, combined with its more recent subjection to priests, enervated its martial virtue: in both republics and principalities, "since the priests and the other citizens did not have knowledge of arms, they began to hire foreigners" (*P* 12). In the *Discourses*, Machiavelli attributes Italy's lack of liberty to the success of the Roman Empire, which, with "its arms and its greatness, eliminated all republics and all civil ways of life. And although that empire was dissolved, the cities still have not been able to put themselves back together or reorder themselves for civil life except in very few places of that empire" (II.2.2). Thus, while subjection to the Holy Roman Empire confirmed Italy's weakness and still longer subjection to priests disarmed it, Rome's imperium established the preconditions for the success of both the Holy Roman Empire and the Catholic Church.[10] Modern Italy's hapless effeminacy necessitated the use of mercenary and auxiliary forces, which Machiavelli condemns as "useless and dangerous" (*P* 12).[11] While mercenary arms are conducive to "slavery and disgrace" (*P* 12), auxiliary arms are even more dangerous: borrowed from one's neighbors, "when they lose you are undone; when they win, you are left their prisoner" (*P* 13). "A wise prince," therefore, "always" flees these arms (*P* 13). Given the broad significance of "auxiliary arms" suggested by Machiavelli's retelling of the David and Goliath story—treated above, in chapter 2—one might conclude that wise princes seek military help from neither neighbors nor God.

Because Cesare Borgia employed auxiliary arms even after he learned of their dangers, he cannot be "a wise prince." Indeed, Cesare depends on defective arms for most of his career; with respect to the use of arms, Machiavelli casts him only as a qualified model of improvement. He began by using auxiliaries, but eventually realized they were dangerous; turning to mercenaries, he soon learned of their defects. After employing auxiliary arms once more, finally, near the end of his career, he "turned to his own arms" (*P* 13). Thus, Machiavelli carefully qualifies his praise of Cesare, judging, "His reputation will always be found to have increased, but he was never so much esteemed as when everyone saw that he was total owner of his arms" (*P* 13).

While auxiliary arms are more dangerous, Italians more commonly employ mercenary arms. In chapter 12, Machiavelli offers an expansive critique of these arms. When they are lackluster, their employment leads to longer and more devastating wars. Mercenaries are more concerned with receiving a paycheck than securing a decisive victory, and both the prince and his people suffer from their disinclination to fight. When they are excellent, however, mercenaries are a threat to subjugate their employers. Machiavelli provides numerous examples of contemporary Italy's risky employment of mercenaries. According to him, Florence was lucky not to be subjected by its mercenary captain.[12] The Venetians experienced success with a mercenary named Carmagnola, but eventually felt threatened by him and were compelled to kill him. Machiavelli reports that his less-than-excellent replacement "lost in one day what they had acquired with such trouble in eight hundred years" (*P* 12). The example of Venice purportedly demonstrates the extreme danger posed by mercenary arms; they can squander even well-established empires.

Yet one cannot attribute Venice's defeat wholly to the uneven virtue of mercenary arms. In the *Discourses*, Machiavelli offers a fuller account of Venice's momentous defeat that identifies a more fundamental defect of Venice—and of all who rely on mercenary arms. He emphasizes that Venice's loss might have been less staggering had the Venetians possessed sufficient virtue: instead, they displayed "cowardice," "submission," and "abjectness of spirit" (III.31.3). With evident disgust, Machiavelli recounts how "they grew so cowardly that they sent ambassadors to the emperor to make themselves his tributaries, and they wrote letters to the pope full of cowardice and submission so as to move him to compassion" (III.31.3). Thus, what Machiavelli characterizes as a "half-defeat" (III.31.3) in the *Discourses*, became a catastrophic loss for Venice.[13]

Machiavelli attributes the Venetians' cowardly and abject spirit to "the quality of their orders, which were not good in the things of war" (III.31.3). Ultimately, these orders issue a defective education that creates men who fail in adversity.

And it will always happen thus to anyone whatsoever who governs himself like them. For becoming insolent in good fortune and abject in bad arises from your mode of proceeding and from the education in which you are raised. When that is weak and vain, it renders you like itself; when it has been otherwise, it renders you also of another fate; and by making you a better knower of the world, it makes you rejoice less in the good and be less aggrieved with the bad. What is said of one alone is said of many who live in one and the same republic: they are made to that perfection that its mode of life has. (III.31.3)[14]

When confronted by adversity—like a "half-defeat"—properly educated men would be able to execute a plan to recover what was lost. They would be able to do so, as Machiavelli explains in the next section, because an adequate education prepares men for war: "the foundation of all states is a good military, and that where this does not exist there can be neither good laws nor any other good thing" (III.31.4).[15]

If states that are not founded on military orders cannot produce anything good, Jesus—the quintessential unarmed prophet—cannot be the source of any good law or education. Indeed, Machiavelli's other more famous critique of modern education establishes that a "Venetian" education is, in fact, a Christian education. In II.2.2 of the *Discourses*, he attributes the "cowardice" of modernity to Christian teachings, and complains that Christianity "places the highest good in humility, abjectness, and contempt of things human"—those blameworthy qualities that a Venetian education produces.[16]

Thinking when it can arise that in those ancient times peoples were more lovers of freedom than in these, I believe it arises from the same cause that makes men less strong now, which I believe is the difference between our education and the ancient, founded on the difference between our religion and the ancient. For our religion, having shown the truth and the true way [*la verità e la vera via*], makes us esteem less the honor of the world, whereas the Gentiles, esteeming it very much and having placed the highest good in it, were more ferocious in their actions. (*D* II.2.2)[17]

As Harvey Mansfield and Nathan Tarcov indicate, Machiavelli's criticism of "our religion" (II.2.2) alludes to John 14:6, in which Jesus proclaims, "I am the way and the truth and the life. No one comes to the Father except through me."[18] Machiavelli thus links the weakness of contemporary Europe—evidenced by a reliance on mercenary arms and a spirit unable to withstand bad fortune—to the success of Christ's teaching in John.

Attention to the context of John 14 confirms that Machiavelli is advancing a radical critique of Christ, and the pernicious effects of his teachings about the world. In this passage, Jesus's disciples evince striking skepticism about his grandiose claim to be "the way and the truth and the life."[19] First, they demand proof (John 14:8). In response, Jesus cites the miracles he has performed and promises, "Whoever believes in me will do the works I have been doing, and they will do even greater things than these. . . . You may ask me for anything in my name, and I will do it" (John 14:12–14). Thus, he intimates that he will offer worldly support to those who "love" him and believe in him (John 14:21). Still, the disciples remain doubtful, asking, "But, Lord, why do you intend to show yourself to us and not to the world?" (14:22). Jesus initially responds by reaffirming the sufficiency of love and obedience to guarantee salvation. Then, he offers a characteristic denigration of "the world" that typifies his disagreement with Machiavelli: "Peace I leave with you; my peace I give you. I do not give to you as the world gives. Do not let your hearts be troubled and do not be afraid" (14:27). In the next chapter, Jesus confirms that he wishes his followers to "esteem less the honor of the world" (D II.2.2) by teaching, "If the world hates you, keep in mind that it hated me first. If you belonged to the world, it would love you as its own. As it is, you do not belong to the world, but I have chosen you out of the world. That is why the world hates you."[20] According to Machiavelli, Christ's commandments to eschew violence, avoid earthly entanglements, and shun earthly honor produce—and indeed, are identical with—the "weak and vain" (D III.31.3) education that dooms Venice. Christ's otherworldly orders ought to be compared with the actions of the founders of chapter 6, who, despite their prophetic pretensions, are engaged fully in the things of this world.[21]

Because good Christians do not pursue earthly success, they do not need to learn its preconditions. Thus does Christ's denigration of the worldly render men poor "knowers of the world" (D III.31.3). Christ's deprecation of worldly honor—in combination with his rejection of violence—explains Italy's lack of arms, the only "sin" (P 12) Machiavelli identifies in The Prince.[22] Dominated by men sworn to imitate the pacific teachings of Christ and corrupted by an education that condemns any preoccupation with the world as sinful, a Christian education is debilitating. The Italian education is particularly effete: while all Christian regimes must labor under the adversity of Christ's otherworldliness, Italy is also saddled with a large and especially powerful priestly class.

Yet as Machiavelli's works confirm, Christians are divided in their allegiance: while they are attracted to Christ's promises of otherworldly triumph, they remain fonts of worldly ambition. These contradictory impulses engender profound ambivalence. On the one hand, Machiavelli repeatedly asserts that human nature had not changed from antiquity: men will still run great risks and commit great crimes to attain worldly goods.[23] On the other hand, passages like this confirm that human education had changed decisively: modern education does not equip men with the knowledge necessary to attain worldly goods, and indeed, inculcates the belief that worldly ambition is sinful. Italy's reliance on mercenary arms is perhaps the most obvious manifestation of this deficient education.

Christianity's ascendancy has left Italy effectively unarmed, but Machiavelli suggests that Christ's effect on the spirits of men is particularly damaging. In particular, his teachings leave men's spirits unarmed against the ravages of fortune: once again, attention to John 14 confirms this. There, Christ teaches men that any earthly success they experience is evidence of his promised support, rather than the product of their own exertions. This perhaps explains why Venetians were insolent in success; they believed that God was on their side.[24] Yet when Christians encounter bad fortune—as all men will—they despair of having been abandoned by God, and become "abject" and "cowardly" (D III.31.3). Their abjectness is perhaps intensified by the reflection that they are being punished for their sinful ambition. Importantly, this despondency is reasonable if one believes Christ's teaching about "the world." A follower of Christ believes that loving him and believing in him are decisive to success: a student of Machiavelli will understand that he ought to believe in his own ability and "never abandon himself" (D II.29.3).[25] Hence, the half-defeated Venetians beg for "compassion" from the pope, while Machiavelli advises that they ought to have redoubled their efforts to strengthen Venice's military orders. This is the weak world into which Alexander VI thrusts his natural-born son. The success of Christianity may explain why Cesare, as son of the pope, was able to survive by deceit, but it also explains the truest cause of his struggle to locate faithful arms. Paradoxically, the success of Christianity helps to explain the failure of the pope's son.

Cesare Borgia's Fatal Belief in Reconciliation

As John McCormick notes, Machiavelli's selective presentation of Cesare's career constitutes a perverse imitation of Christ's: he is the son of the pope, God's representative on earth—by whom he is sent "into the world" to act as his agent.[26] He holds a grotesque "last supper," at which he strangles his guests, rather than promising to sacrifice himself on their behalf; immediately thereafter, Machiavelli reports Cesare's public execution of Remirro D'Orco, whose death liberates the people of the Romagna from their worldly troubles and consecrates their new and lasting pact with Cesare.[27] Machiavelli surely invites a comparison of Christ and Cesare in chapter 7, but he does so to emphasize the deleterious effects of Christ's legacy, rather than any potential value Christian teachings might have for a modern founder. Machiavelli teaches that Cesare was a failure and, moreover, suggests that his chief difficulties proceeded from certain teachings endorsed by the Prince of Peace.

As Machiavelli recounts in detail in chapter 7, Cesare spends most of his career searching for an army on which he could depend. In a province dominated by the Bride of Christ, this is a difficult undertaking. Nonetheless, Machiavelli suggests that Cesare dawdled in his early efforts. Some of Cesare's errors—most notably, his repeated reliance on the auxiliary arms of the French—suggest that he did not understand the urgency of possessing arms of one's own. Indeed, if he had been freed of this concern earlier in his career, he might have been able to accomplish the conquest of Italy. Instead, he wasted crucial months testing the fidelity of auxiliary arms and managing the ambition of mercenaries.

The consequences of Cesare's deficiency became evident when Alexander VI fell ill. In response, Cesare endeavored to secure himself against the new pope. He eliminated the bloodlines of all he had despoiled; he bribed (or eliminated) Roman gentlemen in order to check the new pope's power; he gained partial control over the college of cardinals, whose selection he could reject; and he sought to acquire enough empire to protect himself against foreign and domestic enemies. Cesare failed only to accomplish this last goal.

> If he had succeeded in this (as he was succeeding the same year that Alexander died), he would have acquired such force and reputation that he would have stood by himself and would no longer have depended on the fortune and force of someone else, but on his own power and virtue. But Alexander died five years after he had begun to draw his sword. He left the duke with only the state of Romagna consolidated, with all the others in the air, between two very powerful enemy armies, and sick to death. (P 7)

Cesare's inability to conquer sufficient territory is inextricably related to his inability to secure a faithful army; indeed, the Romagna's faithfulness subsequent to Cesare's execution of D'Orco attests to the value of an army whose loyalty is consecrated in blood and grounded in fear. His actions in the Romagna were those of a "wise prince," yet Cesare, who relied on his fortunate origins, also spent most of his career relying on defective arms.[28] Consequently, he was unable to exploit fully the opportunity presented by his paternity.

Despite the importance of Cesare's defective arms, Machiavelli vacillates in his judgment of the ultimate cause of Cesare's demise. He notes that Cesare might have been able to overcome the death of his father, had he not been "sick to death" himself: Machiavelli reports a conversation with Cesare "on the day that Julius II was created" in which Cesare claimed that he "was on the point of dying" (P 7). Machiavelli himself vacillates in his judgment of the gravity of Cesare's illness: he describes Cesare as unhealthy, "half-alive," and affected by "sickness" (*P* 7). Cesare would, in fact, live for almost four more years, a fact that Machiavelli deliberately omits. Why does Machiavelli underscore Cesare's mistaken belief that he was on the brink of death? It is possible that Machiavelli thinks that Cesare's illness enervated his capacity to act to secure himself. Perhaps the fear of dying obscured his judgment in the selection of a new pope.[29] Whatever the cause, Machiavelli condemns Cesare's decision to assent to the elevation of Giuliano della Rovere to the papacy, since it guaranteed Cesare's political death:

> He made a bad choice; for as was said, though he could not make a pope to suit himself, he could have kept anyone from being pope. And for the papacy he should never have consented to those cardinals whom he had offended or who, having become pope, would have to be afraid of him. For men offend either from fear or for hatred. . . . And whoever believes that among great personages new benefits will make old injuries be forgotten deceives himself. So the duke erred in this choice and it was the cause of his ultimate ruin. (*P* 7)[30]

Reflect on the manifold failings of Cesare. He relied on his father, who was also the pope, throughout his political career. He struggled to create his own arms during the five years he enjoyed good fortune, repeatedly engaging the services of hostile auxiliary arms. In his final act, despite a lifetime of egregious sin, he commits a quintessentially Christian error: like Piero Soderini, he deceives himself by believing "new benefits will make old injuries be forgotten" (*P* 7). This belief leads to his ruin; shortly after his creation, Julius II imprisons Cesare, thus ending his ambitions. Cesare Borgia, who treacherously assassinated his enemies at Sinigaglia, somehow believed that by benefiting Julius, he might be reconciled to the new pope. What can explain this error?

Cesare's fear of imminent death, which Machiavelli carefully emphasizes, perhaps helps explain his unfounded hope in reconciliation. Machiavelli tells us that Cesare was racked by an illness, surrounded by powerful armies, and convinced that he would shortly die. While Machiavelli suggests that Cesare's position was not hopeless, Cesare confided in Machiavelli, "on the day that Julius II was created, that he had thought about what might happen when his father was dying, and had found a remedy for everything, except that he never thought that at his death he would also be on the point of dying" (*P* 7). One might wonder: was this Cesare's despairing response to Machiavelli when the latter warned him against permitting the creation of Julius?

This question is, of course, speculative. It is incontestable, however, that Cesare—whose career is replete with sins mortal and venial—seeks reconciliation with the father of the Church as he nears his supposed death.

While one could argue that his habitual dependence on Church power precipitated this gamble, Machiavelli suggests a different explanation: he believed (*crede*) that he could be reconciled to the new pope.[31] By harboring this belief, Cesare betrays an attachment to a crucial Christian teaching. Christ teaches, "Ask and it will be given to you; seek and you will find; knock and the door will be opened to you. For everyone who asks receives; the one who seeks finds; and to the one who knocks, the door will be opened."[32] In one of his final directives to his disciples, Christ instructs them, "If you forgive anyone's sins, their sins are forgiven; if you do not forgive them, they are not forgiven."[33] This teaching is particularly attractive to the gravely ill, whom Christ frequently heals upon a demonstration of faith.[34] Practicing Catholics seek absolution for their transgressions before they die; Cesare's folly confirms Machiavelli's general judgment that even the most corrupt and nominal of Christians, at moments of great consequence, will succumb to the siren song of Christianity's hopeful promises—including the forgiveness of sins.[35] Machiavelli deliberately suggests that Cesare's illness enflamed these groundless hopes. Duke Valentino believed the new Vicar of Christ would forgive and forget his family's transgressions.[36] This belief dooms him.

Cesare Borgia and Alexander VI: Fresh, but Failed, Examples

In his lengthy praise of Cesare Borgia in chapter 7, Machiavelli opines that those who wish to employ the modes necessary to rule as a new prince can "find no fresher examples than the actions of that man."[37] Yet while Cesare might be a "fresher" example of a new prince, Moses, Romulus, Theseus, and Cyrus remain superior examples. Indeed, it is not clear that any new prince ought to imitate Cesare's attempt to renew "old orders" (*P* 7). Cesare's praiseworthy modes tend only to underscore the defective nature of his orders, which are never actually established, but remain "in the air" (*P* 7) at the death of Alexander. He rose to "empire through fortune and the arms of others" (*P* 7), and his decline coincides with the loss of that fortune. Lacking Cesare's paradoxical and extraordinary fortune, the founders of chapter 6 were compelled to begin their enterprises by acquiring or consolidating their arms: because their exploits proceed from this necessary foundation, they "acquire their principality with difficulty but hold it with ease."

Yet Cesare Borgia is not merely a modern Italian prince who attempted to conquer and unify Italy. Instead, his career represents an attempt by the pope to use his religious position to accomplish the conquest of Italy through an extraordinary son. Machiavelli makes this clear when he writes that Cesare—who employed unchristian tactics ostensibly to advance the interests of the Church—attempted to "renew old orders through new modes" (*P*7).[38] Machiavelli thus invites us to interpret the failure of Cesare Borgia as the failure of Alexander VI, who sought to renew the Church's orders with unchristian modes. The Borgias' career demonstrates the limits of the Church's political power, even under the direction of the canniest and worldliest of popes. Their failure demonstrates richly the consequences of deficient arms, but it also reveals the dangerousness of relying on old, defective, orders.

This reminder of the necessity of new orders requires a return to a discussion of crime, which is central to the foundings praised in chapter 6. Machiavelli teaches that the greatest changes require profound destruction, equivalent to crime. The Borgias—though inveterate sinners—could not perform this act, which would entail the destruction of the Church. Indeed, their criminality appears niggling in comparison to that of the founders. As bad men living amid those educated to be good, they were accustomed to survive by deceit, with an admixture of surreptitious violence. Unlike Moses and the armed prophets, they depended ultimately on the credulity of other men, rather than their own arms, to succeed. However bad the Borgias may have been, they were not bad enough to commit the crime required of a lasting founding: either because they were constrained by their reliance on its orders, charmed by its teachings, or perhaps both, they could not destroy the Bride of Christ. Eventually, when she withdrew her favor and Cesare found himself opposed by her orders, whatever the Borgias had accomplished ultimately "redounded to the greatness of the Church" (*P*11).[39]

The need to eliminate the old order is particularly pressing for any prince who wishes to establish a civil principality. In chapter 9, Machiavelli recommends founding a regime on the people since "one cannot satisfy the great with decency and without injury to others, but one can satisfy the people; for the end of the people is more decent than that of the great" (*P* 9).[40] A prince of a civil order places himself at the peak of political power; all other princes find themselves among unmanageable and ambitious equals who are intent on oppressing others. Due to the humor that inclines them to oppression, the great are a persistent obstacle to the foundation of civil society. Should one become prince with their help, Machiavelli dictates that he "must before everything else seek to gain the people to himself, which should be easy for him when he takes up their protection" (*P*9). For the reasons we have already discussed—Cesare's debilitating reliance on the papacy, his lack of a sufficient faithful army, and his latent belief in the teachings of Christianity—he is unable to pursue a similar strategy against his coconspirators in the Church. In the next two chapters, Machiavelli will counsel a prince whose knowledge of the world inures him to Christianity's seductive and corruptive teachings.

Unarmed Principalities and the Vatican

After offering a faint sketch of how one might found a civil principality by waging war against the great in chapter 9, Machiavelli returns to the subject of the papacy in chapters 10 and 11. Chapter 10 is titled "In What Mode the Forces of All Principalities Should Be Measured." In this summative chapter, Machiavelli judges all principalities according to their autonomy: can they rule alone—that is, can they, with either men or money, field an army adequate to defend themselves? If a principality lacks the means for its own defense, Machiavelli suggests that it lacks true autonomy. Any neighbors that come to its defense will share in its rule. Machiavelli thus rebukes Italian affairs, as disclosed especially in chapters 3 and 7. No Italian principality emerges as truly autonomous; Machiavelli presents the Italian politico-military world as a complex latticework of alliances and counteralliances that change in response to the machinations of the principal powers involved: the Church, Venice, Spain, and France. The Church, which has no army of its own, suffers from a particularly acute dependency. It is the quintessential unarmed principality.

Given the importance of arms, one might conclude that inadequately armed principalities are doomed. Yet in chapter 10, Machiavelli recommends a provisional strategy for securing these regimes. A prince who lacks an army may be "compelled by necessity to take refuge behind walls and to guard [the city]," but if he supplies his town and manages "the governing of his subjects," he will be relatively secure, since "it is not easy to attack one who has a strong town and is not hated by the people" (*P* 10). Given his praise of vigorous preemption in chapter 3 and armed princes in chapter 6, this is very un-Machiavellian advice—for very un-Machiavellian principalities. To provide evidence for his claim, he cites certain "cities of Germany" (*P* 10) that "are very free, have little countryside, and obey the emperor when they want to; they do not fear either him or any other power around, because they are so well fortified that everyone thinks their capture would be toilsome and difficult. . . . They still hold military exercises in repute, and they have many institutions to maintain them" (*P* 10).

Machiavelli cites these German cities, which he elsewhere describes as "republics" (*D* II.19.1), as examples of model political communities. While he traveled in that province, Machiavelli apparently employs them as models that illustrate the problems with contemporary cities and republics.[41] In the *Discourses*, Machiavelli cites them as models of "goodness" and "religion" that highlight the corruption of contemporary Europe: unlike other European communities, they are public spirited, remain free from the scourge of parasitic gentlemen, and are bastions of political and economic equality (*D* I.55.2–4). More relevant to this passage, in the context of a discussion of the decline of Italian military virtue, Machiavelli also describes these republics "maintaining military exercises with the highest seriousness" and as the only in the world that may "succeed in staying quiet and enjoying its freedom and little borders" (II.19.1). All other republics must expand with their armies, or perish, yet "certain conditions" allow the exceptional cities of Germany to pursue the only strategies available to the unarmed: to "put a check on every ambition, regulate one's city inside with laws and customs, prohibit acquisition, and think only of defending oneself and of keeping one's defenses well ordered" (D II.19.1).[42] Machiavelli's lesson is that all other principalities lack the internal conditions—and the geopolitical position—to remain quiet, inadequately armed, and secure. His mention of the cities of Germany in chapter 10 thus underscores the peril of being inadequately armed. An ideal principality may thrive thus, but no real city can imitate this success, which resembles the "middle way" (D II.23.4) that Machiavelli elsewhere condemns.[43]

The most important implication of this argument is that the Vatican—the most prominent walled, inadequately armed city in Europe—is in a perilous predicament. Situated in Rome, amid warring principalities and republics, it cannot hope to be insulated from the ambitious striving of the world. While one might argue that it could, with the help of the Gospels' unequivocal endorsement of humility and poverty, check ambition and the desire to acquire among its own people—the men and women religious who dominate the population of the Vatican and have sworn to imitate the life of Christ—the careers of Alexander VI and Julius II suggest the impossibility of that effort. Human nature cannot be reliably bent to the teaching of the Gospels. The Curiae will seek wealth, priests will seek political power, and popes will sometimes even issue sons. The goodness, religion, and unfailing order possessed by the cities of Germany are chimerical. Any real city that depends on German orders alone for its survival is in jeopardy.

What Men Truly Love

In the final lines of chapter 10, Machiavelli overstates the security of these inadequately armed principalities. He writes that they are difficult to conquer, since they possess great internal strength—especially if a "powerful and spirited prince" (P 10) governs them. He recommends against laying siege to such cities, on the grounds that "worldly things are so variable" as to render a siege of up to a year "next to impossible" (P 10). To an imaginary objector who predicts that the people will be lured outside the walls when the enemy begins to burn their possessions, and that "the long siege and their love for their own [la carità propria] will make them forget the prince" (P 10), Machiavelli suggests that this prince will manage their discontent with a mixture of rhetoric and force.

In this passage, Machiavelli departs from using his usual word for love (*amore*), suggesting instead that "charity for their own" will tempt the people to abandon their prince.[44] This is one of only two appearances of the word "charity" in *The Prince*.[45] As the most common and pregnant Latin version of the New Testament term *agape*, charity describes the disposition of a good Christian toward his fellow man: godly love.[46] As noted in chapter 1 of this work, Christ repeatedly enjoins his followers to imitate him by exhibiting self-sacrificial love toward their neighbors: "My command is this: Love each other as I have loved you. Greater love has no one than this: to lay down one's life for one's friends."[47] Later writers emphasize the central importance of charity, most famously in 1 Corinthians, in which Paul insists that this sort of love "is not self-seeking."[48] Machiavelli's appropriation of this word is thoroughly unchristian. These subjects love that which is their own, rather than their fellow man. This oblique discussion of the Vatican's defenses suggests that among the men and women religious who occupy the Vatican, Christ's teaching on charity does not enjoy authority.[49] In order to prevent defection, a pope must manage them with deceptive rhetoric and by "skillfully securing himself against those who appear to him too bold" (*P* 10). Clandestine violence and clever deceit are surer guards of the unarmed than is love—a fact evidenced by the careers of the Borgias.

Machiavelli insists that an enemy will "reasonably" (*P* 10) aid the efforts of the unarmed prince by ruining the entire countryside upon his arrival. If a prince can maintain control of his city during this period, the community inside the walls will "unite with their prince so much the more, since it appears he has an obligation toward them, their houses having been burned and their possessions ruined in his defense" (*P* 10). The prince's followers—seeing their sacrifices on his behalf—will believe that he is obligated to them, and they to him. They will have nothing to which they might return outside the walls. Solidarity with the prince is an accomplished fact: the sacrifice of that which they love consecrates their union with the prince. Machiavelli thus opines that it is "the nature of men to be obligated as much by benefits they give as by benefits they receive" (*P* 10).

This is the only passage in *The Prince* in which Machiavelli addresses the "nature of men."[50] Yet why do men naturally feel obligated to causes for which they have lost so much? Obligation more reasonably resides with the party that was benefited. Indeed, this claim is in considerable tension with much of Machiavelli's presentation in *The Prince*. In chapter 17, Machiavelli claims that men are "ungrateful, fickle, pretenders and dissemblers, evaders of danger, eager for gain." How do we reconcile Machiavelli's general skepticism about the power of obligation with his claim that it is human nature "to be obligated as much by benefits they give as by benefits they receive"? (*P* 10).

These puzzling and apparently contradictory statements are clarified by a consideration of Christianity, which depends on a belief that mutual sacrifice engenders mutual obligation. At the Last Supper, Christ explicitly argues that his sacrifice obligates him to others: "This is my blood of the covenant, which is poured out for many for the forgiveness of sins. I tell you, I will not drink from this fruit of the vine from now on until that day when I drink it new with you in my Father's kingdom."[51] Men consecrate this reciprocal obligation by imitating Christ's sacrifice: "Whoever wants to be my disciple must deny themselves and take up their cross and follow me. For whoever wants to save their life will lose it, but whoever loses their life for me will find it. What good will it be for someone to gain the whole world, yet forfeit their soul? Or what can anyone give in exchange for their soul?"[52] Paul emphasizes the centrality of sacrifice to Christianity: "Follow God's example, therefore, as dearly loved children and walk in the way of love, just as Christ loved us and gave himself up for us as a fragrant offering and sacrifice to God."[53] Peter instructs suffering Christians to "rejoice inasmuch as you participate in the sufferings of Christ, so that you may be overjoyed when his glory is revealed. If you are insulted because of the name of Christ, you are blessed, for the Spirit of glory and of God rests on you."[54] The promises of the Beatitudes, the instructions to give away wealth, and the injunction to love one's fellow man all indicate that by bestowing benefits—or sacrificing earthly goods—a follower confirms his fidelity to Christ.[55] These self-sacrificial acts cement his obligation to Christ, who has also promised him great rewards.

A cynic might conclude that Christianity can demand sacrifice only because it promises these rewards. Yet can mere calculation really account for the tremendous deprivations to which Christians submit themselves for the sake of Christ? If Christianity is merely a *quid pro quo* arrangement, the *quo* is largely presumptive. Christ's rewards are largely otherworldly. His followers' belief in them depends substantially on faith. While Christ's miracles—including especially his resurrection—may constitute evidence of his ability to deliver his promised rewards, many of his most grandiose promises depend on his word alone.[56] How does the psychological power of "benefits they give" (*P* 10) help explain Christians' stalwart faith in the kingdom of heaven?

The power of self-sacrifice to engender obligation can be explained by extrapolating from Machiavellian psychological principles. Machiavelli's general teaching is that men are primarily self-seeking, rather than self-sacrificial: they most regularly seek "their own utility" (*P* 17).[57] Yet precisely because calculative self-love is the general rule for mankind, men balk at blaming themselves when they are unable to satisfy their selfishness. Instead, they tend to attribute the frustration of their desires to an external person or cause. Yet "*la carità propria*" is not easily thwarted: because they love that which is their own so ardently, hope springs eternal in men.[58] Rather than merely mourn their losses and assign blame—although they are surely capable of this—they tend to renew their hopes by redirecting them to the very cause of their stymied selfishness. In chapter 10, the object of these renewed hopes is the prince of the unarmed principality. Machiavelli's puzzling presentation is coherent if we consider the possibility that these men, having lost that which they truly love (their own possessions, or worldly goods), and yet remaining unswervingly selfish, cannot conceive of a universe that does not support their selfish concern. The fact that *they* lost something leads them to believe that the universe must have a plan to restore their worldly goods. Machiavelli suggests that this subtle calculation engenders a sense of obligation to the cause for which they have suffered, the worthiness of which is made evident by the fact of their sacrifice. Ultimately, then, this obligation is linked inextricably to a belief in their own desert, rather than the merits of the party they have benefited. These men anticipate a just reward for the "benefits they give."[59] Hope leads them to associate their previous loss on the unarmed prince's behalf with a future gain in his name. Indeed, more intense deprivations will likely enflame these hopes, deepen their sense of obligation, and necessitate grander rewards. Seen thus, the radical self-abnegation Christ requires is the principal cause of the incredible faith of Christians. "Hated" by "the world," Christians' self-concern breeds confidence in an extravagant reward for their suffering; Christ's promise to "overcome the world" is that reward.[60] Seen thus, the humility of a Christian—and Christ himself—is a cloak for overweening pride. The language of self-sacrifice is an attempt to satisfy—and ennoble—frustrated selfishness.

The unarmed prince of chapter 10, like Christ, ultimately depends on the selfish concern of the dispossessed, who obligate themselves to him because they believe that having given up so much in his name, a reward must await them. Christ encourages this belief among his followers. Machiavelli, recognizing that men's primary passion is "love for their own" (*P* 10), seeks to exploit this selfish passion in order to enervate the obligation men feel toward their unarmed prince.[61] Any potential conqueror who reads chapter 10 of *The Prince* will know better than to destroy the entire countryside upon arriving at the gates of an unarmed principality. Instead, he ought to deliberately—and slowly—destroy the possessions of those inside the walls, perhaps while promising that no harm will come to the possessions of those who betray the prince. The conqueror will thus seek to enflame the subjects' "charity for their own" at the expense of charity for their prince. When applied to a conquest of the Vatican, Machiavelli suggests that a conqueror ought to hold the possessions of the ecclesiastical order hostage in order to encourage dissension within the walls of the Holy See. By doing so, the conqueror will gain entrance to the walled city

and overcome the powerful political psychology of self-sacrificial obligation that is so crucial to unarmed princes.

When applied to Christianity more generally, Machiavelli is recommending that by enabling men's "charity for their own," one can adulterate their
love of Christ. Since according to Machiavelli, Christ's appeal depends
largely on the deprivation of worldly goods, one can diminish the power of
his hopeful teaching merely by expanding and protecting what men consider most their own—their property, families, and liberty. Christians may
continue to multiply, and even remember Christ's sacrifice by celebrating
the Eucharist, but their way of life will be less Christlike as Machiavelli's
judgments about the primacy of this world take root in their hearts. Importantly, Christ agrees: "Do not store up for yourselves treasures on earth,
where moths and vermin destroy, and where thieves break in and steal. But
store up for yourselves treasures in heaven, where moths and vermin do
not destroy, and where thieves do not break in and steal. For where your
treasure is, there your heart will be also."[62]

By directing men to earthly goods, Machiavelli believes that he is help-
ing them satisfy their true desires. The argument of chapter 10 suggests
that humans seek reward through self-sacrifice only if "charity for their
own" is impossible. Self-sacrificial obligation thus emerges among men
only as a second-best option—or indeed, as the context of this discussion
suggests, it may be adopted only as a last resort. Finding men on earth, but
gazing uselessly at heaven, Machiavelli merely encourages them to fix their
eyes on the true—worldly—objects of their longings. The regular satisfaction of these ordinary desires will enervate their belief that an imitation of
Christ's suffering is necessary to salvation. In its place, Machiavelli offers a
new, unchristian salvation to mankind—understood in worldly, rather than
heavenly, terms. This recommendation to satisfy men's material desires
complements his endorsement of the passions that enable republican liberty—hatred and revenge: these passions inure men to Christianity's most
abject, impoverishing, and slavish teachings.[63]

Exposing the Bride of Christ to Peril

Chapter 10 conveys an implicit teaching about the Vatican, but chapter
11 reveals Machiavelli's explicit judgment of ecclesiastical principalities.
He initially hesitates to undertake this discussion. Employing precisely
the same doubletalk that introduced his discussion of Moses, Machiavelli
comments, "Since they are exalted and maintained by God, it would be
the office of a presumptuous and foolhardy man to discourse on them.
Nonetheless, if someone were to inquire of me how it came about that
the Church has come to such greatness . . . it does not seem to me

superfluous to recall a good part of it to memory" (*P* 11).[64] Machiavelli feigns pious awe.

Ecclesiastical principalities defy Machiavellian political rules.[65]

> They are acquired either by virtue or by fortune and are maintained without one or the other, for they are sustained by orders that have grown old with religion, which have been so powerful and of such a kind that they keep their princes in the state however they proceed and live. These alone have states, and do not defend them; they have subjects, and do not govern them; and the states, though undefended, are not taken from them; the subjects, though ungoverned, do not care, and they neither think of becoming estranged from such princes nor can they. Thus, only these principalities are secure and happy. (*P* 11)

Machiavelli's praise of ecclesiastical principalities is ironic. They appear to do nothing, and yet claim everything. One requires neither virtue nor fortune to maintain them, since "they subsist by superior causes" (*P* 11). They meet none of the usual requirements of political rule, and yet they retain subjects and states. Because they possess "orders that have grown old with religion" (*P* 11), they alone flourish while remaining indolent. Machiavelli wonders at their ability to thrive despite their perpetual torpor. Yet by alerting the reader to their character, he also exposes these principalities to danger. If one can weaken the authority of their old religious orders—as Machiavelli seeks to do in *The Prince*—one can remove the principal prop of their power.

The rest of the chapter consists of a history of the Church's political power, which is plagued by perpetual factional quarrel; in the time about which Machiavelli discourses, the division between the Orsini and Colonna families of Rome kept the Church weak. Fearful of a powerful Church, the other Italian powers assiduously encouraged this quarrel. When a pope who supported the Colonna died, a pro-Orsini pope would succeed him. The short lives of the popes prevented either faction from gaining supremacy. This perennial disorder enervated the Church's power, and caused "the temporal forces of the pope to be held in low esteem in Italy" (P *11*). Although supposedly "exalted and maintained by God," neither "fortune [n]or wisdom" arose to lift the Church from this morass (*P* 11). Thus, the lone principality that "subsist[s] by superior causes" (*P* 11) yielded decidedly inferior temporal results.

The rise of the Borgias altered this pattern. Alexander VI employed money and forces more effectively than any previous pontiff. He used his son to capture the Romagna and end the factional conflict that paralyzed the Vatican (*P* 11). Though his short tenure as pope exemplified the Church's struggle to formulate a consistent papal policy, the Bride of Christ was nonetheless fortunate to be ruled consecutively by two industrious popes.[66] Julius reaped the rewards of the Borgias' labors: while he was himself an exemplary religious profiteer, his "greatness" was enabled by the Borgias, who "had eliminated the barons in Rome, and had annihilated those factions" that had historically infected Rome's political climate and enervated the papacy's power (*P* 11).[67]

In his praise of Julius, Machiavelli casually and indirectly suggests a paradoxical solution to the Vatican's problem of political instability: the cardinals, he says, "are the origin of the tumults among" the barons in Rome. "Nor will these parties ever be quiet as long as they have cardinals; for cardinals nourish parties, within Rome and without, and the barons are forced to defend them. Thus, from the ambition of prelates arise disorders and tumults among the barons" (*P* 11). Alexander sought to eliminate faction by attacking the barons and preventing the Orsini and Colonna from becoming cardinals; this solution was akin to beheading the Hydra. The only permanent solution to the Vatican's factional quarrel is to annihilate the college of cardinals. This solution would transform the Church into a monarchy with no clear line of succession. Because popes do not always have sons, and we cannot presume that the ecclesiastical order would easily consent to so radical a change, this would be a risky act with uncertain consequences. More certainly, the one remedy for the Church's temporal weakness is not practicable for the Vicar of Christ. Such a transformative alteration to the Church would be equivalent to Jesus slaughtering his disciples at the Last Supper—inconceivable and radically self-defeating.[68]

Thus, the most prominent ecclesiastical principality is weak, and is likely to remain so. One ought to note that Machiavelli's teaching on the various kinds of principalities culminates in this teaching about the Church, which he situates between a discussion of the criminal violence required for a founding (chapters 6–9) and the proper foundations of armies (chapters 12–14). The Church, maintained only by the ineffectual attention of God and Christ's vulnerable orders, is helpless against any prince who remains unmoved by its appeals to goodness, love, and faith. Indeed, the current pope's "goodness" (*P* 11) makes him particularly ill-prepared to withstand an assault by a prince who has learned from chapters 10 and 11 of *The Prince*. Neither powerful nor spirited, Leo X is unlikely to manage the intense factional conflict that a prudent siege of the Vatican would surely precipitate. Seen thus, Machiavelli's prayer for Leo's goodness and the Church's veneration is poisonous irony.

Arms, Hope, and the Antichrist: Machiavelli's Summative Critique of Christian Politics

In the first thirteen chapters of *The Prince*, Machiavelli has demonstrated amply his anti-Christian animus. He has routinely praised ancient and pagan politics, while harshly condemning the Christianized politics of Europe; he has named pre-Christian founders as "most excellent" (*P* 6), while offering a discreet critique of Jesus's founding; he has even advanced a radical critique of many of Christ's most important teachings—including the proper roles of acquisition, love, and violence in political life—while proffering his own worldly teachings as a substitute. No innovation is more important and anti-Christian, however, than Machiavelli's new teaching on arms, the possession of which is crucial to Machiavellian political practice. He summarizes this teaching at the end of chapter 13: "I conclude, thus, that without its own arms no principality is secure; indeed, it is wholly obliged to fortune since it does not have virtue to defend itself in adversity. And it has always been the opinion and judgment of wise men 'that nothing is so infirm and unstable as fame for power not sustained by one's own force.'"[69] This summary teaching constitutes a radical critique of the Prince of Peace, who seeks fame as the Son of God, but is wholly dependent on God's force for deliverance. Consequently, he refuses to order his arms so that he might defend himself.

> While he was still speaking, Judas, one of the Twelve, arrived. With him was a large crowd armed with swords and clubs, sent from the chief priests and the elders of the people. . . . Then the men stepped forward, seized Jesus and arrested him. With that, one of Jesus's companions reached for his sword, drew it out and struck the servant of the high priest, cutting off his ear. "Put your sword back in its place," Jesus said to him, "for all who draw the sword will die by the sword. Do you think I cannot call on my Father, and he will at once put at my disposal more than twelve legions of angels? But how then would the Scriptures be fulfilled that say it must happen in this way?"[70]

Jesus's followers flee. He is subsequently interrogated, tortured, and crucified. According to Machiavelli's implicit teaching, the ultimate success of his orders is best explained by the intercession of the Roman Empire and Christ's exploitation of human beings' natural—and ultimately confused—tendency to be obligated by self-sacrifice. Christ might have anticipated the latter effect, but could not have predicted the former event. Because the success of Christian orders depends on a combination of external support and human confusion, it is not prudent to imitate Jesus Christ. Indeed, as numerous nominally Christian reprobates—including Liverotto da Fermo, Giovampagolo Baglioni, and Cesare Borgia—demonstrate by their soft-hearted bungling, it is perilous to harbor even a latent belief in him. Ultimately, chapters 1 through 13 of *The Prince* demonstrate that "nothing is so infirm and unstable" (*P* 13) as projects undertaken in his name.

Machiavelli offers an education designed to counteract the most damaging effects of this Christian education: its effeminacy, lack of knowledge about the world, and persistent attraction to groundless and extravagant

hope. Consequently, he teaches, "One's arms are those which are composed of either your subjects or citizens or creatures: all others are either
mercenary or auxiliary. And the mode of ordering one's arms will be easy
to find if one reviews the orders of the four I named above. . . . I submit
myself entirely to these orders" (*P* 13). Machiavelli thus reminds the reader
that the four pre-Christian prophets of chapter 6 most clearly demonstrate
how to order one's army.[71] At the crucial moment when Jesus's criminal
conspiracy against the older orders is confronted fully, he is utterly without
arms, and doom swiftly follows his arrest. His dismissive teachings on arms
and the world have perpetuated a harmful relationship between arms and
contemporary Christians. Having surveyed the political rubble of Christ's
legacy, Machiavelli proclaims that he prefers to imitate ancient—or, more
precisely, pre-Christian—men. To do so, he needs an army.

Yet while Machiavelli professes his preference for pre-Christian modes,
we must note that he has more in common with Jesus Christ than with
Moses. First, his statement at the end of chapter 13 reminds us that, he,
like Christ, seeks to imitate ancient founders. Second, Machiavelli and
Christ both lack arms; indeed—even more than Christ—Machiavelli relies
on speeches, rather than deeds, to propagate his teaching.[72] Third, Machiavelli and Christ each find themselves alienated from the earthly kingdoms
they seek to subvert. Finally, the remainder of *The Prince* confirms that, like
Christ, Machiavelli places his trust in posthumous success: this book will be
his gospel. With it—in imitation of Christ—he hopes to attract the arms
necessary to institute his new orders.[73]

Machiavelli is also, however, a decidedly anti-Christian imitator of
Christ. Crucial to his plan is his unchristian appropriation of Christ's chief
support: hope. As an unarmed prince, Christ cannily exploited the natural
tendency of human beings to be obligated by deprivation and self-sacrifice.
According to Machiavelli, this sense of obligation among Christians is not
rooted in self-forgetting brotherly love, but in extravagant and ultimately
selfish hopes in a just reward. Because the psychological power of misplaced
hope, in combination with the intercession of the Roman Empire, explains
Christ's success, Machiavelli's evaluation of Christ's career teaches him at
least two lessons. First, he learns from Christ the importance of hope to an
unarmed prophet. Yet he also learns that hope is not enough: the intercession of Romulus's armed orders was necessary to secure Christ's legacy.

Nonetheless, Roman virtue—which, as Machiavelli reveals in chapter 19,
was already in decline—was not able to correct the most damaging effects
of Christ's orders. Instead, Christ's eschewal of arms and trust in God thoroughly corrupted Rome's martial tradition. Machiavelli's survey of Christianized politics confirms this. Yet Christianity did not expunge entirely
men's worldliness. As a result, Christians are painfully divided between
their attraction to this world and their hopes to enter the "kingdom of

God"—a pain only intensified by the reflection that their attachment to the former is an impediment to entering the latter. This ambivalence largely helps to explain Christians' worldly failures. Because Machiavelli's teaching is so thoroughly worldly, his believers will be free of this damaging and painful ambivalence. To epitomize his new, worldly teaching, at the moment that Machiavelli has revealed most fully his conspiracy against the existing order, he departs from Christ: unlike the Prince of Peace, he explicitly calls for arms to be ordered and employed in his name.

Chapters 1 through 13 demonstrate that Machiavelli's attempt to enflame and satisfy men's hopes in this world, rather than the next, is the hallmark of his anti-Christian plan. He offers material prosperity in place of deprivation, selfish satisfaction in place of self-sacrifice, and worldly glory in place of otherworldly triumph. These teachings are anti-Christian. John, when writing of those who possess the "spirit of the antichrist," alerts Christians to their distinguishing marks: "They are from the world and therefore speak from the viewpoint of the world, and the world listens to them."[74] Throughout the first half of *The Prince*, Machiavelli has deliberately confirmed that he is "of the world." In chapter 13, he openly announces his fidelity to mundane orders, and in doing so confirms his lack of faith in the Prince of Peace, who famously proclaims that his "kingdom is not of this world."[75] This anti-Christian argument culminates in chapter 14, where Machiavelli will endorse the worldly prince of war.

CHAPTER FOUR

The Prince of War

With his condemnation of modern Christian politics in chapters 1 through 13, Machiavelli has sought like-minded malcontents. Chapter 14 presents a scheme for their basic training, and establishes an appropriate, non-Christian model of imitation: the Greek prince, Philopoemen. In obedience to ancient orders, Machiavelli discloses the best way to correct the weak and vain education of Christianity: "a prince should have no other object, nor any other thought, nor take anything else as his art but that of war and its orders and its discipline" (*P* 14). The rest of the chapter consists of three sections: an exhortation for princes to think constantly of war; a comparison of war to hunting that reintroduces the landscape metaphor of the dedicatory letter; and finally, a prescription to read histories so that one might correctly imitate ancient men.[1]

Machiavelli asserts that knowledge of the art of war is sufficient "to one who commands" (*P* 14). Being unarmed, on the other hand, makes one "contemptible," since it is not "reasonable" (*P* 14) for the armed to obey the unarmed. Although Machiavelli does not allude to the Gospels here, Christ's relationship to Roman soldiers generally confirms his judgment that being unarmed produces scorn among the armed.

> The soldiers led Jesus away into the palace . . . and called together the whole company of soldiers. They put a purple robe on him, then twisted together a crown of thorns and set it on him. And they began to call out to him, "Hail, king of the Jews!" Again and again they struck him on the head with a staff and spit on him. Falling on their knees, they paid homage to him. And when they had mocked him, they took off the purple robe and put his own clothes on him. Then they led him out to crucify him.[2]

According to Machiavelli, even a prince who is at peace is obliged to think constantly of war.[3] To prepare the body for war, Machiavelli recommends a combination of military exercises and hunting. The latter activity also constitutes mental preparation: while hunting, "he should learn the nature of sites, and recognize how mountains rise, how valleys open up, how plains lie, and understand the nature of rivers and marshes—and in this invest the greatest care" (*P* 14).[4] This knowledge of nature, which Machiavelli identifies as "science" in the *Discourses* (III.39.2), enables one to defend one's country and conquer one's neighbor. Machiavelli's injunction to learn natural sites also ought to remind the reader of the dedicatory letter, in which Lorenzo's ignorance of the valleys revealed his deficient political wisdom.[5]

The Men on the Plains: Philopoemen, Publius Decius, and Machiavelli

Machiavelli evidently regards the knowledge of landscape as important: it is among the few lessons he repeats with precision in both *The Prince* and the *Discourses*.[6] Moreover, in both books, after conveying the general teaching, Machiavelli furnishes an example of a commander who made use of this knowledge of nature. In *The Prince*, Machiavelli cites the Greek prince Philopoemen as one who "in times of peace . . . never thought of anything but modes of war" (*P* 14). In the *Discourses*, Machiavelli names Publius Decius as a captain whose understanding of nature allowed him to succeed in war (III.39.2). Machiavelli presents each while on campaign, and like Machiavelli in the dedicatory letter, each is on a plain, while the object of his scheming is the high place. Decius and Philopoemen each serve as an agent of the Roman Republic, although Philopoemen's support of Rome is qualified by his devotion to Greek liberty. Philopoemen joins Rome to combat Greek tyrants before eventually denouncing Rome's imperial ambitions in Greece; Publius Decius devises a strategy to save the Roman army in a battle against the Samnites.[7] Taken together, they reveal Machiavelli's relationship to Rome, and disclose his broadest goals. Yet Philopoemen is especially important, insofar as his life's work, spirit, and education mirror closely Machiavelli's own.

In *The Prince*, Machiavelli fabricates a conversation between Philopoemen and his friends that discloses both his method for gaining knowledge of sites and the objects of his belligerent thinking.

> And when he was on campaign with friends [*amici*], he often stopped and reasoned [*ragionava*] with them: "If the enemy were on top of that hill and we were here with our army, which of us would have the advantage? How could one advance to meet them while maintaining order? If we wanted to retreat from here, how would we have to do it? If they retreated, how would we have to follow them?" And he put before them, as he went along, all the chances that can occur to an army; he listened to their opinions, gave his own, supported it with reasons, so that because of these continued cogitations

[*continue cogitazioni*] there could never arise, while he led the army, any accident for which he did not have the remedy. (*P* 14)[8]

Philopoemen's dialogic cogitations resemble philosophical activity. As Nathan Tarcov observes, Philopoemen encourages a degree of freedom of inquiry and genuine fellowship that no other prince of the book enjoys, yet "this is the freedom masterfully enjoyed by Machiavelli himself, though exercised with restraint in writing *The Prince*."[9] By writing *The Prince* for "whoever understands it" (*P* 14), Machiavelli, like Philopoemen, seeks friends with whom to reason; like the Achaean, Machiavelli's cogitations are instrumental to a desired good—the defeat of the enemy on the hilltop—rather than for their own sake.[10]

Chapter 14 suggests that Philopoemen's practical philosophy is sufficient preparation for any prince: "there could never arise, while he led the army, any accident for which he did not have the remedy" (*P* 14). With this tantalizing promise of inoculation against "any accident," Machiavelli suggests that men like Philopoemen are models for armed princes. By inviting a comparison of himself to Philopoemen, he suggests that he, too, is an imitative model. Machiavelli's friends can profit from his "continued cogitations" (*P* 14) about war.

Indeed, an important, but largely implicit, lesson of *The Prince* is that "cogitations" about nature can produce friendship, especially if they are intended to engender hope among friends. The nature of the people may necessitate the use of force or fraud to bind them to a prince, but for those who can understand, rational inquiry, employed in a scheme against a common enemy, is sufficient. Machiavelli thus revises the dim presentation on friendship from chapter 3. Yet this revised, quasi-philosophical friendship remains incompatible with Christian charity, according to which one ought to love—rather than scheme against—one's enemies.

While Philopoemen and his friends employ the practical philosophy required for war against the heights, attention to the example of Publius Decius in the *Discourses* illuminates Machiavelli's motive for scheming to secure the hilltop. Publius is a tribune of the Roman army during the war against the Samnites. He advises the consul Cornelius to secure a peak left undefended by the Samnites: "Do you see . . . that peak above the enemy? That is the citadel of our hope and salvation if (because the blind Samnites have left it) we take it quickly" (*D* III.39.2).[11] The presence of the Samnites, who are among Rome's most obstinate foes, is important in at least two respects. First, their defeat is an important moment in Rome's progress toward unifying Italy, a task that Machiavelli explicitly endorses.[12] Second, in Machiavelli's discussion of religion's value to military enterprises in the *Discourses*, their practices emerge as an inferior alternative to Rome's. Machiavelli teaches that the Roman Republic grounded its religious orders in the canny subordination of priestly authority to political elites and military commanders.[13] The Romans exhibit this arrangement in the ultimate battle against the Samnites. While the Roman consul Papirius Cursor employs a combination of violence and deceit to appear to "accommodate his plans to the auspices" and engender hope among the soldiers, the Samnites—before the same battle—commit themselves to the orders of priests, who perform an "ancient sacrifice" "with words of execration and verses full of fright" in order "to induce obstinacy in the sprits of their soldiers" (*D* I.15.1).[14] The Samnites' subsequent loss to the Romans demonstrates perhaps the superiority of the republic that controls its priests, but it vindicates even more clearly the strength of religious practices that engender hope, rather than fear. Decius's successful exhortation to secure Rome's "hope and salvation" (*D* III.39.2) by seizing the aforementioned peak confirms the psychological power of hope. Decius thus aids two projects that Machiavelli supports: the unification of Italy and the triumph of a politically salutary civil religion.

A consideration of the context of Decius's and Philopoemen's careers helps us understand Machiavelli's own relationship to Rome, past and present. Decius is a stalwart captain for the young Roman Republic, while Philopoemen is a conditional Roman ally who opposes its nascent imperialism. Machiavelli famously praises the Roman Republic, but also expresses profound ambivalence about its ultimate legacy: the extirpation of Italian republics, the loss of freedom in Rome, and the ascendancy of the Catholic Church of Rome are the clearest harmful consequences of the Roman Empire.[15] Machiavelli's identification with Decius and Philopoemen reflects his ambivalence toward Rome.

Despite their varied attitudes toward Roman power, these three men on the plains have something important in common. Each man wages war against an enemy hostile to liberty. Lorenzo de' Medici is a hereditary prince whose family ended the Florentine republic and owes its position to the stultifying power of the Church; the expansionary Roman Republic of Philopoemen's time poses a danger to Greek freedom; and the Samnites, although themselves a republic with "so much order and so much force" (*D* II.2.3), when their republic is in its death throes, subject themselves to priests who employ ineffective religious practices that engender terror, rather than hope—while also constituting an obstacle to the Roman unification of Italy.[16]

The Enemy on the Hilltop

Machiavelli's commendation of the "prince of war" complements his critique of Christ in *The Prince*. Indeed, Machiavelli's model prince—who is travelling with his friends, always thinking of war, and conspiring to defeat enemies and capture worldly goods—is a sort of Antichrist.[17] While Machiavelli does not allude directly to Scripture here, a comparison of this prince of war and Christ nonetheless yields pregnant results. While Machiavelli's prince of war conspires on the plains, the Prince of Peace regularly appears on hilltops: Jesus's most important sermon is delivered on "a mountainside";[18] he conveys to his disciples the details of his divine plan to overcome the world on the "Mount of Olives";[19] he is transfigured on a "high mountain";[20] and his all-important death is reputed to have occurred on a hill outside of Jerusalem, the city against which he was conspiring.[21]

While Machiavelli's prince of war devises a battlefield strategy predicated on knowledge of "the nature of sites" (P 14) that might deliver that city, Christ's triumph requires that the laws of nature be controverted.[22] His followers will rely upon the wondrous power of prayer: "Truly I tell you, if you have faith and do not doubt . . . you can say to this mountain, 'Go, throw yourself into the sea,' and it will be done."[23] As he nears his violent end, Christ issues a series of warnings that foreshadow his death and the eventual apocalypse, at which time God and supernatural angels—rather than men—will intervene decisively.[24]

While Christ predicts that his followers will suffer much until his triumphant return—including the reign of the anti-Christian "prince of this world"—he seeks to comfort them with a hope for redemption in the world that is to come, which will be attended by heavenly calamities.[25] Machiavelli, who teaches that those seeking earthly victories ought to heed rational precepts about nature, identifies himself with two pagan princes of the world—a Roman captain who seeks to secure a republic's hope and salvation in this world and a Greek prince whose ambition and independence leads him to think only of war against a universalizing empire—rather than Paul, who preaches, "For though we walk in the flesh, we do not war according to the flesh. For the weapons of our warfare are not carnal but mighty in God for pulling down strongholds, casting down arguments and every high thing that exalts itself against the knowledge of God, bringing every thought into captivity to the obedience of Christ, and being ready to punish all disobedience when your obedience is fulfilled."[26] Machiavelli, who trusts only in the "science" (D III.39.2) of nature and the "weapons of the world," declines to submit his "every thought" obediently to Christ.[27] Instead, he seeks to ensure the triumph of a "prince of this world" by providing him with careful instruction in the nature of sites—and the actions of men.[28]

Histories and Imitation

An education in deeds prepares the mind, but a prince should also "read histories and consider in them the actions of excellent men, should see how they conducted themselves in wars, should examine the causes of their victories and losses, so as to be able to avoid the latter and imitate the former" (P 14).[29] This discernment ought to culminate in the imitation of one "who had been praised and glorified before him, whose exploits and actions he always kept beside himself" (P 14). Machiavelli offers examples of men who imitated glorious predecessors. The first two pairs constitute a consecutive line of imitation: Julius Caesar imitated Alexander the Great, and Alexander imitated Achilles. The third pair— Scipio imitated Cyrus by reading Xenophon's *Cyropaedia*—stands alone.[30] Although the context of this discussion suggests that they are all models for imitation, Machiavelli does not explicitly recommend that any be imitated. Instead, he cites them merely as models *of* imitation: these are men who engaged in the imitative process, but Machiavelli only implies that they correctly imitated worthy objects.

Who are these men?[31] Julius Caesar, who studied Alexander's exploits while on campaign, was the victor in a Roman civil war, and was subsequently named dictator in perpetuity.[32] Caesar's ascendancy and assassination signaled the final demise of the Roman Republic. Machiavelli cites him as a qualified model of liberality in chapter 16, but condemns him as a "tyrant" in the *Discourses* (I.37.2).[33] Nor does his empire appear particularly conducive to a prince's security: in chapter 19, Machiavelli reveals that those who ascend to his royal seat encounter constant dangers.

Alexander the Great conquered much of the known world, and like Caesar, was a successful progenitor of empire.[34] Yet despite his virtue, his accomplishments are not so impressive as those of the founders of chapter 6: as Vickie Sullivan notes—and as Machiavelli reminds us in chapter 4— Alexander owes much of his conquest to the work of Cyrus, whose empire eventually descends to Darius III, whom Alexander defeats to become "lord of Asia."[35] He also profits from the efforts of his father, Philip, whom Machiavelli extols in the *Discourses* (I.20) and in chapter 13 of *The Prince*; as a hereditary prince, Alexander enjoys a species of fortune that diminishes his status and renders him difficult to imitate.[36]

Machiavelli reports that Alexander imitated the ancient warlike Greek hero Achilles, whose exploits he scrutinized by reading a copy of the *Iliad* that—according to Plutarch—had been corrected by Aristotle (*Alexander* 8.2–3). Machiavelli pointedly omits mention of Aristotle's instruction of Alexander, but Plutarch relates that in addition to bequeathing his kingdom, Philip bequeathed an invaluable education to his son. Young Alexander "not only received from [Aristotle] his ethical and political doctrines, but also participated in those secret and more profound teachings which philosophers . . . do not impart to many" (7.3). Alexander reportedly loved Aristotle as a father, and prized his education so highly that he bristled when Aristotle published some of his philosophical works: "Thou hast not done well to publish thy acroamatic doctrines; for in what shall I surpass other men if those doctrines wherein I have been trained are to be all men's common property? But I had rather excel in my acquaintance with the best things than in my power" (8.3, 7.4). Aristotle responded by reassuring Alexander that his published works would be unintelligible to all except those who were "already trained" (7.5).[37] Merely reading his works would be insufficient to learn his wisdom; at some point, readers would need direct instruction from a teacher who was initiated to philosophy.

Why does Machiavelli ignore Aristotle's famous relationship with Alexander, and emphasize instead the influence of Achilles's example? It is not credible to maintain that Machiavelli regards Aristotle's influence as unimportant to Alexander's career. By insisting that Alexander imitated Achilles, he directs the reader to Aristotle's famous correction of Alexander's *Iliad*, and thus, Aristotle's tutelage of the young Alexander. The meaning of this omission, then, depends on one's evaluation of Alexander's career. If Alexander is a problematic model of imitation, Machiavelli might be suggesting that Aristotle's intervention corrupted the teachings of the *Iliad*. We might thus attribute any defects of Alexander's reign to Aristotle's influence. Yet if Alexander is a relatively unproblematic model, then Machiavelli might be suggesting that an education in war that is corrected by private lessons in philosophy is conducive to vaulting political success. Finally, Machiavelli might judge that Aristotle's influence was crucial to Alexander's vast empire and—following Sullivan—that the universalizing tendencies of the Alexandrian world were ultimately a problematic development.[38] In the immediate context, however, it is most clear that Alexander's example demonstrates that classical philosophy can help enable conquest. Machiavelli conceals this fact shabbily, while trumpeting noisily the value of Machiavellian philosophy—and Homeric poetry—to the ambitious prince.

While the presentation in chapter 14 suggests that this line of imitation originates ultimately in Achilles, in chapter 18, Machiavelli discloses that Achilles was also an imitator.

> Therefore it is necessary for a prince to know well how to use the beast and the man. This role was taught covertly to princes by ancient writers, who wrote that Achilles, and many other ancient princes, were given to Chiron the centaur to be raised, so that he would look after them with his discipline. To have as a teacher a half-beast, half-man means nothing other than that a prince needs to know how to use both natures; and the one without the other is not lasting.[39]

This nominally successful line of imitators originates in a beast-man who taught his pupils how to combine these distinct natures. While Machiavelli cites the imitators of chapter 14 as models *of* imitation, he explicitly establishes that Chiron is a model *for* imitation. Importantly, Chiron was not merely an untamed and warlike beast: he was regarded as a wise and gentle centaur, with knowledge of war, prophecy, and medical healing.[40] Chiron embodies the education that Alexander could approach only by combining the glorious history of Homer with Aristotle's philosophical corrective. Julius Caesar—who apparently merely read histories—lacks this philosophical instruction entirely.[41]

As Michael Palmer has observed, by directing ambitious men to imitate Chiron the centaur, Machiavelli recommends the teachings of a wise, prophetic, and warlike beast-man rather than the wise, prophetic, and pacific Son of God.[42] Yet Chiron's differences with Christ are not merely physical and spiritual: Chiron's teachings on worldly ambition and eternal life are also vastly different. Each of Chiron's imitators famously pursues earthly ambition; each dies prematurely; each secures a glorious reputation.[43] These men are all pagans, and in their belligerent worldly ambition, they lead lives that are particularly inconsistent with Christian virtue. Christ's followers exhibit ambition, but their object is otherworldly triumph: he promises eternal life to those who "deny themselves" and follow him, encouraging men to forgo worldly acquisition for the sake of their eternal souls.[44] Chiron's imitators seek to acquire worldly empire and glory. Despite some reservations about their careers, Machiavelli recommends that a novice prince of war follow in their paths by imitating Chiron.

According to traditional accounts, the centaur also contradicts Christ's teaching on eternal life, by discounting its value.[45] Apollodorus, for example, reports that the immortal Chiron, irremediably wounded by one of Heracles's poisoned arrows, willingly chooses to die rather than linger eternally in agony.[46] In an ode to Hiero of Syracuse, Pindar wistfully imagines that a resurrected Chiron, whose "mind was friendly to men," might send a demigod to cure the desire for immortality that infects human beings.[47]

> We must seek from the gods what is appropriate for mortal minds, knowing what lies before our feet, and what kind of destiny we have. Do not crave immortal life, my soul, but use to the full the resources of what is possible. But if wise Cheiron were still living in his cave, and if our honey-voiced odes had cast a spell on his spirit, I would have persuaded him to send even now a healer to cure noble men of their feverish diseases, someone called a son of Apollo or of his father Zeus.[48]

Pindar casts Chiron's teachings as the antidote for the desire for immortality. This antidote consists in worldly conquest and the promise of glory. Machiavelli, who grounds his worldly teachings in "what is possible," resembles the disciple of Chiron for which Pindar longs.[49] This renders Machiavelli an improved version of Achilles, since his preoccupation with knowledge of nature renders him even more similar to Chiron than the Achaean, who is famously preoccupied with war.[50]

Given the fortune enjoyed by Alexander and the problematic consequences of Caesar's success, neither of these men is an unblemished model for imitation. Achilles escapes Machiavelli's disapprobation, but like Chiron, he appears as a highly poeticized model for spiritual imitation rather than a historical figure whose victories in battle might be replicated by an astute imitator. One ought to note, however, that these men are not the only imitators of Chiron to appear in chapter 14. Machiavelli unreservedly praises Philopoemen, whom Plutarch reports as schooled in philosophy, a conscious imitator of Alexander, and an assiduous reader of Homer.[51] Plutarch emphasizes Philopoemen's kinship with Achilles by remarking that he was educated by his foster-father Cleander, "just as Homer says that Achilles was reared by Phoenix."[52] In addition to providing fatherly instruction, Cleander also enlisted the services of philosopher-statesmen Ecdemus and Demophanes to tutor young Philopoemen.[53] Thus, like Alexander and Achilles (but unlike Caesar), Philopoemen received direct instruction in philosophy and war. Despite being an orphan, he thrived.[54]

> He also listened to the discourses and applied himself to the writings of philosophers—not all of them, but those whom he thought helpful to him in his progress towards virtue. And as for the poems of Homer, whatever in them was thought by him to rouse and stimulate the activities of the soul which made for valour, to this he would apply himself. Among other writings, however, he was most of all devoted to the "Tactics" of Evangelus, and was familiar with the histories of Alexander, thinking that literature was conducive to action, unless it were prosecuted merely to while away the time and afford themes for fruitless small talk. Indeed, he would ignore the charts and diagrams for the illustration of tactical principles, and get his proofs and make his studies on the ground itself.[55]

Those who are seeking to imitate the "actions of excellent men" (*P* 14) ought to study the life of Philopoemen, who combined contemplation and action in his stalwart efforts against the Roman Empire.[56] By praising Philopoemen in *The Prince*, Machiavelli announces that he prefers the imitator of Chiron who opposes empire, rather than those who precipitate it.

A Machiavellian Victory in Death

The record of Philopoemen's final days strengthens the proposition that Machiavelli also presents his model prince of war as an alternative to Jesus Christ. At the age of seventy, after a lifetime of defending Greek freedom, Philopoemen was captured by a band of rebellious Messenians as he risked his life in a daring gambit to preserve his cavalry.[57] While his captors initially subjected him to indignities and even threatened him with torture, the people reacted with ambivalence upon viewing the triumphal procession that accompanied his arrival in Messene. Indeed, "the magistrates and principal citizens were afraid that the compassion [*misericordia*] evoked by the sight of so great a man might lead to a disturbance, for whilst some would contrast his former greatness with his present position, others would be moved by the memory of all he had done for them."[58] Consequently, they secreted him in "the public treasury which was an underground chamber, walled with hewn stone. Here he was let down in chains and the huge stone with which it was covered was lowered with pulleys."[59] In the morning, the leaders of the rebellion feared correctly that the people were intent on liberating Philopoemen. Thus, they sent a man with poison to his chamber. The Achaean appeared "overwhelmed with trouble and grief" about the fate of the cavalry he had been trying to save.[60] Upon learning that it had escaped, however, he looked at his executioner and "with a kindly look . . . said to him: 'That is good news, if we have not wholly lost.'"[61] Then, "without the slightest sign of fear," he drank the poison and died.[62]

Philopoemen was quickly and violently avenged. The furious and grief-stricken Achaeans invaded Messene; most of the principal conspirators were executed; those who advocated torturing Philopoemen were enchained; Philopoemen's body was recovered and ceremoniously burned; his ashes were then carried home "with a blending of triumphal procession and funeral rites."[63] After arriving at Megalopolis, the Achaeans "did not shrink from according to [Philopoemen] divine honours"; throughout Greece, men erected statues of him.[64] The prisoners who had advocated torturing Philopoemen lived to regret their temerity. Plutarch reports that they "were stoned to death" at Philopoemen's tomb.[65]

The final days of Christ and Philopoemen exhibit meaningful similarities. Like Philopoemen, Christ is apprehended immediately after guaranteeing the salvation of his followers.[66] The multitude shows deference to each, but each is nonetheless targeted by the conspiracy of a few who are intent on his death.[67] Although he had already expired, Christ is also placed in a crypt hewn of rock, with a large stone sealing the entrance.[68] Finally, each vacates his crypt and is accorded posthumous glory that confirms his divine status.

Their histories differ, however, in important respects. These differences demonstrate the superiority of Philopoemen's worldly and warlike ways. First, despite ardent belief among his partisans, Christ is unable to match Philopoemen's popularity. While Christ is ensnared by a conspiracy of the few, the Gospels emphasize that the people ultimately advocate his death with alacrity.[69] By contrast, within twenty-four hours of Philopoemen's capture, "the whole population" of Messene—nominally, an enemy city—came to conceive of him as their political savior, and was ready to submit the city's recent civil dispute to his judgment.[70] Philopoemen earned more "compassion" (*misericordia*) from his enemies than Christ did from his own people.[71] Indeed, such was the people's faith in Philopoemen that only determined subterfuge by the few ensured his death.

Philopoemen is spared torture. Christ is not.[72] While the elderly Philopoemen's death is quiet, private, and dignified, Christ dies prematurely, publicly, and in agony—and, according to two of the four Gospels, exhibits a striking lack of equanimity on the cross.[73] While Philopoemen's comrades recover his body and carry it in public triumph, Christ's body disappears, and reappears only in clandestine meetings with his partisans before allegedly ascending to heaven.[74] Philopoemen's avenging followers arm themselves in order to torture and kill his executioners; generally, Christ's disciples react to his demise with grief and fear: Peter denies Christ after his arrest and John reports that his followers gathered, "with the doors locked for fear of the Jewish leaders" after his execution.[75] The disciples do not plan revenge, and when Jesus appears in their midst, he vindicates their timorous forbearance. He instructs them only to preach his gospel to "all nations" and pray ardently for his return.[76] Prominent among his final words is the benediction, "Peace be with you!"[77] Perhaps unsurprisingly, Christian tradition holds that most of Christ's disciples subsequently follow their savior to various gruesome deaths.

In chapter 14, Machiavelli has instructed his readers to engage in rational discourse about nature. When judged according to the worldly standards of nature, without reference to Christ's alleged miracles and promised supernatural benefactions—or to the accident of history that led Rome to adopt Christianity—what ambitious student of nature and history would choose to imitate Christ rather than Philopoemen? Philopoemen lived a long life devoted to securing material freedom for the Greeks; in death, his immediate legacy was satisfying revenge, the earthly triumph of his followers, and glory for himself. Christ lived a short life preaching spiritual freedom, while evincing passive hostility toward the powerful of the world. They brutalized and killed him for his efforts; his disciples scattered to the far corners of the known world, where they generally suffered similar ends. Christ's glory was deferred until glorious Rome adopted his teachings.[78] While Christ's alleged miracles were crucial to the resiliency of his teachings during the intervening centuries—and no less crucial to the universality of his fame after Rome's intercession—only under the empire's stern supervision did Christ receive from the world what the Greeks freely gave Philopoemen, when "many statues of him were erected and many honours decreed him by the cities."[79]

By summoning Philopoemen from the vast repository of figures to which Machiavelli's "continuous reading" (*P* DL) of ancient history gives him access, Machiavelli presents an ancient "prince of war," whose life and actions serve as a foil for Christ's life as modernity's "prince of peace." Philopoemen's knowledge of nature, energetic belligerence, and obstreperous refusal to submit to the universal rule of a stronger power contrast neatly with Christ's character, which is marked by an ethereal and pacific humility that eventually ingratiated itself to imperial Rome. By praising Philopoemen at the center of *The Prince*, Machiavelli commends him as a superior spiritual model.

The Perils of Faulty Imitation: *Pietà*, Disorder, and Crime

While Philopoemen is the spiritual hero of chapter 14, Machiavelli's mention of Cyrus reminds us that even more "excellent men" have existed. The line of imitation that begins with Cyrus is indirect. Although all of the imitators in chapter 14 except Achilles relied on histories, Machiavelli emphasizes that Scipio learned about Cyrus by reading Xenophon's account of his life.[80] Thus, Machiavelli stresses in Scipio's case what he implies in Alexander's. Cyrus's appearance is noteworthy, because this is the first time Machiavelli has named a founder since chapter 6, where he insisted that the "particular actions and orders" of each appear "no different."[81] Indeed, Cyrus is not the only founder to have an imitative successor: Numa followed Romulus, and Christ—who seeks "to fulfill" the "Law" and the prophets—is Moses's most famous imitator.[82] Numa's "quiet and religious" (*D* I.11.1) character is comparable to Christ's, but in other ways, Scipio and Christ had more similar careers.[83] For each, many centuries had elapsed since his model lived. Scipio was a Roman, rather than a Persian; Christ, although a Jew, was preceded by a succession of less prominent rabbis, kings, and prophets—and finds himself in a world quite different from that of Moses. Lacking direct access to his model, each relies on an acclamatory written account of his forerunner's "particular actions and orders" (*P* 6).

Unlike in his discussion of Caesar and Alexander, Machiavelli discloses the substance of Scipio's education: "whoever reads the life of Cyrus written by Xenophon will then recognize in the life of Scipio how much glory that imitation brought him, how much in chastity, affability, humanity, and liberality Scipio conformed to what had been written of Cyrus by Xenophon" (*P* 14).[84] With this line, Machiavelli offers his most explicit instruction regarding the reading of histories: he directs his reader to examine the "the life of Cyrus" by Xenophon in order to see how Scipio's "chastity, affability, humanity, and liberality" (*P* 14) might be traced to Xenophon's book. Yet if one recalls Machiavelli's instruction earlier in chapter 14, one realizes that this list of praiseworthy attributes does not constitute praise of Scipio. First, Scipio did not learn from Cyrus the "exploits and actions" (*P*

14) that Machiavelli insists are most necessary, but instead conformed to certain spiritual qualities Xenophon reports Cyrus as exhibiting. Second, unlike Alexander and Achilles, Scipio did not learn directly from one who was wise. Instead, Scipio read Xenophon's often puzzling account of Cyrus, in which Machiavelli elsewhere claims the Greek "toils very much" (*D* III.20) to demonstrate that Cyrus's humanity and affability accrued great rewards.[85] While Machiavelli affirms that "Xenophon writes [*scrive*]" that "affability, humanity, [and] mercy" "were in Cyrus" (III.22.5), he asserts unambiguously that the Greek "shows [*mostra*]" (II.13.1) Cyrus's capacity for necessary fraud.[86] Given the inscrutability of Xenophon's account, one ought to recall Aristotle's response to Alexander when the latter complained that by writing books, the philosopher's teachings lay open to the world: Aristotle insisted that they would be useless to the uninitiated. Although Livy credits young Scipio with cleverness and charisma, we know nothing of Scipio's early education.[87] Could it be that Scipio, like Caesar, was uninitiated to philosophy—and thus failed to distinguish between what Xenophon "wrote" about Cyrus and what he "showed" to be true of Cyrus's actions?[88]

Machiavelli's treatment of Scipio in *The Prince* certainly suggests that Scipio learned the wrong lessons from the *Cyropaedia*. In chapter 17, Machiavelli discloses that any prince in command of armies must exercise cruelty. He praises Hannibal for the "inhuman cruelty" that kept his army ordered in bad and good fortune, and condemns Scipio for his "excessive mercy [*pietà*]," which caused his armies to rebel (*P* 17).[89] Machiavelli thus echoes Fabius Maximus's condemnation of Scipio's conduct in Spain and Locri, where Scipio served as "the corruptor of the Roman military" (*P* 17) while he lived a life of "self-indulgence and effeminacy" that resembled a Greek tyrant's.[90]

Livy's detailed account of Scipio's failings is instructive. The events to which Machiavelli refers in *The Prince* occurred during the Second Punic War. While other generals were opposing Hannibal in Italy, Scipio successfully conquered New Carthage, in Spain. After the city's fall, Scipio grew indolent and his army grew restive. Soon, Rome's allies in Spain began revolting, Scipio's native auxiliary commanders began scheming, and his own troops began to mutiny.[91] Rumors of Scipio's illness and impending death emboldened the conspirators, but Livy emphasizes that "a long period of inactivity had, as usual, demoralised them, and they chafed against the restraints of peace after being accustomed to live on the plunder captured from the enemy" (XXVIII.24). When Scipio recovered, he wished to restore order, but feared meting out "excessive" punishments: "For the present he decided to go on as he had begun, and handle the matter gently [*leniter*]" (XXVIII.25).[92] After using persuasion to end the mutiny quietly, Scipio adopted a strange punitive strategy that combined heated indignation and a detached quasi-Socratic perspective on injustice. He summoned the entire army and hectored them for their ingratitude toward Rome, while simultaneously excusing them, insisting, "No crime is dictated by rational motives" (XXVIII.28) and likening their mutiny to a bodily illness. After expressing more indignation at the low estate of his usurpers, the names of the thirty-five ringleaders were read aloud. Each was dragged to the front of the crowd, stripped, beaten, and beheaded. Livy reports that "the spectators were so benumbed by terror that no voice was raised against the severity of the punishment, not even a groan was heard" (XXVIII.29). After these events, the traitorous auxiliary command-ers pled for clemency, which Scipio granted, exulting in his display of Roman "kindness [*beneficio*]" (XXVIII.34).

This is not the only instance of Scipio's legendary mercy. Machiavelli also directs us to consider the events at Locri, which disclose more fully how Scipio's "excessive mercy" (*P* 17) harms the people under his pro-tection.[93] The small Italian city had fallen to Carthage, but subsequently betrayed that city and sided with the Romans, who put the town under the command of Pleminius, whom Scipio had appointed. When Hannibal attempted to retake the city, Scipio rushed to Locri from Syracuse, where he had been planning the African campaign. After an aborted battle, Hannibal was repelled.[94] Scipio submitted Locri's status to the Roman Sen-ate, and leaving Pleminius in command, he returned to Sicily to resume scheming against Carthage. Once in command, Pleminius directed a cam-paign of cruelty and rapacity that would have made a Carthaginian blush: Livy reports that his tyrannical rule over Locri was characterized by "crimi-nality," "greed," "unspeakable outrages," and even "sacrilege" (XXIX.8 and 16–17). This lawlessness undermined even the highest Roman law: when military tribunes attempted to intervene on the Locrians' behalf, Plem-inius ordered the tribunes seized and beaten (XXIX.9). The army grew indignant at this outrage: "without the slightest respect for the majesty of office or even for humanity, they grossly maltreated the lictors, and then having separated Pleminius from his men and hemmed him in, they slit his nose and ears and left him half dead" (XXIX.9). When Scipio learned of these events, he returned to Locri. After a brief investigation, he acquit-ted Pleminius. He enchained the tribunes before rushing back to Sicily— again, to plan the African campaign. Returned to command and "beside himself with rage" (XXIX.9), Pleminius vented his anger by torturing the tribunes to death and furiously renewing his crimes against the Locrians.

The distressed Locrians now appealed directly to the Roman Senate for relief (XXIX.16–18). Though the Locrians excoriated Pleminius, they declined to prosecute Scipio, attributing his conduct to negligence or a "lack of resolution to inflict punishment" (XXIX.21). This is the context in which Fabius Maximus condemned Scipio: according to him, Scipio's effeminacy and indolence was "not only not Roman, but even unsoldier-like" (XXIX.19). He moved that Pleminius be arrested and Scipio be recalled; if guilty, he proposed that the former ought to be executed and the latter ought to be removed from office. Fabius's efforts failed. Scipio greeted the Senate's investigatory committee with a festival consisting of extravagant military exercises and mock battles; impressed, the senators formally and enthusiastically recommended his invasion of Africa (XXIX.22). Thus did the Roman Senate hide Scipio's "damaging quality" and contribute to his "glory" (*P* 17).

What, then, are the chief effects of Scipio's excessive mercy? A mutinous and ineffective army; political instability within the empire, as allies revolt and ambitious auxiliary captains pursue aggrandizing schemes; the enabling and tacit acceptance of outrageous sacrilege and pointless cruelty by criminal subordinates who do what they can because they are confident of his mercy; and in spite of all of this, glory for Scipio. Machiavelli describes Scipio as "very rare not only in his times but in the entire memory of things known" (*P* 17), but one can recognize the effects of Scipio's merciful rule in Machiavelli's presentation of Christendom. Due to Christ's effeminate and indolent teachings, a good army is impossible to find in Italy, and rare in Europe. Despite the persistent efforts of the Church to establish broader hegemony, affairs among cities remain chaotic and variable, subjected constantly to the harebrained schemes of ambitious and self-aggrandizing princelings, whom Christ's Church cannot reliably check. The people—who have not claimed much attention in *The Prince*—suffer through these tempestuous variations.

In the *Discourses*, Machiavelli offers an even clearer account of how Christianity empowers criminality and harms the people. First, it encourages a "mode of life" that has "rendered the world weak and given it in prey to criminal men, who can manage it securely, seeing that the collectivity of men, so as to go to paradise, think more of enduring their beatings than of avenging them" (*D* II.2.2). Second, the imitation of the "life of Christ" encouraged by Saints Dominic and Francis has empowered the

> dishonesty of the prelates and the heads of the religion . . . [who] give [peoples] to understand that it is evil to say evil of evil and that it is good to live under obedience to them and, if they make an error, to leave them for God to punish. So they do the worst they can because they do not fear the punishment that they do not see and do not believe. (*D* III.1.4)

Machiavelli does not write of "hell" (*inferno*) in either *The Prince* or the *Discourses*, and this appears to be the only indirect reference to hell in either book.[95] Its lone appearance suggests that the specter of its punishments is impotent to deter human wrongs. Christ's subordinates, like Scipio's, are not frightened by the prospect of punishment. Scipio's deputies transgress because they know that Scipio carefully contrives a reputation for kindness, but Christ's "evil [*male*]" (*D* III.1.4) priests appear even less restrained. Machiavelli attributes their transgressions to the fact that they do not "believe [*credono*]" (*D* III.1.4) in Christ's promise of punishment.[96] Their skepticism is perhaps understandable: Christ's promises of punishment in the Gospels are rare, vague, and usually noncorporeal.[97] Yet even if an evil priest begins to fear Christ's judgment or imagine his fate in hell, he will find comfort in the New Testament, which repeatedly invokes Christ's mercy, which encompasses adulteresses, thieves, and even tax collectors.[98] Christ teaches: "[God] is kind to the ungrateful and wicked. Be merciful, just as your Father is merciful."[99] Subsequent books of the New Testament enlarge upon God's mercy for transgressors.[100] Machiavelli's analysis suggests that "excessive mercy" like that practiced by Christ and Scipio creates insecurity and abets criminality: "too much mercy" creates "disorders," "killings," and "robberies," "which customarily hurt a whole community" (*P* 17).[101] Scipio appears to have contracted his "excessive mercy" from an improper reading of Xenophon's *Cyropaedia*; did Christ learn wrongly from Moses's Pentateuch?

Miracles, Mercy, and Credulous Prophets

Chapter 6 of *The Prince* teaches that Moses's virtuous use of arms and prophecy "ennobled" his fatherland, which "became very happy," but we may wonder whether Machiavelli thinks that Moses's fatherland could be described as "very happy" so long as he remained alive to stalk its camps (*P* 6). Indeed, in the *Discourses*, Machiavelli obliquely identifies Moses as a practitioner of cruelty. First, by claiming that Moses "was forced to kill infinite men who, moved by nothing other than envy, were opposed to his plans" (*D* III.30.1), Machiavelli implicates Moses in the deaths of many of his own people. Second, he names the Israelites as a people constrained to flee their ancestral country for another: "when they are great in number, then they enter with violence into the countries of others, kill the inhabitants, take possession of their goods, make a new kingdom, and change the province's name, as did Moses and the peoples who seized the Roman Empire" (*D* II.8.2).[102] Earlier in the *Discourses*, Machiavelli described almost identical modes—to "make in cities new governments with new names, new authorities, new men; to make the poor rich and the rich poor"—as "very cruel, and enemies to every way of life, not only Christian, but human" (*D* I.26).

While Moses does report God's mercy for the Israelites in several important passages, that promise is typically accompanied by incredible violence: for example, God's most generous and explicit promise of mercy occurs immediately after Moses commands the slaughter of three thousand of the Israelites.[103] Most of the public miracles recorded in the Pentateuch coincide with violence or are themselves violent acts.[104] Mosaic law—which demands rigorous obedience to "all" of God's laws and prescribes violent punishments for a variety of transgressions—further testifies to Moses's conviction that exacting punishment, rather than mercy, conduces to stable orders.[105] In sum, Machiavelli's Moses depends routinely on cruelty: he kills the envious among the Israelites, institutes a rigorous and sanguinary legal system to control those who remain alive, and launches inhuman and genocidal wars against foreigners.

Christ heals, rather than kills, infinite men. The Gospels record seven instances in which Jesus miraculously controverts the laws of nature to benefit those present.[106] Jesus heals by faith approximately twenty persons afflicted with various maladies and raises three from the dead.[107] Almost always, these miracles benefit those present immediately and tangibly: frequently, he responds to explicit appeals for mercy.[108] Indeed, Jesus produces only one act of miraculous violence in the Gospels: he curses a fig tree, which subsequently withers.[109] In behaving thus, he does not imitate Moses. Instead, he conforms to an especially meek, merciful, and miraculous version of Moses. Indeed, while he claims he has come "to fulfill" the Law and the prophets, his avowed preference for the modes of love, rather than fear, renders his teachings quite distinct from those of Moses.[110] Yet despite these differences—and his numerous quarrels with the Pharisees— Christ explicitly contravenes Mosaic law only three times in the Gospels. He intervenes to prevent the stoning of an adulteress, issues a general prohibition against divorce, and violates the Sabbath by allowing his disciples to pluck and eat grain.[111] Each act might be construed as merciful: a woman is spared death; faithful wives are protected from the potentially capricious wills of their husbands; and the hungry may eat on the Sabbath. Indeed, when his disciples are accused of the last transgression, Jesus responds: "If you had known what these words mean, 'I desire mercy, not sacrifice,' you would not have condemned the innocent."[112]

Does Christ learn wrongly from the Pentateuch? Does he undertake a comprehensive revision of Moses's example? Or does he believe that he is satisfying the most important explicit promise of the Abrahamic tradition: that God created heaven and earth, made a covenant with Abraham, and that "all nations on earth shall be blessed through him."[113] Understood thus, Moses's cruelty might have been circumstantially necessary—to chasten the hard hearts and bow the stiff necks of the Israelites—but did not represent the true or permanent character of God's relationship with human beings. Christ's insistence that he comes "to fulfill" the "Law" and the prophets and the efforts he undertakes to support his innovative teachings by reference to Old Testament texts support this supposition.[114]

A second possibility is that Christ wished to innovate, but found himself unable to imitate Moses's violent cruelty: thus, like Numa, he eschewed violence and proffered constant miracles because "he wished to put new and unaccustomed orders in the city and doubted that his authority would suffice" (*D* I.11.1). According to this view, Machiavelli might judge Christ as an ambitious religious pretender, no different than Numa, Lycurgus, or Solon. Finally, he might conclude that Christ exhibits a combination of these two positions: he might be an ardent believer who recognizes his own incapacity for violence, and thus alternates between bold prophetic claims and more oblique attacks on the existing political and religious powers.

Whatever the explanation for Christ's mercy, Machiavelli learns from the Old Testament that earthly punishments—whether of human or divine origin—are necessary to restrain human wickedness; truly civil religions sanction the cruelty required of those punishments, which must be made manifest on earth to perform an educative function.[115] Unremitting mercy, accompanied by the promise of an imminent heavenly judgment, is bad political practice. This explains why Machiavelli, who accords much power to fear, nonetheless declines to speak of hell or the devil in either the *Discourses* or *The Prince*.[116] Poets may be fascinated by these phantasms; charismatic priests may be convinced of their power; the people may even be cowed briefly by threats thereof; but Machiavelli's silence suggests that they are politically ineffectual. What, then, did Machiavelli think was Christ's opinion? Did he truly believe in the power of God, the legitimacy of his heavenly mandate, and the existence of the devil and hell? Does his ardent belief excuse his imprudent devotion to mercy, rather than cruelty?

Pretender or Prophet?
The Perplexing Cases of Scipio and Christ

A consideration of Scipio is once again instructive. Machiavelli describes Scipio as "very rare not only in his times but in the entire memory of things known" (*P* 17), but if Scipio's distinguishing characteristic is his *pietà*, this epithet more aptly conforms to Jesus Christ, whose *pietà* is so rare that it "will bring you to eternal life."[117] Scipio is an ambitious commander who wishes to conquer northern Africa and cultivates assiduously a reputation for leniency. Is this so rare, compared to the supremely merciful Christ, who claims to have "overcome the world?"[118]

Yet according to Livy, Scipio possessed one remarkable quality that helps the reader make sense of Machiavelli's hyperbole. Scipio was a religious pretender. He cultivated the belief that he was of divine origin—the product of a pagan virgin birth, of a sort—and throughout his career, he used clever oracular speech to imbue men "with more hopeful confidence than is usually called out by faith in men's promises or by reasonable anticipations of success."[119] While Livy does not openly brand Scipio an imposter, he evinces skepticism about his divine pretensions.

> In his public life he generally spoke and acted as though he were guided either by visions of the night or by some divine inspiration, whether it was that he was really open to superstitious influences or that he claimed oracular sanction for his commands and counsels in order to secure prompt adoption. He sought to create this impression on men's minds from the beginning, . . . for he never undertook any important business, either public or private, without first going to the Capitol, where he sat for some time in the temple in privacy and alone. This custom, which he kept up all through his life, gave rise to a widespread belief, whether designedly upon his part or not, that he was of divine origin, and the story was told of him which was commonly related of Alexander—a story as silly as it was fabulous—that he was begotten by an enormous serpent which had been often seen in his mother's bedroom, but on any one's approach, suddenly uncoiled itself and disappeared. The belief in these marvels was never scoffed at by him; on the contrary, it was strengthened by deliberate policy on his part in refusing to deny or to admit that anything of the kind ever occurred. There were many other traits in this young man's character, some of which were genuine, others the result of studied acting, which created a greater admiration for him than usually falls to the lot of man.[120]

Readers of the Gospels will recognize in Scipio's conduct events from Christ's life. First, the Gospels testify to Jesus's abundant cleverness. He holds the rapt attention of crowds large and small, repeatedly frustrates the Pharisees' attempts to implicate him in crime, and excels at instilling hope beyond what mere reason commends. Like Scipio, he displayed this ability even as a young boy.[121] Second, Christ's entire career is alleged to be divinely inspired; the Gospels even report that he sometimes receives direct supernatural help from angels.[122] Third, like Scipio, "Jesus often withdrew to lonely places and prayed"; often, he does so before important events.[123]

Finally, consider the gravid claim of his supernatural conception. The story about a serpent in the bedroom of Scipio's mother suggests that he is the son of Jupiter, a story that Scipio never confirms explicitly.[124] Matthew and Luke report Christ's Virgin Birth.[125] The story does not appear in the Gospels of Mark or John, and Paul's epistles—which present Christ as David's heir and emphasize the fleshly sinfulness of Christ's body—do not mention its occurrence.[126] Like the story of Scipio's serpent-father, the story certainly has a fabulous quality: could its irregular reception be due to some skepticism about these claims? Importantly, Christ himself never explicitly endorses its veracity.[127] Instead, we learn of these events from the evangelists' narratives and from secondhand accounts contained therein. The angel Gabriel informs Mary that she will give birth to the Son of God; John the Baptist refers to him as "God's Chosen One"; Nathanael, Martha, some disciples, a centurion, several demons, and a voice from the heavens identify him as the Son of God.[128] Even when Peter identifies Christ as the "Son of the Living God," Christ's enthusiastic response stops short of an admission: "You are blessed, Simon son of Jonah, because flesh and blood did not reveal this to you, but my Father in heaven!"[129] He then instructs his disciples to conceal this fact.[130]

This secrecy seems contrived, since Jesus himself certainly implies that he is the Son of God throughout Matthew, Luke, and John, where he repeatedly invokes his heavenly Father. While many times he appears to refer to God promiscuously, as the father to all men, he also frequently describes himself as the Son of God, charged with special knowledge and power: in some of those instances he invokes the phrase "my father" (*tou patros mou* or *a patre meo*) with particular intimacy.[131] In Matthew, for example, he advises, "All things have been committed to me by my Father. No one knows the Son except the Father, and no one knows the Father except the Son and those to whom the Son chooses to reveal him."[132] Nonetheless, when the Pharisees ask him to clarify his pretensions to be sent by his father to be the "light of the world," he offers a cagey response: "'I am one who testifies for myself; my other witness is the Father, who sent me.' Then they asked him, 'Where is your father?' 'You do not know me or my Father,' Jesus replied. 'If you knew me, you would know my Father also.'"[133] Only after he is arrested and questioned by the Sanhedrin does Christ explicitly confess his paternity. Even then, only Mark's Gospel records this reluctant confession.[134]

Both Luke and Matthew report this conversation, but in their accounts, Christ issues no confession: instead, he employs the cryptic and suggestive language that usually attends discussions of his paternity.[135] Importantly, in none of the accounts does Jesus explicitly confirm the truth of his Virgin Birth, and only in the final confrontation with the religious authorities before his execution does he—according to Mark alone—confess openly his divine parentage. When pressed to answer questions about his alleged supernatural paternity, Christ generally conforms to Scipio's practice of refusing "to deny or to admit that anything of the kind ever occurred."[136] Thus, when the chief priests remark of Christ on the cross, "Let God rescue him now if he wants him, for he said, 'I am the Son of God,'" they are not merely lying, but neither are they accurately describing Christ's subtle and insinuating rhetoric.[137]

Scipio, Christ, and Machiavelli's Hostility to Universal Empire

According to Livy, Scipio's oracular pretensions might have been a "deliberate policy" that exhibited "studied acting," rather than "genuine" "divine inspiration."[138] Machiavelli directs us to this skeptical account, and he indirectly invites the reader to compare the careers of Scipio and Christ. An examination of Christ's "exploits and actions" (*P* 14) reveals that he and Scipio conducted themselves in similar ways. Each seeks to enflame extravagant hopes in public speeches. Each undertakes ambitious projects with universalizing implications: while Christ, who claims to have "overcome the world," is the progenitor of the Christian Church that Machiavelli opposes, Scipio's invasion of Africa sets Rome on the path to empire of which Machiavelli is so critical in the *Discourses*; in subsequent years, it would begin the takeover of Greece that would earn Philopoemen's ire.[139] Each employs oracular language and subtly fuels speculation about his divine origins in a way that might help "secure prompt adoption" for his plans.[140] Jesus claims, "The Spirit of the Lord is on me," but Machiavelli—with discretion that exceeds even Xenophon's—leads his more diligent readers of history to wonder whether Christ's divine pretensions might have been a "deliberate policy."[141] Thus, attention to Livy's presentation of Scipio illuminates Machiavelli's most overtly heretical opinion of Christ, which he communicates with a furtiveness fitting of such dangerous thoughts.

Machiavelli's critique of "the princes of the Christian republic" in the *Discourses* (I.12.1) corroborates this claim more obviously.[142] There, citing Camillus's approval of the belief that a statue of Juno verbally assented to her capture by Roman soldiers, he praises the ancient Roman "princes" who "favored and magnified" alleged miracles "even though they judge[d] them false" (*D* I.12.1). Machiavelli then posits, "If such [*quale*] religion had been maintained by the princes of the Christian republic as was ordered by its giver [*datore*], the Christian states and republics would be more united, much happier than they are" (*D* I.12.1).[143] Christianity's "giver" is Christ; Machiavelli thus implicates him in salutary religious fraud.

Despite the numerous similarities between Christ and Scipio, the most obvious common trait remains their "excessive mercy" (*P* 17). While the Roman Senate hid this "damaging quality" of Scipio's and "made for his glory," the Roman Empire accomplished these things for Christ (*P* 17).[144] Having rendered the world servile through its arms, ferocity, and prudence, Rome's conquest abroad—which was accelerated decisively by Scipio himself—eventually led to political corruption and the loss of liberty at home.[145] Amid growing political inequality, Christianity began to find adherents. The weak found in Christ's teachings a triumphal justification of their position; the clever weak found that by exalting lamblike meekness among its adherents, Christianity increased their security and granted them criminal license, with which they further enervated civil society. Thus did Christ become glorious on earth: his ethereal teachings became the most powerful universalizing yoke of the decadent and worldly Roman Empire. Christ's universal pretensions and promises of victory for those who are slaves on earth made him a particularly apt messiah for that empire.[146]

While the Roman Empire eventually disintegrated, Christianity survived its host—and appropriated some of its earthly majesty. Machiavelli lived among the decadent ruins of that mongrel regime. Machiavelli is surely a critic of the temporal power of the Church, but he also seeks to deprive Christianity of its earthly power by inviting men to consider the defects of Christ's life and teachings, while reflecting on the excellence of ancient men. By exhorting men to learn nature, plan for war, and read the histories of ancient men correctly, he hopes to recover the virtue lost over "these corrupt centuries of ours" (D II.19.1). By the end of *The Prince*, like a perverse John the Baptist, Machiavelli will herald the arrival of a Machiavellian prince of war to lead his anti-Christian acolytes. As part of this plan, he must offer a coherent alternative to Christian virtue.

CHAPTER FIVE

Machiavelli's Unchristian Virtue

Chapter 15 commences Machiavelli's teaching on how princes ought to regard—and practice—the virtues and vices.[1] The title, "Of Those Things for Which Men and Especially Princes Are Praised or Blamed," indicates two important features of Machiavelli's subsequent discussion. First, these teachings—unlike the majority located in chapters 1 through 14—apply to all men, and only especially to princes. Machiavelli thus announces his ambition to provide a universal teaching on virtue to "whoever understands it"—although what follows applies especially to princes, insofar as he will seek "what the modes and government of a prince should be with subjects and with friends" (*P* 15).[2]

Second, the title testifies to Machiavelli's attention to the reputation that attends virtue and vice, rather than the practice of the virtues and the avoidance of vices. By presenting virtue and vice as "things" (*P* 15) for which men are praised or blamed, he treats virtue as instrumental to opinion, rather than desirable for its own sake.[3] Because praise and blame illuminate the virtues and vices, the latter are not inscrutable characteristics of one's soul, or evident in one's conduct toward others, but a form of popular moral shorthand that indicates others' perception. In chapter 15, Machiavelli diminishes the moral force of this popular judgment by blurring the distinctions between virtues and vices. He accomplishes this dramatically by providing a convoluted list of paired "qualities that bring [men, and especially princes] either blame or praise" (*P* 15).

> Someone is considered liberal, someone mean. . . ; someone is considered a giver, someone rapacious; someone cruel, someone merciful; the one a breaker of faith, the other faithful; the one effeminate and pusillanimous, the other fierce and spirited; the one humane, the other proud; the one lascivious, the other chaste; the one honest, the other astute; the one hard, the other agreeable; the one grave, the other light; the one religious, the other unbelieving, and the like. (*P* 15)

Machiavelli offers that it would be "praiseworthy" for a prince to possess all of the "above-mentioned qualities that are held good," but due to his obfuscations, it is not certain which qualities Machiavelli endorses as good (*P* 15). By alternating the expected order of the virtues and vices, Machiavelli confuses his presentation.[4] The apparent randomness of his presentation furthers his explicit contention that, when choosing virtue and vice, appearances can be deceiving.

There may, however, be some order to this list. First, he will clarify his judgment of some of these qualities in subsequent chapters: for example, while "easiness" might be construed as a good quality, chapter 17 reveals that it leads to disorder.[5] Second, in a digression about the Tuscan dialect, he introduces the quality of avarice without offering any contrasting alternative. If one includes this among the list of qualities, humanness [*umano*] becomes the central quality in a list of twenty-three qualities; if one includes avarice and disaggregates the collapsed pairs that include effeminacy and pusillanimity, and fierceness and spiritedness, spiritedness becomes the central quality in a list of twenty-five qualities.[6] Given Machiavelli's condemnation of Christ's inhuman pretensions and lamblike meekness in *The Prince*, these qualities—humanness and spiritedness—constitute an appropriate summary teaching on virtue.

After emphasizing that one gains praise from the appearance of virtue, at the close of chapter 15, Machiavelli deprecates the importance of a good reputation. In particular, princes ought to disregard the "fame" (*P* 15) that attends vice. Since some vices are necessary to "save one's state" (*P* 15), they must be practiced without compunction. Indeed, he doubts whether these actions are really vices at all: "for if one considers everything well, one will find something appears to be virtue, which if pursued would be one's ruin, and something appears to be vice, which if pursued results in one's security and well-being" (*P* 15).[7] Although this chapter appears to be about virtue and vice, the only instance of the word "virtue" (*P* 15) occurs at the end of the chapter, and then, Machiavelli emphasizes that it consists of mere perception confirmed by the opinions of others—and that its practice will lead to ruin. Machiavelli thus begins a project to devalue popular opinion that will culminate in chapter 18, where he suggests that it is possible to manipulate popular perception of one's virtue so as to subordinate entirely questions of virtue and vice to the Machiavellian ends of security and success.

The Effectual Truth about Imaginary Principalities

Machiavelli admits that his teaching "depart[s] from the order of others" (*P* 15). While it certainly contravenes important classical conceptions of virtue—perhaps especially by deprecating the importance of one's soul to a consideration of virtue—it more directly contradicts Christ's pronouncements. When asked to disclose the "greatest commandment," Jesus responds: "'Love the Lord your God with all your heart and with all your soul and with all your mind.' This is the first and greatest commandment."[8] The preeminent requirement of Christianity is thus satisfied within the heart, soul, and mind of the believer. It is indifferent to reputation and defies external scrutiny; in this, it is precisely the opposite of Machiavelli's general teaching on virtue. Jesus's condemnation of hypocrites confirms that he privileges the internal disposition of one's soul over external actions or the appearance of virtue: "Be careful not to practice your righteousness in front of others to be seen by them. If you do, you will have no reward from your Father in heaven."[9] Christ's condemnation of the teachers of law and the Pharisees echoes this judgment. "Everything they do is done for people to see," and thus he charges, "You are like whitewashed tombs, which look beautiful on the outside but on the inside are full of the bones of the dead and everything unclean. In the same way, on the outside you appear to people as righteous but on the inside you are full of hypocrisy and wickedness."[10] Upon Christ's return, these men but will be conducted to a place "where there will be weeping and gnashing of teeth."[11] Those who practice "secret" virtue, however, will be rewarded in heaven— precisely because they derive no worldly good from their virtue.[12]

Machiavelli justifies his unchristian attitude toward virtue by condemning traditional accounts as useless.

> But since my intent is to write something useful to whoever understands it, it has appeared to me more fitting to go directly to the effectual truth of the thing than to the imagination of it. And many have imagined republics and principalities that have never been seen or known to exist in truth; for it is so far from how one lives to how one should live that he who lets go of what is done for what should be done learns his ruin rather than his preservation. For a man who wants to make a profession of good in all regards must come to ruin among so many who are not good. Hence it is necessary to a prince, if he wants to maintain himself, to learn to be able not to be good, and to use this and not use it according to necessity. (*P* 15)[13]

This passage has been interpreted as a critique of various imagined regimes, including those found in Saint Augustine's *City of God* and Plato's *Republic*; other possible referents include Aristotle's best regime and the "kingdom of heaven" described by Christ.[14] Machiavelli's basic objection is that imagined regimes create false expectations about human nature. Those who adhere to their rules by making "a profession of good in all regards" are ruined because they must live in regimes that actually "exist in truth" (*P* 15).[15] I argue that Machiavelli's critique applies especially to the imaginary cities of Christianity, and particularly to the "kingdom of heaven" imagined by Christ. Classical philosophers may have imagined republics and cities, but these regimes never required their citizens to make a "profession of good in all regards": Aristotle's best regime must still wage war and judge crimes; the city-in-speech of the *Republic* requires a "throng of lies" and a devious foreign policy.[16] Despite their capacity to inspire political idealism, even a superficial reading of these works confirms that they require men to be bad in some ways. Thus, they agree with Machiavelli's judgment that "human conditions" do not "permit" one to "wholly observe" qualities that are held to be good (*P* 15).[17] Only Christianity's imaginary cities command unequivocal goodness, a position made possible by their supernatural preconditions. God's judgment of human beings winnows the wicked from the population of these cities.[18] The triumphant kingdom of heaven has no enemies to fight.[19]

Jesus invokes the "kingdom of heaven" and "kingdom of God" approximately seventy-five times in the Gospels.[20] His invocations of this imagined city fall into three broad categories: he announces its imminence, describes some of the requirements for entrance thereunto, and sketches its theological rationale with the use of parables.[21] Jesus's audience hears that the kingdom of heaven is near, that believers will populate it, and that God has "prepared [it] for [them] from the foundation of the world" in order to fulfill his covenant with man.[22] In comparison to the intricately described imaginary cities of classical political philosophers, Saint Augustine, or John's Revelation, however, Jesus offers only an extremely rough sketch of his "kingdom of heaven."[23] Preferring to speak in parables, he leaves no detailed account of its ordering. Excepting perhaps the author of the book of Revelation, even the most ardent believer cannot see this murky kingdom, since it will be realized only after the "powers of the heavens will be shaken."[24] Thus, although Christians are confident in its imminence, the kingdom of heaven "has never been seen" by humans "or known to exist in truth" (*P* 15). In Machiavelli's judgment, human beings cannot flourish by imitating this exceptionally imaginary city. Its rules will not inform Machiavelli's teaching on virtue and vice.

Machiavelli's Unchristian Understanding of Possessions

Machiavelli's teaching "On Liberality and Parsimony" (*P* 16) is his first attempt to teach a virtue: how ought one to acquire, employ, and regard wealth?[25] As demonstrated in chapter 1 of this book, the Gospels are unequivocal and emphatic in their condemnation of acquisition. According to Christ, a preoccupation with acquisition signals a deficient faith in God: by hoarding wealth, one betrays doubts about his providence.[26]

Moreover, abundant possessions enervate one's devotion to God: "For where your treasure is there your heart will be also."[27] Consequently, men who imitate Christ exhibit a practiced indifference toward wealth that betrays a profound wariness concerning its worldly charms: "Give to everyone who asks you, and if anyone takes what belongs to you, do not demand it back."[28]

Christ's general teaching on wealth consists, then, of three principles. First, he enjoins men to trust in God, rather than possessions. Second, he recommends honesty: for "if you have not been trustworthy in handling worldly wealth, who will trust you with true riches?"[29] Third, he offers a teaching to the rich: wealth is salutary only insofar as it affords one an opportunity to show compassion by spending it on those who suffer.

> When you give a luncheon or dinner, do not invite your friends, your brothers or sisters, your relatives, or your rich neighbors; if you do, they may invite you back and so you will be repaid. But when you give a banquet, invite the poor, the crippled, the lame, the blind, and you will be blessed. Although they cannot repay you, you will be repaid at the resurrection of the righteous.[30]

John clarifies this teaching: "Jesus Christ laid down his life for us. And we ought to lay down our lives for our brothers and sisters. If anyone has material possessions and sees a brother or sister in need but has no pity on them, how can the love of God be in that person?"[31] The Gospels teach that the greedy, the dishonest, and the calculative—indeed, "whoever stores up things for themselves but is not rich toward God"— imperils his soul.[32] Christ prefers, moreover, that his followers practice their generosity covertly, since secrecy testifies to a praiseworthy indifference to worldly opinion: "when you give to the needy, do not let your left hand know what your right hand is doing, so that your giving may be in secret. Then your Father, who sees what is done in secret, will reward you."[33]

Machiavelli contradicts entirely these Christian teachings. While both Machiavelli and Christ acknowledge that it is "good to be held liberal" (P 16), Machiavelli attends to the opinion of men, who see "how you appear" (P 18), rather than God, "who sees what is done in secret."[34]

> I say that it would be good to be held liberal; nonetheless, liberality, when used so that you may be held liberal, hurts you. For if it is used virtuously and as it should be used, it may not be recognized, and you will not escape the infamy of its contrary. And so, if one wants to maintain a name for liberality among men, it is necessary not to leave out any kind of lavish display, so that a prince who has done this will always consume all his resources in such deeds. (P 16)

Machiavelli's assessment of the problem of liberality is strikingly unchristian. First, since liberality is a reputational good, Christ's recommendation to secret liberality is folly. Second, he maintains that "lavish" (*P* 16) liberality is self-defeating, since it threatens what is prior to, and more important than, liberality: wealth. Unlike Christ, Machiavelli presumes the necessity of wealth: men and especially princes need money. If they spend it on someone, they will need to take it from another—through taxes and "other things" (*P* 16), which are likely to generate hatred. If the extravagant liberality Christ recommends is unaccompanied by acquisition, it breeds poverty, which makes men "little esteemed" (*P* 16). In Machiavelli's judgment, the liberal Christian endangers himself uselessly. Men cannot follow Christ's commandments and maintain their reputations. The Christlike prince can maintain neither his reputation nor his state.

Machiavelli's initial solution to the problem of liberality is to recommend "meanness" (*P* 16). Indeed, by prudently managing his finances, the "parsimonious" prince will "be held more and more liberal" "with all those from whom he does not take, who are infinite" (*P* 16). Paradoxically, the reputation for virtue—or its approximation—does not require its practice, but its opposite: hoarding treasure gains the prince a reputation for something akin to liberality among those who expected him to act rapaciously. Those who had expected gifts will be disappointed and consider him mean, but Machiavelli describes meanness as "one of those vices which enable him to rule" (*P* 16).

Managing One's Reputation:
Avarice, Meanness, and Different Modes of Rapacity

Machiavelli next provides a list of three successful princes who are "considered mean" (*P* 16): Julius II, Louis XII, and Ferdinand of Spain. While the examples appear to be equivalent, they betray important differences. Only Louis XII practiced consistent and efficient parsimony: the other two examples illuminate modes for getting and spending wealth that transgress the bounds of liberality, meanness, and parsimony. While Julius II cultivated a reputation for liberality while trying to attain the papacy, "he did not think of maintaining it later" (*P* 16). Machiavelli implies that he adopted strict parsimony, but recall that in chapter 11 Machiavelli disclosed that Julius followed a "path still open to a mode of accumulating money never used by [Pope] Alexander"; Harvey Mansfield reasonably identifies this mode as "the sale of ecclesiastical offices or indulgences."[35] Is this not a particularly shameless mode of avarice?

Of Ferdinand, Machiavelli announces only that he is not "held liberal" (*P* 16). From this, one can infer that Ferdinand did not practice consistent meanness or parsimony, although many may have "considered" (*P* 16) him mean. How, then, did Ferdinand fund his many campaigns? In chapter 21, Machiavelli reveals Ferdinand's other sources of income: the Church funded some of his enterprises and he gained even more wealth by expropriating the *conversos*, Muslims, and Jews he expelled from Spain.[36] Thus, Ferdinand was able to avoid burdening most of his people by securing funds from the Church and exercising rapacity against a propertied domestic minority. He could remain "mean" (*P* 16) with all subjects whom he did not rob or kill, yet because the whole world witnessed his rapacity—concealed only shabbily under the "cloak" of religion—he could not be "held liberal" (*P* 21).

Machiavelli does not disclose Ferdinand's rapacity in chapter 16. Instead, he cites Cyrus, Caesar, and Alexander as preeminent examples of rapacity. Unlike Ferdinand, however, they did not rob their own subjects.

> And for the prince who goes out with his armies, who feeds on booty, pillage, and ransom and manages on what belongs to someone else, this liberality is necessary; otherwise he would not be followed by his soldiers. And of what is not yours or your subjects' one can be a bigger giver . . . because spending what is someone else's does not take reputation from you but adds it to you; only spending your own is what harms you. (*P* 16)

Rapacity toward foreigners adds to the prince's reputation because it enables him to be liberal without impoverishing himself. Practiced in any other way, liberality is harmful—either by making a prince "poor and contemptible" or compelling him to be "rapacious and hateful" (*P* 16). Thus, when he condemns rapacity at the end of chapter 16, Machiavelli is either flatly contradicting the previous sentence or—as is more likely—distinguishing between rapacity toward one's subjects—as practiced by Ferdinand—and rapacity toward foreigners—as practiced by princes whose reputations were burnished by conquest-fueled liberality. Indeed, the final line of chapter 16 suggests that ambitious princes ought to practice rapacity abroad rather than unswerving meanness or rapacity at home. The "most excellent" founders of chapter 6 practiced the former, as did the glorious (although problematic) imitative models of chapter 14.[37] The best that one can earn from meanness, however, is "infamy without hatred," while domestic rapacity like Ferdinand's "begets infamy with hatred" (*P* 16).

Yet while rapacity abroad benefits princes, it also imperils republican government. Caesar, because he "wanted to attain the principate of Rome" (*P* 16), used his wealth to enrich his soldiers and induce the people of Rome to support him. His behavior is identical to that of Julius II; like the latter Julius, Caesar could not have continued with this policy had he lived long enough to rule. Eventually, his intemperate expenditures "would have destroyed that empire" (*P* 16). Caesar exemplifies the twin political dangers of liberality: those who practice liberality create partisans, whose support they can use to satisfy private ambition.[38] This is fatal to republican government. Yet because liberality is not sustainable, its practitioners also expose the state to considerable danger in other ways. First, their actions threaten to impoverish the community. Second, liberality creates expectations that cannot be satisfied reliably: this conduces to disappointment and political instability, as a people accustomed to liberality will tend to seek new benefactors. According to Machiavelli's account, Christ's exhortation to unrestrained liberality is a dangerous policy for princes that perpetuates instability and conflict. Princes cannot imitate his liberality without losing their positions; republicans who tolerate Christlike liberality in their captains lose their liberty; men accustomed to liberal princes are always scanning the horizon for their next benefactor. Christ appears aware of this last tendency, and warns his hopeful followers: "Watch out that you are not deceived. For many will come in my name, claiming, 'I am he,' and, 'The time is near.' Do not follow them."[39]

The Cruel Mercies and Pious Cruelties of Christianity

Chapter 17 of *The Prince* teaches that the cost of maintaining the appearance of mercy is frequently too high, and thus, one ought not to shrink from necessary cruelty. Thus, while it "is desirable to be held merciful and not cruel," one should "take care not to use his mercy badly" (*P* 17). As discussed in chapter 1 of this work, the word that Mansfield translates as "mercy" is "*pietà*"—a word that might be translated as compassion, pity, or even piety.[40] Machiavelli's warning therefore suggests that piety itself is hazardous for princes. Given the centrality of mercy to Christ's teaching (discussed especially in the previous chapter), Machiavelli's skeptical account of mercy implies particularly pointed doubts about the prudence of adhering to Christian piety.

Admittedly, *pietà* is not a clear substitute for the word translated as "mercy" in English versions of the New Testament.[41] That word—in Latin and Italian—is *misericordia*. It does not appear in *The Prince* and appears only once in the *Discourses*—and with important implications. Machiavelli opines that the prosecution of the calumniator Manlius Capitolinus, during which the Romans uniformly declined to "beg for pity [*misericordia*]" on his behalf, demonstrated "the perfection of that city and the goodness of its matter" (*D* III.8.1).[42] Thus, the lone appearance of *misericordia* in *The Prince* and the *Discourses* teaches emphatically that "the goodness" of republican orders is demonstrated best by the absence of mercy and the rigorous application of the law. In *The* Prince, Machiavelli will advance his critique of Christianity by offering a critical account of *pietà* (hereafter translated as "mercy").

As Clifford Orwin notes, in the subsequent discussion Machiavelli reveals "a kind of cruelty as the compassion of princes."[43] Mercy cannot contend reliably with "disorders" (*P* 17). "Too much mercy" exacerbates instability, from which arises "killings or robberies" that "hurt a whole community" (*P* 17). Cruelty, however—when practiced with deliberate precision against one or few—can produce virtuous results. Indeed, while meanness produced only the reputation for an approximation of liberality, the practitioner of cruelty exhibits actual mercy: "with very few examples he will be more merciful [*sarà più pietoso*] than those who for the sake of too much mercy allow disorders to continue" (*P* 17).[44] Machiavelli's readers encountered this argument in chapter 8, in which he explained how Agathocles managed to prosecute foreign wars, stymie domestic conspiracies, and live a long life "secure in his fatherland," after having perpetrated "infinite betrayals and cruelties" (*P* 8).

> I believe that this comes from cruelties badly used or well used. Those can be called well used (if it is permissible to speak well of evil) that are done at a stroke, out of the necessity to secure oneself, and then are not persisted in but are turned to as much utility for the subjects as one can. Those cruelties are badly used which, although few in the beginning, rather grow with time than are eliminated. Those who observe the first mode can have some remedy for their state with God and with men, as had Agathocles; as for the others it is impossible for them to maintain themselves. (*P* 8)[45]

Grand acts of necessary cruelty allow a prince to secure himself. Moreover, "by not renewing them, [he] secure[s] men and gain[s] them to himself with benefits" (*P* 8). Those who are incapable of executing necessary cruelties in a single "stroke" will find themselves compelled to inflict "fresh and continued injuries" (*P* 8). Machiavelli attributes this incapacity to either "timidity" or "bad counsel" (*P* 8).

Christ, who commands, "Be merciful, just as your Father is merciful," therefore provides "bad counsel" to princes.[46] His uncompromising support of mercy might also account for the timid cruelty of a Christian: considering that Christ's extraordinary mercy extends even to those who perform his cruel execution, how could one of his followers justify cruelty?[47] Christianity teaches that men will be judged scrupulously according to both their deeds and the disposition of their hearts—and consequently emphasizes that the necessity to abstain from wickedness is absolute.[48] Thus Paul, who believes there "will be a resurrection of both the righteous and the wicked," strives "to keep [his] conscience clear before God and man."[49] A Christian prince seeking justification for necessary cruelty will find nothing in Christ's life to justify cruel actions undertaken "out of the necessity to secure oneself" (P 8).[50] The sacraments of the Church exacerbate the problematic effects of this prohibition: Catholics are required to examine their consciences before confessing their sins; indeed, confession helps form one's conscience, and fortifies a Christian against recurring in sin. Such rigorous self-examination, combined with Christ's unswerving commandment to show mercy, is likely to induce squeamishness among those who are solicitous of the fate of their souls.

Yet if cruelty is incompatible with Christianity, how does one explain Ferdinand's "pious cruelty" against the Muslims, Jews, and *conversos* of Spain? Machiavelli describes Ferdinand as "the first King among the Christians" (P 21). How was he able to reconcile cruelty with Christian mercy?

Machiavelli's teaching seems to be that he did not. Ferdinand's poorly formed—or, perhaps, nonexistent—conscience enabled his unchristian contrivance of extreme cruelty in the name of a supremely merciful God. Machiavelli writes of Ferdinand that he "never preaches anything but peace and faith, and is very hostile to both. If he had observed both, he would have had either his reputation or his state taken from him many times" (P 18).[51] In matters of faith, Ferdinand is an inveterate dissembler. His striking lack of faith enables him to appropriate Christ to justify his pious cruelty. Thus, when Machiavelli writes of Ferdinand's pious cruelty "nor could there be an example more wretched and rarer" (P 21), he might be commenting on his ghastly combination of actual cruelty, accompanied by sham mercy—or the spirit required of the prince who shamelessly enacts this policy. Yet however cruel, Ferdinand's cruelty is not "well used" (P 8). Spain "persisted in" (P 8) the use of religious pretense to imprison, torture, and expropriate Spanish subjects throughout his reign.[52]

Yet men who care neither for the state of their souls nor Christ's teachings, while wretched, are also rare in Christendom.[53] Most men will be more earnest Christians than Ferdinand. Their belief poses a different challenge to well-used cruelty. When blood must be spilled to secure one's life and state, not even the most Catholic of princes can remain abstemious. The cruelty required of political life will trouble the conscience of a Christian who believes he ought to imitate Christ's extraordinary mercy. Paul works assiduously to fortify that conscience by reminding men of the fruits of evil: "God 'will repay each person according to what they have done.' To those who by persistence in doing good seek glory, honor and immortality, he will give eternal life. But for those who are self-seeking and who reject the truth and follow evil, there will be wrath and anger."[54] The Christian conscience, especially, vitiates the cold-bloodedness that well-used cruelties require. In an effort to limit the damage to his soul, the prince with a troubled conscience is likely to perform halfhearted—that is, badly used—cruelty. Thus, Machiavelli's analysis of cruelty and mercy suggests that Christianity's apparently virtuous devotion to mercy accomplishes two vicious results. First, it commonly prevents good men from enacting well-used cruelty. Second, it more rarely enables unrepentant pretenders to practice especially wretched and rapacious cruelty. Both of these effects ultimately intensify cruelty and increase suffering. Thus, contradicting Paul, Machiavelli concludes that only those who practice efficient cruelty have remedy "with God and with men" (*P* 8).[55]

Love, Mercy, and the Original Carthaginian

The example of Dido illuminates the damaging consequences of relying on love and mercy to secure one's state. Machiavelli cites Virgil, who "says in the mouth of" the queen of Carthage: "The harshness of things and the newness of the kingdom compel me to contrive such things, and to keep a broad watch over the borders" (*P* 17).[56] This quote—one of only five in *The Prince*—ostensibly supports Machiavelli's contention that it is "impossible for a new prince to escape a name for cruelty because new states are full of dangers" (*P* 17).[57] Those familiar with the *Aeneid* know that Dido had good reason to be watchful. She had absconded with her murderous brother's fortune before founding Carthage.[58] Yet the *Aeneid* reveals that Dido is an obviously inappropriate example of a cruel new prince: she is doomed by a fatal combination of mercy and love and is herself a victim of cruelty.[59]

Aeneas and his companions are driven to Dido's shores by divine agency. Once ashore, Aeneas's mother, Venus, conceals him and one of his companions in a mist, allowing them to travel throughout Carthage undetected (I.410–14). Aeneas finds Carthage a well-defended and efficiently managed city, headed by a majestic and well-armed queen (I.418–46). He travels to the Temple of Juno, where the unconcealed Trojans beseech Dido to succor them until they can continue to Italy. While Aeneas remains hidden, Dido welcomes the Trojans with the words quoted by Machiavelli. Her profession of watchfulness is ironic, given Aeneas's concealment.

The deceptions of Dido proliferate. When Aeneas finally appears, he is rendered more beautiful by Venus (I.548–93). Aeneas flatters Dido, praising her as the only person who has pitied (*miserata*) the Trojans (I.597). Venus resolves to deceive Dido further with Cupid's help (I.673–75): Cupid impersonates Aeneas's son, and infects Dido with a poisonous (*veneno*) love for Aeneas (I.688). As the love-stricken Dido contemplates a marriage to Aeneas, Carthage's defenses are left unimproved and unmanned (IV.1–53 and 86–89; cf. IV.259–64). Eventually, thanks to the intervention of the gods, Aeneas and Dido share a bed (IV.167–72). Dido considers them married; Aeneas does not. Urged by Mercury to depart for Italy, Aeneas plots to leave Carthage in secret (IV.279–330). When Dido learns of his plans, she reproaches him for his cruelty (*crudelis*) (IV.311; IV.661) and appeals to his pity (*miserere*) (IV.318). Aeneas receives both her recriminations and her pleas coldly, whereupon Dido laments his lack of pity (*miseratus*) and describes her decision to receive him as foolish (IV.369). Yet Dido still hopes that pity can rescue her marriage: in a desperate final attempt to stay Aeneas's departure, she repeatedly invokes the pity he ought to feel for her (IV.416–36). Aeneas nonetheless departs. Dido is left with bitter regrets: she laments that she had not served Aeneas's son as the main dish in a gruesome welcoming banquet for the Trojans, whom she subsequently might have slaughtered to a man (IV.597–606). Yet rather than race to the sea to burn Aeneas's fleet, she commits suicide (IV.665).

The obvious lesson of Dido's story is that mercy is a perilous policy. This is perhaps especially true of mercy offered to a Roman.[60] Yet Machiavelli's reference to this story also invites us to consider: what is the connection between mercy and love? If one treats the intervention of the gods as superfluous to the events of the *Aeneid*—and Machiavelli always treats pagan accounts thus—one sees only that Dido's mercy precedes her love for Aeneas. Indeed, Virgil emphasizes that the practice of mercy may have fostered romantic love for the eventual founder of Rome: having assumed care for Aeneas, and having been charmed by his manipulative and motherless son, she comes to love the Trojan (I.721–22). Thus, while it is her romantic love—and the expectation that Aeneas would reciprocate her love—that most clearly invites disaster, her mercy seems inextricably linked with—and perhaps, even responsible for—that love. Yet it is love, rather than mercy, that leads her to abandon her native caution and neglect her spiritual defenses. Even as Aeneas sails away, Dido can muster only empty threats of revenge; readers know that she loves him too much to harm him.

The *Aeneid*'s course of events conforms to Machiavelli's previous teaching on "*la carità propria*" (*P* 10), observed in chapter 3 of this book.[61] There, it appeared that men tend to love that which is their own, and that any sacrifice of that which men truly love—namely, their property—engenders a sense of obligation that proceeds (often, unconsciously) from the expectation that any sacrifice on their own part will be rewarded or reciprocated. While wiser princes exploit this psychological tendency to their advantage, Dido is ensnared by it. Dido's confidence that her mercy will be rewarded—or at minimum, not exploited—is suggested by her extraordinarily generous welcome of the shipwrecked Trojans, during which she offers her "wealth" (I.569) and announces: "The city I build is yours; draw up your ships; Trojan and Tyrian I shall treat with no distinction" (I.570–74).

According to Machiavelli's reasoning on love, Dido's generous mercy toward the Trojans produces immediate psychological effects. First, it certifies her high opinion of the Trojans and Aeneas. Self-love—or a belief in her own worthiness—persuades her that she would only give so much of her own to a people worthy of her generosity. Thus her mercy fosters a love for Aeneas that leaves her undefended against his schemes. Is this also true of the mercy and brotherly love commanded by Christ? Can we display necessary circumspection with men to whom we are habituated to give freely and love as ourselves?[62] Or does obedience to Christ's second most important commandment only prepare one to be deceived? Within a dozen lines of Dido's appearance in *The Prince*, Machiavelli casts human beings as "ungrateful, fickle, pretenders and dissemblers, evaders of danger, eager for gain" (*P* 17).[63] Had Dido reminded herself of this rule, she might have inoculated herself against the self-deceptions attendant on mercy and love, and remained secure on her throne. Indeed, Machiavelli's pointed denigration of human nature seems designed to puncture any hope that reciprocal trust and love will guide relations among princes—or even, perhaps, men.

The queen's fruitless rage at Aeneas's betrayal depicts the consequences of allowing mercy and love to guide the affairs of one's state, but it also demonstrates that mere claims of justice are impotent to correct human wrongs.[64] Dido's generous mercy engendered a conviction that the Trojans owed her something and would strengthen Carthage by settling in her kingdom. Aeneas profits from her belief, which he does not share. Aeneas's concern was founding Rome, rather than strengthening Carthage. His departure confirms that interest—rather than love, mercy, or justice—is decisive in foreign affairs.[65] When strangers wash upon one's shores, a prince ought to behave as Dido says, rather than as she does.[66] She ought to have left the gates of Carthage—and her heart—closed to Aeneas. Better yet, by cutting Aeneas and his companions to pieces, she would not only have saved her life, but made impossible Rome's eventual conquest of her city, which was accomplished by another silver-tongued Roman.

Virgil's account suggests that when a stranger invokes a sense of pity that arouses feelings of tender and intimate love, one ought to remain circumspect: "He should be slow to believe and to move, nor should he make himself feared, and he should proceed with a temperate mode with prudence and humanity so that too much confidence does not make him incautious and too much diffidence does not make him intolerable" (*P* 17).[67] Those who do not follow Machiavelli's advice will, like Dido, regret their intemperance. Indeed, the indignation they feel at having been deceived in their affections may inspire greater cruelty toward their beloved, as they seek to punish him for his injustice.[68]

Machiavelli's exhortation to spiritual circumspection is incompatible with Christ's teaching.[69] By directing the reader to a story of spurned mercy and false love, he makes this clear. The dangers attendant on love and mercy explain Machiavelli's final judgment: "Of Cruelty and Mercy, and Whether It Is Better to Be Loved Than Feared, or the Contrary" (*P* 17).[70] He teaches that cruelty and fear are surer guards of a prince's security. The "dread of punishment" invoked by fear "never forsakes you" (*P* 17). Hannibal's "inhuman cruelty" (*P* 17) is superior to the mercy and love displayed by his Carthaginian predecessor. The examples of love and mercy offered by Christ and Scipio offer the tantalizing promise of glory, but Dido—whose "damaging quality" (*P* 17) is not concealed, but exposed, by virtuous Rome—demonstrates the uncertainty of their modes.

Fearsomeness, Astuteness, and the Perverse Power of Faith

In chapter 18 of *The Prince*, Machiavelli returns to the theme that introduced his discussion of "qualities that bring [all men and especially princes] praise or blame": how to maintain the appearance of virtue, while practicing those vices that are necessary to "save one's state" (*P* 15). Indeed, chapter 18 constitutes Machiavelli's summary teaching on virtue, although that word does not appear in the chapter.[71] He reveals two aspects of this teaching: he discloses the most important qualities one should appear to have, while also describing the spiritual requirements of the consummately virtuous prince. This man can maintain the appearance of virtue and goodness, while adhering resolutely to the practices and qualities conducive to security, even if they appear vicious—or are, in fact, evil.

Chapter 18 is entitled "In What Mode Faith Should Be Kept by Princes." Machiavelli's first, most tentative teaching is that astuteness triumphs over faith.[72]

> How praiseworthy it is for a prince to keep his faith [*la fede*] and to live with honesty and not by astuteness, everyone understands. Nonetheless one sees by experience in our times that the princes who have done great things are those who have taken little account of faith [*della fede*] and have known how to get around men's brains [*cervelli*] with their astuteness [*l'astuzia*]; and in the end they have overcome those who have founded themselves on loyalty. (*P* 18)

By recommending astuteness, Machiavelli refers to a sort of calculation that allows one to outthink one's companions.[73] He does not describe this quality as dishonesty, but nonetheless opposes it to both honesty and loyalty. His basic point is that those who prize fidelity over canny prudence lose. Read narrowly, this might be construed as a reluctant concession to the claim that a prince cannot maintain strict morality.

Yet Machiavelli's teaching becomes more radical as the chapter progresses. To explain his contention that faithlessness prevails, Machiavelli discloses "that there are two kinds of combat" (*P* 18).[74] Men use laws; beasts use force. Laws depend on fidelity that princes cannot always expect, and are thus "often" (*P* 18) insufficient to secure victory.[75] The prince must therefore "know well how to use the beast and the man" (*P* 18). It is here that Machiavelli introduces Chiron the centaur, the "half-beast, half-man" (*P* 18), as a model. Offering a teaching that he claims "was taught covertly to princes by ancient writers," Machiavelli claims, "a prince needs to know how to use both natures; and the one without the other is not lasting" (*P* 18). Machiavelli's recommendation to imitate a "half-beast, half-man" (*P* 18) is problematic advice for men commanded to imitate the fully human, fully divine Christ.[76]

The beasts that Machiavelli recommends imitating are the lion and the fox. He argues that since the "lion does not defend itself from snares and the fox does not defend itself from wolves," "one needs to be a fox to recognize snares and a lion to frighten the wolves" (*P* 18). While imitating either animal exclusively is insufficient, using only the lion appears especially so. Princes appear prone to make this mistake, but "the one who has known best how to use the fox has come out best" (*P* 18).

While Machiavelli introduced this discussion by claiming that beasts are models of how to make combat by force, neither of the beasts he cites confirms this claim. Lions use merely the threat of force to frighten wolves; the fox's wariness also serves defensive purposes.[77] The ways of these beasts become powerful offensive weapons, however, when human beings use them. A lion may roar to frighten wolves, but the wolves do not, presumably, thereafter lie frightened in their dens at night, certain that the lion is coming to get them. Princes who roar like lions can, however, inspire precisely this sort of fear among men. Human imagination, combined with knowledge that human beings (and especially princes) often act on motives apart from narrow self-preservation, multiply our fears. Human nature also amplifies the power of the foxlike astuteness, since human beings can set, as well as recognize, snares.

Faith-breaking (*fedifrago*) is, however, a decidedly human quality.[78] Abandoning his earlier reticence, Machiavelli now recommends it freely. Since the prince is surrounded by men, who "are wicked and do not observe faith," he "cannot observe faith, nor should he, when such observance turns against him, and the causes that made him promise have been eliminated" (*P* 18). This teaching complements his assessment of "wicked" human character in chapter 17.

Somewhat paradoxically, Machiavelli teaches that faith-breaking is empowered by the tendency of men to trust others. While men's wicked and calculative character often renders them faithless, they are also "so simple and so obedient to present necessities that he who deceives will always find someone who will let himself be deceived" (*P* 18). One can account for these contradictory tendencies of human nature by noting that it is difficult to calculate and secure one's interest; this is truer of humans than animals, since human imagination and ability produce complicated, lofty, or even unattainable hopes. Most men, when faced with this uncertainty, will cooperate with others to accomplish these ends. This requires trust, which is based on a belief—or hope—that the other party will satisfy his promises and help meet "present necessities" (*P* 18). A faith-breaker can exploit these hopes by astutely setting snares.

The nature of the lion's mode of combat defies concealment, but Machiavelli insists that a human being who "use[s] the fox" must "color this nature," and "be a great pretender and dissembler" (*P* 18). Like all effective snare-setters, the faith-breaker must conceal his astute deceptions, because even the most gullible human will learn to avoid snares set by one who has a reputation for faith-breaking. Luckily for the faith-breaking prince, humans—despite our ability to pretend, dissemble, and deceive—are also credulous beings. Machiavelli's teaching on faith has progressed: he begins the chapter with a reluctant concession to the necessity of breaking faith; he abandons his reluctance in his second statement on faith-breaking, then recommends that one's faith-breaking be concealed—and thus perfected—by pretensions of fidelity.

Lions, Foxes, and the Lamb of God

By recommending the imitation of lions and foxes, Machiavelli departs from Christianity's allegorical teaching, which enjoins men to imitate Christ, whom John the Baptist describes as the "Lamb of God."[79] Jesus himself describes his followers variously as lambs, sheep, and a vulnerable flock.[80] He is certainly aware of the dangers to which he exposes his imitators, who are stalked by enemies described as ravenous beasts. To his disciples, he acknowledges, "I am sending you out like lambs among wolves"; he warns that, after his death, "false prophets," who wear "sheep's clothing, but inwardly . . . are ferocious wolves," will besiege his flock.[81] Early Christians understood the peril of imitating Christ: "For your sake we face death all day long; we are considered as sheep to be slaughtered."[82]

The meekness enjoined by Christ means that the lion—an animal whose admirable qualities are often ascribed to virtuous men in the Old Testament—is an inapt allegorical model for Christians. While some Old Testament writers—and especially David—associate the lion with the wicked enemies of Israel, most attribute to lions majesty, ferocity, and justice.[83] In the Old Testament, leonine qualities are even ascribed to God.[84] By contrast, the New Testament contains strikingly few references to lions.[85] In a departure from his immediate and most prominent prophetic predecessors, Jesus never refers to the lion in his speeches and sayings. Indeed, excepting several obscure references in the Book of Revelation, the lone original reference to a lion in the New Testament occurs in 1 Peter, where the apostle gives advice to the shepherds of Jesus's flock. He instructs them to remain humble and warns them of a sinister predator that preys upon the unvigilant: "Your enemy the devil prowls around like a roaring lion looking for someone to devour."[86] The devil—that being who tempts Christ with the promise of earthly rule, robs men of their belief, corrupts Judas Iscariot, and whom Christ calls "the father of lies"—is the lion of the New Testament.[87] To those stalked as prey by the diabolical lion, Peter recommends humility, faith, and patient suffering. Machiavelli, however, recommends that a prince imitate this famed predator of Christians.

Machiavelli's recommendation to imitate the fox is also problematic, given the New Testament's treatment of that animal.[88] Christ's judgment of the creature is critical. He mentions the fox in two contexts. When a man promises to follow Christ, he replies by reminding the man of his remarkable poverty: "Foxes have dens and birds have nests, but the Son of Man has no place to lay his head."[89] Christ's deprivations are worse than those of the lowly fox. Christ's second—and more important—reference to a fox ascribes its qualities to a man: King Herod.[90] When Pharisees advise Jesus to flee before Herod kills him, Jesus replies: "Go tell that fox, 'I will keep on driving out demons and healing people today and tomorrow, and on the third day I will reach my goal.'"[91] Herod—whom the New Testament records as the executioner of John the Baptist, wily conspirator against Christ, "friend" to Pontius Pilate, and persecutor of early Christians—is the fox of the New Testament.[92] Machiavelli teaches that the most successful princes imitate this animal.

With sinister playfulness, Machiavelli thus offers an anti-Christian allegorical teaching: one ought to use "the beast" (la bestia) for the purpose of combat.[93] By recommending the use of the lion and the fox, Machiavelli endorses indirectly the imitation of Christ's most important opponents on heaven and earth: the angelic being who opposes the Christian God and the first earthly king to persecute the Christian Church. One must therefore consider whether the general superiority of the fox also indicates that Herod surpassed the devil as Christ's antagonist. Recall that Herod famously refused to seek Christ's execution, and attacked Christianity directly only after Christ's martyrdom had strengthened it: might Machiavelli be suggesting that the foxlike Herod recognized that Christ's execution was a snare that ought to be avoided?[94] This teaching, although concealed within an allegory, discloses Machiavelli's anti-Christian spirit.

Flexible Spirits or Firm Hearts?
Christianity, the Limits of Probity, and Machiavellian Virtue

Despite the anti-Christian implications of Machiavelli's allegorical teaching on the beast, his most blasphemous teachings in chapter 18 are his exhortation to radical faithlessness and his description of the spirit required to practice Machiavellian virtue.[95]

> Thus, it is not necessary for a prince to have all the above-mentioned qualities [that are held to be virtuous] in fact, but it is indeed necessary to appear to have them. Nay, I dare say this, that by having them and always observing them, they are harmful; and by appearing to have them, they are useful, as it is to appear merciful, faithful, humane, honest, and religious, and to be so; but to remain with a spirit built so that, if you need not to be those things, you are able and know how to change to the contrary. This has to be understood: that a prince, and especially a new prince, cannot observe all of those things for which men are held good, since he is often under a necessity, to maintain his state, of acting against faith, against charity, against religion. (*P* 18)

In one way, this is a more pointed restatement of the teaching he offered in chapter 15.[96] Because some of these qualities—mercy, faith, humanity, honesty, and religiosity—are harmful, the appearance of virtue is often preferable to its possession. Yet this is not a moderate, but regrettable, concession to political realities: seeking merely the appearance of these qualities obliterates them as Christian virtues. Christ's condemnation of the Pharisees as hypocrites demonstrates that the possession of virtue is all that matters. Indeed, Christ condemns those who maintain only the appearance of virtue most harshly: "Well did Isaiah prophesy of you hypocrites, as it is written, 'This people honors me with their lips, but their heart is far from me; in vain do they worship me.'"[97] Jesus confirms his low opinion of artifice by proclaiming, "Blessed are the pure in heart, for they will see God."[98] Throughout the Gospels, Christ indicates that when discerning righteousness from sin, and good conduct from evil, the disposition of one's heart is decisive, "for the mouth speaks what the heart is full of."[99]

Christ offers no comfort to the dissembling Machiavellian prince. Lying is associated with the devil, truth with God.[100] By juxtaposing the utility of being virtuous with the claim that you need to be able to "change to the contrary" "if you need not to be those things" (*P* 18), Machiavelli confirms that his understanding of virtue contradicts Christ's. The Christian does not "have a spirit disposed to change as the winds of fortune and the variation of things command him" (*P* 18). He has a heart and soul that "stand firm."[101] Because "God knows [our] hearts," Paul teaches that the Christian's salvation depends on his probity.[102]

> You were taught, with regard to your former way of life, to put off your old self, which is being corrupted by its deceitful desires; to be made new in the attitude of your minds; and to put on the new self, created to be like God in true righteousness and holiness. Therefore each of you must put off falsehood and speak truthfully to your neighbor, for we are all members of one body.[103]

The heart and soul of the Christian believer is engaged in a community that is superintended watchfully—and judged ultimately—by God. Thus, he ought to remain truthful and "stand firm."[104] Machiavelli, by contrast, judges that astute flexibility is the most necessary spiritual quality of a prince; deceptive physical contortions of the brain are necessary in communities of men, "where there is no court to appeal to" (P 18).[105] Whereas Christ instructs his disciples to pray so that God might "lead us not into temptation, but deliver us from the evil one," Machiavelli instructs his reader "not [to] depart from good, when possible, but know how to enter into evil, when forced by necessity" (P 18).[106]

Christian Princes and the Vulgar Many

Despite his injunction to enter into necessary evil, Machiavelli acknowledges that one should appear "all mercy, all faith, all honesty, all humanity, all religion" (P 18).[107] The appearance of religiosity is an especially necessary quality. Machiavelli's high praise of the armed prophets of chapter 6 prepares the reader for this judgment, yet his cynicism here is nonetheless striking. "Men in general" are vulgar; they are easy to deceive; they trust what they see and what they hear; and when their opinion is protected by "the majesty of the state," the few—who actually "touch what you are" and might therefore contradict the positive judgment of you that prevails among the vulgar—are silenced (P 18).[108] Machiavelli thus concludes, "In the actions of all men, and especially princes, where there is no court to appeal to, one looks to the end. So let a prince win and maintain his state: the means will always be judged honorable, and will be praised by everyone" (P 18). By asserting that the judgment of "men in general" (P 18) is dispositive to questions of virtue, Machiavelli supervenes Christ's claims that "what people value highly is detestable in God's sight" and that God the Father "has entrusted all judgment to the Son, that all may honor the Son just as they honor the Father. Whoever does not honor the Son does not honor the Father, who sent him."[109]

Machiavelli's teaching on virtue is not a halfhearted concession to amoral, but necessary, means for the sake of successful ends; the prince's means are not justified, but ennobled, by success.[110] According to Machiavelli's amoral view of virtue, cruelty, infidelity, inhumanity, and irreligion require no apology. While the prince who appears "all religion" will find it easier to do what is necessary to "win and maintain his state," even the honor and praise accorded to his means depend on the earthly success of his enterprise (*P* 18). No judgment awaits princes in heaven; "men in general" (*P* 18) constitute the court of last resort.[111] Machiavelli's prince ought therefore to disregard the restrictive moral requirements of Christianity, and execute instead what is necessary to win and maintain his state. By maintaining the appearance of virtue, Machiavelli's prince condescends to the vulgar, who cannot understand what is necessary to achieve good things.

An important implication of this argument is that the claim of divine sanction alone is insufficient to win glory. What, then, of the life and reputation of Christ? Without the establishment of the powerful Church of Rome, would Christ's self-sacrifice—if remembered at all—be regarded as reckless and blameworthy? Subsequent historical events render this question hypothetical, but this much is clear: for Machiavelli, not death but blame "is swallowed up in victory."[112]

Obvious and Effective: The Paradoxical
Success of Religious Pretenders in Christianity

In chapter 18, Machiavelli cites two Christian princes as religious pretenders. Pope Alexander VI was an unrivaled oath-breaker; Machiavelli's language suggests that Alexander's boundless capacity for deceit was well known.[113] Why, then, did men continue to believe him? Machiavelli confirms his earlier judgment, when he explained how Alexander VI persuaded Louis XII to give him an army, although doing so contradicted Louis's interests: Alexander's success depended on his position as pope.[114] He specifies that Alexander "always found a subject [*subietto*]" (*P* 18) whom he could deceive.[115] The pope's subjects are the men and women of Christendom; those outside that world—or those who resolutely disbelieve— would never subject themselves to the obvious deceits of Alexander. While a believing "subject" might persuade himself that ascending to the throne of Peter had transformed Rodrigo Borgia's character, those inured to the siren song of Christian piety would know better. Thus the success of Alexander's inveterate faithlessness depended largely on the misplaced faith of his partners, rather than astute artifice on his part.[116] A damaging belief in the need for papal dispensations is merely the most prominent example of this misplaced faith.

The other Christian prince is unnamed: "A certain prince of present times, whom it is not well to name, never preaches anything but peace and faith, and is very hostile to both. If he had observed both, he would have

had either his reputation or his state taken away from him many times"
(*P* 18). As Mansfield notes, Machiavelli appears to refer to Ferdinand of
Spain, "whom [he] unhesitatingly names" in chapter 21.[117] Machiavelli's
discretion is thus halfhearted: here in chapter 18, he identifies himself as
one of "the few" who opposes "the opinion of the many," but does not dare
to disclose his judgment (*P* 18); in chapter 21, however, he announces that
judgment openly.[118] So while Ferdinand may conceal his faith-breaking
more completely than Alexander VI, his deception is nonetheless open to
the world. Perhaps if he had appeared "all religion" (*P* 18)—as did, for
example, Christ or Moses—Machiavelli would not dare to brand him a bra-
zen pretender.[119]

The two religious pretenders of chapter 18 are both inexpert—and both
Christian. What explains Christian princes' inability to conceal entirely
their faithlessness? Christianity's devotion to probity partly explains their
inability, but to answer this question fully, Machiavelli will discourse on
apparently disparate subjects over the next three chapters: the problem
of conspiracies, the varied modes adopted by Roman emperors, the dangers of fortresses, the political limitations of the papacy, and the strange
fruits produced by Ferdinand, "the first king among the Christians" (*P* 21).
These diverse subjects are unified by Machiavelli's critique of the Church,
Christianity, and its founder, which reveal the impossibility of a successful
and genuinely Christian prince.

CHAPTER SIX

Christ's Ruinous Political Legacy

Over the next three chapters, Machiavelli suspends his more direct critique of Christ in order to offer a critique of Christ's political legacy. He elaborates the political weakness of the papacy, the pernicious effects of its most popular politico-military strategy, and the ghastly consequences of acquiescing to the rule of the "first king among the Christians" (*P* 21). Using Italian and ancient examples, Machiavelli teaches a prince how to purge Italy of the corrupting influence of the Church and repel incursions by the ascendant Spanish Empire, whose success destroys the very foundations of civil society.

The title of chapter 19 is "Of Avoiding Contempt and Hatred." Because the model Machiavellian prince described in chapter 18 would govern with Machiavellian virtue and would therefore "be praised by everyone," one might ask why this advice is necessary. The consummate Machiavellian prince is famous, rather than infamous. Since the prince addressed here seems incapable of the height of Machiavellian virtue, chapter 19 appears to represent a descent in the argument.[1]

This prince has not learned to abstain from taking his subjects' property and women.[2] He must "contrive" (*ingegnarsi*) to appear strong, grave, and spirited (*P* 19).[3] While Machiavelli promises that the mere appearance of these qualities will prevent subjects from thinking "either of deceiving him or of getting around him" (*P* 19), that advice is conspicuously insouciant about the dangerous ambition of the few. Although Machiavelli cites two "failed" (*P* 19) conspiracies as evidence that conspiracies are difficult to accomplish, these offer little comfort: though their efforts are bungled, the conspirators nonetheless succeed in killing their respective targets.[4] Machiavelli's advice to this defective prince is misleading. It betrays his hostility to those in power and prepares the reader for Machiavelli's conspiracy against the religious status quo, which emerges at the end of this chapter.

Internal and External Conspiracies

Machiavelli furthers his disingenuous teaching on conspiracies in the next paragraph. He notes that conspiracies can arise from within and from without. To combat "external powers," one needs "good arms and good friends" (*P* 19). Machiavelli reassures the reader that the former are a sufficient guarantee of the latter. This teaching on the sufficiency of arms appears at first glance to be a variation of one that he has already offered in *The Prince* (*P* 12), but closer inspection reveals that it is not. In chapter 3, Machiavelli teaches that a prince (and perhaps, especially, a new prince) must benefit those he hopes to befriend. But since, due to the lofty expectations of friends and the self-defeating nature of liberality, he cannot satisfy his friends "in the mode they had presumed" (*P* 3), Machiavelli eventually cites the "dread of punishment" (*P* 17) as a surer guarantor of men's good word. Yet force employed to inspire fear does not so much guarantee friends as stupefy subjects and deter enemies, thus making both "hesitant" (*P* 17) to offend the prince. To describe those who do not dare to conspire against a prince as his "friends" is too cynical even for Machiavelli—for whom friendship requires at least the illusion of mutual benefit. How, then, do arms secure friends? Chapter 16's teaching on liberality offers a clue: a prince may create approximate friends by transforming his subjects or creatures into armed partisans, willing to employ force under his direction, for partisan benefit. A prince seeking friends must thus behave as Machiavelli informs us Cyrus, Caesar, and Alexander—and the founders—behaved: he must put himself at the head of a rapacious and pillaging army (*P* 16).[5]

This implicit recommendation is in considerable tension with what is required to avoid domestic conspiracies: "Things inside will always remain steady, if things outside are steady, unless indeed they are disturbed by conspiracy" (*P* 19). The prince needs friends; to acquire them, he must equip them and pay them; to do these things, he must feed them "on booty, pillage, and ransom" (*P* 16); yet by exercising external rapacity, he ensures that the "things outside" (*P* 19) will remain unsteady.[6] Although Machiavelli suggests that the prince who finds himself in this predicament ought to trust in the people as Nabis did, Nabis's assassination demonstrates the riskiness of that advice—and confirms the necessity of a personal army or bodyguard.[7] Machiavelli's summary advice is dubious, if not downright conspiratorial:

> I conclude, therefore, that a prince should take little account of conspiracies if the people show good will to him; but if they are hostile and bear hatred for him, he should fear everything and everyone. And well-ordered states and wise princes have thought out with all diligence how not to make the great desperate and how to satisfy the people and keep them content, because this is one of the most important matters that concern the prince. (*P* 19)

This advice contradicts what Machiavelli has taught regarding the humors of the people and the great and establishes an impossible task for the obedient but undiscerning reader. The people do not demand much, but the prince confuses their passivity with fidelity at his own peril (*P* 3). More importantly, one does not need to make the great desperate to enflame their desire to rule (*P* 9). They are born desperate. Indeed, Machiavelli's teaching has been that the prince should not make the people desperate and that there is no way to satisfy the great, since they want what he has.

Machiavelli's account of the difficulties that attend conspiracies thus teaches the ambitious and alert that while conspiracies are dangerous to undertake, they are not impossible. The conspirator's first task is to locate a "rare friend" or "obstinate enemy of the prince," with whom he can safely conspire (*P* 19).[8] This is also Machiavelli's task in *The Prince*, as he invites readers who second his critique of Christ to join his conspiracy.

A Defective Principality:
Roman Emperors and the Problem of the Army

One might conclude that Machiavelli wishes merely for the lackluster prince to fail. But in chapter 19, he also offers practical advice to the reader who is attuned to the contradictions in his teaching. To this end, Machiavelli entertains an objection: he will explain why certain Roman emperors who possessed great "virtue of spirit" (*P* 19) nonetheless failed.[9] Machiavelli suggests that these men were excellent, but for their failure. This formulation is in considerable tension with Machiavelli's general teaching that virtuous princes are able to remedy every accident.[10] Yet this subject is an important one for the second-rate prince: he undoubtedly considers himself excellent, and yet finds ruling and maintaining his state very difficult. Based on the preceding paragraphs, the likely sources of his difficulties are his unwillingness to abstain from taking the property and women of his subjects and his inability to eliminate the great. It is ostensibly for this prince that Machiavelli will explain the causes of the emperors' successes and failures; in this discussion, Machiavelli discloses another, less glorious way for these inferior princes to maintain power. Insofar as it lacks any promise of transcendent glory, this model for imitation appears to depart significantly from the model founders of chapter 6 and the model prince of chapters 15 through 18. It nonetheless lays bare the requirements of founding and the limitations of Christian principalities.

Machiavelli announces: "And I want it to suffice for me to take all the emperors who succeeded to the empire, from Marcus the philosopher to Maximinus: these were Marcus, Commodus his son, Pertinax, Julianus, Severus, his son Antoninus Caracalla, Macrinus, Heliogabalus, Alexander, and Maximinus" (*P* 19).[11] This discussion of Roman emperors—which appears to follow the account of the historian Herodian—is indicative of the descent that has occurred in the book as a whole.[12] These emperors are neither prophets nor founders; they did not create new orders, and in some cases, rose to the principate by mere inheritance.[13]

Machiavelli begins by revealing that these emperors had to contend with something hitherto unmentioned in Machiavelli's musings about the people and the great, but nonetheless alluded to in his previous discussions of arms: the cruelty and avarice of their "soldiers" (*P* 19). The history to which Machiavelli refers reveals that the "soldiers" (*soldati*) to whom Machiavelli refers are members of the Praetorian Guard, rather than the regular army.[14] Praetorians were elite military men who also served as the emperor's personal bodyguard. Machiavelli's imprecision obscures the crucial importance of a prince's elite forces and personal bodyguard, which appear especially necessary but difficult to manage.

Machiavelli reveals that the desires of these Roman soldiers were sometimes contrary to—or in tension with—the desire of the emperor. All but two of these Roman emperors struggled to control their armies, who sought to terrorize and rob the people. Emperors who lacked a "great reputation" (*P* 19) were unable to manage the soldiers: they did not truly possess their "own arms" (*P* 13). Their difficulty was in some ways understandable: the Praetorian Guard—composed of Roman citizens who were nonetheless officially subject to the emperor, increasingly accustomed to the booty and pillage that accrued from imperial conquest, and frequently representing an interest separate from both the people and the emperor—possessed the mixed characteristics of citizens, subjects, creatures, mercenaries, and auxiliaries. How was one to manage them?

Of the three humane emperors who were "lovers of justice" (*P* 19), only Marcus Aurelius died of natural causes: the soldiers murdered Pertinax and Alexander for their efforts to restrain the army.[15] This is the first time the word "justice" appears in the book—and it appears in the context of failure.[16] In particular, justice is felled by cruelty and avarice. What, then, explains Marcus's ability to survive? Machiavelli offers that Marcus was a hereditary prince "with many virtues that made him venerable" (*P* 19), yet he has also shown that mere inheritance is insufficient to maintain authority. Could it be that his philosophical training—combined with the authority of his hereditary position—allowed him to succeed as a lover of justice? At the end of chapter 19, Machiavelli will suggest a solution to this puzzle.

The others, fearing revolt by the Praetorian Guard, allowed them to satisfy their malignant desires. Machiavelli judges that this decision was sensible. He thus revises the teaching of chapter 17, which held that a virtuous prince must exercise cruelty to discipline his army and should avoid being hated by his citizens. Now Machiavelli asserts that one cannot avoid being hated by someone: princely rule—and perhaps politics—requires the prince to harm someone. Thus, Machiavelli concludes that the prince ought to avoid being hated by those who are most dangerous. Yet one wonders whether this advice applies only to defective princes, who are incapable of sufficient cruelty, and thus do not possess arms that are truly theirs. If these emperors had possessed an army composed entirely of their "creatures" (*P* 13), would they find themselves in this quandary? As we learn from Machiavelli's praise of Hannibal in chapter 17, to transform the army into one's own requires great, "inhuman" cruelty and great virtue. Only one of these emperors displayed these qualities: Septimius Severus.

The Best of the Worst: Severus

Machiavelli's discussion of the emperors after Marcus suggests that all but Severus were princes of limited promise. Most inherited mongrel armies, who were "acquired at a price [i.e., the rape of the people] and not with greatness or nobility of spirit" (*P* 17). Lacking the ability to reorder or even discipline the army, these emperors could not establish new orders with their forces. Of the emperors who glutted the avarice of their soldiers, only Severus died of natural causes. The rest were doomed by a conspiracy of their soldiers. What, then, allowed Severus to succeed?[17]

Machiavelli writes that Commodus, Severus, Caracalla, and Maximinus were all "very cruel and very rapacious. They would not spare any kind of injury that could be inflicted on the people" (*P* 19). Severus alone succeeded because he possessed "so much virtue that, by keeping the soldiers his friends [*amici*], although the people were overburdened by him, he was always able to rule happily because his virtues made him so admirable in the sight of his soldiers and the people that the latter remained somehow astonished and stupefied, while the former were reverent and satisfied" (*P* 19).[18] Readers of Machiavelli will recognize this formulation from Machiavelli's discussion of Cesare Borgia's execution of Remirro D'Orco, in chapter 7. Borgia's exploitation of his cruel subordinate was an example of well-used cruelty: the brief episode pacified the province, increasing his own security and that of his people.[19] Machiavelli intimates in chapter 17 that because of this episode, Borgia was both loved and feared by his people; in this respect, Borgia's behavior appeared to be a model.

Yet here, in chapter 19, Severus emerges as an alternate model.[20] The presence of the indolent Julianus on the Roman throne offered Severus an opportunity to satisfy his ambition. According to Herodian, he concealed his ambition in pious pretensions of fidelity to the memory of the murdered Pertinax; claiming oracular inspiration, he marched on Rome.[21] By feigning piety and pronouncing invectives against the imperial guard, he rallied the Illyrian army—on which he would rely throughout his reign—to his cause (*History* II.10.1–9). With a loyal army at his side, Severus exhibited foxlike skill in manipulating Albinus in the west (II.15.1–5), which afforded him an opportunity to attack Niger in the east (III.2.3–5; III.5.3–7). When Niger was defeated, he contrived an excuse to fight and kill Albinus (III.4.6–7).[22]

Because satisfying the soldiers was the most pressing concern of these emperors, Severus's ability to manage the armed elite is particularly striking. Herodian also reports that Severus is the only emperor after Marcus who could check the Praetorian Guard: as he marched on Rome, they deserted Julianus "because they were afraid of Severus" (II.12.6). After arriving in Rome, Severus cashiered the Praetorian Guard that had been responsible for Pertinax's death in a particularly memorable way (II.13.2–12). Commanding them to appear unarmed before him in an arena, he then surrounded them with armed soldiers. He pronounced that they deserved destruction for their perfidy, but—citing his "philanthropy" (II.13.8)—nonetheless spared them.[23] Stripping them of their arms and insignia, Severus chased the ex-Praetorians into Rome's winding streets.

Yet Severus did not wish to change fundamentally the nature of the imperial power: unlike Hiero, Severus does not orchestrate the slaughter of the parasitic military class in order to make broader use of the citizenry.[24] Of course, unlike Hiero, he never intended to transform Rome into a "free state."[25] Indeed, Severus was not animated by even vaguely republican intentions. He selected the most trusted and capable men from his own army to populate the new Praetorian Guard, thus transforming them into an army of his "creatures."[26] He could not imitate Hiero, since slaughtering the soldiers would have established a precedent that would have discomfited his personal bodyguard and undermined his criminal schemes.

Though antirepublican and inhumane, Severus is nonetheless a model of how to deal with the people. Herodian reports that "the Romans were absolutely terrified" when Severus arrived in Rome; the fact that he had achieved the throne "so effortlessly and with so little bloodshed" imbued their fear with a tremulous sense of awe.[27]

> Thus, whoever examines minutely the actions of this man will find him a very fierce lion and a very astute fox, will see that he was feared and revered by everyone, and not hated by the army, and will not marvel that he, a new man, could have held so much power. For his very great reputation always defended him from the hatred that his people could have conceived for him because of his robberies. (*P* 19)[28]

Thus, Severus's reputation for cruelty and rapacity enabled him to rule. He satisfied the avarice of his soldiers and robbed his people.[29] He was a criminal, and the scale of his criminality stupefied the people: he was loved by the soldiers and gaped at by the people—like a lion, he was so feared that the people's hatred withered under his stern glance. His foxy astuteness only amplified his power. Indeed, Herodian's depiction of Severus's capacity for deceit resembles closely Machiavelli's dark ode to Alexander VI: "He was an absolute expert at deception and giving assurance of his goodwill, but he had no respect for an oath if, after he had lied to secure some advantage, he had to break it. He would make protestations by word of mouth which did not represent his true feelings."[30]

In one way, Machiavelli's praise of Severus in this chapter would seem to be a logical consequence of the teaching of chapters 15 through 18. Although Severus is a criminal of the highest order, he was successful— indeed, his many "robberies" (*P* 19) were the cause of his success. Since one "should not care about incurring the fame of those vices without which it is difficult to save one's state," Severus's actions appear worthy of imitation for princes of "effectual" principalities (*P* 15). Crime succeeds, and therefore takes its place among the acceptable means to power.[31] This argument is not, of course, new to *The Prince*. Machiavelli hinted at this conclusion when he praised the violent and destructive founders, in chapter 6, and Agathocles, in chapter 8; his deconstruction of classical and Christian virtue in chapters 15 through 18 also prepared the reader for this conclusion.[32] In chapter 19, however, Machiavelli abandons any halfhearted concessions to conventional virtue: Severus made himself secure and happy by criminality, and Machiavelli praises him without compunction.

One who views Machiavelli as unflinchingly republican might here object that Severus cannot be a model for princely behavior, since by "teaching the [soldiers] to be greedy for riches and seducing them into a life of luxury," he destroyed utterly the tattered remnants of Rome's republican military orders.[33] Severus is surely antirepublican, but Machiavelli's praise of him completes his most comprehensive teaching on mercenary arms. Under the direction of the deficient princes of Italy, mercenary armies are undoubtedly useless and dangerous. They are absolutely poisonous to republican government. Yet Severus demonstrates that under the direction of a man of sufficiently inhuman virtue, mercenaries are conducive to a prince's—and especially a founding prince's—security.[34] Indeed, this teaching is not new to *The Prince*, but is now, rather, more fully revealed. The imitative models Philip of Macedon, David, and Philopoemen acted as mercenary captains.[35] Xenophon was a mercenary. Agathocles's first conspiratorial action was to select a corps of soldiers who "were very firmly attached to [him], having received many benefits from him during the campaigns"; subsequently, he enlists mercenaries to cull the ambitious and envious from Syracuse.[36] Cyrus, Caesar, and Alexander each sought "booty, pillage, and ransom" in order to "be followed by his soldiers" (*P* 16); so, too, do Moses, Romulus, and Theseus pillage their neighbors for the benefit of their armies.[37] Even

Machiavelli's preeminent example of staunchly antimercenary behavior communicates covertly the value of mercenaries. Hiero earns praise because he "cut to pieces" (*P* 13) Syracuse's mercenaries, yet Polybius reports that after this act, Hiero enlisted "on his own account a sufficient body of mercenaries, [and] he thenceforth carried on the business of the government in security."[38]

Like the founders to whom he has "some proportion" (*P* 6), Hiero needed his own arms. While Machiavelli suggested casually in chapter 6 that arms accompany virtue, in the second half of *The Prince*, he has demonstrated with increasing candor what he meant when he identified virtue with one's own arms: because armies cohere especially to leaders who conduct successful criminal enterprises, one also finds preeminent Machiavellian virtue among men who are nominally criminals. Christ's categorical rejection of worldly goods—and studiously formal obedience to all laws—helps to explain his inability to attract arms to his cause.[39]

Yet one ought to resist the temptation to conflate Machiavelli's praise of Severus with the fundamental reorganization of Machiavelli's political universe.[40] The example of Severus reveals the radical limitlessness of Machiavelli's new virtue and the criminal requirements of founding, but Severus's criminality is not the peak of Machiavellian political practice. Indeed, in chapter 7, Machiavelli suggests that these Roman emperors relied on fortune, insofar as their positions depended on "corrupting the soldiers" (*P* 7); moreover, unlike the princes of chapter 6, Severus did not "introduce any form [he] pleased" (*P* 6).[41] While his criminal methods might be identical with those of the founders, who destroy old orders without regard for conventional virtue, importantly, Severus created neither new modes nor new orders. Indeed, he did not even destroy old orders. Instead, he accomplished the takeover and consolidation of the Roman Empire by glutting the cruelty and avarice of his army. It is true he possessed considerable astuteness, but ultimately, one must remember that he is comparable to Agathocles, rather than Moses, Romulus, Cyrus, or Theseus: although he founded the Severan dynasty, the account in chapter 19 reveals that those rulers were all deficient, and Machiavelli elsewhere acknowledges his reputation as a criminal.[42]

While Herodian reports that Severus was attuned to the requirement that a prince should appear pious, Severus never claimed to be commanded by divine necessity: that is, he declined to don fully the justificatory cloak of prophecy.[43] In Machiavelli's political world, men like Severus are likely to be more common than the founders, but they possess less virtue and less vaulting ambition. They conspire to satisfy their worldly desires with consummate skill, but their unwillingness—or inability—to found new and prophetic orders means that they leave no lasting benefit to their fatherlands.[44] These princes are the primary audience of chapter 19, and with his praise of Severus, Machiavelli encourages the canniest of them to remedy their inability to avoid hatred by venting fully their soldiers' avarice and cruelty. This is a simple, but harrowing, solution to a difficult political problem posed by their lesser ambition or deficient natures.

The Rest of the Worst: Caracalla, Commodus, and Maximinus

The audacity of Severus's methods perhaps explains why Machiavelli attempts to conceal—somewhat halfheartedly—this teaching from his reader. He softens his amoral presentation when he discusses the other emperors who employed the army to secure themselves. In his discussion of Caracalla, Commodus, and Maximinus, Machiavelli attempts to give the impression that it is possible to err by being excessively cruel and rapacious; attention to the text, however, confirms the lesson of Severus's example. These emperors possessed most of Severus's virtues, but emerge as insufficiently foxlike; they could not avoid the snares attendant on this method of rule.

Antoninus Caracalla was a hard and spirited man of "most excellent parts," yet Machiavelli intones that he was of such cruelty and ferocity that "he became most hateful to all the world" (*P* 19), and was killed by a centurion. Machiavelli initially suggests that no prince can guarantee his security against a determined and suicidal assassin, but then he admits that Caracalla might have avoided his fate. His assassin, Machiavelli discloses, was the brother of a man "he had put to death with disgrace" (*P* 19). Caracalla threatened the surviving brother every day, thus giving him two good reasons to kill the emperor.[45] Caracalla's daily threats indicate that he perceived the danger posed by the surviving brother, yet he apparently believed that his ferocity and his cruelty secured him against such threats; consequently, he allowed both to rage, unrestrained. His violent rage overwhelmed his calculation.[46]

Next, Machiavelli discusses Commodus. Machiavelli's altered chronology moves Commodus from his natural position. Instead of appearing after a discussion of his father, Marcus, Commodus appears between Caracalla and Maximinus. This choice obscures the important fact that Commodus is the first of the "bad" emperors and he follows the last of the successful "good" emperors.[47] Thus, one should consider his example carefully. Among other things, Machiavelli's consideration of Commodus helps one discern the cause of Marcus's success.

According to Machiavelli, Commodus was largely responsible for tarnishing the reputation of the emperors.

> It was enough for him only to follow in the footsteps of his father, and he would have satisfied both the soldiers and the people. But since he had a

cruel and bestial spirit, so as to practice his rapacity on the people, he turned to indulging the armies and making them licentious. On the other hand, by not keeping his dignity, descending often into theaters to fight with gladiators, and by doing other very base things hardly deserving of the imperial majesty, he became contemptible in the sight of his soldiers. And since he was hated on one side and despised on the other, he was conspired against and put to death. (*P* 19)

Machiavelli writes that Commodus was "bestial"; his practices rendered him "contemptible" to his soldiers, whom he had empowered to vent their criminal desires (*P* 19).[48] Yet in comparison to Severus, his criminality and bestiality appear niggling; consequently, the people were not awed, but hated him.

Thus one learns why Marcus was able to succeed, despite his humanity and justice. Commodus's degradation of the "imperial majesty" (*P* 19) made the rule of the Pertinaxes and the Alexanders of the Roman Empire impossible.[49] Subsequent emperors could not rely on the deference traditionally shown to the emperor. Here, it should be noted (although Machiavelli does not note this) that Roman emperors after Augustus were commonly viewed as divine.[50] Though they did not rule by divine right, they often tolerated and encouraged the existence of imperial cults; moreover, they associated themselves with imperial forebearers, many of whom had been apotheosized after death. Indeed, Commodus diligently cultivated this semidivine image, often appearing as Hercules in official statues. But can human beings view a leader who descends into the gladiatorial ring as godlike? Commodus undermined his pretensions of divinity, and failed to contrive to render himself magnificent in the eyes of his army in any other way. Marcus was the last emperor who plausibly could claim semidivine authority.[51] The example of Commodus demonstrates what is perhaps the fatal problem with hereditary divine right: an office that is created for a godlike man is often occupied by a beast, who works to squander the reputation secured by his ancestors.[52]

Machiavelli proceeds to discuss Maximinus. Although he was sufficiently cruel, Machiavelli laments that he failed to go to Rome and seize the throne formally and was, in addition, "of very base origin" (*P* 19). These failings, combined with a protracted siege of Aquileia, turned the army against him. They killed Maximinus as enemies, representing the entire Roman world, surrounded him. Machiavelli stresses that the "baseness of his blood" (*P* 19) contributed significantly to Maximinus's demise, but the reader ought to recall that Agathocles, though of very base origin, nonetheless succeeded.[53] One thus suspects that Maximinus's principal error was his failure to go to Rome: an imperial procession bristling with soldiers would have quieted complaints about his ancestry. His indiscretion in consolidating the empire contrasts neatly with Severus's discretion: Severus manipulated the Senate to help him deceive and kill his rivals; the same Senate rebelled against the dilatory Maximinus.[54]

Chapter 19—the longest chapter of *The Prince*—is a discussion of the perils of ruling as a prince of deficient virtue. Ultimately, it discloses the limits of what such princes may accomplish, and implicitly encourages ambitious potential princes to avoid most—but not all—of their methods. The Roman emperors' deficient virtue is evident most clearly in their inability to control their armies, which generally satisfy their desires to rob and rape the Roman people, while doing nothing to perpetuate lasting orders. By describing and praising the actions of Severus, Machiavelli offers to princes like these a method of overcoming their inadequate control over the army. Yet Severus's method is fraught with dangers. Moreover, while it can make one powerful and secure, Severus is neither "held in veneration" nor "honored and happy" (*P* 6). Chapter 19 thus echoes Mansfield's judgment that "Machiavelli shows how a founder is affected by his reputation, in particular, how he can be hampered by an evil reputation as a tyrant."[55] One must add to this that the helpful example of Severus is surrounded by much dubious advice; the defective prince must read carefully if he is to avoid the fate of a Pertinax or a Caracalla. In this way, chapter 19 serves as a proving ground for second-rate princes; if they can avoid the snares Machiavelli describes—and the snares he lays—they can aspire to live a life of crime and die a natural, if inglorious, death.[56]

The Roman Empire, Old and New: The Significance of Chapter 19

It is odd that Machiavelli devotes so much space to a discussion of second-rate princes; indeed, he underscores the strangeness of his discourse when he concedes that the Roman emperors' examples are unhelpful to modern European princes, who "have less of this difficulty of satisfying the soldiers by extraordinary means in their governments . . . because none of these princes has armies joined together which are entrenched in the government and administration of provinces" (*P* 19). In Machiavelli's time, princes must "satisfy the people rather than the soldiers" (*P* 19). Having begged the question, Machiavelli indicates the relevance of his digression with considerable circumspection. First, he observes that only the Ottoman Turk and the Sultan of Egypt currently rely on the army for their security, as did the Roman emperors. Second, he comments that the rule of the Sultan of Egypt "is similar to the Christian pontificate" (*P* 19).

For it is not the sons of the old prince who are the heirs and become the lords, but the one who is elected to that rank by those who have the authority for it. And this being an ancient order, one cannot call it a new principality, because some of the difficulties in new principalities are not in it; for if the prince is indeed new, the orders of that state are old and are ordered to receive him as if he were their hereditary lord. (*P* 19)

Thus Machiavelli discloses the relevance of this obscure discussion of the Roman emperors, by way of a discussion of two Muslim princes: the late corrupt Roman Empire, led by the emperor, is comparable to the Catholic Church, led by the pope. The seemingly disjointed arguments of chapter 19 have prepared the reader for Machiavelli's conspiratorial revelation of the radical defects of papal rule, which may be discerned by comparing these emperors to Catholic popes.

This comparison has four important implications. First, Machiavelli views the Church as a defective principality, in which the pope leads an army, over which he has uncertain control—and to which he owes his position and security. This describes the ecclesiastical order. Machiavelli views this priestly army as a potential threat to the pope's security—and even his life.[57] Consequently, the pope is interested primarily in satisfying his priests, bishops, and cardinals, and not the people. His lack of a regular army only deepens his peril, as he must rely on mercenaries or auxiliaries to defend his life and prosecute his worldly schemes. Second, the divine mandate that might have empowered early popes, and served to restrain the ecclesiastical order, was made implausible by subsequent corrupt popes. Machiavelli does not name a culprit here, as he names Commodus, but given his appraisal of the deceitful Pope Alexander VI in chapter 18, he clearly believes that modern popes must be corrupt to succeed.[58] Third, a consequence of the corruption of the papacy is that good, just, and humane popes cannot succeed. "Good" (*P* 11) popes like Leo X will be doomed by the cruelty and avarice of the ecclesiastical order; they will lack the cruelty and ferocity necessary to instill order in their priestly armies.[59] Compounding their difficulty, every pope—good and bad—will struggle to prevent priests from conspiring with the princes of their home countries. Popes who act resolutely to curb the injustice of the ecclesiastical order will face conspiracies from within and without.

The final implication of Machiavelli's argument is that when faced with the loss of the imperial majesty of the papacy, successful popes turned to crime. The venality and voracity of the Church of Machiavelli's time testify to this development. Yet can a pope behave like Severus? From its introduction in chapter 8 to its bestial manifestation in chapter 19, Machiavelli has associated cruelty with criminality. Can a pope adopt, as a policy, either inhuman cruelty or massive criminality? Alexander VI would appear to be a potential model of criminal behavior, yet even he attempted to preserve a brittle veneer of religiosity. It is one thing to be cruel and ferocious in the Roman world, with its martial violence; it is quite another to be the same in the Christian world, with its exhortations to meekness and charity. The Roman emperors were constrained to behave as gods, but at least their gods were fond of meting out sanguinary punishments. Popes, however, are constrained—even more than Christian princes—to imitate the life of Christ, and Machiavelli's analysis has demonstrated that such a life is not conducive to earthly success, because "human conditions do not permit it" (*P* 15). Consider: could any Christian claim the throne of Peter by imitating Severus? Probably not: such an audacious enterprise would weaken the "orders that have grown old with religion" (*P* 11), which sustain the Church: the papacy thus taken would delegitimize—and divide—the Church. The Church's reliance on spiritual power thus renders it less resilient than the Roman Empire. And even if a "Severan" pope gained the throne, Severus's own example suggests that he could not effect a permanent change to the Vatican. Eventually, a papal version of Caracalla or Alexander would cede power back to the ecclesiastical order, which no pope can do without.

Because they can imitate neither Marcus nor Severus, popes cannot escape contempt and hatred. Importantly, they cannot benefit from Machiavelli's advice in chapters 15 through 18. In part, chapter 19 is written to elaborate their insoluble predicament, which appears similar to, but worse than, that of the later Roman emperors. Indeed, during Machiavelli's life, the Church was weakened by popular disgust with its perceived criminality and the incredulity that resulted. Neither professions of goodness nor acts of cruelty could save its power. Its decline would precipitate the Protestant Reformation. Machiavelli's analysis predicts this decline.

The political defects of the Church appear impossible to remedy without dramatic revision of the New Testament. Jesus's original commission to Peter and the apostles justifies the powers of both the papacy and the college of cardinals; the scourging of Christianity requires the scourging of that Church, which established the authority of a group of men whose power is inconsistent with the decent civil life that the people desire.[60] Popes who imitate Christ's meekness, indifference to the world, and mercy will be ineffective and short-lived; those who vent the criminal desires of the ecclesiastical order will burden the people. In either case, the people lose: they love civil "quiet" and "modest princes" (*P* 19). The Church's corrupt orders guarantee the opposite.

The defects of both popes and Roman emperors explain why Machiavelli abandons any pretension of giving advice to second-rate princes at the end of the chapter. He instead decides to advise "a new prince in a new principality" (*P* 19). Neither Marcus nor Severus is a sufficient model for such a prince. Instead, he must "take from Severus those parts which are necessary to found his state and from Marcus those which are fitting and glorious to conserve a state that is already established and firm" (*P* 19). Hence, a new prince must behave like the criminal, Severus, but contrive to invoke the dignity—and perhaps the divinity—of Marcus.[61] This task is, as Machiavelli disclosed in chapter 6, exceedingly difficult: this consideration of chapter 19 reminds us of the rarity of such men in a Christian world, and confirms with certainty that they will not be found at the head of the Catholic Church.[62] With its unruly and rapacious religious army led by a nominal prince of peace, it lacks the virtue required to remedy Europe's afflictions and is incapable of providing for Europe's political salvation.

The Empire and the Incubation of Christianity

Although Machiavelli does not report this fact, the period of Roman history that he discusses in chapter 19 coincided with the growth of Christianity in Rome. The progress of the early Christians does not concern Herodian, on whose text Machiavelli apparently relies, but it is a minor theme of the *Historia Augusta*, a late-Roman collection of imperial biographies with which Machiavelli was almost certainly familiar.[63] Only three of these accounts discuss the fate of early Christians: the lives of Severus, Heliogabalus, and Alexander.

According to the *Historia Augusta*, of all the emperors Machiavelli discusses, Severus alone "forbade conversion to Judaism under heavy penalties and enacted a similar law in regard to the Christians."[64] In different ways, Heliogabalus and Alexander each encouraged the worship of Christ. The religious eccentric Heliogabalus included among his schemes a plan to subordinate all existing religions of Rome—including the "religions of the Jews and the Samaritans and the rites of the Christians"—to the god that shared his name.[65] Alexander, who showed deference to all religious authorities indiscriminately, "respected the privileges of the Jews and allowed the Christians to exist unmolested."[66] He even maintained a private sanctuary, in which he worshipped the figures of deified emperors, Roman gods, and his ancestors alongside "Christ, Abraham, Orpheus, and others of this same character" (29.2): "He also wished to build a temple to Christ and give him a place among the gods. . . . Alexander, however, was prevented from carrying out this purpose, because those who examined the sacred victims ascertained that if he did, all men would become Christians and the other temples would of necessity be abandoned" (43.6–7). Alexander nonetheless encouraged the proliferation of Christian churches in Rome (43.6). He also prized Christ's teachings.

He used often to exclaim what he had heard from someone, either a Jew or a Christian, and always remembered, and he also had it announced by a herald whenever he was disciplining anyone, "What you do not wish that a man should do to you, do not do to him." And so highly did he value this sentiment that he had it written up in the Palace and in public buildings. (51.7–8)[67]

Attention to the *Historia Augusta* helps us understand why Machiavelli—abandoning the ambivalence of the historians—praises Severus so highly. Although the corruption of Rome made his rule possible, he undertook efforts to stop corrupting incursions by foreign religions. He evidently agreed with Machiavelli's judgment that "princes of a republic or of a kingdom should maintain the foundations of the religion they hold."[68] Alexander's augurs were, of course, correct: once it found a purchase within Roman society, Christianity would undermine the foundations of the pagan religion. The strident monotheism of the Abrahamic tradition and the universal character of Christianity do not admit equality with other gods easily.[69]

Reading the *Historia Augusta* also helps explain why Machiavelli distorts the histories of Heliogabalus and Alexander. He incorrectly reports that Heliogabalus was so "contemptible" that he was "immediately eliminated," when in fact he ruled for almost five years—five times longer than his fellow "contemptible" emperors, Julianus and Macrinus (*P* 19). His penchant for religious spectacle, which evidently fascinated Romans of all classes, may have helped him to stay a conspiracy by his well-paid soldiers.[70] Machiavelli, who undoubtedly takes a dim view of Heliogabalus's eccentric endorsement of Christianity, discounts his success.

Machiavelli includes Alexander among the "lovers of justice" (*P* 19) who came to a bad end. While he acknowledges that he ruled for fourteen years, he does not note that this makes him the longest-serving emperor on Machiavelli's list, after Marcus and Severus.[71] Neither does Machiavelli report fully the cause of Alexander's demise. Alexander's "humane and kind" (*P* 19) disposition proved ill-suited for combat: in his first significant battle against Rome's enemies, he faltered. Required to advance his army against the Persians, he remained paralyzed, either "due to fear" or because "his mother may have restrained him because of her womanly timidity and excessive love for her son."[72] Barely surviving this engagement, when the Germans immediately attacked a different front, "Alexander attempted to buy terms from them rather than risk the danger of war" (VI.7.9). Avaricious soldiers used these failures as a pretext to kill him, although they had always despised him for the reasons Machiavelli indicates (VI.9.6–8).

Although he describes Alexander as "effeminate" (*P* 19), Machiavelli uncharacteristically overlooks the notable defect of spirit and error in judgment that precipitated his death. Instead, he emphasizes his "good-ness" (*P* 19), which Machiavelli opposes to his effeminacy and his subjec-tion to women—despite the fact that Herodian explicitly attributes many of the good features of his rule to the women in his life, and especially his grandmother.[73] This appraisal of Alexander immediately follows Machia-velli's repetition of the advice from chapter 15: "a prince who wants to maintain his state is often forced not to be good" (*P* 19). While the context suggests that this judgment applies to kindly old Pertinax—whose career Machiavelli had just summarized—the language Machiavelli employs in his depiction of Alexander highlights the contrast between that emperor's life and Machiavelli's teaching on virtue. After all, Machiavelli's original rec-ommendation "not to be good" occurred in the context of his critique of imaginary principalities—of which Christ's "kingdom of heaven" is most prominent. Effeminate and good, Alexander tried to abide by the central precept of that imaginary principality: the Golden Rule, which "sums up the Law and the Prophets."[74] The emperor's definite limitations—and the limitations of his favorite prophet's favorite law—become evident when necessity constrains him to make war.

Reading the lives of Heliogabalus and Alexander in the *Historia Augusta* reminds readers that Christianity found powerful supporters in Rome long before it became respectable enough to be considered the official religion of the state. Examining the lives of the two emper-ors who were among Christ's earliest—though unorthodox—devotees, Machiavelli judges that one was contemptible and the other exhibited a fatal combination of goodness, effeminacy, and subjection to women. By recommending that princes imitate the life of Severus, Machiavelli summons them to reflect not only on that emperor's qualities, but also on his negative judgment of Christianity, to which Machiavelli is sympa-thetic. Severus, as "a very fierce lion and very astute fox" (*P* 19) stalked the nascent Christian flock.[75]

Italy, a Mixed Principality

Chapter 19 explicated the insoluble predicament of the papacy; chapter 20 describes the practical political and military consequences of that predica-ment, and invites foreigners to exploit the weaknesses attendant on Ita-ly's perilous political arrangement. Titled "Whether Fortresses and Many Other Things Which Are Made and Done by Princes Every Day Are Useful or Useless," this chapter, like the previous one, seems to address a hodge-podge of subjects; yet the several subjects of chapter 20 are unified by a broad critique of the Catholic Church's political and military strategies, the failure of which serve to inform superior princes.[76]

Chapter 20 introduces Machiavelli's treatment of fortresses, which appears related to his discussion of fortified cities in chapter 10. Chapter 10 taught that fortified cities are preferable only for those "who cannot appear in the field against an enemy, but are compelled of necessity to take refuge behind walls to guard them"; all others should either raise or purchase an army. *The Prince* has demonstrated that the Catholic Church lacks an army of its own and struggles even to equip adequate mercenaries.[77] It is the most prominent unarmed principality of Europe. While in chapter 10, Machiavelli sought to undermine the obligation men customarily feel to the unarmed prince of Christianity, chapter 20 demonstrates the uselessness of the unarmed prince's chief politico-military strategy: the building of fortresses.

Continuing with the ascent that began at the end of chapter 19, Machiavelli addresses his advice in chapter 20 especially to new princes. After a brief introductory paragraph, Machiavelli reminds readers of the central lesson of chapter 19. His repetition here signals the importance of this advice:

> There has never been, then, a new prince who has disarmed his subjects; on the contrary, whenever he has found them unarmed, he has always armed them. For when they are armed, those arms become yours; those whom you suspected become faithful, and those who were faithful remain so; and from subjects they are made into your partisans. And because all subjects cannot be armed, if those whom you arm are benefited, one can act with more security toward the others. (*P* 20)

This is a central argument of *The Prince*, and Machiavelli has repeated a variation of it throughout the book.[78] The only alternative to forming one's own army is to resort to mercenary or auxiliary arms, which Machiavelli has deemed useless or dangerous.[79]

The unarmed prince of chapter 10 sought to engender obligation by way of mutual sacrifice: having lost so much on his behalf, his subjects would remain united with him, in the expectation of a just reward. Here, however, Machiavelli suggests that arming some of one's subjects is a superior way to engender obligation: "the difference in treatment that they recognize regarding themselves makes them obligated [*obligati*] to you; the others excuse you, judging it necessary that those who have more danger and more obligation [*obligo*] deserve [*merito*] more" (*P* 20).[80] The armed prince has soldiers who are obligated to him and subjects who are unarmed, but nonetheless recognize that the arrangement is in accord with a sort of justice, or merit. If any malcontents arise among the unarmed, "one can act with more security toward" them (*P* 20). This provides far more security to all parties: the prince is adequately defended; the army enjoys the sense of distinction—and the material rewards—that service provides; most of the unarmed also enjoy greater security, since they may be defended by an actual army, rather than mere professions of obligation, consecrated by mutual sacrifice, and accompanied by promises of grand, but ever deferred, rewards.

The remainder of chapter 20 will describe how to use one's own arms in conquest. Specifically, Machiavelli stipulates what is to be done by a "prince [who] acquires a new state that is added as a member to his old one" (*P* 20). Readers will recognize that he is describing a "mixed principality," the subject of chapter 3. There, Machiavelli described a mixed principality as "not altogether new but like an added member." His repetition invites a comparison of chapters 3 and 20. The main subject of chapter 3 was Louis XII's invasion of Italy, which was foiled by Alexander VI's canny double-dealings. Ultimately, the Church was the only beneficiary of these maneuvers: the affair ended with the expulsion of Louis, the death of Alexander, and the defeat of Cesare Borgia (*P* 11). Given Machiavelli's economy, why return to the subject now?

He does so to provide his clearest plan yet for the conquest of Italy and the destruction of the Catholic Church.[81] Having argued that the Church is incapable of redeeming anything in chapter 19, Machiavelli offers a plan for conquering it in chapter 20. This plan will employ Louis XII's failed campaign as a foil for a superior, Machiavellian plan. Critical to its success is Machiavelli's elaborated critique of fortresses, which one finds at the end of the chapter.

First, however, Machiavelli offers several strategies for conquering a country like Italy. They are the opposite of those pursued by Louis XII in chapter 3. Machiavelli's first directive is to disarm the newly acquired state as quickly as possible—and then to rearm it as your own, thus unifying the state. He insists that it is not sufficient to keep your new state weak by encouraging internal division; eventually, the weaker party will seek foreign allies, creating disorders that invite potential conquerors.[82] Second, Machiavelli recommends that a prince contrive to increase his reputation for greatness by nourishing "some enmity so that when he has crushed it, his greatness emerges the more from it" (*P* 20). Thus Machiavelli endorses the propagandistic value of enemies of the state. Moses opposed Pharaoh; Caesar opposed Pompey; Severus opposed Albinus: should Louis XII have opposed Alexander VI, whom he might have branded as a rogue pope?

Machiavelli's third recommendation concerns the allies one ought to cultivate in newly acquired territories. He suggests one ought to rely on those who initially oppose his conquest, provided that they "are of such quality that to maintain themselves they need somewhere to lean" (*P* 20). Those who helped you enter the state cannot be trusted, since as ambitious malcontents, they want more than you can provide. Those who opposed you, however—provided they are of a certain "quality" (*P* 20)—have greater cause to fear you, which creates a stronger obligation, and makes them more ingratiating.[83]

The Conquest of "Fortress Italy"

Thus far, the advice in chapter 20 is an elaborated recapitulation of the lessons of chapter 3; Machiavelli's discussion of fortresses, however, departs from the earlier argument. He begins by praising fortresses, since they have been employed "since antiquity" (*P* 20). In the very next sentences, however, he remarks that three Italians have recently destroyed fortresses in order to hold their states. Importantly, in the *Discourses* (II.24.2), Machiavelli stipulates that the Church built or occupied each of these fortresses. While Machiavelli concludes that "fortresses are thus useful or not according to the times, and if they do you well in one regard, they hurt you in another" (*P* 20), one ought to be skeptical of this equivocation: in chapter 20, Machiavelli will name no fortress that conduces to security. Machiavelli predicts Francesco Sforza's fortress will bring him ruin; the countess of Forli, though initially saved by her fortress's walls, eventually falls to Cesare Borgia. The clear lesson of chapter 20 is that the destruction of these bastions of papal power is crucial to the security of princes who aspire to rule in Italy.

In the *Discourses* (II.24.2), Machiavelli explains why a prince ought to raze any fortress he finds. According to him, they encourage violence from the prince, breed hatred among the people, and are always inferior to an army of one's own.[84] In chapter 20, Machiavelli pronounces that the only prince who ought to build a fortress is he "who has more fear of the people than of foreigners."[85] These are extremely defective princes, who lack even the army possessed by the defective Roman emperors who were "lovers of justice" (*P* 19). Popes, of course, are diligent builders of fortresses. Machiavelli's advice to the bishop of Rome is to flee his principality entirely, because if a virtuous prince follows Machiavelli's advice concerning fortresses, he can conquer the Vatican with ease.

The countess of Forli is the only Italian named in chapter 20 who benefits—albeit temporarily—from a fortress. Machiavelli thus invites the reader to consider her brief success. An examination of the darkly comic events that led to her salvation confirms that fortresses constitute a poor defense for the defective prince.

Machiavelli recounts her story in the *Discourses* and in the *Florentine Histories*.[86] The countess's husband, Count Girolamo, was a cruel prince, and the people of Forli came to hate him. One leading citizen was repeatedly threatened by the count, and thus resolved to kill him (*FH* VIII.34). This he did after dinner one evening; soon thereafter, he and his companions killed several servants and a prominent military official. A proto-republican uprising blossomed in Forli, as the assassins threw the count's head from the window with cries of "Church and Liberty!" (*FH* VIII.34). The people armed themselves and rallied in support of the conspirators. They captured the countess and her two young children, and proceeded to the fortress.

> Since it appeared to them that they could not live secure if they did not become masters of the fortress, and the castellan was not willing to give it to them, Madonna Caterina (so the countess was called) promised the conspirators that if they let her enter it, she would deliver it to them and they might keep her children with them as hostages. Under this faith [*sotto questo fede*] they let her enter it. As soon as she was inside, she reproved them from the walls for the death of her husband and threatened them with every kind of revenge. And to show that she did not care for her children, she showed them her genital parts, saying that she still had the mode for making more of them. So, short of counsel and late to perceive their error, they suffered the penalty of their lack of prudence with a perpetual exile. (*D* III.6.18)[87]

The pope did not send an army to aid the uprising, but the countess's uncle sent an army to her aid (*FH* VIII.34). The conspirators gathered their possessions and fled.

Machiavelli judges that these conspirators were "short of counsel" (*D* III.6.18). What, then, were their principal errors? First, like the Canneschi conspirators of Bologna (*P* 19), they failed to eliminate the hereditary ruler's bloodline.[88] Second, they believed wrongly that they needed the fortress to accomplish their revolution; instead, Machiavelli suggests that they might have starved its inhabitants while preparing for the city's external defense. Third, they trusted that the countess would show good faith—both to them and to her own children. This mistaken belief that she would remain faithful might have been reinforced by her designation as the "Madonna Caterina"—a name that pointedly evokes images of the Virgin Mary. Yet they underestimated dramatically her depravity—or, as Harvey Mansfield suggests, her ambition and her desire for revenge.[89] Fourth, they believed that Caterina's mere presence in the fortress gave her a decisive strategic advantage. The citizens were armed and united—and could have fought against the army of the countess's uncle while Caterina slowly succumbed to starvation within the fortress walls—but they elected instead to disband and flee. They overestimated the true powers of fortresses. Machiavelli's counsel would have corrected their misunderstanding; indeed, Cesare Borgia's defeat of Caterina six months later testifies to the little help—and the false sense of security—fortresses provide princes.

Why cite this story as the lone qualified example of the utility of fortresses? I argue that Machiavelli does so to instruct the reader about how the most consistent and successful of fortress-builders—the Catholic Church—manages to survive, despite its numerous material disadvantages. Without an army at her disposal, and shut up within the walls of a fortress, Caterina's predicament resembles the pope's: weak to the point of actual effeminacy, and charged with the care of children that lie outside of her walls, she must survive by deceit and her enemies' consistent misapprehension of her character and predicament. They are mistaken about the power attendant on her possession of a fortress; they are deceived by her pretensions to good faith; and they overestimate dramatically the love she has for her own children.[90] Machiavelli invites us to view Caterina as a religious figure by noting that the conspirators "begged" or "prayed" for her help, and subsequently believed in the "good faith" of "Madonna Caterina" (*FH* VIII.34).[91] Machiavelli's implicit lesson is that Italy's invaders ought not to trust in the "good faith" of the pope or any paternalistic professions of the care he has for his "children." Nor, presumably, should they be overawed by his possession of St. Peter's Basilica, which, in the absence of an army to defend it, provides him no lasting security.

Thus, like chapter 19, chapter 20 ends by disclosing—albeit indirectly—a lesson about the Church's perilous predicament in Italy. The virtuous prince of chapter 18 will benefit from these lessons; the Church—and the hereditary principalities it supports—will not. By exposing the weakness of the Church's military strategy in chapter 20, after exposing the defects of papal rule of Italy in chapter 19, Machiavelli provides a plan for a successful conquest of the Vatican and its fortress-bound supporters.

Machiavelli teaches that princes who rely on fortresses eventually lose everything—to either their own people, or the enemy. Thus, he insists that a "wise and good" (*D* II.24.2) prince will never build a fortress, but will instead arm his own people. Jesus, who abjures violence, never arms his own people and builds no fortresses. The former decision demonstrates his lack of wisdom; the latter might constitute evidence of his goodness—yet in place of earthly fortresses, he repeatedly invokes the God of the Psalms, who is described as "my rock, my fortress and my deliverer; . . . in whom I take refuge, my shield and the horn of my salvation, my stronghold."[92] Do God's fortifications escape Machiavelli's general critique of fortresses? Or might they be a hallmark of violent tyranny, as evidenced by the repeated and precipitous "crushing" (*D* II.24.2) of the Israelites?

Wretched and Rare: The Exemplary Christian Principality

While popes may be incapable of combining the methods of Severus with the appearance of Marcus, one Christian prince emerges as potentially successful in this regard: Ferdinand of Spain. Already praised by Machiavelli in chapter 18 for his ability to pretend to be a faithful Christian, Machiavelli chronicles Ferdinand's successes more thoroughly in chapter 21. His high praise leads one to ask: Is Ferdinand the model Christian prince—or the model prince, simply? Do his exploits prove that Christian princes can escape the predicament of the popes, described in chapter 19?

Ferdinand remained at war throughout his career, which helped him expand his power and check the ambition of the Spanish nobles. He funded his army with money from the Church and used Christianity instrumentally: he ascribed his ambition to attack Africa, Italy, and France to religious motives, using Christianity as a "cloak" (*P* 21) for his actions. Machiavelli opines: "nor could there be an example more wretched and rarer" (*P* 21) than the expulsion of the Marranos—during which Jews and Muslims were either forcibly converted or deprived of their property and expelled from Europe. Ferdinand's efforts led to the death of many innocents, and the relocation of entire communities. For these actions undertaken in the name of Christianity, Innocent VIII named him "Ferdinand the Catholic."[93]

Machiavelli describes the expulsion of the Marranos as a "pious cruelty" (*P* 21)—which is a cruel action, undertaken to secure oneself, but justified by religious pretense. While Machiavelli does not explicitly criticize Ferdinand for his cruelty (which Machiavelli has judged necessary to successful princes), he does describe it as "wretched" (*P*21). Nonetheless, Ferdinand's willingness to exploit the religious beliefs of others for the sake of personal power distinguishes him from myriad examples of failed Christian princes in *The Prince*. Though he lacks the stature of a Machiavellian founder, he is able to combine Christianity and worldly success to a degree that no other Christian prince can. His "pious cruelty" helps him accomplish this.

Yet the expulsion of the Marranos was not the only—or even the most famous—"pious cruelty" undertaken by Ferdinand; by referring to the expulsion, Machiavelli alludes to wider cruelties of the Spanish Inquisition.[94] This movement was approved by Pope Sixtus IV in 1478 and carried out by priests under Spanish control; it allowed Ferdinand to persecute men for heresy and other thought crimes against Christianity.[95] The general Inquisition would thus appear to benefit Ferdinand in a way that the expulsion of the Marranos could not: it allowed him to eliminate and intimidate domestic political enemies, regardless of their ancestry. Thus, "pious cruelties" are critical to the success of the most successful Christian prince, Ferdinand of Spain. As maintained above, these are precisely the sorts of actions that the pope—who is constrained to a degree that Christian princes are not—will find difficult to accomplish.[96] A consideration of Ferdinand's success thus reminds one that it is impossible for the papacy to unite Italy, as Ferdinand has united Spain.

Because "pious cruelties" are crucial to the success of Ferdinand, the lone unqualified example of a successful Christian prince in *The Prince*, we may conclude that "pious cruelties" are thus conducive to Christian princes' security, just as "avarice and cruelty" (*P* 19) contributed to that of the Roman emperors of chapter 19. Yet, importantly, Ferdinand is not an unqualified model of success. The limits attendant on his rule disclose the limits of what Christian principalities may accomplish, more generally. To discern these limits, one must understand the particularly pernicious effects of "pious cruelties," which enable Christian princes to "carry on great enterprises" (*P* 21).

At the end of chapter 21, in the context of discoursing on the model prince, Machiavelli describes what civil policies a prince ought to pursue:

> A prince should also show himself a lover of the virtues, giving recognition to virtuous men, and he should honor those who are excellent in any art. Next, he should inspire his citizens to follow their pursuits quietly, in trade and in agriculture and in every other pursuit of men, so that one person does not fear to adorn his possessions for fear that they may be taken away from him, and another to open up a trade for fear of taxes. But he should prepare rewards for whoever wants to do these things, and for anyone who thinks up any way of expanding his city or his state. Besides this, he should at suitable times of the year keep the people occupied with festivals and spectacles. And because every city is divided into guilds or into clans, he should take account of those communities, meet with them sometimes, and make himself an example of humanity and munificence, always holding firm the majesty of his dignity nonetheless, because he can never want this to be lacking in anything. (*P* 21)

Machiavelli is describing here a meritocratic commercial monarchy with an open society that spurs innovation.[97] The citizens receive benefits from the state, and thus seek to return the favor. They trust their prince, and appear happier than any other people described in *The Prince*; this principality has little in common with the corrupt principalities discussed in the book. Indeed, with its penchant for expansion, acknowledgment of diverse communities, and relative freedom, this principality more closely approximates the Roman Republic Machiavelli describes in the *Discourses on Livy*. This may be an "imagined" principality, but crucially, it rests on the worldly foundations of personal security, material wealth, and earthly goods; the reader, immersed in the dark intrigues of princely politics, enjoys only fleeting glimpses of this sort of political life in *The Prince*.[98]

Most importantly, however, this principality cannot describe Ferdinand's Spain. In Spain, Ferdinand deprives an entire community of their livelihoods, and in some cases, their lives; these people are secure in their private possessions, and in their lives. Ferdinand takes money from the people and Church to expand Spain's power with a military; this prince seeks to expand the state through commerce, rather than taxes and war. Ferdinand persecutes as heretics men who seek political and scientific innovation; this prince, whose religion is not identified, rewards the same men for their contribution to the reputation of the state. Ferdinand employs "pious cruelties" to exploit divisions within Spain, breeding an atmosphere of fear and distrust among communities that nonetheless conduces to his security; this prince condescends to meet with the various communities, exhibiting a combination of "humanity" and "dignity" (*P* 21) that Ferdinand cannot contrive.[99]

Ferdinand of Aragon, the model Christian prince, is not a model prince, simply. A comparison of Ferdinand's kingdom with the imagined principality described at the end of chapter 21 reveals the unpalatable fruits of Christian rule, even under the most capable prince. Ferdinand cannibalizes his own kingdom: his "wretched" (*P* 21) actions do not ennoble his fatherland. Moreover, because Ferdinand decided to use Christianity to secure himself, he remains constrained by that decision. According to the argument of chapter 19, Ferdinand, having conspired with the Catholic Church to consolidate his power, now remains wedded to that institution. Machiavelli's analysis predicts that like all Roman emperors following Commodus, Ferdinand's successors will struggle to escape the constraints imposed by their predecessor. Commodus's successors struggled with the cruel and rapacious army that Commodus unleashed; Ferdinand's will struggle with an ecclesiastical order accustomed to venting its cruelty and avarice in Spain, and in the broader world. Based on Machiavelli's critique of papal influence in Italy, we can expect that Ferdinand's employment of Christianity will serve to retard progress in Spain, and enervate that civil society. Certainly, Spain's success abroad will mean the end of a free way of life, at home and abroad; given its modes of rule, Spain's recent interest in Italian affairs would certainly alarm Machiavelli.[100]

Loving One's Fatherland More than One's Soul: Messer Bernabò and the War of the Eight Saints

Machiavelli's subsequent praise of the obscure Messer Bernabò da Milano highlights Ferdinand's deficiency. He cites Bernabò as a prince who gave "rare examples of himself in governing internally" (*P* 21). Machiavelli cites no specific instance of Bernabò's praiseworthy "mode of rewarding or punishing"; indeed, in Machiavelli's chief works, he mentions Bernabò most often in connection with his own assassination, carried out by a usurping nephew.[101] The only reported action of Messer Bernabò that one might construe as "punishment" is a war against Pope Gregory XI in which he assumed a leading role. Gregory had given criminal license to one of his legates; that man had attempted to starve the people of Tuscany in order to "make himself lord" (*FH* III.7) of that region.[102] In reaction to the Church's cruelty, Bernabò, along with "all the cities hostile to the Church" (*FH* III.7), formed a military alliance against Gregory. Eight citizens from the various cities were selected to direct the war; among their dictatorial powers was the authority to tax the clergy.[103] Machiavelli opines that the war

> was administered with such virtue and with such universal satisfaction that the magistracy was extended to the Eight every year; and they were called Saints even though they had little regard for censures, had despoiled the churches of their goods, and had compelled the clergy to celebrate the offices—so much did those citizens then esteem their fatherland than their souls. And they showed the church that just as before they had defended it as friends, so now as enemies they could afflict it. (*FH* III.7)

Machiavelli invites the reader to consider this war against the Church as a "rare example" of "internal" governance, which punished the Church for its "extraordinary" effort to work some "ill" in "civil life" (*P* 21). While Ferdinand conspires with the Church to corrupt civil life, the Eight Saints—who "esteem their fatherland [more] than their souls"—demonstrate that a healthy civil life requires a war against that Church (*FH* III.7).[104] While Ferdinand provided examples of which none was "more wretched and rarer" than his "pious cruelty," Messer Bernabò provided only "rare examples" that might have earned him "the fame of a great man and of an excellent talent" (*P* 21). Machiavelli's lesson is plain: rather than conspire with the Church, princes ought to conspire against it. They ought to regard the pope as a temporal prince, and his churches as taxable commercial ventures. As a necessary condition to the Church's presence in their realms, priests ought to be rendered agents of the civil authority, who can be commanded to perform Mass at its will.[105] Thus is Bernabò's War of the Eight Saints exemplary. Yet perhaps because that war is eventually lost, Machiavelli will recur to a more radical strategy against the Church.

Whom to Trust?

Within this critique of the Church's effect on civil society, Machiavelli locates advice about the importance of trust to foreign relations. By suggesting that a "prince is also esteemed when he is a true friend and a true enemy, that is, when without any hesitation he discloses himself in support of someone against another" (*P* 21), Machiavelli appears to be offering a sound moral lesson. Yet he describes this only as a "more useful" strategy than neutrality, since if the victor is "of such a quality" that you have cause to fear him, "you will always be prey" (*P* 21). Thus, Machiavelli's initial teaching is that a prince ought to ally himself resolutely against those whom he has the greatest cause to fear.

The example of Rome's war with Antiochus, which Machiavelli cites in support of his argument against neutrality, complicates his presentation of the dangers attendant on neutrality. Antiochus had marched his army into Greece at the request of the Aetolians, who wished to drive Rome out of the area.[106] Representatives from these powers beseeched the Achaeans, who had allied with Rome in its efforts against the Spartan tyrant Nabis, to remain "aloof" during the coming war against Rome.[107] Yet the Roman representative, a consul named Quinctius, also offered a speech, the closing words of which Machiavelli reproduces here: "As to what they say, moreover, that you should not intervene in the war, nothing is more alien to your interests; without thanks, without dignity you will be the prize of the victor" (*P* 21).[108]

Quinctius's speech was, however, more nuanced than Machiavelli suggests. He began with a lengthy and thorough denigration of the Syrian and Aetolian forces; evidently, he needed to establish that his enemies were unlikely to defeat the Romans in order to dissuade the Achaeans from adopting neutrality. Then, immediately before the pronouncement Machiavelli quotes, Quinctius exhorted the Achaeans to recall the good offices performed by Rome: "You must not, therefore, let yourselves be deceived; trust rather in the good faith [*fidei*] of Rome, of which you have had actual experience."[109]

The Achaeans immediately agreed to join Rome, but Quinctius's full speech reveals that the decision to join or abstain from wars is more complex than Machiavelli's presentation suggests. Calculations of relative power require considerable prudence, especially since these calculations are not merely mathematical: often, subjective determinations of fidelity and trust are required. Yet Machiavelli proclaims that he who "discloses himself boldly" ultimately encourages the good faith of the victor:

> If the one to whom you adhere wins, although he is powerful and you remain at his discretion, he has an obligation to you and has a contract of love [*è contratto l'amore*] for you; and men are never so indecent as to crush you with so great an example of ingratitude. Then too, victories are never so clear that the winner does not have to have some respect, especially for justice. (*P* 21)[110]

A "contract of love," Machiavelli claims, will restrain the victor from crushing its allies; failing that, the uncertainty of all victories—and the fear that one might need one's allies in the future—will lead the victor "to have some respect for justice." If this is indeed the rule of international relations, the Achaeans ought to have fared well in the years following Rome's defeat of Antiochus. They did not.

Almost immediately, the alliance between the Achaeans and the Romans began to crumble. When the Achaeans, under the direction of Philopoemen, besieged Sparta in response to an alleged treaty violation, the Spartans sought protection from Rome.[111] Both sides sent emissaries to Rome; the faithful Achaeans, represented by Philopoemen's lieutenant Lycortas, "pleaded that as the Senate had been the instrument of their freedom, so they should preserve that freedom for them undiminished and unimpaired."[112] The Senate's initial response was ambiguous: when the Achaeans seized the opportunity to raze Sparta's walls, expropriate many of its slaves, and dissolve the orders of Lycurgus, the Spartans responded by complaining only more loudly to Rome.[113]

Despite growing misgivings about the treaty with Rome, the Achaeans appeared before a Roman commission charged with settling the dispute.[114] They arrived to an inauspicious sight: two condemned Achaean traitors were among the commissioners (Livy XXXIX.36). Lycortas nonetheless offered an impassioned defense of the Achaeans' faithful conduct as Rome's ally, and beseeched Rome to maintain their "sacred and inviolable" treaty (XXXIX.37). He even addressed directly the precarious status of the Roman-Achaean alliance: "The treaty, you say, is on the face of it just to both sides. As a matter of fact, the Achaeans enjoy a precarious freedom; the supreme power rests with the Romans. I am sensible of this. . . . What satisfies the victors is too little for the vanquished; enemies demand more than allies receive" (XXXIX.37).

The Roman consul's sinister response demonstrates the insecurity that a "contract of love" (*P* 21) affords: he "said he would strongly advise the Achaeans to court the favour of the Romans whilst they could do so of their own free-will, lest they should soon be compelled to do so against their will."[115] Rome thereafter assumed direction of the Spartan affair, which signaled its increasing control over Greek affairs. Achaean power waned; immediately, after these events, Livy reports the circumstances that led to Philopoemen's death.[116]

Prudence, Contracts of Love, and Italy's Limited Promise

Machiavelli's reference to this failed treaty reminds us that Philopoemen— whom Machiavelli praised so highly in chapter 14—failed to check Roman power and preserve freedom for his native province. Nonetheless, he did not necessarily blunder, since it is not clear that the Achaeans had any other choice.[117] As Rome's ally against Nabis, they had observed the quality of its armies; if they agreed with Quinctius's assessment of Antiochus's army, neutrality would have been a self-defeating course. Machiavelli's practical wisdom accommodates such predicaments, and encourages daring action, despite long odds: "Nor should any state ever believe it can always adopt safe courses; on the contrary, it should think it has to take them all as doubtful. For in the order of things it is found that one never seeks to avoid one convenience without running into another; but prudence consists in knowing how to recognize the qualities of inconveniences, and in picking the less bad as good" (P 21).[118] According to Plutarch, Philopoemen embodied this practical wisdom: against ascendant Roman power, "Philopoemen, like a good helmsman contending against a high sea, was in some points compelled to give in and yield to the times; but in most he continued his opposition, and tried to draw to the support of freedom the men who were powerful in speech or action."[119] The Achaean experience suggests that in foreign affairs, no course is free from danger—although Machiavelli nonetheless will suggest later that the Achaeans might have erred in their decision to ally with Rome against Antiochus.

Both Erica Benner and Vickie Sullivan have noted that Machiavelli's discussion of the Greek city-states parallels his discussion of the Italian city-states: each region fights against a grabby adversary with imperial pretensions; each suffers from crippling disunity; each region is championed by a man whose support of Rome is conditioned upon its support of a free way of life.[120] The Greeks ought to have crushed tyranny at home before resolutely opposing all foreign powers including ancient Rome: could the modern Italians unite against their many foreign enemies after subduing their grabbiest, most tyrannical, and most divisive domestic adversary, the Vatican?[121] Messer Bernabò's War of the Eight Saints appears to be a potential model for action against the Church, but that effort failed. The intervening 150 years do not appear to have made Italians less corrupt. It is difficult to imagine the cities that Machiavelli describes in *The Prince* accomplishing anything of importance, including especially the task of freeing Italy from the miasmic political influence of the Vatican and the debilitating conditions of its "contract of love."[122]

As "the last of the Greeks," any hope for pan-Hellenic freedom died with Philopoemen.[123] Like the Greek city-states of Philopoemen's time, the Italian cities appear trapped by circumstances that seem destined to keep them in servitude, of which Christianity and the Christian Church are the chief architects. While Philopoemen enlisted men who "were powerful in speech or action" to his cause, this is a more difficult task for Machiavelli: he must contend with the corrupting effect of the Christian education, which saps the strength of the powerful with its exhortations to meekness.[124] Because Machiavelli doubts that such "powerful" men exist in sufficient numbers to resist Rome successfully, he offers another, more radical, plan for Italy's redemption in *The Prince*'s closing chapters: its subjection to a redeeming prince.[125]

Advisers and *The Prince*

This redeeming prince will need advisers. Or will he? Machiavelli's chapters on advisers underscore the difficulty of finding fidelity and capacity in one's advisers. His ultimate lesson is that unless a prince possesses the first kind of brain—"one that understands by itself"—he risks being exploited by his advisers (*P* 22). He may even become the instrument of a wise adviser, who conceals his ambition in pretensions of pusillanimity. Indeed, Machiavelli encourages this result: while he suggests that one should reward richly advisers who "think always of the prince" (*P* 22), men who know human nature will realize that such selfless devotion is impossible; an adviser who appears to offer wholehearted devotion is lying or conspiring.[126]

The "secretive" (*P* 23) Emperor Maximilian appears to be among the deceived. The reader learns that in his court, "the things he does on one day he destroys on another, that no one ever understands what he wants or plans to do, and that one cannot found oneself on his decisions" (*P* 23). Machiavelli's source for this secret information is "Father Luca," who serves as "a man" of Maximilian's (*P* 23).[127] Note that Father Luca reveals his derogatory judgment of the emperor's court to a Florentine, while also serving as Maximilian's adviser. This falseness is the hallmark of a flatterer. A prince seeking to learn "In What Mode Flatterers Are to Be Avoided" learns at least one concrete lesson from chapter 23: he ought to regard priests with the same—or greater—circumspection with which he should regard any other man.

Embedded in his dissimulating advice concerning flattery is sounder advice: "For this is a general rule that never fails: that a prince who is not wise by himself cannot be counseled well, unless indeed by chance he should submit himself to one alone to govern him in everything, who is a very prudent man" (*P* 23). This statement has important implications for Machiavelli's project in *The Prince*. The prince who submits to Machiavelli's advice is performing Machiavelli's will, rather than his own. Yet by following Machiavelli, he does not imperil his rule: Machiavelli's decision to publish *The Prince* posthumously means that a prince who reads Machiavelli's work learns from a Florentine who is among the ranks of departed historians, rather than an ambitious political operative whom he ought to suspect and fear. Like Christ, Machiavelli will achieve his ambitions only through the efforts of his followers. They will accrue all material rewards that Machiavelli's "long experience with modern things and continuous reading of ancient ones" (*P* DL) can earn a man.[128] Machiavelli discloses his anti-Christian plan for these men most clearly in the final chapters of *The Prince*, in which he contemplates the harsh necessities required of Italy's redemption. These considerations confirm that one cannot accomplish this task by imitating Christ.

CHAPTER SEVEN

The Harrowing Redemption of Italy

Chapter 24 commences the conclusion to *The Prince*. Machiavelli indicates this by remarking that the "new prince" should observe "prudently" the "things written above" (*P* 24).[1] Indeed, since the last paragraph of chapter 19, Machiavelli has addressed especially the new prince, who, if he has penetrated Machiavelli's ironic dissimulations and is of sufficient ambition, is now plotting to secure an army of his "creatures" (*P* 13) with which he might seize absolute power in Italy. The closing chapters offer anti-Christian psychological training to that prince, and suggest how he might contrive to earn a reputation akin to the humane and just Marcus, despite the necessity of conforming to so many of Severus's bestial and criminal modes. In short, Machiavelli teaches Italy's conquering prince how he might construct a glorious and humane edifice upon a foundation composed of the bones of Italians. In doing so, he recommends the imitation of Moses, rather than Christ, and reveals that his patriotism is qualified radically by his hope that virtue might finally triumph in Italy.

Machiavelli informs the new prince that if his actions are recognized as virtuous, "they will take hold of men much more and obligate them much more than ancient blood" (*P* 24). This argument is explicitly hostile toward hereditary princes; yet by emphasizing the weakness of obligations engendered by blood, Machiavelli may also be referring obliquely to the Eucharist, the obligations of which appear to be supervened easily by the sight of virtuous worldly actions.[2] Machiavelli encourages this conclusion with his next pronouncement: "For men are much more taken by present things than by past ones, and when they find good in the present, they enjoy it and do not seek it elsewhere" (*P* 24). Christ, whose many good deeds attracted followers, offers his "blood of the covenant" to his beleaguered disciples in order to oblige them "until that day when I drink it new with you in my Father's kingdom."[3] His priests seek to remind Christians of this obligation by performing this blood rite "in remembrance of" him.[4] Machiavelli suggests that Christ's past good deeds might be supervened easily by "good in the present," but can "present things" (*P* 24) so easily deter one from seeking the future goods that Christ promises?[5] According to Machiavelli's general assessment of human nature, the answer is no.

> Human appetites are insatiable, for since from nature they have the ability and the wish to desire all things and from fortune the ability to achieve few of them, there continually results from this a discontent in human minds and a disgust with the things they possess. This makes them blame the present times, praise the past, and desire the future, even if they are not moved to do this by any reasonable cause. (*D* II.1.3)

The Prince generally confirms that this restless desire to improve their future condition frequently leads men to seek goods "elsewhere."[6] Dire circumstances engender perhaps the most fabulous hopes, but Machiavelli's general presentation testifies to the intoxicating power of hope, even in times of quietude. The regular satisfaction of material desires—namely, the desires for property, security, and liberty—can do much to bridle hope, since by directing men to that which is attainable, one can diminish their preoccupation with the future, yet nowhere does Machiavelli suggest that one can extinguish all hopes for the future by bestowing merely material blessings upon civil society. Machiavelli's silence about men's hope for future goods in chapter 24 testifies to the problem that all new princes face: keeping men occupied with "present things" (*P* 24) is not enough to guarantee the prince's security.[7] Material goods can adulterate his subjects' love of Christ, but they cannot extinguish entirely their attraction to his most grandiose promises. How can a prince contend with men's tireless attraction to promises of future goods—for which they will "willingly change their lords" (*P* 3)?

Severus demonstrates that oppressive fear can remind most men that present goods are precarious—and therefore, precious. The founders of chapter 6 demonstrate that claims of divine support can do the same, and for centuries after the prince has laid down his arms and died: divine justification for earthly violence—if it also orders human life—will lead most men to conceive of the armed prophet's orders as a legitimate part of the cosmic order, in which their security on earth and in the afterlife is guaranteed, provided that they adhere to his rule. Yet Machiavelli's pregnant discussion of "blood" obligations reminds the reader that the promise of a shining future sometimes persuades men to abandon established orders, even in the absence of "present" goods that might verify that future (*P* 24). How can Machiavelli compete with a lord who promises everything, delivers nothing, and is nonetheless believed and obeyed?

Machiavelli provides a final answer to this question in chapter 26, but for now, he offers only that the new prince who supervenes the obligations of "ancient blood" has much to win: he promises him a "double glory" that contrasts with the "double shame" of the defeated hereditary prince (*P* 24). In this context, Machiavelli describes the "beginning of a new principality"; the new prince will have "adorned it and consolidated it with good laws, good arms, good friends, and good examples" (*P* 24). Machiavelli does not specify which of these are crucial to consolidation, and which constitute mere adornment. One needs arms to consolidate a new principality, yet Machiavelli has also insisted elsewhere that arms guarantee good laws and good friends.[8] Good laws and good friends thus appear to be "adornments"—consequent to the primary act of consolidation. What, then, of "good examples" (*P* 24)?

The word "example" (*esemplo*) has appeared dozens of times in *The Prince*.[9] Most often, Machiavelli uses it to introduce a particular prince, province, or episode that supports his argument.[10] While the founders of chapter 6 are the "greatest examples" of new princes, on four other occasions Machiavelli has described as an "example" the actions of a lesser prince as it relates to his reputation among his own people or their civic education. Machiavelli names Ferdinand as one who gave "rare examples of himself," of which at least one—the expulsion of the Marranos—was especially "wretched" (*P* 21). Machiavelli contrasts Ferdinand's "wretched" and "rare" example with the "rare" example of internal governance practiced by Messer Bernabò—presumably, in his war against the Church (*P* 21). In the same chapter, Machiavelli describes a prosperous imaginary principality in which the prince makes "himself an example of humanity and munificence" (*P* 21) by encouraging the peaceful arts and commercial enterprise.[11] Cesare Borgia's actions are also an example: his execution of Remirro D'Orco is especially worthy of "being imitated by others" (*P* 7), because it kept "his subjects united and faithful" (*P* 17). One might add to this list Machiavelli's casual naming in chapter 26 of the things "brought about by God" to herald the arrival of Italy's redeeming prince, although these exemplary and legitimizing miracles are purportedly "without example."

Three of these examples—Cesare's, Ferdinand's, and Bernabò's—require arms, and appear crucial to consolidation of one's principality, although Ferdinand does not appear to be a "good" example (for the reasons discussed above). The sterling reputation of the imaginary kingdom is not due to the possession of arms; neither does the claim of miracles performed on behalf of the redeeming prince require arms.[12] They appear instead to be adornments—necessary to those who seek glory, but unnecessary to consolidation. A differentiated list of Machiavellian "good examples" thus emerges. These are necessary and sufficient for consolidation: cruel acts that unify a people and render them faithful at the beginning of one's rule; and armed resistance directed against the powerful status quo, which subordinate that power to one's authority. Other examples, however, are necessary to imitate if one wishes to adorn his principality: domestic policies that enrich a people, render them secure in their possessions and persons, and contribute to material progress; and audacious claims of divine support. While the latter are not strictly necessary, they are required if one seeks lasting orders, and thus glory.

Christ, who is entirely without arms and insists, "My kingdom is not of this world," exhibits none of the qualities required to consolidate his rule or ensure material prosperity.[13] He claims only to perform miracles that are "without example" (*P* 26), while promising that his followers will receive a heavenly kingdom. While the armed prophets "remain powerful, secure, honored, and happy" (*P* 6), Christ achieves only honor.[14] By way of these examples, *The Prince* has reminded the reader of the superiority of armed prophets—and of the defects of Christ's orders.

Tyranny's Resiliency

Machiavelli next attempts to explain the reasons that "the lords in Italy . . . have lost their states in our times"; he cites the duke of Milan, the king of Naples, and unnamed "others" as proof that "a common defect as to arms" and an inability "to secure themselves against the great" have led Italian princes to lose their states (*P* 24). Importantly, Pope Alexander VI's ambition to conquer Italy is the indirect cause of each of these defeats.[15] So while Machiavelli suggests that better arms might have enabled these princes to defend themselves, the circumstances of their defeats suggest that "the great" (*P* 24) against whom they needed security was the Church.

Machiavelli cites Philip V of Macedon as a superior model for Italian princes. He was able to resist ancient Rome and subject much of Greece "because he was a military man and knew how to deal with the people and secure himself against the great" (*P* 24).[16] In the *Discourses*, Machiavelli elaborates Philip's admirable qualities with more precision. He reports that Philip was a trenchant critic of mercenary arms, and praises his practice of "abandoning and despoiling" the countries he could not guard, since it is better to destroy a city than leave "it in the prey of the enemy" (*D* III.37.2).[17] Machiavelli relies on Livy's account for these reports about Philip, and attention to the context of each of these episodes illuminates more precisely how Philip's example serves as an instructive model for modern Italians.

Philip denigrates mercenary arms in peace negotiations with Rome, during which he elects to stay aboard his ship and shout terms to the Roman envoy on shore, rather than disembark and expose himself to danger. Philip was skeptical of the good "faith" (*fides*) of those in attendance—both the Romans and the mercenary Aetolians.[18] Given Rome's notable lack of faith in Greece, this was prudent.[19] An Aetolian responded, however, by condemning Philip as "deceitful and tricky[;] in war he does not encounter his enemy on fair ground or fight a set battle. He keeps out of his adversary's way, plunders and burns his cities, and when vanquished destroys what should be the prizes of the victors."[20] In *Discourses* III.37, Machiavelli praises these practices, which Philip used against his own allies while retreating from Rome.[21] Livy reports that "these measures were extremely distasteful to Philip, but as the country would soon be in possession of the enemy he was determined to keep the persons, at all events, of his allies out of their hands."[22]

Philip also employed this destructive strategy against his enemies' possessions—including their temples.[23] Philip subjects the Athenians to extraordinary punitive measures after they perpetrate a pious cruelty against his allies. While visiting Athens, curiosity led two Arcarnian men to wander into a temple during a celebration of the Eleusinian mysteries; the Athenians charged them with impiety and executed them as though they had committed an "unspeakable crime."[24] The excessive and cruel punishment of a religious crime aroused Philip's wrath. When he eventually joined the Arcarnian battle against Athens,

> he determined to leave nothing free from profanation and gave orders for the temples which the people had consecrated in every deme to be destroyed and set on fire. The land of Attica was famous for that class of building as well as for the abundance of native marble and the genius of its architects, and therefore it afforded abundant material for this destructive fury. He was not satisfied with overthrowing the temples with their statues, he even ordered the blocks of stone to be broken in pieces lest if they retained their shape they might form imposing ruins. When there was nothing left on which his rage, still insatiate, could wreak itself he left the enemy's territories.[25]

Philip may not have defeated Rome, but Machiavelli nonetheless exhorts Italian princes to imitate his military policies in their efforts against modern Rome. These instructions include to be wary of mercenaries; never trust envoys from Rome; burn your own cities rather abandon them to the Roman enemy; and respond to pious cruelties by razing every consecrated building and destroying every sacred icon that one encounters. Italian princes who react thus to modern Rome's artful incursions may not defeat it entirely, but they might, like Philip, be able to retain their kingdoms.

In his resistance to a universalizing empire, one ought to compare Philip's policies with Philopoemen's. Both faced the nascent Roman Empire: while Philopoemen attempted to preserve Greek freedom by engaging in careful diplomacy with Rome, Philip abjured diplomacy in favor of open hostility.[26] Indeed, Polybius reports that Philip even attempted unsuccessfully to "rouse the Achaeans against Rome" during Philopoemen's tenure as general of the Achaeans.[27] The Achaeans' refusal is plainly an error, although whether Philopoemen is to blame is unclear. Perhaps he was overruled in assembly; or perhaps his reflexive opposition to tyranny clouded his judgment. Philip's reputation for faithlessness probably made him a dubious ally, and Philopoemen had spent his entire career waging war against tyrants. To join Philip against the Romans would have required a spiritual flexibility that Philopoemen may have lacked.

Whatever the reason, Machiavelli's explicit openness to tyranny improves upon Philopoemen's unswerving republicanism, insofar as it accommodates the canny prudence of the tyrant, as well as the spirited contentiousness of republics. Livy and Polybius confirm that Philip's dramatic measures avoid the peril of Philopoemen's wary prudence: by allying with Rome, Philopoemen created a legitimate entrée for Rome, which the empire subsequently exploited.[28] Philip's hostile policy deprives Rome of a chance to conquer his kingdom by dividing its loyalties. Machiavelli, whose critique of modern Rome alternates between violent boldness and diplomatic circumspection, employs both of these strategies in his writing.

In his reaction to religious cruelty, one also ought to compare Philip's retributive harshness with Bernabò's "War of the Eight Saints" (*FH* III.7). While the latter sought to subordinate those complicit in pious cruelty to civil authority, Philip sought to destroy all earthly manifestations of the offending religion. The insufficiency of Bernabò's strategy is evident: Bernabò's efforts only slowed the Church's progress in Italy; the "War of the Eight Saints" weakened, but did not destroy, its power in Tuscany. Philip, by contrast, transformed Athenian temples to rubble.

Machiavelli attributes Philip's political longevity to his military acumen and canny understanding of the people and the great. Machiavelli does not report—as does Polybius—that as Philip's reign progressed, he ceased to resemble a king and adopted increasingly the modes of a tyrant.[29] This transformation coincided with his long war with Rome, and key events from his history suggest that Roman military pressure actually precipitated his tyrannical behavior.[30] Philip's anti-Roman resolve even led him to execute his own son, who had been taken hostage as a young man and thereafter advocated a pro-Roman policy for the Macedonian kingdom.[31] While Polybius is critical of Philip, his account also suggests that if Philip had not adopted tyranny at home, Rome would have infiltrated his kingdom and deprived him of his throne. If the princes of Italy need to imitate Philip in order to retain their principalities against the machinations of modern Rome, then Machiavelli's lesson is clear—and sinister: they must abandon the warm but fickle affection that sustains hereditary principalities and embrace icy fear, which is always the reassuring foundation of tyrannies. Their first task will be to cull from their people anyone whose loyalties are divided between their tyrant and Rome.

Deceived by the Sparrow and the Wildflowers: Indolence and the Problem of the Future Good

In the final lines of chapter 24, Machiavelli turns from a critique of the military tactics of Italian princes to condemn their psychology. In particular, he ascribes the failures of Italian princes to their "indolence" (*P* 24). When times are "calm," they do not prepare for the "storm" that fortune inevitably brings, which Machiavelli describes as a "common defect of men": "For one should never fall in the belief [*credere*] you can find someone to pick you up. Whether it does not happen or happens, it is not security for you, because that defense was base and did not depend on you. And those defenses alone are good, are certain, and are lasting, that depend on you yourself and your virtue" (*P* 24).[32] Machiavelli alludes to one of the Psalms' most common teachings: "The LORD makes firm the steps of the one who delights in him; though he may stumble, he will not fall, for the LORD upholds him with his hand."[33] Indeed, the Psalms are written as odes to God's concern for his people, and generally encourage the belief that God will rescue the afflicted among them. Machiavelli discourages this belief.

Christ quotes from the Psalms more frequently than any other Old Testament text, and it is the most quoted Old Testament book in the New Testament.[34] This is perhaps sufficient evidence of the influence of the Psalms' generally optimistic view of divine protection on New Testament writers. For example, although the crucified Christ describes himself as "forsaken," the Psalm from which he quotes also contains the hopeful plea that the Lord might "Deliver me from the sword, my precious life from the power of the dogs."[35]

Christ punctuates his general teaching on divine providence with metaphors that enjoin his disciples to trust in God's protection. To the apostles he sends into the world, he asks: "Are not two sparrows sold for a penny? Yet not one of them will fall to the ground outside your Father's care. And even the very hairs of your head are all numbered. So don't be afraid; you are worth more than many sparrows."[36] Rather than labor industriously to feed and clothe themselves, Christ instructs his apostles to imitate the "wild flowers," which do not "labor or spin," yet nonetheless receive all that they need.[37] Later New Testament writers echo Christ by testifying abundantly to God's ability to "keep you from stumbling" or protect you in times of danger.[38]

With his critical allusion to the belief that the "Lord upholds all who fall," Machiavelli identifies Italian indolence with the biblical notion of divine protection offered in the Psalms, and championed by Christ.[39] The New Testament teaches Christians that God, who counts "even the very hairs of your head," is never far away.[40] Just as he saved Christ from ultimate destruction, Christ—who can miraculously calm any storm that might arise—will save believers.[41] Faithful Christians are "convinced that neither death nor life, neither angels nor demons, neither the present nor the future, nor any powers, neither height nor depth, nor anything else in all creation, will be able to separate [them] from the love of God that is in Christ Jesus our Lord," since Christ "always lives to intercede for them."[42] Machiavelli's commendation of "those defenses alone . . . that depend on you yourself and your virtue" (*P* 24) constitutes an implicit rejection of this pious belief. According to him, the belief that anyone—and perhaps especially God or Christ—will intervene to save your principality "is not security for you" (*P* 24).[43]

God Makes the Rain Fall, but Fortune Is a River

Having associated the belief in divine providence with the failure of Italian princes, Machiavelli deconstructs that belief in chapter 25, entitled "How Much Fortune Can Do in Human Affairs, and in What Mode It May Be Opposed."[44] This is the first title in which the word "human" appears; this suggests that Machiavelli's teaching applies to the broadest possible audience.[45] According to Machiavelli, "many" hold that "worldly things are so governed by fortune and by God that men cannot correct them with their prudence, indeed they have no remedy at all; and on account of this they might judge that one need not sweat much over things but let oneself be governed by chance" (*P* 25). While in the previous chapter Machiavelli suggests discreetly that God's rule over the universe discourages preparative action, here he explicitly attributes men's indolence to a corrupted version of this opinion. Apparently, no men believe in a God of maximum providence: all attribute to "fortune" some worldly events.[46] Machiavelli emphasizes men's uncertainty about what governs the universe by stipulating that while they believe God and fortune govern the world, they let themselves be governed by "chance" (*sorte*).[47] This ambiguity reflects perhaps the incoherence of common opinion, but it also attests to its corruption. Men do not have full confidence in God's power to rule the universe. The belief that God's sovereignty is abrogated by fortune undermines the glory that the Bible accords to God, due to his alleged power.[48]

Machiavelli thus reveals casually that the common notion of piety is corrupt—and even admits that he "sometimes" has "been in some part inclined" to this opinion (*P* 25). Yet rather than accede to this corrupted view, or come to the defense of the God whose majesty has been impugned, Machiavelli concludes that the main problem with this view of the world is that it stifles human agency beneath the oppressive forces of both fortune and God. His effort to free men from their effects signals his hostility to God: "Nonetheless, so that our free will not be eliminated, I judge that fortune is arbiter of half our actions, but that she also leaves the other half, or close to it, for us to govern" (*P* 25).

In defense of "free will," Machiavelli advances a view of the universe that denies God's governance of "worldly things" (*P* 25). In Machiavelli's first explicit discussion of a theological concept in *The Prince*, he confirms his antitheological perspective with harsh irony.[49] The God of maximum providence is not generally credible—less so in "our times," which are subject to variation "beyond human conjecture" (*P* 25). Nonetheless, even the corrupted belief in an expansively providential God prevents men from acting resolutely to affect worldly things. Consequently, Machiavelli excises God from his cosmology.

The reader ought to be prepared for Machiavelli's shabby treatment of the God of Abraham.[50] Thus far, he has appeared in four chapters. In chapter 6, Machiavelli implies that while God may have instructed Moses, his influence was negligible, since the pagan founders "appear no different." In chapter 8, he opines that those who employ well-used cruelties "have some remedy for their state with God and with men," even if they are infamous criminals. In chapter 11, he declines briefly to discuss the political operations of the Church because it is "exalted and maintained by God," but nonetheless proceeds to offer a withering indictment of its orders. In chapter 12, God is unable to instill fear in mercenary arms. While God will appear six times in chapter 26, those appearances do nothing to change Machiavelli's generally poor accounting of the supreme deity, who appears neither particularly effective nor especially sensitive to claims of justice.[51]

In his next gambit to encourage human action, Machiavelli seeks to demystify the fearsome power of fortune by offering a practical account of its powers. He describes "her" as a "violent river" whose floods destroy human constructions, transform the landscape, and prompt men to "flee" (*P* 25).[52] Notably, fortune's effects parallel those wrought by Christ's death, at the moment of which the temple curtain is torn, the landscape is transformed miraculously, and people are prompted to flee.[53] Machiavelli's attribution of floods to fortune also ignores the Bible's repeated claims that God controls the weather—including especially the rains. The book of Job offers an account of this power, which the author juxtaposes to a critique of Machiavellian types: "He performs wonders that cannot be fathomed, miracles that cannot be counted. He provides rain for the earth; he sends water on the countryside. The lowly he sets on high, and those who mourn are lifted to safety. He thwarts the plans of the crafty, so that their hands achieve no success."[54] In response to fortune's destructive capacity, Machiavelli recommends neither awe, nor prayer, nor despair, nor flight. Men must instead create dikes, dams, and canals to limit fortune's destructive power and transform its deluge into something that supports human flourishing. Machiavelli thus emphasizes that fortune is not random chance: as a river, it may flood its banks or alter its course, but its path is never absolutely random. Thus, for men of sufficient virtue, fortune's flood signals an opportunity to improve their material condition. Machiavelli's allusion to the death of Christ suggests that the early Christians, confronted with the death of their alleged savior, failed to exploit the opportunity presented by that event. Rather than use Christ's example to build a new world, they scurried away in fear, generally remaining fixated on Christ's promises of heavenly salvation and otherworldly glory—even as they preached the gospel "to the ends of the earth."[55] As a result, after living for a time at the margins of the civilized world, they eventually followed Christ to their own gory deaths. They could not imitate the founders, for whom adverse fortune constituted an opportunity.

Neither can Italy claim anyone of the founders' virtue. It is, instead, part of the problem: in a strange phrase that reminds one of the pope's claim to universal rule from the Holy See (*la Santa Sede*), Machiavelli describes Italy as "the seat [la *sedia*] of these variations" (*P* 25).[56] There are other reasons to conclude that Machiavelli refers here to the Church. *The Prince* has demonstrated that while the rest of world meddles liberally in Italian affairs, Italians are not generally sufficiently organized to exert much influence outside the country. The notable exception is the Church, which as *la Santa Sede* of Christendom has aided a French invasion of Italy, empowered Spanish domination, and can even claim a counselor in Emperor Maximilian's court. Indeed, nothing of consequence appears to flow from Italy *but* the Church's influence—and that influence has precipitated ceaseless political change, both in Italy and Europe. *The Prince* teaches that the Church is the chief cause of Italy's chaotic recent history; as part of its strategy, it has endeavored to keep Italy weak and divided. Hence, Italy is "a country without dams and without any dike" (*P* 25).[57] Given the corruption and effeminacy that prevail in Italy, due to a combination of a history of servitude and Christianity's debilitating teachings, it is likely to remain so.

The Fixity of Human Nature and the Variability of the Good

The denial of God's governance of the universe and the elevation of fortune's power constitutes an unmistakable opportunity for human beings. Fortune, unlike the Abrahamic God, may be opposed successfully. Yet the second half of chapter 25 suggests that men are only rarely capable of exploiting that opportunity.

Machiavelli begins his narrower discussion of fortune by critiquing the ways men seek "the end that each has before him, that is, glories and riches" (*P* 25). With this blithe assertion, Machiavelli presumes what Christ condemns: men seek money and earthly glory.[58] His appraisal of men's efforts to accomplish these ends, however, reveals a litany of blameworthy practices: men rely on fortune to sustain them; they do not understand that "the good" varies; they do not observe sufficiently "the quality of the times" when selecting their "modes" of action; and they do not "change" their natures "with the times and with affairs" (*P* 25). If a man would heed Machiavelli's advice, his "fortune would not change" (*P* 25).

Machiavelli's deconstruction of classical and Christian virtue in chapters 15 through 18 prepared the reader for his assertion that "the good" varies with the times (*la variazione del bene*).[59] That this is familiar ground for Machiavelli, however, ought not to diminish its shocking quality. Christ was no relativist. The preeminent Christian good, which a man ought to seek always, is the salvation of his soul and the eternal life it guarantees.[60] Christ, who proclaims himself the "way and the truth and the life," directs men to that good: "Just then a man came up to Jesus and asked, 'Teacher, what good thing must I do to get eternal life?' 'Why do you ask me about what is good?' Jesus replied. '"There is only One who is good. If you want to enter life, keep the commandments."'"[61] This rule is not circumstantial, since "whoever believes in the Son has eternal life, but whoever rejects the Son will not see life, for God's wrath remains on them."[62] Contrary to Christ, Machiavelli thinks that "glories and riches" are the truly constant ends of human life; all other notions of "the good" are subordinate, circumstantial, and ephemeral (*P* 25).

Chapter 18 also prepared the reader for the necessity of changing one's nature; there Machiavelli described the consummate prince as one who possessed "a spirit disposed to change as the winds of fortune and the variation of things command him." In chapter 25, Machiavelli emphasizes the difficulty—but not, as some scholars have argued, the impossibility—of this task. Those who are inclined to caution might be especially susceptible to spiritual intransigence, but this teaching apparently applies to all men.

> Nor may a man be found so prudent [*prudente*] as to know [*sappi*] how to accommodate himself to this, whether because he cannot deviate from what nature inclines him to [*la natura lo inclina*] or also because, when one has always flourished by walking on one path, he cannot be persuaded [*persuadere*] to depart from it. And so, the cautious man, when it is time to come to impetuosity, does not know [*sa*] how to do it, hence comes to ruin. (*P* 25)[63]

Nature inclines, but does not command. The principal defect among these men is their lack of knowledge, or their inability to be persuaded—which might result from a natural inclination, in combination with a lack of understanding. Machiavelli's language here does not preclude the existence of a man who can "change his nature" (*P* 25), but instead explains why such men are so rare.[64] Indeed, Polybius informs us that Philip V of

Macedon possessed this ability: "When king Philip had become powerful and had obtained supremacy over the Greeks, he showed the most utter disregard of faith and principle; but when the breeze of fortune again set against him, his moderation was as conspicuous in its turn. But after his final and complete defeat, he tried by every possible expedient to consolidate the strength of his kingdom."[65] In response to his changing fortunes, Philip transformed himself from audacious conqueror, to potential ally in a grand Greek alliance, to wily cunctator, to harsh tyrant. The rarity of men like Philip helps explain Machiavelli's preference for republican government, which can "accommodate itself better than one prince can to the diversity of the times through the diversity of the citizens who are in it" (*D* III.9.2). Yet the rarity of virtuous men with flexible spirits and changing natures does not obviate their necessity. Such men must rule if human beings are to resist the relentless efforts of universalizing empire. They are also required so that human beings can accomplish the greatest action of which men are capable: the founding of new modes and orders.

Impetuosity, the Young, and the
Spirit Required to Command Fortune

Inflexibly impetuous men also encounter difficulty. They possess a spiritedness that is conducive to success in certain times, but struggle to change their modes when necessary. Machiavelli's lone example in this chapter is one of impetuosity: Pope Julius II.[66] His discussion of Julius confirms two lessons from the chapter. First, an episode from Julius's career demonstrates dramatically how the Holy See operates as "the seat" of the variations that inundate Machiavelli's time: his furious effort to expel Bentivoglio from Bologna prompts France to move its army across Italy and enflames Spain's desire to possess all of Naples. Second, Machiavelli implies that his teachings on the power of fortune, the impotence of God, and the crucial importance of human effort also apply to the pope: God did not—and could not—aid Pope Julius. His impetuosity succeeded merely because the times were "in conformity with his mode of proceeding"; had times changed, Machiavelli pronounces, "his ruin would have followed" (*P* 25). God would have remained dormant as fortune swept away the Vicar of his "only begotten son."[67]

Despite its limitations, Machiavelli nonetheless prefers impetuosity to caution,

> because fortune is a woman; and it is necessary, if one wants to hold her down, to beat her and strike her down. And one sees that she lets herself be won more by the impetuous than by those who proceed coldly. And so always,

like a woman, she is a friend of the young, because they are less cautious, more ferocious, and command her with more audacity. (*P* 25)

Machiavelli's infamously stated preference for impetuosity appears to reflect a conviction that these men are more likely to oppose fortune successfully—perhaps because those inclined to impetuosity are less likely than the plodding cautious types to remain "obstinate in their modes" (*P* 25). This might also explain why fortune is a "friend of the young": those not yet habituated by a long life to a particular mode of proceeding are better equipped to nurture the spiritual flexibility necessary to change one's nature—especially if they are fitted with an education that teaches them to "know how to do it" (*P* 25). But why does Machiavelli link these qualities with violent and sexualized audacity against women? *Fortuna* may have been a female Roman deity, but why is it necessary to exhort the young to rape her?

First, note that Machiavelli attenuates his misogyny with professions that fortune "lets herself be won" and is a "friend" to her assailant (*P* 25).[68] More importantly, however, one ought to view Machiavelli's exhortation as part of his broad effort in *The Prince* to encourage manliness among his readers. This effort has generally remained implicit, but consider his repeated exhortations to imitate ancient men, for whom manliness is much more important than it is for Christians; his critique of the "cowardice," "submission," and "abjectness of spirit" (*D* III.31.3) that characterize a Christian education, the chief evidence of which is Italy's defective arms; his condemnation of effeminacy; and the fact that, of the emperors listed in chapter 19, the two who encouraged the growth of Christianity—Heliogabalus and Alexander—were also the only two who subjected themselves to women.[69] These observations support Machiavelli's general complaint in the *Discourses* that by the success of Christianity, "the world appears to be made effeminate and heaven disarmed" (*D* II.2.2). Machiavelli's extreme rhetoric in chapter 25 is calculated to overcome Christianity's effeminizing tendencies with a rhetorical appeal to men's—and especially young men's—basest and most constant inclination: the desire for sex.

Machiavelli thus acts as a tempter. His exhortation to rape fortune seeks to enflame sinful desires, and contrasts starkly with Christ's persistent meekness toward, and deference to, women, which are exemplified both by his warning that one should not even look "at a woman lustfully" and by his mother's important role in his career.[70] Christ's apparent indifference to sex appears connected to his gentle treatment of women.[71]

Machiavelli's endorsement of a crude and violent notion of manliness appears necessary to counteract Christianity's most debilitating effects, but one might also observe that by contemplating the rape of a Roman goddess at the end of chapter 25, Machiavelli prepares the reader for the attack upon the Bride of Christ that he will encourage in chapter 26. This aspect of Machiavelli's political plot requires men who exhibit the daring and cruelty that usually attend such extreme manliness.

The Harsh Requirements of Italy's Redemption

The Prince ends with chapter 26, an "Exhortation to Seize Italy and to Free Her from the Barbarians."[72] While this language echoes the patriotic language of Julius II, Machiavelli also identifies Italy's cause with that of the Greeks, for whom the Romans were barbarians; finally, he distinguishes himself from the popes of his time, nearly all of whom offered ineffective exhortations to wage war against the infidel Turks.[73] Although Machiavelli wonders briefly "whether there is matter to give opportunity to someone prudent and virtuous to introduce a form that would bring honor to him and good to the community of men" in Italy, he concludes "that so many things are tending to the benefit of a new prince that I do not know what time has even been more apt for it" (*P* 26). Is Machiavelli undeterred by the cavalcade of failed Italian princes who have stumbled through the pages of this book? No: Italy's extreme corruption is a founder's golden opportunity: "To know the virtue of an Italian spirit, it was necessary that Italy be reduced to the condition in which she is at present, which is more enslaved than the Hebrews, more servile than the Persians, more dispersed than the Athenians, without a head, without order, beaten, despoiled, torn, pillaged, and having endured ruin of every sort" (*P* 26).

Machiavelli cites Moses, Cyrus, and Theseus as men who overcame Italy's many problems severally. For Italy suffers from extreme misfortune in triplicate: it is enslaved by a more exacting Pharaoh, subject to an empire more expansive than that of the Medes, and more radically disunited than the Athenians. Who, then, is Italy's Pharaoh? What is the empire to which Italy remains in servitude? What tears Italy asunder? Unsurprisingly, all roads lead to Rome: as the Vicar of Christ, the pope's commands are especially absolute; as the putative head of Christianity, he leads the only truly universal empire; as a political actor within Christendom, he keeps Italy radically divided. Yet, paradoxically, perhaps because his powers are almost exclusively spiritual, Italy remains "without a head" (*P* 26). Insofar as the Christian Church is Italy's greatest affliction, the Bride of Christ is the barbarian against which a founder must direct his efforts. The redemption of Italy will mean the defeat of the most prominent earthly manifestation of the Christian God: the Church dedicated to his Son's ministry.

Machiavelli's exhortation to action confirms that the redemption he envisions is political, rather than spiritual. While Mary's Magnificat betrays significant hopes for earthly vindication, Christ's redemptive promise is overwhelmingly spiritual.[74] Rather than constitute new earthly institutions that will order human life, Christ offers a redemption that will free believers from earthly powers and culminate in the satisfaction of the most grandiose promise of Christianity: "But now that you have been set free from sin and have become slaves of God, the benefit you reap leads to holiness, and the result is eternal life."[75] Christian redemption will save believers from God's wrath by subjecting them wholly to his rule.[76] Yet since Christianity's ultimate redemption occurs only at the end of the world, at which time there will be "great distress in the land and wrath against this people," it requires—rather than remedies—political dysfunction.[77] Christ will only redeem Italian political life by ending it. In the meantime, his pacific teachings aggravate the only "sin" (*P* 12) that Machiavelli identifies in *The Prince*: the astonishing incapacity of Italian arms.

Machiavelli excludes Romulus from the list of founders an Italian might imitate. By doing so, he indicates that Italy's freedom requires the prolonged absolute rule of a single man.[78] Moses, Cyrus, and Theseus each ruled alone—or with the help of a small band of armed men. While each left lasting orders, none bequeathed to his people a republic. Neither shall Italy have a healthy republic in the near future. This conclusion ought not to be surprising. Machiavelli has demonstrated that modern Italians, unlike their ancient counterparts, lack the virtue necessary to constitute a republic, a development for which Christianity is largely to blame. Italian corruption means that Italy requires a "kingly hand . . . with absolute and excessive power" to give it the "order" that is always a precondition to "a political way of life" (*D* I.55.4).[79]

The next section of the exhortation recounts the failures of those who have tried to redeem Italy. Italians have mounted hapless efforts—but so, too, has the Christian God. While "a glimmer has shone in someone who could judge that he had been ordered by God for her redemption, yet it was seen that in the highest course of his actions, he was repulsed by fortune" (*P* 26). This is an allusion to Cesare Borgia's failed plot to conquer Italy; Machiavelli implies that either Borgia's judgment or God's power was insufficient, since God's orders were ultimately thwarted by fortune. This failure—which was really the failure of Pope Alexander VI—only intensified Italy's suffering by leaving her "lifeless" (*P* 26), and unable to resist the depredations that Spain and the Church visited upon her.[80] While Italy "prays to God to send her someone to redeem her from these barbarous cruelties and insults," the best that he can provide is yet another Medici: "Nor may one see at present anyone in whom she can hope more than in your illustrious house, which with its fortune and virtue, supported by God and by the Church of which it is now the prince, can put itself at the head of this redemption" (*P* 26).[81] Although Machiavelli's happy juxtaposition of the "fortune and virtue" of the Medicis is perhaps sufficient evidence of poisonous irony, note also that none of the parties to Italy's purported redemption have demonstrated an ability to improve anyone's condition—other than, perhaps, their own. The Medici destroyed the Florentine republic in order to gratify familial and factional interests; the Church survives as a petty criminal enterprise that exploits its flock and weakens Italy; and God, despite his grandiose claims to justice, remains idle as fortune overwhelms what little virtue remains in Italy. There will be no Medicean redemption of Italy, a fact that the existence of a Medici pope merely confirms.

God's Severe Friendship

While a redeeming Medici may be a chimera, Machiavelli uses the occasion to remind the reader of what is required to redeem a corrupt province. One must imitate the founders "named above" (*P* 26). Nor should one be awed by their claims to semidivinity or their alleged friendships with God. Although they were "rare and marvelous, nonetheless they were men . . . , nor was God more friendly to them than to you" (*P* 26).

Machiavelli is guilty of at least three blasphemies. First, he humanizes these founder-prophets in a blithely irreligious way. Second, abandoning the careful equivocation of chapter 6, he implies the same God befriended all three (or four) of these men, and is, moreover, no "more friendly" to them than to the upstart to whom chapter 26 is devoted; Machiavelli's God, unlike the God of Abraham, is not especially choosy about his friends.[82] Finally, Machiavelli justifies the redemption of Italy in a way that departs dramatically from the prophets. God's alleged sanction justifies their enterprises: as Paul comments, "Who will bring any charge against those whom God has chosen? It is God who justifies."[83] Machiavelli substitutes in the place of divine justification a rational one: "Here there is great justice: 'for war is just to whom it is necessary and arms are pious when there is no hope but in arms'" (*P* 26).[84] This quote is from Livy, and appears within a Samnite speech that promises that the gods will ally with the Samnites against the intransigent Romans.[85] Deprived of this context, however, the quote clearly subordinates piety and justice to necessity. Machiavelli teaches that if necessity commands, God will follow obediently. Italy needs this war; hence its piety and justice are assured.

Yet neither the Samnites' pious claims, nor Machiavelli's religious language in chapter 26—where God appears more frequently than in the rest of the book combined—are merely superfluous. First, pious professions attract the support of the nominally pious by clothing and thereby concealing naked necessity, which is often ugly. Second, the example of the founders demonstrates that prophetic claims conduce to more lasting orders because they confer glory upon the founder and his orders, while giving future generations a divine object on which to fix their future hopes. Machiavelli's religious rhetoric thus conforms to his earlier promise to "submit myself entirely" (*P* 13) to the orders of the founder-prophets. His inelegant assertion of divine sanction suggests, however, that such professions need not be especially artful.

> Besides this, here may be seen extraordinary things without example, brought about by God: the sea has opened; a cloud has escorted you along the way; the stone has poured forth water; here manna has rained; everything has concurred in your greatness. The remainder you must do yourself. God does not want to do everything, so as not to take free will from us and that part of glory that falls to us. (*P* 26)

This is a list of miracles from Exodus, and their intrusion is abrupt and incredible.[86] They purportedly presage the arrival of Italy's redeemer, but Machiavelli provides no corroboration for his account. He merely insists that God has demonstrated his support by bringing about these miracles that no one else has seen. The implication is clear: justice and piety adhere to armed prevaricators, while he who is merely armed frequently earns the reputation of a tyrant.

By exhorting his reader to commence a prophetic war against the status quo, Machiavelli, perhaps playfully, assumes the role of God in Exodus. Even after God appears to Moses in a burning bush, Moses remains a reluctant prophet.[87] God overcomes Moses's self-doubt by hectoring him for his lack of confidence, promising "I will help you speak and will teach you what to say," eventually offering him the superfluous assistance of his well-spoken brother, and promising miracles that will demonstrate that his prophetic claims are genuine.[88] Excepting the guarantee of Aaron's assistance, Machiavelli has imitated God precisely.[89] This is indicative of Machiavelli's grandiose impiety, but it also discloses his most vaulting ambition.[90]

Baptizing Italy in a River of Blood

As Harvey Mansfield notes, Machiavelli presents these miracles out of order; as Christopher Lynch observes, they appear in this order in Psalm 78.[91] Machiavelli's allusion to the saving miracles performed during the Exodus appears to confirm the notion that he is seeking a "new Moses" to lead Italy out of servitude: these miracles allow the Israelites to escape (and quickly thereafter, crush) their enemies and sustain their bodies.[92] They also inaugurate their marauding passage to the promised land, during which they will conquer and expropriate all whom they encounter.

Machiavelli's vision of Italy's future is not millennial, but Mosaic. Rather than an enthroned Christ solemnly judging "all the nations," Italians will be fighting for their lives.[93] Indeed, many are likely to be slaughtered by their Mosaic redeemer, as he culls the envious from their midst and struggles to make them conform to the "political way of life" (D I.55.4) that he wishes to impose.[94]

In this regard, Machiavelli's allusion to Psalm 78 is even more telling: as Lynch notes, the psalm alternates among accounts of God's miracles, the persistent perfidy of his "stubborn and rebellious" people, and God's wrathful punishment of their disobedience: "In spite of all this, they kept on sinning; in spite of his wonders, they did not believe. So he ended their days in futility and their years in terror. Whenever God slew them, they would seek him; they eagerly turned to him again. They remembered that God was their Rock, that God Most High was their Redeemer."[95] Given the context of this allusion to Psalm 78, Machiavelli's implicit lesson is that the saving miracles of Exodus are not sufficient to bind Italy to God—or his redeeming prince. The God who befriends Italy's founder will demand the deaths of "the sturdiest among them" for generations.[96]

Particularly meaningful is the punishment for military cowardice to which Psalm 78 alludes. It recounts how "the men of Ephraim, though armed with bows, turned back on the day of battle," rather than come to the aid of Jepthah's army.[97] As Lynch once again notes, Judges reports that after Jepthah won the initial battle, he waged war against these cowardly forces. Once the Ephraimites were defeated, a throng of stragglers sought to cross the Jordan to flee home. Jepthah's forces culled every last Ephraimite from this mass: if an escapee proved to be an Ephraimite, they "seized him and killed him at the fords of the Jordan. Forty-two thousand Ephraimites were killed at that time."[98]

Psalm 78 is an ode to King David's rule, and claims to disclose "hidden things, things from of old."[99] Although their tale is told outside the Pentateuch, the Ephraimites are, strangely enough, the first example offered of a people who broke "God's covenant and refused to live by his law."[100] Is punishment of their ilk David's first priority? This appears to be the lesson to which Machiavelli directs his reader: he ought to imitate Jepthah's annihilation of unfaithful arms. Machiavelli explicitly commended this policy in his earlier praise of Hiero (P 13): given the dismal state of Italian arms, however, its redeemer might need to kill many more than forty-two thousand. The unchristian implications of this particular exhortation are especially pointed. Christ famously inaugurates his ministry by submitting to baptism in the Jordan River; Jepthah filled the same river with the blood of cowards.[101] The deaths of the Italian redeemer's lukewarm supporters will accomplish more worldly good than "the blood of Jesus," which "purifies us from all sin"—but nonetheless leaves us "as sheep to be slaughtered."[102]

If Italy imitates the history reported in this psalm, this cycle of bloodletting will culminate in the rule of a king who claims to enjoy divine support. Psalm 78 closes by endorsing the reign of David, who serves as "shepherd of [God's] people."[103] It is notable that David, whom Machiavelli praises for his radical self-sufficiency, is a markedly different sort of shepherd than Christ—the rare "good shepherd" who "lays down his life for the sheep."[104] *The Prince* has demonstrated that Christ's self-sacrifice has devastating implications for worldly governance: while the Israelites will be ruled "with integrity of heart [and] skillful hands," Christians must "wait for the blessed hope—the appearing of the glory of our great God and Savior, Jesus Christ, who gave himself for us to redeem us from all wickedness and to purify for himself a people that are his very own, eager to do what is good."[105] In the meantime, they remain subject to a long succession of deficient earthly rulers, to whom they are commanded to remain obedient.[106] They do this in imitation of Christ, who "learned obedience from what he suffered," and was consequently "made perfect."[107]

The Problem with Italy's Heads

The list of miracles is the first rhetorical peak of chapter 26. Machiavelli thereafter descends to discuss Italy's wretched condition for one last time in *The Prince*, in order to explain why "it always appears that military virtue has died out in her" (*P* 26). Machiavelli's first explanation is that "her ancient orders [*ordini antiqui*] were not good" (*P* 26).[108] This constitutes blame of the Church, since Machiavelli has used this phrase almost exclusively to describe its orders throughout the book.[109] It also constitutes blame of Christ, insofar as he is the originator of these "ancient orders." Other than the Church, the republics of chapter 5 are the only other regimes to which Machiavelli ascribes "ancient orders [*ordini antichi*]."[110] Machiavelli invites the reader to compare the defective "ancient orders" of Christianity with the superior "ancient orders" of republics, whose martial obstinacy is sustained by the unchristian passions of hatred and revenge. While the latter always enables rebellion in "the name of liberty" (*P* 5), the former produces a military policy that leads to "slavery and disgrace" (*P* 12). What Italy most needs, therefore, is to rid herself of the ancient orders of Christianity: honor awaits the man who will introduce "new laws and the new orders found by him" (*P* 26).

Machiavelli appears to qualify his critique of Italian arms by offering next an image of Italy as a body. He exonerates individual Italians of the charge of martial haplessness by insisting "there is great virtue in the limbs, if it were not lacking in the heads [*capi*]" (*P* 26).[111] Italians excel in duels and brawls, but are hapless when formed into an army: "everything proceeds from the weakness of the heads [*capi*], because those who know are not obeyed."[112] Machiavelli's condemnation of "the heads" would appear consistent with his critique of the Church in this passage, but for the fact that he uses a plural noun and had insisted at the beginning of the chapter that Italy was "without a head." While one might reasonably conclude that he refers to the leaders who place themselves at the head of Italian armies, the context of the passage—in which Machiavelli heaps blame upon Italy's ancient Christian orders—suggests a more radical and sinister critique. One needs only to recall that the New Testament proclaims "that the head of every man is Christ, and the head of the woman is man, and the head of Christ is God."[113] Christ's preeminent position testifies to his power over men, which is granted by God. It dwarfs the piddling exertions of Italian patriots.

> That power is the same as the mighty strength he exerted when he raised Christ from the dead and seated him at his right hand in the heavenly realms, far above all rule and authority, power and dominion, and every name that is invoked, not only in the present age but also in the one to come. And God placed all things under his feet and appointed him to be head over everything for the church, which is his body, the fullness of him who fills everything in every way.[114]

If one is mindful of his critical allusion to this New Testament teaching, one sees how Machiavelli's apparent defense of Italian virtue only sharpens his condemnation of Jesus Christ, who is "the head of every man" in his Church, while also serving as head of the Church itself.[115] In those capacities, he corrupts the minds of Italians by his exemplary lack of arms, his general weakness, and his support of the corruptive institution that bears his name. The effectual truth of Christ's reign is that Italy is left "without a head" (*P* 26). The remedy for these Christly afflictions is to obey "those who know" about arms (*P* 26).

War, Peace, and Redemption

Immediately after this critical allusion to Christ, the most famous unarmed prophet, Machiavelli repeats the central lesson of the book: "Thus, if your illustrious house wants to follow those excellent men who redeemed their countries, it is necessary before all other things, as the true foundations of every undertaking, to provide itself with its own arms; for one cannot have more faithful, nor truer, nor better soldiers" (*P* 26). Machiavelli claims that when the soldiers "see themselves commanded by their prince, and honored and indulged by him" (*P* 26), this redeemer will be able to defend

Italy from foreigners. It is not clear on the basis of this passage, however, that the new prince will indulge his army by directing their avarice and cruelty against foreigners exclusively. The chapter has intimated that much Italian blood must be shed in order to begin this enterprise; surely, like Moses's Levites, the new prince's faithful and keenly acquisitive army will be eager to aid this endeavor, which will culminate in "a regeneration of arms and a change in orders" (P 26).[116]

According to Machiavelli, Italy will greet its redeemer with an assortment of passions, including faith, piety, and tears.[117] But most immediately, Italy's redeemer will find a people thirsting for revenge, a passion that Christ attempts to stifle by imposing meek forbearance.[118] One ought to doubt Machiavelli's insinuation that no Italian would chafe under the bridle of this redeemer's rule, just as one should remain skeptical of the purported ease of this "just enterprise," under which "this fatherland may be ennobled" (P 26). Machiavelli's general teaching on the requirements of founding presumes the existence of faithlessness, ambition, and envy among the people who become subject to a founder. Yet for well-armed men of sufficient virtue, even the most ungrateful and fickle people constituted "the matter enabling them to introduce any form they pleased" (P 6). The truly virtuous prince can mold a people much like the God of Genesis molds men.[119]

Machiavelli closes *The Prince* with a quote from Petrarch's *Italia Mia*: "Virtue will take up arms against fury, and make the battle short, because ancient valor in Italian hearts is not yet dead" (P 26). Machiavelli's use of Petrarch suggests that they agree: the union of arms and virtue can resuscitate ancient Italian valor. While each critiques mercenaries and each laments the despoilment of Italy at the hands of foreign powers, Petrarch's *canzone* indicates that Italy's political salvation depends on the will of the Christian God and Italians' return to Christ's pacific ways.[120] Machiavelli holds the opposite view. Petrarch appeals to the "*pietà*" of the "ruler of heaven," who will remedy the afflictions of his "dear" land.[121] Machiavelli insists that Italy's redemption depends on human effort. For Petrarch, Italy's cause is that of Christianity: Italy's enemies are "savage beasts" who sleep in the pens of "gentle flocks"; Machiavelli infamously encourages men to imitate the lion and the fox—two beasts that, by stalking the flock of believers, represent Christianity's most stalwart enemies.[122]

Yet the lines that immediately precede the passage Machiavelli quotes illustrate most vividly Machiavelli's rejection of the Christian humanist's hopes for Italy: "In God's name may your mind for once be moved by this, and look with *pietà* upon the tears of all your grieving people who, after God, look only to you for hope. If only you would show some sign of *pietate*, then virtue against rage will take up arms, and battle will be short, for all that ancient valor in the Italian heart is not yet dead?"[123] Petrarch's grand hopes lie in the quality of the soul that Machiavelli rejects as the cause of "disorders" (*P* 17) like those that afflict Italy: pity, or mercy. Petrarch also advises Italians to forbear "hatred and disdain" in favor of a peaceful way of life that will lead them "to heaven" (*del ciel*); Machiavelli, by contrast, has endorsed hatred and revenge as superior bonds for political communities that enjoy the free way of life (*P* 5).[124] Petrarch's closing lines typify his disagreement with Machiavelli, and serve to highlight Machiavelli's rejection of Christianity as a solution to earthly problems. Petrarch instructs his "song" to pacify "haughty [*altero*]" Italians, "whose wills are still so full of that ancient, most vicious of all habits, always truth's enemy. But you must try your fortune among the valiant few who love the good; tell them: 'Who will protect me? I go my way beseeching: Peace, peace, peace.'"[125] Machiavelli, who famously extols the superiority of the "ancient" customs that Petrarch denigrates, rejects this solution. In *The Prince*, he seeks to enflame the indignation Italians ought to feel at the "barbarian domination" (*P* 26) of Christianity, the Christian Church, and its founder, Jesus Christ—while crying out loudly for war.

CONCLUSION

Machiavelli's Gospel

I love my native city more than my own soul.

In the *Discourses*, Machiavelli opines that religious sects "vary two or three times in five or in six thousand years" (II.5.1). This means that Machiavelli believed that Christianity—which "come[s] from men" (*D* II.5.1) and is thus subject to this general rule—would survive between approximately 1,666 and 3,000 years. This explains his flexible approach when combating Christ: sometimes, he intimates that the destruction of Christ's legacy is imminent; at other times, he proposes a more covert, long-term strategy to defeat the Prince of Peace.[1]

In either case, once Christianity is destroyed, Machiavelli does not think it will come back from the dead. While he concedes that one might renew sects by leading them "back towards their beginning" (*D* III.1.2), the examples of Saint Francis and Saint Dominic prove that a renewal will not remedy Christianity's defects, precisely because its founder is so lacking. Nor is a renewed Christianity likely to find another earthly dynamo like the Roman Empire to supplement its effeminate meekness with ferocity and order: because it has rendered the world "effeminate and heaven disarmed" (*D* II.2.2), virtue reigns only in the ancient histories that it failed to extirpate—or in provinces untainted by Christianity.[2] This explains why Machiavelli invokes a Mosaic redemption at the end of *The Prince*. Just as Rome had to return to the example of the "fierce and bellicose" Romulus, rather than "quiet and religious" Numa (*D* I.19.1), Christians must look to the ancient example of the unchristian and inhuman Moses to renew their religion.[3] Failing that, the bellicose orders of the ascendant Ottoman Empire of "the Turk"—following Moses's most faithful imitator, Muhammad—stand poised to inundate Italy with its superior arms, orders, and virtue.

The Prince is written to demonstrate the insufficiency of Jesus Christ, the Prince of Peace, as a model for human life. Machiavelli's commendation of the prince of war, which occurs at the center point of the book, is important evidence of this effort.[4] Yet the strongest evidence of Machiavelli's anti-Christian plan consists in his repeated contradictions of the New Testament and his critical allusions to the life and teachings of Christ. While not every opinion contained in *The Prince* is intended to contravene Christ's commandments, the cumulative effect of Machiavelli's persistent and "destructive analysis" of Christian virtue constitutes compelling evidence of his anti-Christian plan.[5] His biting critique of the Church corresponds to his devastating judgment of Christ, but is not identical with that judgment.

Machiavelli communicates hostility toward Christ and his Church that is difficult to reconcile with the notion that he adheres to some variety of Christianity. Efforts to protect Machiavelli from the charge of radical impiety have been largely unconvincing. The claim that Machiavelli, in thrall to the muddled religious world of Renaissance theology, was unaware of the anti-Christian nature of his teachings is not credible; neither Machiavelli's principal sources, nor the passages that allegedly demonstrate his belief in supernatural occurrences, nor contemporary accounts of his character and writings, nor the early reception of his books support this thesis. The claim that ardent patriotism led Machiavelli to critique the religion that he otherwise loved also encounters important difficulties. First, *The Prince* demonstrates that Machiavelli's love of Florence and Italy is attenuated by his attraction to ancient men and adulterated by his withering appraisal of contemporary Italy. Interpreters who excuse his impiety by citing his patriotism cast the man who claims "I do not judge nor shall I ever judge it to be a defect to defend any opinion with reasons, without wishing to use either authority or force for it" (*D* I.58.1) as a mere provincial. Contrary to the claims of many recent interpreters, there exists no evidence in either *The Prince* or the *Discourses* that Machiavelli sought to rescue "true" Christianity from false interpreters who had corrupted Christ's orders. This book has demonstrated that each time Machiavelli appears to defer to Christianity's *datore*—including especially in chapter 2 of book 2 of the *Discourses*—an examination of the text with reference to the New Testament reveals his profound anti-Christian animus. More than anything else, Machiavelli seeks a worldly, violent, and manly founder. In his view, Christ is ethereal, pacific, and effeminate; even worse, he encourages his followers to be the same. One must labor strenuously to cast Machiavelli as a Christian—or Christ as a militant patriot. In sum, neither Machiavelli's alleged patriotism, nor his alleged obeisance to Renaissance theology, nor his several feints concerning the renovation of Christianity exonerates him from the charge of grave impiety.

Those who claim that Machiavelli's true concern is the resuscitation of pagan or classical virtue ought to consider more carefully the link between this affinity and Machiavelli's anti-Christian political thought. By assessing Machiavelli's judgment of how to read ancient political thought—on display in his commentary on Livy, Polybius, and Herodian, and to be discerned especially by his explicit statements regarding Xenophon—one can begin to see why Machiavelli prefers to comment on Roman histories rather than Greek philosophy. While Roman historians often require a Machiavellian corrective, their relatively staid presentations of ancient history are not so susceptible to corruption by Christian writers as the imagined principalities and princes created by Plato, Aristotle, and even Xenophon. One might add that many of the Roman histories, including the *Historia Augusta*, shed unedifying light on Christianity's origins. The comparative beauty of Greek philosophy made it an attractive object for appropriation by Christian writers. One ought to consider: to what degree did Christianity's appropriation of classical thought taint those sources of ancient wisdom, thereby diminishing their utility to Machiavelli?

Machiavelli conspires against Christianity because he thinks that it serves to retard human progress: it directs people to chimerical other-worldly concerns, thereby encouraging idleness and intensifying poverty; it instructs them to forgo a spirited defense of their lives and possessions, thereby giving license to petty criminals; it enervates the virtues required for civil society and human flourishing. Reading *The Prince* alongside the New Testament supports the argument that Machiavelli identifies Christianity's defects with those of its founder, rather than any subsequent "interpreters" (*D* II.2.2). By remaining attuned to Machiavelli's artful critique, one sees that more than any other actor—including the Church, the hapless princes of Christendom, or the decadent Roman Empire—Jesus Christ is to be blamed for "these corrupt centuries of ours" (*D* II.19.1). His damaging example necessitates a new model.

Why Tyranny? A "Kingly Hand" and the Miasma of Christianity

The founders of chapter 6 are the preeminent models of political and religious action. Yet by creatively appropriating the examples of other ancient men—especially Hiero, Agathocles, Philopoemen, Hannibal, Severus, and Philip V of Macedon—Machiavelli establishes a rich array of anti-Christian models that princes of lesser excellence and lesser ambition might imitate. This does not mean that Machiavelli abandons his famous devotion to republics, of which his identification with Philopoemen and his persistent praise of Romulus are perhaps sufficient proof. Machiavelli surely appeals to ardent defenders of republicanism, but *The Prince* privileges the rule of one man—and for good reasons.

First, Machiavelli appeals to ambitious princes and tyrants because his observations suggest that their transgressive and spirited natures might inure them to the siren song of Christian piety. With their spirits thus armed, they will be equipped to mount a transformative war that will culminate in a new founding. Machiavelli confirms the superior resiliency and foresight of spirited individuals in his covert critique of the Roman Republic's conduct in Greece, where by transforming itself into an empire, it extirpated the free way of life in that province. Machiavelli's various comments on Greece reveal conclusively that the efforts of a single wise and spirited man were Greece's best defense against the encroaching Roman Empire. Both Philopoemen and Philip V of Macedon were capable of detecting Rome's threat, yet only the increasingly tyrannical and always mistrustful Philip succeeded in preserving nominal autonomy from Rome. That he did so by employing a brutality that betrayed no "pious respect" confirms that he is a particularly helpful model for modern princes beset by Roman calls to adhere to the faith.[6] Indeed, by encouraging modern princes to imitate Philip in chapter 24, Machiavelli seeks a prince with a spirit capable of accomplishing the "enterprise" that the tyrant Giovampagolo Baglioni failed to carry out: to "crush" the heads of the ecclesiastical order (*D* I.27.2).

Second, the corruption engendered by Christianity, which assumed the mantle of the already corrupted Roman Empire, means that contemporary Europeans—and especially Italians—lack the stuff of republican governance. Republics require virtuous peoples, and many even more virtuous captains. In the *Discourses*, Machiavelli repeatedly and pointedly identifies the corruption of contemporary Europe with the ascendancy of Christianity as a political and spiritual power. *The Prince* seconds this judgment dramatically: Machiavelli cites no Christian prince or captain as an unqualified success, and indeed, almost all are ridiculous failures. The ascendancy of Christ's Church coincided with a decline in arms, which are the essential precondition for a free way of life; and the effeminate Italian republics that linger on find themselves at the mercy of mercenaries who exhibit a dangerous combination of fecklessness and grandiose ambition. The republican Christianity that some identify with Italy's political salvation is, in fact, a symptom of Italy's corruption. It is "a country without dams and without any dike"—a country without virtue (*P* 25). Those who judge Machiavelli as resolutely republican may divine Machiavelli's political sentiments, but they do not consider adequately the chief implication of the severe corruption that he observes in Italy and Europe: redeeming a corrupt province like Christendom requires a "kingly power" (*D* I.18.5) capable of making it "reborn with many dangers and much blood" (*D* I.17.3). Nor should one conclude that patriotism forbids this judgment: love of one's fatherland often coincides with the harshest judgments of its corruption. Indeed, Machiavelli loves his fatherland so much that he awaits its bloody earthly redemption as eagerly as faithful

Christians await "the Son of Man coming on the clouds of heaven, with power and great glory."[7]

The necessity of a new founding for Christendom largely explains Machiavelli's appeal to potential tyrants. Founders must act alone, at the head of their "own arms" (*P* 26), in order to destroy existing orders and thereby redeem a corrupt province.[8] From the perspective of the status quo, these men are indistinguishable from criminals.[9] Machiavelli appeals directly to ambitious men with criminal spirits; he intimates that despite their criminality, they might secure glorious reputations by successfully founding new modes and orders amid the pulverized rubble of Christianity. Indeed, Machiavelli's reading of history confirms that only such grand criminals can reliably secure such vaulting glory.

Yet the most important anti-Christian model in *The Prince* is Machiavelli himself. He assembles and presents models for men and especially princes; though uniformly ancient, he uses these examples to suit his purposes, thereby rendering them new. Indeed, like Christ, he orchestrates a conspiracy to make everything new, while armed with words alone. To punctuate this blasphemy, by the end of the book he even assumes the role of Moses's God, encouraging an unchristian redeemer to don the cloak of prophecy and found a new order in Italy.

In doing these things, Machiavelli presents himself as a model for subsequent philosophers, who might imitate his decision to apply "judicious" (*D* III.30.1) and "continuous reading" (*P* DL) of ancient histories to this-worldly problems. They might continue his project to found and propagate a new education, based on a true knowledge of histories and the study of the "the nature of sites" (*P* 14)—which aim to make men "better knower[s] of the world" (*D* III.31.4). Christ teaches his followers that "you do not belong to the world": since Machiavelli judges that this education is "weak and vain" (*D* III.31.3), and largely responsible for the decline of prosperity, martial virtue, liberty, and general human excellence, he opposes it with an exhortation to practice science and study history.[10] By insisting that a new education—based largely on the wisdom of the ancients, but directed more energetically to worldly causes—is necessary to correct the corruption of his times, Machiavelli attempts to create the fundamental precondition for truly republican orders: a truly virtuous education.

Finally, the moral and political revolution that Machiavelli envisions in *The Prince* cannot be accomplished without either the destruction of the Catholic Church or its subjection to earthly powers. Either accomplishment would signal the end of the Church's quasi-universal influence, but the former exploit is the surest remedy to Europe's political ills. Even if a new pope and college of cardinals were to spring from the Bride of Christ's bleeding corpse, a notable example of ecclesiasticide would prove that the Church is not sacred and inviolable—and that earthly powers have ultimate recourse against its pious charms. It would demonstrate to everyone "how little is to be esteemed whoever lives and reigns as they do" (*D* I.27.2). Therefore, at several points in *The Prince*, Machiavelli intimates what is required to destroy the Church. Mere Italian patriotism does not lead Machiavelli to encourage this result; nor is he moved especially by the particularly fetid corruption of the contemporary ecclesiastical order. Indeed, his assessment of the reign of the most successful Christian prince, Ferdinand of Aragon, confirms that unpalatable fruits attend Christian rule even—or especially—under "good" popes like Leo X: among these are the persecution of minorities, the triumph of ignorance, the rule of petty criminals, and the enervation of civil society—a judgment confirmed by his implicit comparison of the Catholic Church to the decadent Roman Empire in chapter 19.

Spain's interdependent relationship with the Church reminds one that the destruction of the Church would amount to the radical reformation of European politics, since it would banish Christianity from political decision-making, and create the preconditions for a freer and more innovative civil society. Machiavelli encourages an assault on Catholic Italy in the closing chapters of *The Prince* because he judges it to be the surest way to accomplish this salutary reform. The defeat of the chief bastion of *pietà* would weaken Spain's most effective—and destructive—weapon: "pious cruelty" (*P* 21).

La Carità Propria and the Making of the Modern World

Yet perhaps because he harbors doubts about his ability to attract a man of requisite badness from the ranks of Christian princes, Machiavelli also offers a plan for covert spiritual warfare against the Vatican. One could also use this strategy to undermine Christ's teaching more directly. In his discussion of unarmed principalities, he suggests that by encouraging "charity for their own [*la carità propria*]" (*P* 10), rather than charity for their fellow man, a prince might not only breed dissension within a besieged Vatican, but also induce Christians in general to abandon freely the life of self-sacrifice and patient suffering that Christ enjoins, and that so few Christians actually practice.[11] This spiritual warfare is perhaps even more dangerous to Christ's legacy than an armed assault on the Vatican: because it is a plan to increase the common benefit, it creates no martyrs. Because it appeals to men's constant and universal desires for "glories and riches" (*P* 25), it corrupts surreptitiously men's appreciation of Christ's mortifying example of self-sacrifice. In doing so, Machiavelli imitates Christ's corruptive appropriation of Moses: while Christ sought to render Moses's people meek and effeminate, Machiavelli seeks to render Christians lovers of money and glory.

The history of early modernity vindicates the appeal of this strategy: the irrepressible appeal of scientific and economic progress—which was under way in Machiavelli's lifetime, but would blossom fully in the following centuries—compelled Christianity to conform increasingly to a life of material prosperity and comfortable self-preservation that modernity embraced. In the theological world, this first entailed a rebellion against the authority of the Catholic Church; later, it required theological arguments more friendly to wealth and a more forward defense of good earthly government.[12] In the philosophical world, Machiavelli's works commence a grand project to render otherworldly Christian principles consistent with worldly reason; Bacon, Hobbes, and Locke are among the first to engage in this project. Their various appropriations of the New Testament adapt—and thereby corrupt—Christ's teachings in notable ways.[13]

Machiavelli's anti-Christian orders encourage men to value this world, rather than the next. These orders require men to care more for their material condition than for their souls. I take this to be the truest meaning of Machiavelli's confession that "I love my native city more than my own soul."[14] For followers who might bring his plan to completion, Machiavelli seeks the strong, healthy, and proud, rather than the weak, sick, and humble sought by Christ. Unlike Christ, who commends patient suffering, Machiavelli seeks to encourage those with audacious spirits to work assiduously to exploit fortune's floods for the common benefit. With his wisdom, he seeks to empower these men in their attempts to conquer their world. This prescription for the union of power, wisdom, and daring is identical with the beginning of the modern world. Attention to Machiavelli's *The Prince* demonstrates most clearly that this transformation to modernity requires the rejection and the overcoming of the example of Jesus Christ.

Notes

Introduction

1.   Unless otherwise noted, excerpts of Machiavelli's *Discourses on Livy* (1996) are from Harvey C. Mansfield and Nathan Tarcov's translation (hereafter cited in text as *D*). In this passage (*D* I.12.1), it is unclear whether Machiavelli is referring to the Church, Christianity, or both.

2.   Matthew 16:24–26; Mark 8:34; Luke 9:23. All biblical passages are drawn from the New International Version, unless otherwise noted. Throughout, I have consulted the Greek, Latin, and Italian versions of the Bible where appropriate.

3.   Machiavelli strays twice from his condemnation of the Church and its teaching (*D* II.2.2; *D* III.1.4). While these vacillations are often cited as evidence of his hope that Christianity might be politically useful (see esp. Viroli 2010), I argue in chapter 1 that each passage actually demonstrates the impossibility of a truly Christian renewal.

4.   Sullivan's (1996) work is the leading representative of the first approach; de Grazia's (1994), Parel's (1992), Nederman's (2009), and Viroli's (2010) works advance the latter arguments, or some combination thereof.

5.   This line of interpretation, pursued most famously by Strauss (1958), Mansfield (1996), and de Alvarez (2008), is considered below. After a series of careful equivocations (1958, 9–12), Strauss concludes that this interpretation of Machiavelli, while important to consider seriously, is insufficient. Instead, a "considerate ascent from [this traditional opinion] leads to the core of Machiavelli's thought" (13; cf. 295). Hulliung (1983, 56 and 168) deems Machiavelli unchristian, but obviously so: he rejects Strauss's approach as an "overly subtle search for covert significations" (1983, 239).

6.   Machiavelli 1988b, "Niccolò Machiavelli to Francesco Vettori," December 10, 1513. Xenophon deserves particular attention: he is the only ancient thinker to whose works Machiavelli explicitly refers the reader in *The Prince*, doing so in chapter 14. Yet as an anonymous reviewer suggested, Moses, David, Virgil, Marcus Aurelius, and Petrarch—all authors of significant works— also are named by Machiavelli. For an exhaustive and judicious account of Machiavelli's likely influences, see Rahe 2009; cf. Benner 2009; Brown 2010b; and Palmer 2014, 81–88. Benner (2013, xix–xxix) offers a helpful and brief account of Machiavelli's life and times, but Connell (2005, 1–31) especially highlights the disturbing novelty of Machiavelli's book; for a general biography see Ridolfi 1963.

7. Unless otherwise noted, excerpts of Machiavelli's *The Prince* (1998) are from
    Harvey C. Mansfield's translation (hereafter cited in text as *P*); *P* 15; see also
    D I.P.2. Hulliung (1983, 175) condemns this trope as evidence of Machia-
    velli's tendency for "myopic polemics."
8. Machiavelli's presumed private attitudes toward religion are beyond the
    scope of this study; the evidence concerning his belief is fragmentary and cir-
    cumstantial, but those who are interested in this question ought to compare
    Brown (2010a, 164–65) with de Grazia (1994, 58–59, and 89).
9. Bacon, *Advancement of Learning* II.21.9. The italicized passage is drawn from
    Proverbs 18:2. By writing of the combination of "serpentine wisdom with the
    columbine innocency," Bacon refers obliquely to Matthew 10:16.
10. Bacon, *Advancement of Learning* II.21.9. Bacon's provocative allusion to
    Matthew 10:16 prompts one to ask: who is the fool? Is it he who possesses
    a "corrupted mind" or he who evinces "columbine innocency"? Both men,
    according to this argument, lack understanding. By associating Christlike
    innocence with folly, as condemned in Proverbs, Bacon responds to Erasmus,
    who praises Christ for his childlike folly—exhibited most clearly in his lack of
    worldliness (Erasmus 1688, 58–60).
11. Whitfield 1947, 62.
12. The former view is most famously elaborated by Gilbert (1938), Pocock
    (1975a), Skinner (2000), and Viroli (2010). The latter view is proposed by,
    among others, Mansfield (1996), McIntosh (1984), Hariman (1989), Forde
    (1992 and 1995), and Patapan (2006). Hulliung (1983, 158–66) denies that
    Machiavelli is a realist, but also offers (24) a pithy critique of Gilbert's (1938)
    identification of Machiavelli with Christianity.
13. A full elaboration of this debate is beyond the scope of this project; in any
    case, much has already been written on this subject: see Rahe 2009 and
    McCormick 2003 and 2011a (8–11) for recent appraisals of this debate.
14. Mansfield 1975a and 1975b. There are, however, important differences
    between Mansfield's and Strauss's presentations. While Strauss's (1958)
    account ruminates on the ambiguities of Machiavelli's intentions and the
    problematic implications of his project, Mansfield (1975b and 1996) tends
    to resolve those ambiguities, and offers a much more forceful—and slightly
    more friendly—exposition of Machiavellian political thought. See Pocock
    1975b (385–401) for a pointed critique of Strauss, Mansfield, and the Strauss-
    ian approach to Machiavelli.
15. For these reasons, Cambridge school scholarship on Machiavelli tends to be
    grounded in a comparatively broader reading of Machiavelli's works: while
    the Straussians, looking to Machiavelli's own pronouncements (*D* DL; *P* DL)
    that the *Discourses* and *The Prince* are his most comprehensive works, tend
    to focus on these two books, representatives of the Cambridge school are
    far more likely to turn to Machiavelli's minor works, including his private
    correspondence and poetical works, to explain his intentions. Viroli (1990,
    1998, 2010, and 2014), whose works reflect an encyclopedic knowledge of
    Machiavelli's writings, is the signal scholar in this regard. Nederman (2009,
    viii–ix) also observes this characteristic of the literature. Yet as Nathan Tarcov
    (1982, 693) observes, this method "assumes that the historian is *more* able

to construct a consistent doctrine than the thinker he studies." Despite the Straussians' general tendency to hew to *The Prince* and the *Discourses*, many are quite familiar with Machiavelli's minor works and private letters and believe, moreover, that they can help one understand Machiavelli's political thought. See, for example, Mansfield 1996, 289; and Strauss 1958, 193, 223–25, 241, and 285–86.

16.   Indeed, there appears to be much evidence in support of this view in *The Prince* (see Pocock 1975a; Dietz 1986; Skinner 2000 and 2002; McCormick 2011a). As I shall argue below, however, I judge that these apparently patriotic passages actually reveal a deep hostility to Italian politics, as practiced in the Florentine republic and throughout Italy.

17.   See esp. Strauss 1958; Mansfield 1996; and Sullivan 1996.

18.   Pocock (1975a, 158) casts it as a "mere typology of innovators and their relationships to *fortuna*" (cf. Hale [1961, 23; quoted in Hulliung 1983, 25], who notes that "because of its formal resemblance to old manuals . . . , Machiavelli's *Prince* was like a bomb in a prayer-book"; cf. Gilbert's (1939) more subdued claim of *The Prince*'s novelty); Skinner (2001, 28) views the book as a job application—despite the fact that the book was not published widely until after Machiavelli had died, long after it would have been useful to him in that regard (cf., however, Machiavelli 1988b, "Niccolò Machiavelli to Francesco Vettori," December 10, 1513, 143); and Benner (2013, xxi–xxii) regards it as a "masterwork of ironic writing with a moral purpose." Skinner's view is perhaps the most representative of the Cambridge school. Dietz (1986) confronts the protyrannical elements of *The Prince* more directly, and concludes that Machiavelli's apparent support of tyranny is, in fact, evidence of a conspiracy against tyrants, in the name of Italian republicanism. See also McCormick 2011a. Cf. Tarcov 2007, which offers a carefully qualified account of the prorepublican character of *The Prince*.

19.   I am indebted to Alexander Duff, who suggested this framework in response to a presentation of an early draft of this work.

20.   See esp. Mansfield 1996 (4–5), Rahe 2009 (86), Palmer 2001, and Patapan 2006, 91.

21.   In his seminal book, Strauss (1958, 13) claims that Machiavelli's "diabolical" teaching is aimed at pupils who live outside the Florentine and Italian communities, and represents an important—and bold—break with the politico-philosophical tradition that preceded him. He notes (68–69) that both *The Prince* and the *Discourses* feature a damning critique of the Church and its deleterious effects on Italy; each encourages (78) men to abandon the Christian teaching concerning human nature, in favor of an understanding taught covertly by ancient writers; and each offers (176; 186) an account of religion as an instrumental, rather than an intrinsic, good. Strauss identifies Machiavelli's project as predicated on "post-Christian" reason, describing it as a "war of anti-Christ or the devil . . . against the army led by God or Christ" (171). He identifies (286–94) Machiavelli's instruction on the requirements of successful founding—and the revision of virtue a founding necessarily entails—as the crucial contribution of *The Prince*. While Strauss praises Machiavelli's elegance and insight, his final judgment of Machiavelli

is, nonetheless, ambivalent (295)—constituting what Hancock (2000, 47) describes as an "ultimately deconstructive appreciation."

Mansfield (1996, 4) notes that Machiavelli's "anti-Christian presumption" informs his political philosophy—and his reform of virtue, in particular. Like Strauss, Mansfield (1996, 280; see also Mansfield 1979, 27) considers that Machiavelli's innovations are responsible for many of the horrors of the twentieth century, and seems to alternate between approbation and condemnation of Machiavelli's project. Mansfield's scholarship (1979, 194–96) attends especially to Machiavelli's judgment of Christianity's deleterious effects on modern men and concludes that Machiavelli's project is identical with a conspiracy against Christianity, identified as the "malignity of the times" (*D* 1.P.2; Mansfield 1979, 27). See also Orwin 1978, which presents a brief, but excellent, elaboration of this thesis.

In several articles (see esp. Tarcov 2000, 2006, 2013a, 2014, and forthcoming) on Machiavelli's thought, Tarcov addresses most directly Machiavelli's critique of Christianity and Christ. He judges (2000, 30) that "before [Machiavelli] can lay the foundations of *our* modernity, he must overturn the foundations of *his* modernity, the theology, morality, and politics of his at least nominally Christian world." He explicates (2006, 82–86) how Machiavelli replaces divine providence with the concept of fortune, which connotes a world in which "amoral prudence and an order of variability" are sovereign (85). His exhaustive account (2013b) of Machiavelli's use of the personal pronoun in *The Prince* doubles as a pithy and valuable presentation of Machiavelli's core teachings, many of which contradict important Christian precepts (see esp. 2013b, 108, 110, and 113). Tarcov (2014, 213) summarizes Machiavelli's approach to Christianity thus: "His praise of the Christian religion enables him to criticize the church; his praise of a patriotic Christian religion enables him to criticize actually existing Christianity; and his praises of Moses and David, of pagan religion, and of religion in general further enable him to criticize the Christian religion and to conceal his critique of religion in general and his praise of radical human self-reliance." Tarcov nonetheless judges that Machiavelli also contemplates a radical reinterpretation of Christianity, and "aspire[s] through his writing to replace the classical and biblical writers in ruling over ordinary princes" (forthcoming).

According to de Alvarez (2008, vii, 140), Machiavelli's book represents a clarion "call for spiritual warfare." Although de Alvarez is not usually considered a Straussian, his account of Christianity in *The Prince* imitates Strauss's inscrutable style. Consider the following illustrative example. In his discussion of chapter 19, de Alvarez (2008, 99) intimates that Machiavelli most clearly reveals his plan for the Church in his discussion of the Turks and Cyrus. Yet rather than elaborate the implications of this discovery, de Alvarez ends with a leading question: "May not *The Prince* as a whole be thought of as reasoning about Cyrus?" (99). Hence, while de Alvarez's work is the most thorough treatment of *The Prince* to date, his laconic style leaves work remaining for subsequent scholars.

Rahe (2009, 86–99) and Palmer (2001) also address directly Machiavelli's judgment of Christ and the weakness his teachings engender. Like many of the Straussian political theorists, the historian Rahe (2009, 56) concludes that Machiavelli is engaged in an "elaborate program" that is hostile to Christianity. Looking to Machiavelli's familiar account of the political devastation wrought by Christianity and the Church, he concludes that the Florentine seeks to have "the Christian religion radically reinterpreted or replaced" (92). Palmer's (2001, 80) brief summary of *The Prince* argues that Machiavelli is an "atheist" who is "more anti-Christian than antipapist, anticlerical, or antireligion; above all, he is radically anti-Christ." Palmer's pithy article sketches the main contours of Machiavelli's anti-Christian argument in *The Prince*. His excellent and provocative undergraduate lectures inform my own inquiry, and constitute the original impetus for this study. Of thinkers within this group, Mansfield (1996, 4.), Rahe (2009, 86), Palmer (2001), and Patapan (2006, 91) most clearly address Machiavelli's critique of Christ.

22.   Strauss 1958; Sullivan 1996. Like Strauss, Tarcov (esp. 2000, 2006, and 2014) combines both of these perspectives—as does Rahe (2009, 92), in a more limited way. While Sullivan acknowledges that Machiavelli contemplates the destruction of the Church in *The Prince*, she also suggests that Machiavelli undertakes a project to reinterpret Christianity to serve his own political ends (1996, 40). Thus, she argues that Machiavelli seeks to subvert Christian teachings in order to reform—and secularize—the corrupt politics of his time. According to her, the central innovation of this temporal Christianity is Machiavelli's recommendation to exercise cruelty against the young ambitious men of the republic. This cruelty is necessary to guarantee the republic's liberty, and fulfill the "grandiose promise" of a "perpetual republic" (Sullivan 1996, 154; *D* III.22.3). Sullivan claims that Machiavelli, rather than draw divine inspiration from the example of Christ's life (as did Saints Dominic and Francis), looks to Christ's death for political inspiration. Just as humans were granted eternal life through Christ's death, a republic may be made perpetual by the timely deaths of its most ambitious sons (see also Beiner 2011, 43–44). Particularly valuable are Sullivan's ruminations on the ambiguity of Machiavelli's ultimate intentions regarding the Church and Christianity: wondering whether Machiavelli hopes that a man might arise to "slaughter the idle and rich rulers of the Church," or if his more modest hope is to harden the hearts of the perennially deceived Italians against the pious machinations of the Church and its surrogates (1996, 131), she concludes that "on this particular question, it is difficult to say what practical effects Machiavelli intended" (131). See Sullivan 1996 (121) for the quintessential statement of this ambiguity in Machiavelli's writing on Christianity.

Fontana (1999) advances a less equivocal thesis. He recognizes Machiavelli's critique of Christianity's unworldly character, but concludes that he aims to transform Christianity into a politically vigorous religion, which operates in the "sphere of human *virtù* and human activity" (652). Fontana's artful comparison of Moses and Christ (652–54) reveals important dimensions of Machiavelli's critique of Christianity; he asserts: "That such a reinterpretation will vitiate the original principles of the founder does not concern Machiavelli" (654). Cf. Beiner 2011, 19–20.

Hulliung criticizes much of the existing scholarship for its "misplaced determination to prevent Machiavelli's thought from being the scandal he intended it to be" (1983, ix). He judges that Machiavelli is unchristian, but nonetheless "hoped to absorb Christianity into a new paganism" (208) that would culminate in a "Machiavellian ruler, preferably Florentine by birth, wearing papal robes" (207). Machiavelli's many amoral lessons are thus intended to liberate the "incipient power politics of ancient pagan culture" (228) from the shackles of classical philosophy and Christianity. Hulliung's book is distinguished by its unequivocal rejection of the notion that Machiavelli was some sort of Christian: "[Machiavelli's] anticlericalism . . . marks only the first layer of his condemnation of Christianity. . . . Machiavelli generalized his disdain for the prelates to the point of naming Christianity in general, the Christianity that is true to its values no less than the overtly corrupt Christianity of the papacy, as a general cause underlying the phenomenon of Italian corruption" (66; cf. 227). Hulliung thus concludes that for Machiavelli, "Christian virtue is not *virtù*; it is the very opposite, its corruption" (67). Compare both Hulliung 1983 and Sullivan 1996 with Germino's (1972, 42–43) less radical thesis: "At the most [Machiavelli] seeks to supplement the morality of the gospel with the martial vigor of Ancient Rome" (43).

Rahe (2009, 92) and McCormick (2011b) also contemplate whether Machiavelli might intend to radically revise and thereby appropriate Christianity. While Rahe thinks Machiavelli hostile to Christianity, in his brief article on *The Prince*, McCormick (2011b, 1) indicates that he is skeptical of scholars who interpret Machiavelli as anti-Christian. Instead, he locates in *The Prince* high praise of the theological politics of Christianity, concluding that the book is pregnant with religious imagery that suggests the political utility of Christianity, properly utilized (15–18).

Korvela's (2006) study of Machiavelli's relationship to Christianity is also worth noting. In a dissertation published online by his university, Korvela (5; see also 75–83 and 152) notes that Machiavelli's aim was to "interpret Christianity in such a way that it would exalt this life over the other"; however, unlike Viroli (2010) and de Grazia (1994), Korvela recognizes that this effort subverts "the very essence of that religion" (11; see also 144). Korvela's study is a competent evaluation of much of the literature that articulates the tension between Christ's teachings and Machiavelli's, but it makes few original observations regarding Machiavelli's texts.

23. According to Pocock's (1975a, 193–94) strikingly dismissive account of Christianity in Machiavelli's thought, the faith is counterproductive to republican virtue: Pocock finds in Machiavelli's works a full-throated endorsement of pagan civil religion, which seeks to support political life, free of the enervating effects of otherworldly concerns (213–18). Despite the shocking implications of this argument, Pocock generally deemphasizes Machiavelli's novelty: because he thinks that Machiavelli's general republican philosophy is consonant with that of the Atlantic republican tradition, Machiavelli's harsh judgment of Christianity's failures is rendered less problematic (cf. Viroli 2010, 23–24).

Skinner's (2001) efforts to situate Machiavelli's thought in the context of civic humanism also tends to mute the anti-Christian elements of Machiavelli's thought, of which Skinner is nonetheless aware (2001, 42; 2002, 180–83). Thus, while he recognizes the gulf between Machiavelli's teaching and Christian teaching, he chooses to emphasize the importance of Machiavelli's agreement with neopagan civic humanists, rather than his break with the dominant religion of the day. According to Skinner, Machiavelli is a "neo-Roman theorist" who identifies the superior political utility of pagan religions (2002, 184); Skinner eschews a searching consideration of the gulf between Machiavelli's recommendation and the religious status quo. As Nathan Tarcov (1982, 708) trenchantly observes, "Skinner is less interested in Machiavelli's contradicting the Bible, Plato, or us, than his contradicting Pontano or Patrizi [two minor Italian thinkers]." Cf. Sullivan 1996, 162–71. See also McCormick 2011a (8–11) for a succinct critique of the weaknesses of this approach.

Berlin's (1979) searching examination of Machiavelli's intention defies easy categorization. He ruminates on the ambiguity of Machiavelli's attitude toward Christianity, and ultimately concludes that Machiavelli opposes pagan virtue and the ends of classical republicanism with Christian virtue and its lofty ends, and endorses the former as attainable, but not necessarily superior (1979, 54–55 and 57–58). Berlin notes Machiavelli's novelty (36) and claims that Machiavelli believed that "no satisfactory human community" (45) could be constructed upon Christian principles, but also claims that Machiavelli held that certain Christian virtues remain good, despite their lack of utility (46): hence, "he rejects the rival scale—the Christian principles of *ozio* and meekness—not, indeed, as defective in itself, but as inapplicable to the conditions of real life" (57). By the aid of such careful distinctions, Berlin casts Machiavelli as primarily concerned with the restoration of Italy than with the destruction of the Christian order.

Najemy's (1999) judgment resembles Berlin's careful appraisal, concluding "that the reason for the diversity, brevity, and even elusiveness of [Machiavelli's] statements about the Christian faith was not some secret plan to undermine it or even replace it with a new religion but deep ambivalence about both Christianity and religion in general, a conflictedness which made him sometimes skeptical and sometimes hostile but which never permitted him to make a formal break with the religious culture that surrounded him" (664). He nonetheless notes that Machiavelli's approach to religion seems "comparative and almost anthropological" (668), and that his goal is the interpretation of Christianity according to necessity, or virtue (680–81). In concluding thus, he resolves the productive tension at the core of Berlin's (1979) essay.

24.   Brown 2010b, 5–12. Brown acknowledges that Machiavelli was not "typically devout" (2010b, 81), and attributes his heterodoxy to the influence of Lucretius (2010b, vii–viii; 2010a, 160; see also Palmer's [2014, 86] analysis of the marginalia found in copies of Lucretius's text, which leads her to a more reserved judgment of Machiavelli's heterodoxy), along with other sources of ancient wisdom that became available in the Renaissance (2010b, 66; see

also 44–51 and 68–87). Brown's attempt to chart Lucretius's influence on Machiavelli's thought is largely convincing. Unlike many in the Cambridge school, she is attuned to the "fact that religion was seen to be an impediment to humanist studies" (2010b, 5), and reveals how Christian belief was often strained or subverted by adherence to ancient philosophy. Like Parel, Brown thinks that "Machiavelli accepted the important role played by astrology in our lives" (2010b, 85), but nonetheless judges that Lucretius's influence led him to endorse a notion of free will consistent with the Epicurean's claim that a "swerve of atoms within a materialistic world" (85) can alter the course of nature. For Machiavelli's exceptional interest in Lucretian atomism, see Palmer 2014, 85–87.

25. De Grazia acknowledges Machiavelli's anticlericalism (1994, 4), but unlike most scholars, he thinks that Machiavelli "does not disapprove of the church's temporal power; he disapproves of the inept use of it" (1994, 92; see also 103–4 and 119–20). Hence, *The Prince* culminates, according to de Grazia, in a call for a heroic "messianic new prince" (1994, 152 and 235–36) to redeem Italy with the help of a reinvigorated Church (171 and 382) and the "friendship of God" (51), a term de Grazia locates in the long history of Christian theology and the broader Western tradition (50–53), but especially in the person of Moses (56).

For de Grazia, Machiavelli and God are naturally friends: Machiavelli loves Italy (1994, 144–46), while "God favors country" (194). Both do so because "country ultimately seeks the common good" (194), which is furthered by the organization into a community of "rational brutes hell-bent for ruin" (270). De Grazia is unfazed by the unchristian implications of Machiavelli's claim that the "greatest good that one can do is that which one does for one's country" (quoted in de Grazia 1994, 268; cf., for example, John 15:13). Indeed, he views much of Machiavelli's immoral advice as a regrettable necessity—or a consequence of living among "rational brutes," whose management compels a new prince to adopt the "rhetoric of imposture" (1994, 296; but see also 280–317), a term that de Grazia attempts to distinguish from deceit (302).

Because de Grazia's God exhibits "secular favoritism" (1994, 382), the new prince's unchristian behavior is an impediment neither to glory nor to heaven (terms de Grazia [308] conflates). While de Grazia recognizes that Machiavelli subverts the Golden Rule (299–302), he defends its subversion as necessary: de Grazia characterizes Jesus's second most important law (Matthew 22:36–40) as a "forlorn hope" (299–300) that works only in dreams; hence, de Grazia casually endorses Machiavelli's "un-Golden rule" (299) of canny suspicion and violent preemption.

While de Grazia concedes that some doubted Machiavelli's piety, he denies that he was ever "accused of impiety" (1994, 4). Instead, Machiavelli's "many references to God" (58) constitute evidence of the Florentine's belief; indeed, de Grazia identifies in Machiavelli's discussion of God a "conventional reverent attitude" (59). Machiavelli's "Exhortation to Penitence," a work written for a religious confraternity, provides important evidence of this piety (58–61; see also 115; cf., however, Mansfield 1975b, 375; and Ciliotta-Rubery 1997 [22–26, 31–33, and 39–40], which persuasively problematizes

Machiavelli's apparently pious argument in the *Exhortation*). De Grazia thus concludes: "For Niccolò, all religions great and small are false; the exception is Christianity" (1994, 89; cf. Ciliotta-Rubery 1997, 17).

Yet de Grazia's Machiavelli is an unorthodox Christian: he believes promiscuously in God, saints, spirits, astral forces, and fortune's wheel (1994, 69 and 208–16). Traditional Christian ethics are also strained by de Grazia's interpretation: he argues that Machiavelli's "new ethics" (315)—which recommend cruelty and faithlessness—lend a prince "greater moral confidence. It liberates him from the hobbling morality of the princely rule-book writers. Viewing the good qualities as merely apparent goods and as means to an end, he will learn to choose the proper good. He will be more truly religious than the sanctimonious. Though nothing but compassion, good faith, and religion pass his lips, in truth he is not playing false" (316; cf. Fontana 1999, 640). Only de Grazia's poeticized and sophistic presentation of Christianity permits this conclusion.

De Grazia's license also leads him to revise hell. While the people might still fear hell as a manifestation of their fear of God (324; but cf. 383–84), heroes—or those who love their country more than their soul—have nothing to fear. For them, "Hell is an exclusive club" (323) "for real men alone" (339 and 348). Italy's redeemer "must enter into evil and risk his soul," and so de Grazia's Machiavelli relieves heroes of the fear that Christ encourages (see, for example, Matthew 10:28): whatever their crimes, God's true friends will "gain immediate access to heaven" (356; cf. Korvela 2006, 108).

De Grazia gives relatively equal weight to all of Machiavelli's writings, yet he considers neither Machiavelli's text nor the New Testament with particular care (see, for example, 1994, 100). Most importantly, he often neglects the context of Machiavelli's claims—especially those regarding the divine and the supernatural (see 79–80; compare 1994, 65, with *D* I.56). The result is a largely poetical and inferential account of Machiavelli's thought (1994; see esp. God's alleged gift of free will, 87; Machiavelli's alleged belief in Christian saints, 100–101; de Grazia's attribution of "the idea of fall" to Machiavelli, 265–66; de Grazia's account of Machiavellian heroes, 359; and Machiavelli's alleged receipt of grace, 372). Too often, *Machiavelli in Hell* (1994) sacrifices Machiavelli's precision and clarity on the altar of de Grazia's concepts of patriotism and religion.

Nederman (2009) insists that "Machiavelli's writings—most especially that supposedly irreligious tract, the *Prince*—embrace the medieval theological doctrine that the human will is able to defeat external circumstance and to triumph over adversity when it accepts and cooperates with God's grace" (1999, 621). While he acknowledges Machiavelli's virulent anticlericalism, he nonetheless concludes that "[Machiavelli's] views on 'the heavens' and their relation to the earth might be better described as a sort of reconstitution and reinvigoration of Christian doctrines by supplementing them with the political virtues of Roman civil religion in order to promote a conception of actions that permit the overcoming of fortune. In sum, he advocated a 'politicized' version of Christianity suitable for an active civil life" (2009, 37).

Viroli (2010) argues that Machiavelli, while critical of the Church's role in Italian politics, remains convinced that Christianity can nurture and strengthen republican politics, if properly interpreted. This study resembles Sullivan's (1996) in its attempt to explain the relationship between republican politics and Christianity, yet Viroli's conclusions differ starkly. He denies that the encouragement of a "civic Christianity" requires a radical transformation of the religion, insisting instead that Machiavelli "believed in . . . the possibility of a civic interpretation of Christianity similar to the one that he knew existed in his Florence" (2010, xiii and 65–66). This interpretation would replace idleness with action, vice with virtue, and weakness with worldly strength. It would be opposed to Vatican teaching but consistent with Christ's teachings (9).

Viroli acknowledges that Machiavelli was not particularly pious (2010, xiii, 34–35, and 27), but he concludes, nonetheless, that Machiavelli's devotion to politics is consistent with a Christian republicanism (xix, 36, and 49). Thus, according to Viroli, Machiavelli is neither an atheist nor a pagan, but a patriotic Florentine, whose patriotism is itself a species of Christian devotion—and indeed, represents a "return to the genuine principles of the Christian religion" (2010, 8, 86, and 153). His argument depends on two crucial—and dubious—claims: his novel definition of "charity," which he claims is "for all political writers of Christian and classical interpretation, the heart of the love of the fatherland" (68; cf. Luke 10:25–37), and his deliberate conflation of Moses and Christ (61–63 and 105–6). His argument culminates with the claim that Machiavelli's judgments of the world were shaped decisively by Christian concepts and that his republican political aims were consistent with a reformation of Christianity that excised the most damaging false interpretations promulgated by the Church (243). In his most recent work (2014, 45), Viroli invests maximum importance in the exhortation of chapter 26, claiming that Machiavelli wrote *The Prince* "to invoke a redeeming prince." Indeed, he views the book as a work of rhetoric, designed to summon a "new Moses" (53; cf. Hulliung's [1983, 21] diminution of the importance of Machiavelli's rhetoric) to lead Italy to liberty. As I argue below, Viroli presumes a happy coincidence of Mosaic founding and republican Christianity that strains the bounds of each. By viewing Christian teachings through the lens of Italian patriotism, Viroli dissolves the thorniest problems posed by Machiavelli's anti-Christian arguments (cf. Brown 2010b, 5).

Colish (1999) blunts Machiavelli's criticism of Christianity by immersing it in a partial and dubious context: according to her, Machiavelli's attacks on Christianity are truly aimed at Savonarolan republicanism (601), which threatened the health of republican orders in Florence. Otherwise, he (603–5) tends to express "conventional Christian ideas"—especially in his minor works—and believes that "Christianity, if properly used, could promote desirable political outcomes" (608).

Parel (1992, 1) also thinks that Machiavelli's religious opinions are conventional, but his eccentric study defies classification: he maintains that Machiavelli is neither a conventional Christian nor a protomodern atheist, but a believer in conventional premodern cosmology and humoral medicine. Rahe's careful (2009) study effectively refutes Parel's thesis; see also Brown

2010b, 72–73. Von Vacano (2007, 95–96) defends much of Parel's thesis, while nonetheless pointedly observing Christianity's "emasculating" effects.

Benner (2009) adheres entirely to neither interpretive school in her highly original book, *Machiavelli's Ethics*. She argues that Machiavelli is deeply influenced by ancient political and moral thought—Plato, Thucydides, Aristotle, and especially Xenophon. Major (2007) undertakes a similar effort, but his claims about Machiavelli's reliance on ancient thinkers are more guarded. While Major wonders whether Machiavelli seeks to encourage the "far-seeing and armed prudence of the new man (178)," Benner maintains that Machiavelli undertakes a "fresh reconstruction of very ancient teachings about political order and virtue" (2009, 11). Neither work addresses directly Machiavelli's approach to Christianity, except insofar as each stresses his grounding in ancient philosophy.

In Benner's more recent (2013) work, she argues that *The Prince* is a "masterwork of ironic writing with a moral purpose," namely, to convey a "biting critique of both ruthless *realpolitik* and amoral pragmatism" (xxi–xxii) that leads the reader—in a way that is both dialogic and subtle—through myriad poisonous ironies and rhetorical feints to understand the "powerfully reasoned undercurrents" in favor of republics that feature "reciprocal trust between leaders and citizens/subjects, and between states and their external allies" (326). For Benner (see also 2009), Machiavelli is a moral thinker, in the tradition of ancient political thought. Benner's argument generally attends to Machiavelli's political and moral thought, broadly conceived; yet her efforts to link Machiavelli's thought to the classical world leads her to neglect his contested relationship with Christianity (although she remains attuned to Machiavelli's critique of the Church [2013, 150–53]). For example, in her discussion of virtue (2013, 179–224), Benner keenly detects Machiavelli's consonance with certain ancient teachings—while nonetheless understating his dissonance with Christian virtue and blurring distinctions among Greek and Roman, and private and civic, notions thereof.

Tarcov, whose work tends to stress Machiavelli's dissonance with Christianity (forthcoming), argues that Machiavelli's teaching "indicates a more general rejection of ancient virtue as understood by the ancient writers." Hence, he maintains that Machiavelli engages in a "two-front war" against the classical and Christian traditions and that it may be the "common ground between classical philosophy and Christianity that led Machiavelli to reject them both and make his modern turn."

26. See, for example, Viroli (2010, 185–88), whose rich knowledge of Machiavelli's efforts to build a decent Florentine militia leads him to understate the severity of Machiavelli's condemnation of Italian arms and overstate the political utility of Christianity, the general belief in which Machiavelli relied on when building his militia (187; see also de Grazia 1994, 97).

I offer a thorough treatment of these passages in chapters 1 and 3. Cf. *Discourses* 1.27, in which Machiavelli reports that a group of diplomats to which he was a party were shocked by the fact that an incestuous and parricidal tyrant could not bring himself to slaughter an unarmed Pope Julius II, who had barged into the tyrant's court to remove him from power.

27.   Parel (1992), Nederman (1999), Skinner (2001), and Viroli (2010) argue for a contextual reading of Machiavelli's religious views; cf. Wolin 1960, 197–99; and Geerken 1999, 580. De Grazia, in particular, places Machiavelli's arguments in conversation with Saint Augustine (for example, 1994, 265–66). There appears to be good reason to compare Machiavelli's thought to Augustine's, whose arguments he often appears to contradict (Warner and Scott 2011; Rahe 2009, 96–98). In addition to the Gospels, I sometimes rely on other works of the New Testament; aware of the perils of conflating those Christian texts with the Gospels, I do so deliberately and, whenever possible, sparingly. Compare this method with Lynch's (2006) survey of Machiavelli's use of the Old Testament. See also Korvela 2006, 61.

28.   I treat Machiavelli's principal critique of Savonarola (*P* 6; *D* III.30.1) below, in chapter 2. I treat his ambivalent view of Saint Gregory (*D* II.5) in chapter 1. I treat his subversive critique of Saints Francis and Dominic (*D* III.1.4) in chapters 1 and 4. I offer an account of Machiavelli's selective and perverse quotation of Petrarch (*P* 26) in the closing chapter. I do not treat Machiavelli's use of Dante, whom Machiavelli quotes in the *Discourses* (*D* I.11.4; *D* I.53.1); but see Shell 2000, 209n24.

29.   I am indebted to an anonymous reviewer for this judgment.

30.   For an example of the latter tactic, see his account of the fate of Manlius Capitolinus, which Machiavelli obscures by offering two different accounts (*D* 1.8.1 and 1.58.1; cf. Mansfield 1979, 35). For a trenchant account of Machiavelli's approach to the Old Testament, see esp. Lynch 2006; see also Hulliung 1983, 167; and Tarcov's (forthcoming) discussion of Machiavelli's curious relationship to his historical sources, and its implications for Machiavelli's modernity.

31.   As Nathan Tarcov observed in reviewing the present study, the notable exception to this rule would be Machiavelli's works, which he heartily recommends to his readers. Machiavelli offers the clearest justification for this strategy in chapter 14 of *The Prince*. Hulliung (1983, 151–67 and 59–62) is critical of Machiavelli's "profoundly unhistorical" (167) use of history. Indeed, he claims that Machiavelli's "monumental history" (151–67) evades the question of whether one ought really to imitate Rome (59).

32.   For Machiavelli's skeptical accounts of miracles, see esp. *D* I.12.1 and *D* II.5.2 (cf. Tarcov 2014, 198). For his firsthand appraisal of Savonarola's miraculous claims, see Machiavelli 1988b, "Niccolò Machiavelli to Ricciardo Bechi," March 9, 1498, 85–89; cf. *D* I.11.5. See also *D* I.56, and cf. Strauss 1958, 210–15; and Parel 1992, 39–40.

33.   *D* III.1.4.

34.   See esp. *P* 3, *P* 16, *P* 7, *P* 8, and *P* 14. Fontana (1999, 638–52) also employs this method, but in a more limited study.

35.   *P* 16, *P* 17, *P* 26, and *P* 6.

36.   See also McCormick 2015, 31. I discuss chapter 14 in chapter 4.

37.   I will depart rarely from these two texts, which Machiavelli identifies as his most important (*D* DL; *P* DL).

38.   Machiavelli uses the term "arms" (*armis*) to signify armed soldiers (1992, 264; hereafter cited as *Opere*), but *The Prince* gradually discloses a broader

meaning of the word. As Mansfield (1996, 4) observes, his discussion of arms culminates in chapter 14, where "to be armed means to have the art of war, a feat of study and intellect, rather than arms." See my discussion in chapter 4 of this book.

39.   This term is Tarcov's (forthcoming), who uses it in a different context.

Chapter One

1.   See esp. Strauss (1958, 56–59 and 189–91), Skinner (2001, 70 and 99), Scott and Sullivan (1994, 887 and 891–93), Sullivan (1996, 17–54), Mansfield (1996, 10, 275), de Alvarez (2008, 3–24), and Rahe (2009, 56–95). Others (Nederman 2009, 36; and Viroli 2010, 6) also observe Machiavelli's hostility to the Church, but deny that the Florentine's position is informed by anti-Christian sentiments.

2.   A notable exception is Tarcov 2000, esp. 38–42; and 2007, 122–35. See also Major 2007, 174.

3.   "Founder" (*fondatore*) is the term Machiavelli uses to describe an originator of a civilization (see, for example, *P* 6; *Opere*, 265; or *D* I.10; *Opere*, 91). I discuss this term in chapter 2 of this book.

4.   As Benner (2013, 3) recounts, although Florence was nominally a republic, the Medici exercised princely control after the republic fell in 1512; by addressing Lorenzo as a prince, Machiavelli rejects the fiction that Florence had retained its republican character. For Machiavelli's disposition toward Lorenzo, see also Tarcov 2013b, 101–7; de Alvarez 2008, 4; and McCormick 2011a, 38; cf. Benner (2013, xxvii), who nonetheless detects the "irreverence" of Machiavelli's posture (3).

5.   Hence, in his undergraduate lectures, Clifford Orwin has described chapter 2 of *The Prince* as a sinister "lullaby" for the unambitious hereditary prince. Tarcov (2000, 41) presents the errors of hereditary princes thus: "he puts his faith in a future good, miracles, and rules that never fail, whether divine commandments or natural laws. All these errors are of a piece, reflecting a kind of laziness most fully developed in Christianity." See also de Alvarez 2008, 3–5; Mansfield 1996, 176–82; and Sullivan 1996, 17–19.

6.   Cf. Germino 1972, 25–26. It is not certain that Machiavelli ever sent the book to any prince (cf., however, Machiavelli 1988b, "Niccolò Machiavelli to Francesco Vettori," December 10, 1513, 143–44, which attests to Machiavelli's ambivalent attitude toward the Medici; and the anecdotal account of Riccardo Riccardi, presented in Connell 2005, 142). Lorenzo died in 1519, yet Machiavelli did not revise the dedicatory letter. This supports the thesis that the letter is meant as a general critique of princes like Lorenzo, and undermines the claim (de Grazia 1994, 42–49; Skinner 2000, 88; and Nederman 2009, 9) that Machiavelli wrote the book as a job application. See also Viroli 2010, 123–25; cf. Viroli 2014, 46–50.

7.   See also Mansfield 1996, 48–49; de Alvarez 2008, 9–11; and Tarcov 2000, 30. Cf. Benner (2013, 15–17), who notes that Machiavelli rejects the existence of

a truly mixed government and thus reveals the ambiguous status of Medici princes in the Florentine republic (14 and 23).

8.   Plato, *Republic* VIII; Aristotle, *Politics* III.7.

9.   The "Turk" refers to Sultan Selim I of the Ottoman Empire; the "Sultan of Egypt" is apparently the Mamluk sultan of Egypt and Syria. *P* 19, 81n23.

10.   Matthew 22:21; see also John 18:36 and 19:11.

11.   Romans 13. Despite the claims of Puritan ministers under the influence of Locke (see Mayhew 2007), the meaning of the text is clear: men ought to submit to earthly government. While they may seek to "overcome evil with good," they ought to remember that heaven, and not earth, is the proper concern of Christians.

12.   Romans 7:1–14.

13.   Romans 13:11. By announcing the imminence of the kingdom of heaven, Paul follows Christ's explicit statements (see, for example, Mark 9:1; Luke 9:27; or Luke 21:30–32).

14.   Matthew 6:33. Cf. Mansfield 1996, 4–5. As de Alvarez (2008, 11) notes, the new and mixed principalities Machiavelli mentions in chapter 1 are examples of the acquisition of northern and southern Italy. De Alvarez also observes that Machiavelli does not offer an example of the conquest of central Italy— Rome and Tuscany. In his characteristic cryptic style, de Alvarez seems to imply that the rest of the book might offer such an example.

15.   Mansfield (1996, 16) and Strauss (1958, 269) each offer an account of this teaching. In staking this position, Machiavelli prepares the way for modernity's embrace of acquisitiveness. See esp. Strauss 1958, 291–99; and Mansfield 1996, 258–94. Strauss (1958, 290–92) also endeavors to link this teaching with Xenophon's.

16.   1 Timothy 6:10. Consider also the context in which this injunction appears.

17.   Luke 12:15.

18.   Matthew 19:16–30 and 6:19–21; Mark 10:17–31; John 2:13–17. See also James 5:1–6; and Hebrews 13:5.

19.   Matthew 6:24.

20.   Luke 12:34; Matthew 19:23–30. While despising earthly wealth, Christ conspicuously promises hundredfold material prosperity as a reward in heaven—to complement the gift of eternal life. Must even Christ appeal to this "natural and ordinary" desire?

21.   Mark 11:15–19. See also Matthew 21:12–13; John 2:13–17 (where he arms himself with a whip); and Luke 19:45–46. A fuller treatment of Christ's teaching on violence is presented below, in chapter 2.

22.   See *D* 2.2.1–2. See also *P* 16 and *P* 25.

23.   Machiavelli's discourse on gift giving in the dedicatory letter might constitute the first moral teaching. See Mansfield 1996, 90–91; friendship is a central theme of de Grazia's (1994) and Viroli's (2010) works, but each attends primarily to the friendship he observes between God and Machiavellian founders (62); de Grazia, Viroli, and Parel (1992, 57 and 96) conclude that this friendship is consistent with a Christianity that is amenable to republicanism. See also Geerken 1999, 584–87.

24.   *Opere*, 258.

25. John 15:12–13.

26. Mathew 7:12. See also Luke 6:31.

27. Matthew 5:43–48. See also James 3:13–4:12.

28. As Steven Kelts noted in a review of an earlier draft of this work, the concept of self-benefit was also important to Aristotelian friendship (*Nicomachean Ethics* VIII.13). It is noteworthy, however, that while Aristotle describes this sort of friendship as deficient, Machiavelli identifies it as characteristic of friendship, simply. Major (2007, 177) notes Machiavelli's departure from "classical and Christian moral thinking." Machiavelli amends his notion of friendship in chapter 14, where he discusses Philopoemon, whose friendships appear to escape these limitations.

29. I am indebted to Clifford Orwin's formulation of this argument.

30. *Opere*, 258.

31. Consider Aristotle's discussion of friendship in the *Nicomachean Ethics* (VIII.1). I am indebted to Benjamin Mitchell for this observation.

32. Matthew 26:50; see also 26:17–24.

33. An application of his reasoning on friendship to the relationship between Judas and Christ yields provocative results: there is circumstantial evidence to suggest that Judas was of the opinion that Christ could not benefit him in the way he expected, and thus betrayed him. Famously, Judas never calls Jesus "Lord," but only "Rabbi" (see, for example, Mark 14:45). This might constitute evidence of his lack of belief in Christ—and his lofty promises of reward. Seen thus, Judas's betrayal might be understood as emblematic of the calculative nature of friendship: he resolves to accept thirty pieces of silver rather than unsubstantiated promises of a charismatic rabbi (see John 12:4–6). A fuller account of Judas's betrayal is presented below, in chapter 2.

34. John 15:15.

35. For Machiavelli's pithy estimate of human nature, see *P* 17. Indeed, instead of imitating godly love in his "friendly" relations, the prince must act "against faith, against charity, against humanity, against religion" (*P* 18). Thus he will violate the dictates of humanity, as well as the Christian God. I discuss Machiavelli's revision of virtue in chapter 5 of this work.

36. 1 John 4:18.

37. His correspondence with Vettori attests most clearly to the importance of Machiavelli's philosophical friendships (Najemy 1993). In his *Art of War*, Machiavelli commends Cosimo Rucellai's extreme devotion to friendship: yet Cosimo's friendship appears valuable precisely because he ignored Christ's teaching on the supreme value of the soul (Matthew 16:26). Of Cosimo, Machiavelli writes, "For I do not know what was so much his (not excepting his soul) that it would have been willingly spent by him for his friends; I don't know of any good that would have frightened him wherein he had recognized the good of the fatherland" (*Art of War* I.2). I am indebted to an anonymous reviewer who directed me to this passage.

38. John 15:13. As Mansfield (1979), Hulliung (1983), McCormick (2011a), and Sullivan (1996) agree, Machiavelli's republic is grounded on mutual suspicion, tension, and the threat of violence, rather than friendship among those who love liberty.

39.   See Strauss 1958 (65–69), Parel 1992 (114), Sullivan 1996 (20–29), de Alva-
      rez 2008 (16–19), and Nederman 2009 (106–12), each of which offers an
      analysis of Louis XII's failed invasion of Italy. Parel departs from the scholarly
      consensus by identifying Louis XII's failure to "satisfy the Milanese" as the
      chief cause of Louis's failure (1992, 114).
40.   For a pithy treatment of Roman imperial policy, see esp. Sullivan 2013.
41.   Ferdinand of Spain is the only successful modern Christian conqueror, and
      as I argue in chapter 6, his problematic success defines the limits of what
      modern Christian princes can accomplish; consider, however, that the Turk is
      also successful (*P* 13).
42.   See Tarcov 2000 (38–39) and 2014 (200–201), which note the importance
      of this error. Among the other errors committed by Louis was the division
      of the kingdom of Naples with Spain and his premature betrayal of Venice,
      along with his failure to create colonies or come to live in Italy. Colonies may
      have been feasible, but it is not clear how the king of France could have lived
      in Italy and maintained control over France, which Machiavelli describes as
      filled with "malcontent" (*P* 4) barons.
43.   See also Strauss 1958, 68; Mansfield 1996, 182; and Sullivan 1996, 2.
44.   *Opere*, 262.
45.   I discuss the other example in chapter 7 of *The Prince* in chapter 3 of this
      work. I treat the example from the *Discourses* (1.27) below, in this chapter.
46.   Earlier in chapter 3, he describes colonies as "more faithful" (*piu fedeli*)
      (*Opere*, 259; *P* 3). Tarcov's (2013a, 576) distinction between faith and religion
      in Machiavelli's thought is particularly helpful to understanding the perni-
      cious effects of "the faith."
47.   Matthew 7:12.
48.   *Encyclopedia of World Biography*, s.v. "Louis XII," http://www.encyclopedia.
      com/topic/Louis_XII.aspx.
49.   De Alvarez 2008, 18.
50.   *Encyclopedia of World Biography*, s.v. "Henry VIII," http://www.encyclopedia.
      com/topic/Henry_VIII.aspx.
51.   See also Tarcov, 2000, 41. One might reasonably object that this plan would
      be much more dangerous for Louis than for Henry; as a Continental power,
      and as the events of 1511 would demonstrate, France was much more vul-
      nerable than England to an attack of combined Church-led powers. Indeed,
      even though the island nation enjoyed greater distance from Rome, England
      would be roiled by religious disputes for more than 150 years. Had Louis
      pursued this strategy, the rest of his life, and the lives of his successors, would
      likely have been consumed by efforts to consolidate the French king's power.
52.   See Sullivan 1996 (20–28), but also her (2013) discussion of the "depen-
      dency" that excellent princes—and especially the Roman Republic—lack; see
      also Mansfield's (1979, 59–69) discussion of *Discourses* I.11–15.
53.   For an account of Rome's mode of expanding, see *D* II.4. I am indebted to an
      anonymous reviewer who corrected this presentation.
54.   Machiavelli indicates, however, that the Roman religion was not purely
      national in character: at certain times, it defers to international oracles.
      Camillus, whom Machiavelli describes as "the most prudent of all the Roman

captains" (*D* III.12.3), uses foreign oracles to spur conquest (*D* I.12.1 and I.13.1) and rigorously obeys them (*D* I.55.1, III.2, III.23, and III.29). I am indebted to Nathan Tarcov, who alerted me to the relevance of these passages. Tarcov also notes that the Christian God employs precisely those strategies Machiavelli recommends for holding a mixed principality: "He tried coming to live here but was put to death by the Romans. He sent a colony occupying a very small part of the earth, but they were dispersed into exile by the Romans. Now he rules by garrisons (centered in the Rome abandoned by Constantine), who are faithful to his kingdom as their true home, and by their means he defends the weak, puts down the strong, and excludes other powerful foreigners" (2000, 41).

55.   See Sullivan 2013 for a discussion that addresses the importance of these Greek examples.

56.   Indeed, perplexity about this curious feature of chapter 4 has led many scholars (see esp. de Alvarez 2008, 19–21; and Sullivan 2013) to offer sustained contemplation of the chapter's significance. The starting point for most of these reflections may be located in Strauss's (1958, 65, 66) work, where he opines that while in chapter 3 "Machiavelli undoubtedly gives advice to foreigners contemplating conquest in his own fatherland," the proper way to accomplish this invasion "is taken up in an oblique way" in chapter 4. Strauss (1958, 67) also considers Machiavelli's reasons for concealing this advice, which originate in a desire to conceal the "base and dark" methods needed to accomplish the "noble and shining" project of the liberation of Italy.

57.   Cf. *D* I.16 and *P* 5.

58.   A fuller discussion of republics appears at the end of this chapter.

59.   Ágoston and Masters 2009, 207.

60.   Ágoston and Masters 2009, 207.

61.   Ágoston and Masters 2009, 207.

62.   Some bishops even ruled their cities (Nicholas 2014, 79–80).

63.   Popes only rarely have arms of their own; Alexander VI (*P* 7 and 11) is an exception, but Machiavelli will nonetheless characterize his arms as deficient.

64.   See also Scott and Sullivan 1994 (892–93), which makes a similar argument about chapter 4. A fuller discussion of Machiavelli's critique of Christ's teaching on violence is presented below, in chapter 2.

65.   Orwin (2014), describing Baglioni as an example who would have been merely the "first" to demonstrate the weakness of the papacy, notes that Machiavelli might have doubted whether Baglioni's enterprise would have constituted a permanent conquest. Many scholars have treated this passage. Strauss (1958, 69) describes Baglioni as insufficiently courageous and "vile"; Mansfield (1979, 100–101) attributes Baglioni's failure to a species of "pious respect" (101); de Grazia (1994, 116) attributes his failure to "cowardice"; Parel (1992, 88), with important textual evidence in support of his claim, attributes Baglioni's failure to insufficient daring unconnected to any religious scruple; Sullivan (1996, 45–47 and 129–30) notes Baglioni's "cowardice" and disinclination to extreme badness, but argues that Machiavelli ultimately blames "modern education—and thus the Christian education—for the inability of modern people to imitate the deeds of the ancients"

(46); Viroli (2010, 183–84) maintains that Machiavelli relates the stories of Baglioni and Porcari in order to encourage efforts to thwart the temporal power of the papacy.

66. Unless otherwise noted, excerpts of Machiavelli's *Florentine Histories* (1988a) are from Laura F. Banfield and Harvey C. Mansfield's translation (hereafter cited in text as *FH*), VI.29.

67. This translation is mine, from the *Opere* (785). Here, Mansfield and Banfield (*FH* VI.29) translate *"poca fede"* as "faithlessness," although they generally adopt the phrase "little faith." In the *Florentine Histories*, they translate *poca fede* as "lack of faith" once (IV.31) and as "faithlessness" twice (the other instance appears at VII.3). Importantly, Machiavelli's language here is identical to certain passages in Italian translations of the New Testament in which Jesus rebukes his followers—and especially his disciples—for their "little faith." See esp. Matthew 6:30, 8:26, 14:31, and 16:8; and Luke 12:28 (the Greek reads *oligopistoi*, and is rendered in Latin as *"minimae* [or *modicae* or *pusillae*] *fidei,"* and in Italian as *"poca fede"*). Jesus also accuses his followers of "faithlessness" (*apistiav* or *incredulitatem*); Italian translations do not always reflect this distinction (see esp. Matthew 17:17–20). See also John 6:64–71, in which Christ acknowledges that one of his disciples is a "devil" who does not believe.

68. Many scholars have examined this story. Mansfield (1996, 34–35) describes the Porcari affair as a "ridiculous failed conspiracy" (34) that demonstrates the necessity for a new Italian *spirito*; de Grazia (1994, 116) describes it as an admiring account of a "failed" attempt; Viroli (2010, 183–84) views Porcari as a praiseworthy (though unsuccessful) example who demonstrates that poetic exhortations can inspire Italy's redeemer (2014, 41–44; see also Varotti 2011); for Sullivan (1996, 34–35 and 130) the story promises glory to those who would dare remove the papacy (see also Scott and Sullivan 1994, 891); de Alvarez (2008, 136) attributes Porcari's failure to a lack of "knowledge and prudence." None identifies the Porcari affair as an allusion to Christ's betrayal and execution.

69. Like Christ, he makes an ostentatious appearance in the city from which he is estranged (Matthew 21:1–11; Mark 11:1–11; Luke 19:28–44; John 12:12–17). For an account of the events preceding Christ's arrest, see esp. Matthew 26:26–55; Mark 14:22–52; and Luke 22:20–53. Both are doomed by a murky alliance between hostile authorities and the insufficiently faithful (see esp. Matthew 26:3–5 and 14–16). For an account of Jesus's estrangement from Jerusalem and the authorities' awareness of his movements, see esp. Mark 11 and Luke 13:31–35. Judas betrayed Christ, but the Gospels emphasize that his very presence in Jerusalem was dangerous (Matthew 26:3–16). The passage in Mark also reveals that Christ did indeed travel to and from his city in one day; Mansfield and Banfield note (Machiavelli 1988a, 264n5) that Machiavelli's tale of Porcari is suspect, insofar as Machiavelli reports that he made return day trips from Bologna to Rome—a journey that would be impossible to complete in one day. Perhaps Machiavelli attributes this miraculous feat to Porcari in order to emphasize this comparison? Christ, like Porcari, also has a history of remaining in the city surreptitiously (Luke 2:43).

70.   *FH* VI.29. Matthew 27:24; Mark 15:14; Luke 23:13–24; John 18:28–40); *FH* VI.29. This would vindicate the superior humanity of the Romans, noted by Mansfield (1979, 399–400), among others.

71.   For a fuller discussion of the importance of a subject's virtue, see Sullivan 2013.

72.   Surprisingly, scholars have not explored the unchristian implications of this argument. Strauss (1958, 27), Parel (1992, 116), and de Alvarez (2008, 22) treat this passage briefly, but offer little comment on the significance of hatred and revenge to republican governance. Viroli (2010, 145–46) addresses this penchant for revenge and hatred within republics, but does not note its dissonance with traditional Christian virtue. Instead, he (62–65) concludes that republican politics is animated by aversions to injustice and cruelty, and an attraction to Christian charity, which Viroli redefines as "love of the Fatherland" rather than a universal love of one's fellow man (68). Viroli's (2010, 5, 36–61, and esp. 62–65) interpretation of Christian charity as patriotism is strained, and depends on two problematic claims: the alleged crucial importance of Christ's lament for Jerusalem (23) and Moses's presumed display of Christian charity (61–62). Hulliung's Machiavelli always prefers republics to tyrannies (1983, 10 and 31–32), and his characterization of republican life is more conspiratorial than those of recent scholars (Viroli 2014; and Benner 2013; cf., however, Mansfield 1979; and Coby 1999) imagine it. For Hulliung, Machiavelli's republic is a "republic of whispers" (1983, 23), in which the few conspire to maximize their self-interests and launch empires (31): republics are predatory, especially when "untroubled by a Christian conscience" (26). While he identifies Christianity as a source of modern corruption throughout his work, he nonetheless locates in contemporary Florence Machiavelli's hopes for the future (Hulliung 1983, 30; for Florence's alleged military promise, see 93).

73.   Cf. *Discourses* I.26.1, in which Machiavelli intimates that these methods "are very cruel, and enemies to every way of life, not only Christian but human; and any man whatever should flee them and wish to live in private rather as king with so much ruin to men." Machiavelli follows by acknowledging that men who cannot found a "civil" way of life are nonetheless constrained to exercise this cruelty. In this context, see also Tarcov (2014, 202–3), who observes that Moses's orders appear even more resilient than those of republics.

74.   Cf. *Discourses* II.2.2, in which the Roman Republic shares the blame for the servitude of the modern age for its role in crushing republics and "all civil ways of life."

75.   See also *D* I.16.

76.   Cf. Machiavelli's critique of mercy (*Misericordia*) in republican politics, evident in his discussion of Manlius Capitolinus's trial (*D* III.8.1) and discussed below, in chapter 5 of this work.

77.   Matthew 5:3–10.

78.   Matthew 5:44. Cf. Mansfield's (1996, 167–68) discussion of the "politically unmanageable" effects of divine retribution.

79. Matthew 5:38–40. The embedded quote is drawn from Exodus 21:24, Leviticus 24:20, and Deuteronomy 19:21. See also Luke 9:51–56. When Christ is not welcomed by a Samaritan village, the apostles ask whether they ought to "call fire down from heaven to destroy them" (Luke 9:54). Christ responds by rebuking them.
80. Matthew 6:14–15.
81. Romans 12:9, 21.
82. Romans 12:17–19. Cf. *D* III.1.4.
83. Romans 12:21.
84. 1 Peter 2:13–21. Attention to the original Greek complicates Peter's commendation of servitude, insofar as the "slaves" referred to in 3:16 (*douloi*) are carefully distinguished from the "slaves" (*hoi oiketai*, or "household slaves") of 3:18. He uses the former term to describe the relationship of Christians to God; the latter term refers explicitly to the "household slaves." As Peter makes clear, it is the household slave who is to endure beatings for the sake of reward; all other Christians must merely submit—although the surrounding language suggests that suffering will accompany their submission. The Latin translation, upon which Machiavelli probably relied, does not preserve this distinction, using the term *servi* (slave) in both cases. Cf. also Ephesians 6:5, Luke 12:47–48, and John 8:32–36; in the last passage, Jesus describes Jews as "slaves to sin" who may only be liberated through his intercession (John 8:36).
85. 1 Peter 2:19–21. Machiavelli's language varies slightly from Peter's. Peter describes that which is suffered as *kolaphizomenoi* (to strike with a fist); in Latin, *colaphizati* (to box one's ear or cuff); in Italian, *castigo* (to chastise or scourge). Machiavelli employs *battiture* (to beat) in this passage. Cf. Fontana 1999 (652–53), which does not note the similar language in these particular passages. Cf. Mansfield's (1979, 195) comment that "the fault of Christianity is not so much in discouraging the honorable contention and moderate independence of free life as in taming the ferocious vengeance of those who are defending their liberty." See also 194–96; and Tarcov 2014, 197–98.
86. This brief vacillation constitutes crucial evidence for de Grazia's (1994, 103–12 and 376–79) and Viroli's (2010) claim that Machiavelli thinks that Christianity can support civic virtue, and the starting point for Sullivan's (1996) astute ruminations on the potential political utility of Christianity. Cf. also Skinner's (2002, 180–82) account of this passage, in which he recognizes Machiavelli's critique of Christianity, but then moves to a discussion of the requirements of a truly civil religion (182–83), without considering whether Christianity, if properly interpreted, might ever satisfy those requirements. Mansfield (1979, 195) is perhaps most dismissive of this vacillation.
87. To explain how this weak and effeminate religion gained adherents among the ferocious Gentiles, Machiavelli casually reveals that the Roman Republic eventually extirpated the "free way of life" of the ancients (*D* II.2.2 and II.2.3). While the ferocity of the ancient religion allowed some cities—most notably the Samnites—to resist the Romans for a time, eventually the "extreme virtue" of the Romans led to the enslavement of the known world—thus

preparing the way for a religion that "glorified humble and contemplative more than active men" (*D* II.2.2).

88. Matthew 16:18–19.

89. I concede that it is anachronistic to use these titles to describe Christ's charge to Peter; nonetheless, they originate in the New Testament passages in which Christ confers his authority on Peter. De Grazia (1994, 119–20), however, thinks that Machiavelli diminishes the authority of popes as Christ's representatives.

90. Matthew 16:18.

91. Mansfield 1979, 195.

92. Compare also with the bloody animal sacrifices of the Israelites (see, for example, Leviticus 8:14–25); see Geerken's (1999, 592–93) account of this passage. An anonymous reviewer noted that the Romans sometimes also sacrificed human beings (Livy XXII.57)—but not, of course, to invoke pity. When I refer to Livy's original Latin text, I have relied on Weissenborn and Muller's (*Ab Urbe Condita Libri*, 1911) version of the text.

93. See John 1:29–36; Romans 8:36; 1 Corinthians 5:7; and 1 Peter 1:19.

94. See McCormick's (2011a) account of chapter 7 of *The Prince* for a recent presentation of the first position; Sullivan (1996, 156–59 and 171) offers the quintessential account of the potential value of human sacrifice to republican politics. See also Rahe 2009, 88–89.

95. Matthew 26:17–30; Mark 14:22–24; Luke 22:19. Cf. de Grazia 1994 (102), which notes the problem with the Eucharist, but attributes its humility to subsequent "interpretations," rather than to Christ. Christ's resurrection also diminishes the sacrifice; I discuss the implications of his resurrection and the hope it engenders in his followers below, in chapter 3.

96. 1 Peter 2:20. The crucifixion is an educative model throughout the Gospels (see esp. John 3:16 and Matthew 20:28), but especially in the rest of the New Testament (Romans 3:25–28, 5:6–10, and 6:3–11; Galatians 3:10–14; Ephesians 2:13–16; Philippians 3:10–12; Colossians 1:20–22; Hebrews 2:9; 1 Peter 1:3, 2:24, and 3:18; 1 John 4:9–10). Cf. Romans 8:35–39, where Paul insists that Christians are ultimately conquerors.

97. Cf. Bacon, *Advancement of Learning* I.3.2. See Rahe 2009, 98–99; and Sullivan 1996, 15–59 and 119–90. See also Hulliung's (1983, 67) account of the hollow victory of these "anti-worldling" orders. Cf. Wolin 1960, 237; and Colish 1999, 602. Brown (2010b, 80–81) views Machiavelli's praise of the mendicants as genuine.

98. *Opere*, 196.

99. Machiavelli opines that "it is therefore to be believed" (*D* II.5.1) that the Gentiles also persecuted previous sects, but Diodorus Siculus, whom Machiavelli cites as a "mendacious" historian in the very next sentence, refutes this (*Library of History* I.23.8).

100. As Vickie Sullivan has noted, Machiavelli seeks to redirect men's extravagant hopes with his "grandiose promise" of a "perpetual republic" (1996, 154). This worldly good replaces that promised by Christ.

101. Romans 12:21. Cf. Strauss 1958, 182.

102. See also Hulliung 1983, 26; de Alvarez 2008, 22–25; and Wood 1990, xii. Cf. Machiavelli's critical account of "the Christian republic" in *Discourses* I.12.1.

Chapter Two

1. Machiavelli refers to these men as "the greatest examples" (*grandissimi esempli*), "the most excellent" (*li piu eccellenti*), "new princes" (*nuovo principe*), "the introducer" (*lo introduttore*), and "innovators" (*innovatori*), before identifying them as "prophets" (*profeti*) near the end of the chapter. Throughout the chapter, he refers to the founders as "men" (*uomini*) (*Opere*, 264–65).

2. The latter three were also progenitors of empire. Moses's military exploits, which emerge as a model for founders, nonetheless produced uncertain worldly results: many cities fell to his armies before and after his death, but the Israelites could never claim the temporal holdings of Persia, Greece, or Rome. Instead, Moses's spiritual empire—which extended to Machiavelli's own time, and is inextricably linked with the rise of both Christianity and Islam—marks his founding as particularly impressive. See also Lynch 2006, 167–77. For the context of Machiavelli's use of Moses, see Lynch 2006 (162–63) and Brown 1988 (57 and 64–65). Throughout his works (see, for example, *P* 6 [*Opere*, 265]), Machiavelli uses the word "orders [*ordini*]" to signify that which constitutes and animates a new civilization.

3. One possible explanation is that Machiavelli declines to discuss Christ because his example is too lofty, and declines to discuss Muhammad because he considers him a charlatan beneath consideration. The first argument—which is not represented explicitly in the scholarship, but would be most consistent with the claim that Machiavelli is a conventional Christian—encounters an important difficulty: despite some initial hesitation, Machiavelli discusses Moses, a prophet holy to Christianity. The second argument is also problematic, since Machiavelli freely discusses—and praises—pagan founders, who, despite the claims of Nederman (1999), Christians must consider "false prophets" (excepting possibly Cyrus, for reasons I discuss below). Indeed, interpretations that argue that Machiavelli conflates Moses and Christ (Nederman 1999 and 2009; Viroli 2010; Parel 1992), and thus that his praise of Moses is evidence of his support for Christianity, are rendered most problematic by attention to chapter 6 of *The Prince*, which implicitly establishes important differences between the two prophets. Attention to chapter 6 thus confirms Strauss's (1958, 175–77) suggestion that Machiavelli's teaching becomes clearest when one compares it to Christ's.

   Somewhat surprisingly, Muhammad receives scant attention in the literature on Machiavelli: Strauss (1958, 84) claims Machiavelli "could not help thinking of Mohammed when speaking of armed prophets"; he also notes that the Florentine (144) compares Islam favorably to Christianity, noting that the former's armed conquest allowed it to supplant the language of conquered people, thus strengthening the foundation of its regime. Mansfield (1996, 4; see also Fontana 1999, 640n9) notes in passing that Muhammad and Moses are armed prophets who may be contrasted with Christ; Rahe (2009, 86) notes that early readers of *The Prince* recognized the implications of its argument for Islam, and suggests that their puzzlement led them to wonder, "Did Mohammed, the armed prophet par excellence, in any way outdo Christ?" Beiner (2011, 32) claims that "the whole logic of Machiavelli's analysis points toward Mohammed as an archetypal armed prophet."

4.   The first chapter prepared the reader for the opposition between virtue and fortune that Machiavelli observes here. Machiavelli has used the word "virtue" only two other times prior to chapter 6 (in which it appears ten times): in chapter 3 he says that the Romans exhibited virtue in their foreign policy and in chapter 4, in a passage in which the Romans make a conspicuous and puzzling appearance, he implies that successful conquest depends on the virtue of the conquered (Sullivan 2013, 525–27). The scholarship has attended meticulously to Machiavelli's account of virtue: Strauss 1958, passim, but esp. 246–47; Orwin 1978; Mansfield 1996, 6–56; de Alvarez 2008, 75–100; Palmer 2001, 85–88. Cf. Viroli 2010 (53), which claims that Machiavelli believes "that the true Christianity is Christianity interpreted in terms of virtue."

5.   Machiavelli does not report that Cyrus also enjoyed the favor of the biblical God (Isaiah 45:1–6; Ezra 1:1–11).

6.   De Grazia (1994, 52–53) and Nederman (2009, 47) conclude on the basis of this passage that all had divine support. Cf. Tarcov 2013a (575) and 2014 (201–3), which establish Moses's similarity to the pagan founders. De Alvarez (2008, 27) describes Machiavelli's argument as "extraordinary blasphemy." See also Geerken's (1999, 580–83) account of Moses's interactions with God.

7.   Cyrus is reputed to have enjoyed divine favor (Isaiah 45:1–6; Ezra 1:1–11; Josephus, *Antiquities of the Jews* 11.1); Theseus was reputed to have descended from the gods, and slew the mythical Minotaur (Plutarch, *Theseus* 2.1, 19.1); Romulus was suckled by a she-wolf and benefited from numerous auguries (Livy I.4–8). Cf. de Alvarez 2008 (26), which suggests that Romulus's meager opportunity suggests that extraordinary fortune is not so necessary to founding as Machiavelli suggests. See also Tarcov 2014 (201), which notes that Moses's orders are his, rather than God's.

8.   Mansfield notes the ambiguity of the Italian here (*Opere*, 265n3).

9.   Considering Moses's career in particular, Machiavelli clearly alludes to those passages from the Pentateuch in which Moses uses arms against his own people in order to consolidate his rule (Exodus 32; see also Numbers 25:3–9). These incidents are discussed below, in this chapter. Cyrus invoked divine sanction when purging his political enemies (Herodotus I.209). The story of Romulus alternates between fabulous claims of divine origin and sanction and accounts of successful military exploits; indeed, Romulus's rule is consolidated by an augury of questionable veracity that is eventually vindicated by Romulus's murder of his own brother (Plutarch, *Romulus* 9.4–7 and 10.1). The inclusion of Theseus is puzzling. Early in his career, he exhibits many feats of strength by battling and slaying various creatures and men (Plutarch, *Theseus* 8–12). During his first attempt (*Theseus* 24.3) to consolidate his rule of Athens, he adheres to Machiavelli's general rule: "Some he readily persuaded to this course, and others, fearing his power, which was already great, and his boldness, chose to

be persuaded rather than forced to agree to it" (24.3). Toward the end of his career, however, when Theseus attempted to recover the preeminent position in Athens, Plutarch writes that "he was overpowered by demagogues and factions," and went into exile (*Theseus* 35.3). Theseus's story thus confirms the necessity of force to founders, while perhaps diminishing his status among the virtuous. We ought to remember, however, that Romulus closed his career by placing government in the hands of Romans before vanishing mysteriously (*Romulus* 27.3–8). Clinging to power until death is not a requirement for a Machiavellian founder, particularly if he is a founder of a free regime. Plutarch also reports that both might have been murdered, and subsequently revered as semidivine (*Theseus* 35.4–5; *Romulus* 27.3).

10. Weinstein (2011) provides a lively account of Savonarola's prophecies (for example, 65–68 and 75–103), confrontation with the papacy (226—49), and death (294–97). Cf. Machiavelli's appraisal of his career in the *Discourses* (I.11.5, I.45.2, and III.30). For a general survey of prophecy in Renaissance Italy, see Niccoli 1990.

11. For Savonarola's oblique claims to be a "new Moses," see Brown 1988, 60–64. Many scholars note Savonarola's significance as the lone Christian example (Strauss 1958, 83–84; de Alvarez 2008, 28–29 and 58–59; Palmer 2001, 82; Tarcov 2013a, 575 and 578); Hulliung (1983, 62–63), however, does not connect his critique of the "dupe" Savonarola to Christ.

12. Weinstein 2011, 217–18. For evidence of Savonarola's penchant for prophecy, see Brown 2010b, 54–55.

13. While Jesus refuses to perform a miracle after his arrest (Luke 23:8–9; Matthew 26:59–63; see also Mark 16:62, in which Jesus confesses to be the Messiah), Savonarola's attempt is thwarted by the heavens themselves. In 1498 he was dared by a priestly rival to demonstrate the truth of his prophetic claims by submitting to a trial by fire (Weinstein 2011, 267–68). When torrential rains extinguished the fires, Savonarola was deemed to have failed the test (271–76). McCormick (2011a, 131–33) claims that Savonarola might have succeeded had he relied resolutely on the "favor of the people" (2011, 132).

14. Matthew 26:57–68 and 27:11–44; Mark 14:53–65 and 15:1–32; Luke 22:63–71 and 23:1–43; John 18:19–40 and 19:1–16.

15. See, for example, Luke 1:26–38; and Matthew 3:13–17 and 4:23.

16. Luke associates the rule of earthly kingdoms with the rule of the devil, insofar as the devil tempts Christ with the "kingdoms of the world" (Luke 4:5–6; Cassidy 2001, 20). Jesus's opportunity might also lie in his dubious patrimony. The Virgin Birth resembles the abandonment of Moses, Romulus, and Theseus. I am indebted to Nathan Tarcov, who made this observation in response to a draft of this work.

17. For an account of how Rome's economic and political structures conduced to inequality, see McCormick 2011a, 86–90 and 96–97; for an account of how Rome's religious and political structures conduced to the same, see Sullivan 1996, 102–17.

18. John 19:16.

19. See esp. Matthew 5–7.

20.   Matthew 5:17.

21.   During the Exodus, Moses transforms the Israelites into an armed camp, but the Levites are his most important arms (the Israelites' first war occurs in Exodus 17; for the importance of the Levites, see esp. Exodus 32:25–29 and Deuteronomy 33:8–11). I treat Machiavelli's judgment of the psychological power of hope and the devastating spiritual consequences of Christianity in chapter 3.

22.   Moses's confrontation with Pharaoh is reported in Exodus 6:28–12:30. For Jesus's confrontation with the religious authorities, see Matthew 16:1–12, 22:15–46, and 26:57–68; Mark 11:27–33, 12:1–40, and 14:53–65; Luke 20 and 22: 47–53; and John 8 and 18:19–24. For his confrontation with the existing political order, see Matthew 27:11–26; Mark 12:13–17; Luke 22:66–23:25; and John 18:31–40.

23.   Exodus 2:11–17; Matthew 4:23; Mark 1:21–28; John 2:1–12. In all accounts, Christ undertakes his first act after his baptism, his trial in the wilderness, and the assembling of disciples. The Gospel of Luke features a particularly long account of Jesus's childhood, in which many signs of his divine purpose are made evident, yet despite numerous early public statements in Luke, his first act (4:33) is to purify an unclean spirit.

24.   Exodus 6:28–12:30.

25.   Matthew 4:12; Mark 1:14; Luke 4:14. The Gospel of John presents a different account of Jesus's early activity. It begins with a short theological treatise and reports that his first public act was a miracle (the wedding at Cana), rather than a speech at Galilee. In John, Jesus also confronts the old religious order much earlier in his career (John 3). For Jesus's more direct confrontations with the old religious order and the existing political order, see note 22 above. Cf. Machiavelli 1988b, "Niccolò Machiavelli to Ricciardo Bechi," March 9, 1498, 85–89.

26.   Matthew 6:14.

27.   Matthew 5:38–48; Luke 6:27–36. See chapter 1 for a more thorough examination of Christ's directives in these passages.

28.   Matthew 5:38–39. Cf. Exodus 21:24; Leviticus 24:20; and Deuteronomy 19:21.

29.   Luke 22:51. A follower injures the servant in the Gospels of Matthew (26:47–54), Mark (14:43–49), Luke (22:47–51), and John (18:2–11). In Luke (22:51), Jesus heals the injured man; in Mark (14:48–49), Jesus says nothing about his arrest.

30.   John 18:36; Luke 22:42–44.

31.   Matthew 21:12–13; Mark 11:15–19; Luke 19:45–46. In John (2:13–17), Jesus actually fashions a whip, which he uses to drive the beasts and the merchants from the temple. In an adjacent passage (Matthew 21:18–22; Mark 11:12–14; 20–25), Christ curses, and thereby kills, a fig tree that has not born fruit. This, too, may be understood as a violent act, although the meaning of this passage is obscure. It is perhaps an allusion to Judgment Day, when men will be judged according to whether they provided the Son of Man with food when he was hungry (Matthew 25:34–36).

32.   Matthew 10:1–24; Luke 22:36.

33. Luke 22:38. Cf. Moses's instruction to the Levites in Exodus, where, faced with a crisis of belief among his own people, he instructs each of his partisans to "strap a sword to his side" (32:27).

34. Matthew 10:34. See also Luke 12:49–53.

35. Matthew 10:38–39.

36. Matthew 5:10–12 and 10:22; Luke 9:23–25 and 14:27. See also 2 Timothy 2:3.

37. Exodus 32:24–31. See Lynch 2006 for a thorough and penetrating account of this passage, and of Machiavelli's judgment of Moses. In his account of chapter 6, Tarcov (2014, 202) notes "Machiavelli's brutal emphasis on the use of force" to compel obedience and, more importantly, belief; cf. Mansfield's (1979, 71) judgment (in a different context) that "civilization, it appears, is imposed by forced oaths to God." See also Brown's (2010b, 78–79) account, which emphasizes the value of fear but neglects Machiavelli's artful appropriation of hope.

38. Exodus 32:26–27.

39. Cf. Viroli's (2010, 63–65) justificatory account. See also Geerken 1999, 581.

40. Exodus 32:35. For Moses's wars against foreign peoples, see esp. Deuteronomy 1:26–46, 2:24–36, 7, 20; and Numbers 31:1–7 and 35:50–55. For Moses's use of violence against the Israelites, see also Numbers 25:3–9. Miraculous and violent judgments often accomplish Moses's grim work: for example, Numbers 16:12–35 recounts the story of an earthquake swallowing rebellious Israelites (see also Numbers 16:35 and 26:10; and Deuteronomy 11:6). In his discussion of how force might compel belief, Tarcov (2013a, 578) notes, "It is not clear whether force produces true lasting belief in the goodness of the founder's new orders or merely belief that it is good to obey those orders rather than be forcibly punished for disobedience, which would last only as long as the threat of force remains."

41. John 12:37–50. Although this passage appears to refer to the crowds that followed Jesus, it directly precedes Jesus's revelations that Peter will deny him and that he will be betrayed (John 13).

42. Peter's denial appears at Matthew 26:69–75; Mark 14:26–72; Luke 22:54–62; and John 18:13–27. In Matthew, Jesus claims foreknowledge of Peter's denial (26:31–35) and Judas's betrayal (26:17–24).

43. For Satan's alleged involvement see Luke 22:3–6; for Judas's possible pecuniary motives, see John 12:1–8; and Acts 1:18. Cf. Matthew 26:6–13 and Mark 14:3–9.

44. Matthew 16:18 and 26:69–75.

45. Luke 22:41–43. Matthew (27:31–32), Mark (15:20–21), and Luke (23:26) report that Simon of Cyrene is compelled to help Jesus; John (19:17) omits mention of Simon. The Gospels do not all agree about whether the sour wine is intended to help (Matthew 27:48; Mark 15:23; John 19:28–30) or mock (Luke 23:34–37) Christ.

46. Deuteronomy 30–34. In Moses's final words about the Levites, he reminds the audience of their armed support of his orders: "[Levi] did not recognize his brothers or acknowledge his own children, but he watched over your word and guarded your covenant. He teaches your precepts to Jacob and your law to Israel" (Deuteronomy 33:9–10).

47. Deuteronomy 34:7.

48. Matthew 6:33. Cf. Fontana's (1999, 654) critique of Christ's emphasis on one's "interior (or simply spiritual) life" rather than Moses's more "public" conception of truth.

49. See esp. Deuteronomy 1:26–46, 2:24–36, 7; 20; and Numbers 31:1–7 and 35:50–55.

50. Matthew 5:17.

51. Strauss 1958, 49. In his account of this chapter (1979, 99–101), Mansfield points out that this "is Machiavelli's striking way of saying the new prince must imitate God rather than obey him" (99).

52. Luke 1:51–52.

53. Machiavelli also cites Philip of Macedon as an example. Unlike David and Moses, Romulus, Theseus, and Cyrus were able to transcend these cruel modes by founding republics or kingdoms. Machiavelli thus indicates their superior humanity (see Wolin 1960, 223).

54. Matthew 5:1–11.

55. Matthew 8:11. See chapter 1 of this work for a discussion of Jesus's attitude toward political life. For Christ's preoccupation with the kingdom of heaven, see Matthew 4:17; Mark 9:1; and 1 Corinthians 15:24. For his indifference to the temporal world, see Matthew 22:15–22; and Luke 4:5–8 and 10:10–12. He nonetheless claims to have the power of God on several occasions (see, for example, Matthew 12:53; and John 10:25–30; see also Colossians 1:15–17).

56. On the problem of envy, cf. *P* 6. Many scholars (for example, Strauss [1958, 51–52 and 183], Viroli [2010, 126–28], Mansfield [1996, 77–78], and Lynch [2006]) have discussed this aspect of Machiavelli's thought. Although Strauss (1958, 53) declines to discuss this passage in detail, Machiavelli's "judicious" and blasphemous reading of the Bible is a central theme of his analysis. Cf. *D* III.30.1, I.23.4, and I.P.2. Geerken (1999, 580) implausibly claims that Moses shows "the need to use violent means to achieve lawful ends."

57. *Opere*, 237. For the execution of Israelites allegedly commanded by God, see Leviticus 24:10–23; and Numbers 11:1–4, 15:32, 20:22–29, and 25:3–5; for the death of Israelites by natural disaster or allegedly divine scourging, see, for example, Leviticus 10:1–4; and Numbers 14:36 and 16:12–35. See also Deuteronomy 28:15–68.

58. Mansfield (1979, 400) questions whether Machiavelli's account is simply complimentary. While Moses is certainly superior to Savonarola and Soderini, Mansfield suggests that Machiavelli's comparison of Moses and Camillus vindicates the superior humanity of Roman orders (*D* I.8 and I.24.2). This critique of Moses is not new; see Diodorus Siculus, *Library of History* XL.2–3.

59. See Brown's (1988, 60–65) account, which details Savonarola's appropriation of the Mosaic model, his critique of forgiveness (63), and his unflattering comparison of Christian and Muslim arms (63); she credits Savonarola (64–65) as the source for many of Machiavelli's "'modern'" (65) ideas.

60. 1 Corinthians 1:18–31. In the Greek and the Latin, the phrase is rendered as "the wisdom of the world" (*ten sophian tou kosmou toutou*; the Vulgate reads, "*sapientiam huius mundi*"). Machiavelli's reference to the "wise of the world"

(*savi del mondo*) is thus an allusion to scripture, rather than a direct reference (*D* III.30.1).

61. 1 Corinthians 1:22–30.
62. See esp. Matthew 25:31–46 and 26:52. Machiavelli recounts the actions of several bellicose popes (*P* 7, 11, 18, and 25), but their difficulties attest to the problem of reconciling a Christlike comportment with armed belligerence.
63. See esp. his third sermon on Exodus, delivered on February 27, 1498 (Savonarola 2006, 315–35). Savonarola begins by commenting that he is "on a battlefield to fight against the lukewarm" (315) before exhorting his followers to imitate the works detailed in the Psalms (322–35). Brown (1988) sketches Savonarola's worldliness, and notes briefly the constraints imposed by his priestly vows (57).
64. The context certainly suggests that Machiavelli intends to attribute these defects to Soderini, but the Italian (*Quell'altro credeva*) is not explicit, and the condemnation of Soderini is cast in vague terms. See Mansfield's critical discussion of Soderini's inability to dissemble and his intemperate humility (1979, 310–12 and 349–50); McCormick (2011a, 119–38) also offers a long and illuminating account of Soderini's mismanagement of the ambitions of the great in Florence. Neither identifies Machiavelli's critique of Soderini with a critique of Christ.
65. Mark 13:33; Luke 22:31–33.
66. For Christ's exhortations to goodness see esp. Matthew 5:16 and Mark 12:28–34; for his trust in God, see esp. Matthew 17:20 and John 14:1; Christ's many miracles and promises of reward (Matthew 5:1–12) are the clearest indications of his desire to eliminate envy by benefiting others. For the importance of goodness in the New Testament, more generally, see Romans 15:14 and Galatians 5:22.
67. Matthew 10:7.
68. Matthew 27:46.
69. Psalm 22:4–5.
70. *Opere*, 278.
71. Virtuous minds think alike: one ought to compare Hiero's butchery of Syracuse's mercenaries (Polybius, *Histories* I.9) with David's conspiracy against Uriah (2 Samuel 11:3–21; found in Ciliotta-Rubery 1997, 30), whose wife he had bedded. Machiavelli conceals the fact that according to Polybius (I.9), Hiero subsequently enlisted "on his own account a sufficient body of mercenaries, [and] he thenceforth carried on the business of the government in security." I discuss Machiavelli's eventual revision of the teaching on mercenary arms below, in chapter 6.
72. For discussions of the passage in 1 Samuel 17, see esp. Sullivan 1996, 144–46; Lynch 2006; Mansfield 1996, xxii; 1996, 214; de Alvarez 2008, 61–63; Viroli 2010, 62, 127–28; and Tarcov 2014, 206–7.
73. 1 Samuel 17:39–40.
74. Strauss (1958, 51–52 and 162–63) intimates that Machiavelli's "judicious" reading of the Bible was informed by his examination of Livy, whose account of the history of Rome is filled with pagan myths that Machiavelli omits in the *Discourses*. Strauss's suggestion seems to be that a Christian who reads of

pagans' manipulations of religious belief and the political effects of incredible miracles might develop a cynical understanding of prophecy, in general. See also Tarcov 2003 (118), which notes the impious implications of Machiavelli's argument in chapter 13.

75. Machiavelli also links King David and Hiero when he quotes an unnamed source as saying of Hiero "that he lacked nothing of being a king except a kingdom" (*P* 6 and 25). Cf. 1 Samuel 18:8, where the jealous Saul wonders, "What more can he get but the kingdom?" I am indebted to Nathan Tarcov, who noted this possibility in his comments on a draft of this work. Mansfield (*P* 6 and 25n5) identifies this, and other, possible sources for this quotation.

76. Polybius, *Histories* I.9. Tarcov (2003, 118; 2014, 206–7) also notes Hiero's apparent misplacement, but his analysis focuses primarily on David.

77. De Alvarez (2008, 38–39) suggests that Machiavelli intends comparison of these "captains," whose careers reveal crucial characteristics of the "most excellent" examples and demonstrate the limits of virtue, especially insofar as one wishes to secure glory.

78. Polybius, *Histories* I.8; Livy XXIV.4. Despite his neglect of prophecy, his history is not without divine intervention. Justin (*Epitome* XXIII.4) reports that although exposed at birth, Hiero was sustained by the labors of honeybees.

79. Tarcov (2014, 205) also notes that Agathocles's irreligiousness limits his reputation, although Machiavelli expresses his belief (*credo*) that Agathocles's success is due to the practice of well-used cruelty (Tarcov 2013a, 582–83). Scott and Sullivan (1994, 895) attribute Agathocles's diminished status to his failure to "employ necessarily violent means toward ultimately humane ends." Compare this opinion, however, with Polybius (*Histories* IX.23), who writes that Agathocles "became to all appearance the gentlest and mildest of men" after his cruel founding. Polybius (XII.15) also recounts Agathocles's other admirable qualities, which led him to undertake ambitious exploits (XV.35). McCormick (2015) mines these histories to argue that Machiavelli's praise of Agathocles is consistent with the Florentine's democratic thought: for him, "Agathocles overthrew an oligarchy that had formerly been a democracy." By comparing Agathocles's career to Scipio's, McCormick (44) concludes that the Sicilian is denied glory because he could not live under republican orders. McCormick nonetheless overstates the popular character of Agathocles's army (compare McCormick 2015, 34, with Diodorus Siculus, *Library of History* XIX.6.1–3) and his commitment to democratic reform, which he undertakes only haphazardly in the days after he was poisoned fatally (compare McCormick 2015, 39, with Diodorus Siculus, *Library of History* XXI.16.4–6); neither does he note Diodorus Siculus's (*Library of History* XIX.1.5) dim estimation of Syracuse's capacity for self-government. I undertake a discussion of Machiavelli's unchristian support of Agathoclean cruelty in chapter 5 (cf. de Grazia 1994, 85–86). Hiero's criminality (I.9) appears lesser, insofar as he directs his violence against foreign mercenaries, rather than Syracuse's republican institutions. For Machiavelli's identification with Agathocles's "hardships and dangers" (*P* 8 and DL), see McCormick 2014, 137; and 2015, 33.

80. Polybius, *Histories* I.8; Livy XXIV.4.

81. Livy XXIV.4–39. See also Mansfield's (1979, 22–23) discussion of Hiero as a potential model for the addressees of the *Discourses*. McCormick (2011a, 196n5) articulates Hiero's limits as a potential founder.
82. Xenophon (*Cyropaedia* VIII.8.1–2) attributes the failures of latter-day Persians to their impiety.
83. Livy I.8 and I.16. Cf. I.36. By contrasting him with the religious pretender Numa, Machiavelli appears to deny that Romulus used prophecy (*D* I.11.2). Plutarch, however, reports that Romulus was "fond of sacrifices and of divination" (*Romulus* 7.2).
84. Plutarch, *Theseus* 2.1–2.
85. Deuteronomy 31:1–7; for Joshua's military prowess, see esp. Numbers 14–15.
86. Livy XXIII.21. Livy intimates that Hiero was willing even to murder members of his own family in order to preserve his alliance with Rome (XXIII.30).
87. Matthew 16:13–20. Cf. Matthew 8:29.
88. Theodosius I ended Rome's support for pagan religions, which Christianity had slowly eclipsed over the previous one hundred years. *The Discourses* best explains how the prophet known as the "Prince of Peace" could capture martial and imperial Rome (see esp. Mansfield 1979; and Sullivan 1996); cf., however, *P* 19, which supplements this teaching. Tarcov (2014, 203) observes that Rome's adoption of Christianity might indicate Moses's superiority to even Romulus.
89. Plato, *Republic* 373d–e and 414a–415d.
90. Plato, *Laws* 624a–632c. Eventually, the Athenian Stranger persuades the interlocutors that war is insufficient means to establish a city; civic life requires the inculcation of other, less martial, virtues.
91. Hesiod, *Theogony* 685–95; Homer, *Iliad* 8.1–20.
92. Thucydides, *History of the Peloponnesian War* I.4 and I.8. At I.17, Thucydides reveals that eventually tyranny outlived its usefulness. See also 6.53–57, where Thucydides offers qualified praise of Athenian tyrants, who appear especially pious.
93. Machiavelli's account of Camillus's career (*D* III.23) also attests to this temptation.
94. Matthew 5:19–20, 7:21–27, and 23:1–3; Mark 10:17–31; Luke 13:22–30; John 14.
95. Luke 14:27.
96. The Crusades (*FH* I.17) appear to disprove these rules, yet Machiavelli stresses that they were directed against non-Christians and resulted in only temporary conquests, which were then lost to the superior virtue of the infidel.
97. 1 Corinthians 1:23.

Chapter Three

1. Strauss 1958, 54–58 and 71–72; Mansfield 1996, 260; de Alvarez 2008, 25–26. De Grazia (1994, 30–57), Nederman (2009, 45–47), and Viroli (2010, 62–64)

recognize the importance of the chapter, but attribute the greatness of the founders to God's friendship. Cf. Benner 2013, 69–84.

2. See Gilbert 1938, 42. Viroli (2010, 114–18) thinks Borgia's career confirmed for Machiavelli the value of the "rhetorical art" (116) and "statesmanship" (117); Parel (1992, 58) judges Borgia's career as proof that even God's help cannot overcome the power of fortune. Compare these with other, less flattering treatments of Borgia: see esp. Strauss 1958, 58, 66–67; Von Vacano 2007, 47–55; de Alvarez 2008, 32–36; Rahe 2009, 67–69; and Benner 2013, 87–110. Sullivan (1996, 18–25) offers a contextualized presentation of Borgia's career, but Scott and Sullivan (1994, esp. 894–98) offer a lengthier and more penetrating account of Cesare's career. See also McCormick 2011b, discussed below. Surprisingly, little has been written on Sforza's importance to *The Prince* (see Lynch 2012).

3. See Strauss 1958, 214.

4. See also Scott and Sullivan 1994, 896.

5. While the Church employed mercenary arms during Machiavelli's lifetime, these mercenaries were typically purchased by their allied powers—especially France. The Pontifical Swiss Guard, formalized by Julius II, was a corps of approximately 250 soldiers. It was a bodyguard for the pope, but of insufficient size to meet the requirements of the "adequate army" described in chapter 10. When the Vatican was assaulted in 1527, it swiftly fell—despite its impressive fortifications and superior artillery power (McBrien 1997, 278–79).

6. One must consider the temerity of Alexander's support of Louis XII's invasion. In chapter 3, Machiavelli opines that Louis XII's conquest of Italy might have been lasting had he not erred by giving aid to the pope. Instead, Louis XII's concern for his "reputation" was exploited by Alexander VI (*P* 3 and 18).

7. Liverotto meets his doom alongside Vitellozzo Vitelli, "who had been [Liverotto's] master in his virtues and his crimes" (*P* 8; cf. McCormick 2014, 153). The latter nonetheless prayed for pardon from the pope while desperately fending off his murderers, while Liverotto blamed Vitellozzo for any harm done to Borgia. Neither, reports Machiavelli, spoke as one might have expected (1989, 1:168–69). From this, we might conclude that Liverotto was usually inclined to boasting, while Vitellozzo was disinclined to prayer. See McCormick 2014 (150–56), which discusses how Liverotto's failure reflects the deficient virtue of Christian princes, who are "constantly shadowed by papal authority" (152), the representatives of which are "shallow, impotent imitations of their ancient, pagan namesakes" (155).

8. McCormick (2011b, 5) describes this dinner as a grotesque "last supper" that Cesare was able to organize with the help of a "converted" Signor Paolo—or "Mr. Paul" (see also 2011b, 16).

9. Cf. *P* 17 and 9. See also Mansfield 1996, 186–87. Machiavelli juxtaposes the creation of a "civil court" (*P* 7) with Remirro's demise, but does not explicitly indicate that Remirro was judged guilty (see also de Grazia 1994, 327). The people's surprise at his execution suggests that Remirro's killing might have been entirely extrajudicial, but since the court was created because of

Remirro's "excessive authority," my interpretation seems tenable (*P* 7). As McCormick notes (2011b, 7), Cesare delivers the Romagna from its terror on December 26—or Boxing Day—a day on which Christians would typically receive gifts. McCormick (2011b) also notes the similarities between Christ's death and D'Orco's execution. See also de Alvarez 2008, 35.

10.   Cf. *D* I.16.

11.   By way of contrast, he cites ancient Rome, Sparta, and Switzerland as regimes that are "armed and free" (*P* 12). These are regimes that arm the citizenry. France, which might have been "unconquerable" if it had maintained Charles's preference for its own arms, nonetheless succumbed to mercenaries (*P* 13). Was its obliviousness to this "poison" due to its spiritual subjection to the Church (*P* 13)? Colish (1999, 601) describes Machiavelli's position on the weakness of arms within Christendom argument as "bizarre."

12.   Cf. Mansfield 1996, 44.

13.   Machiavelli's harshness in this passage is striking. Within approximately forty lines, he accuses the Venetians of cowardice four times. Cf. Mansfield's account of this passage (1979, 402–4). See also *D* III.10.1, in which Machiavelli condemns the "idle princes" and "effeminate republics" that do not imitate ancient military practices.

14.   See also *Discourses* II.2 (treated later in this chapter); III.27.2; and III.30.1 for Machiavelli's discussion of Christianity's education and its effect on the virtue and spirit of citizens. Other works (see esp. Strauss 1958, 177–80; Mansfield 1979, 400–404; Sullivan 1996, 45–55; and Hulliung 1983, 66–68) have noted this critique. Cf. de Grazia 1994, 104–6.

15.   Machiavelli invites the reader to compare *D* III.31 and *P* 12 by offering this lesson in each passage. See Tarcov 2006, 77–90.

16.   See also Korvela 2006, 97–101.

17.   *Opere*, 149. For Christianity's enervating effects on martial virtue, see also *Art of War*, bk. 2, lines 304–9 (cited in Hulliung 1983, 13 and 62). On the general critique of Christianity in the *Art of War*, see also Lynch 2003, 217–19; cf. de Grazia's (1994, 65) more partial presentation.

18.   *D* II.2.2n12; John 14:6. See also Strauss 1958, 177; and Fontana 1999, 648–50.

19.   John 14:6.

20.   John 15:18–19. For other evidence of Christ's denigration of the "honor of the world" (*D* II.2.2), see also John 16:25–33 and 17:16. Matthew 4:4–11 and Luke 4:5–13 may be interpreted as evidence of Christ's indifference to worldly honor; for the relative importance of one's soul to worldly honor, see Matthew 16:26; Mark 8:36; and Luke 9:25. Even in the Gospel of John, which announces that Christ arrived to redeem the world, Christ opines, "Anyone who loves their life will lose it, while anyone who hates their life in this world will keep it for eternal life" (John 12:25). See also Romans 12:2; 1 Corinthians 1:20–28; 1 Timothy 6:7; James 4:4–5; and 1 John 2:15–17 and 5:19.

21.   See Tarcov 2006, 80–81.

22.   Cf. Hulliung 1983, 205.

23.   For Machiavelli's judgment of the constancy of human nature, see esp. *D* I.P.2; II.P.2; and I.39.1.

24. *D* III.31.3; of course, overconfidence can also attend virtue (III.23). This might explain why Venetians showed contempt for the Church and referred to France as the mere "son" of San Marco, Venice's patron saint (III.31.3). See esp. Mansfield's (1996, 167–68) discussion of the political effects of divine retribution.

25. In the text, Mansfield and Tarcov translate *"non si abbandonare mai"* (*Opere*, 190) as "never give up." I have elected to use a more literal translation (also offered by Mansfield and Tarcov, in a footnote) since it more clearly communicates what is lost to those who falter in bad fortune (*Opere*, 190).

26. McCormick 2011b; John 3:16–17.

27. While employing rich Christian imagery, McCormick argues that Cesare's actions depart importantly from Christ's (2011b, 15–17). Cesare does not defer to heaven for punishment of oppressors, and rather than sacrifice himself for their redemption, Cesare chooses to slaughter other men—most prominently, Remirro D'Orco—in order to deliver the people from their worldly troubles (15–17). Despite these departures, McCormick acknowledges that Cesare appears convinced of the possibility of forgiveness, and thus remains (partially) in thrall to Christianity (16). Ultimately, McCormick (7–10) views Cesare's actions in the Romagna as reflective of the requirements of modern state-building, which comport with McCormick's generally popular understanding of Machiavelli's thought (McCormick 2011a), and suggests the political utility of Christianity. McCormick (2011b, 16) even characterizes Cesare's disappearance from the text as an allusion to Christ's disappearance from the tomb. In order to suggest that Cesare represents a model of "prophetic statebuilding," however, McCormick problematically understates the seriousness of Cesare's errors—most notably, the defective foundation of his rule and his persistent belief in the "possibility of reconciliation," to which Machiavelli attributes Cesare's ultimate failure (16). See also Rahe 2008, 88–89; and Sullivan 1996, 171.

28. Cf. McCormick 2011b, 7–9. Orwin (2014) has noted that the Romagna's "more than a month" of faithfulness ought to be contrasted with the lasting orders of the founders, whose peoples remain faithful for centuries—or even millennia.

29. Pius III served as pope for twenty-six days, following the death of Alexander VI; in that capacity, he strengthened Cesare's position. Julius II succeeded him, and proved very hostile to Cesare. See Scott and Sullivan's (1994, 896) brief account of this period of ecclesiastical intrigue.

30. Machiavelli repeats this teaching in *Discourses* III.4. Scott and Sullivan (1994, 888) suggest that Cesare needed to abolish the papacy in order to succeed. I concur in their judgment that Cesare was incapable of this act.

31. In criticizing Cesare, Machiavelli condemns any "who believes [*crede*] that among great personages new benefits will make old injuries be forgotten" (*P* 7 [*Opere*, 269]). Cf. Tarcov 2013a (580), which also emphasizes this error, and identifies Cesare's latent belief in Christianity as "the cause of his ultimate ruin." According to Mansfield (*P* Glossary), this is the third context in which "belief" (*credere*) has arisen in *The Prince*. In the first instance (*P* 3), Machiavelli suggests that men will be disappointed by their belief that a new "lord"

will improve their condition; in the second instance (*P* 6), Machiavelli treats belief as unreliable, in the absence of force. After its appearance here, it recurs in chapter 8 where Machiavelli introduces his discussion of well-used cruelties with "I believe" (*credo che*) (*Opere*, 270; see also Tarcov 2013a, 582).

32.   Matthew 7:7–8. See also Matthew 6:14–15; and Mark 11:25.

33.   John 20:23.

34.   Mark 2:1–11, 2:17, 5:30–43, and 9:23. For Christ's most extravagant promise of forgiveness, see Matthew 26:26–30; Luke 24:47; and Acts 10:43; see also Luke 15:11–32. Cf. the earlier discussion of Christianity's relationship to hope, and its symbiotic relationship with human misery, in chapter 1 of the present study.

35.   Matthew 6:12. Cf. Machiavelli's account of Giavampagolo Baglioni in the *Discourses* (I.27), discussed in chapter 1.

36.   Among the Borgias' transgressions was an assassination plot against della Rovere that caused him to flee to France in 1494; in exile, he encouraged the king of France to depose Alexander VI (McBrien 1997, 270). During the conclave that led to his unanimous election, della Rovere purportedly promised an ecclesiastical preferment to Cesare (270). Given Julius II's notable impetuosity (*P* 25), he is perhaps an especially problematic vessel for Cesare's hopes; Machiavelli's preference for impetuous men appears closely connected to their willingness to contravene the regnant morality.

37.   Machiavelli describes Cesare's actions as the "*più freschi esempli*" (*Opere*, 268), while the founders are the "*grandissimi esempli*" (264). Compare the foregoing account with Machiavelli 1988b, "Niccolò Machiavelli to Francesco Vettori," January 31, 1515, 186. De Grazia (1994, 171) concludes that Borgia's career enflamed Machiavelli's hopes for Italian unity under the auspices of the Church.

38.   In chapter 11, Machiavelli concedes that Alexander's "intention might not have been to make the Church great, but rather the duke." Thus, it is possible that Alexander attempted to renew old orders that were not identical with those of the Church. Given his ambitions in Italy, Alexander may have been intent on reestablishing the Roman imperium, but under the direction of Cesare and his heirs. Machiavelli's use of *innovare* preserves this ambiguity: it could mean that Cesare intended to replace old orders or that he intended to renovate (renew) them (*Opere*, 268). Machiavelli also uses *innovare* when discussing the malcontent barons of the "French" kingdom; the context suggests that the barons seek to renovate, rather than replace, the orders of the French king (263). See also Strauss 1958, 283–84.

39.   Cf. Hulliung's (1983, 207–9) more optimistic account of the political promise of the corrupted Church.

40.   This chapter is commonly read as evidence of Machiavelli's support for republics (see esp. McCormick 2011a, 21–24). De Alvarez (2008, 32–36) also identifies a populist argument in chapter 9, but believes Machiavelli's aim is politically and morally ambiguous (46). See also Strauss 1958, 75–77; Hulliung 1983, 43; and Benner 2013, esp. 127–30. The civil principality first appears as a way to avoid crime, but Machiavelli discloses that it is, in fact, a way to limit the target of one's crime to those among the great (See also

McCormick 2011a, 31, which nonetheless overstates both Machiavelli's insistence that violence against the great be institutionalized and the certainty of his republican aims); thus, chapter 9 is an addendum to chapter 8—which also featured crimes directed at the great. This chapter is not so much a praise of the people, the protective capacity of which Machiavelli overstates (compare his account of Nabis with *D* III.6; see also Benner 2013, 130–32), but an indication of the proper initial target of founders: first the great must fall, and then things must be ordered in such a way that the people come to depend on the state (de Alvarez 2008, 46). In this context, see Parel's (1992, 100–112) interesting examination of humoral politics.

41. Cf. Viroli 2010, 85–86; see also Mansfield 1979, 160–62, 249–50; and Strauss 1958, 159.

42. These "certain conditions" (*D* II.19.1) appear to be a careful balance of power (II.19.3) moderated by an imperial authority that remains constrained by the Swiss.

43. See also *D* I.6.4; I.26.1 and III.23.3.

44. *Opere*, 273. Compare the discussion of charity that follows with Orwin 1978, 1222–23.

45. The other occurs in chapter 18. There, Machiavelli opines that a prince must sometimes act "against charity." I also discuss Machiavelli's unchristian view of charity in chapters 1 and 5 of this work. See esp. Orwin 1978.

46. In the Gospels, *agape* is more often translated as *dilectio* (see, for example, Matthew 5:43); subsequent books translate *agape* more regularly as *caritas* (see Kyle 1986, 176). Despite the confusion perpetrated by the Vulgate's inconsistent translation, *caritas* has unmistakably Christian connotations.

47. John 15:12–13, where the Latin uses *dilectio.* See also John 3:16 and 13:34–35; Matthew 5:43–48 and 22:34–40; and Mark 12:28–31.

48. 1 Corinthians 13:5, where the Latin reads, "*caritas.*" See also 1 John 4:7–8; Romans 5:8 and 13:9–10; Galatians 6:1–5; and Philippians 2:1–4.

49. Cf. *D* I.12.2.

50. The Italian reads: "*la natura degli uomini*" (*Opere*, 273); Machiavelli does discuss the "nature of peoples" (*natura de' populi*) in chapter 6 (*Opere*, 265). De Alvarez (2008, 48) does not note the uniqueness of this formulation; nonetheless, he helpfully observes that this act of self-sacrifice transforms the inhabitants of the walled city from subjects to "citizens" (48). Cf. Tarcov 2003, 115–16.

51. Matthew 26:28–29. See also Mark 14:24; Luke 22:20; and John 1:29, 3:16–17, 14:1–4, and 17:9–12. For evidence that Paul understands that Christ's sacrifice entails a future obligation, see Galatians 3:13–14. See also Hebrews 9:28. Cf. Matthew 9:12 and 12:7, in which Christ expresses a preference that his followers exhibit mercy, rather than self-sacrifice.

52. Matthew 16:24–26.

53. Ephesians 5:1–2.

54. 1 Peter 4:13–14.

55. For his promise to the poor, meek, and suffering, see Matthew 5:11–12; for his instruction to the wealthy, see Matthew 19:29 or Luke 12:33, for example; for one of many statements on the requirement of love, see John 13:34–35.

See also John 15:2; Romans 8:35–36; 2 Corinthians 4:7–12; and Colossians 1:24 for Christianity's embrace of sacrifice, and its relationship to an ultimate reward.

56.   For the importance of the resurrection to faith, see esp. Luke 24:37–53. For Jesus's promises that are unaccompanied by miraculous signs, see esp. Matthew 10:39 and 25:31–34; Mark 14:25; Luke 21:27–31; and John 14:6. While Christ's miracles and a few of his teachings (see esp. Matthew 6:33 and John 14:12–14) suggest that he also can benefit men in this world, the most important rewards lie in the next world.

57.   For other indications of man's general self-concern in *The Prince*, see *P* 3, 6, and 15.

58.   *Opere*, 273. Brown (2010b, 55) attributes a similar judgment to Lucretius. Compare this discussion with Wolin's (1960, 212–13) illuminating account of "the forms of illusion springing from man's tendency to project a world distorted by his own excessive ambitions, hopes, or fears," of which the most persistent form was belief in the "armed fortress" (212).

59.   For Machiavelli's view on the natural origins of justice, and its relationship to gratitude and selfishness, see *Discourses* I.2.2. Orwin (1978, 1224–25) notes the prevalence of this psychology in a different context. See also de Alvarez 2008 (83), which insists that a prince "must not only benefit [a people] but also make them suffer for him."

60.   John 15:18 and 16:33.

61.   Recall Machiavelli's famous proclamation that "men forget the death of a father more quickly than the loss of a patrimony" (*P* 17; cf. *P* 24). Does the relative weakness of blood ties mean that the obligations engendered by taking the blood of Christ are also weak, in comparison with men's pressing and insatiable need for property (cf. de Alvarez 2008, 83)? Christ also diminishes the obligation of "blood ties," but suggests that he and his followers constitute a new, superior family (Matthew 12:48–50 and 19:29). I am indebted to Robert Fullilove, who directed me to this passage.

62.   Matthew 6:19–21.

63.   *P* 5.

64.   *P* 11; cf. *P* 6. Fontana (1999, 641) notes that Machiavelli thus "explodes the medieval duality between church and empire."

65.   The only example Machiavelli offers in this chapter is the Catholic Church, yet the title and the language of the first paragraph suggest that he is offering an analysis that applies to multiple principalities. Most of the previous chapter titles (*P* 1–3, 5–8, and 10) employed the plural form and discussed multiple examples. Chapters 4 and 9—each of which conveys an important theoretical teaching—employ the singular form, but nonetheless discuss multiple examples. How do we make sense of this puzzle? Perhaps the governance of the Church has varied so widely that by discussing different popes, he is, in effect, discussing multiple examples of ecclesiastical principalities. Another possibility is that Machiavelli's teaching on ecclesiastical principalities applies to only two principalities: those of the Church and its founder.

66.   Tarcov (2003, 116) notes an important aspect of what he describes as "manifestly heavy irony": despite the Church's alleged reliance on superior causes,

it nonetheless grew ascendant by using "money and arms." Alexander and Julius are consecutive in Machiavelli's account only because he omits discussion of the brief reign of Pius III. Machiavelli also omits discussion of Innocent VIII, who served as pontiff between the "spirited" Sixtus IV (whom Machiavelli mentions in this chapter) and Alexander VI (*P* 11). While Pius's short reign renders him insignificant, Innocent VIII had a busy career: he lived as a worldly prince, persecuted alleged witches, and granted Ferdinand and Isabella the title "Catholic Kings" for their expulsion of the Moors from Granada, which Machiavelli describes as a "pious cruelty" (McBrien 1997, 267; *P* 21). Sixtus IV also accomplished much in his thirteen years as pope, during which he also "reigned as a Renaissance prince" (McBrien 1997, 266); most portentously, he "confirmed the infamous Tomás de Torquemada as grand inquisitor" of Spain (265). That man would eventually orchestrate the Inquisition, which Machiavelli surely considers a pious cruelty (*P* 21). Given his critical view of Ferdinand's legacy (which I treat in chapter 6), the careers of Popes Sixtus IV and Innocent VIII demonstrate the damaging consequences of a powerful papacy. We may add to this consideration the fact that Sixtus's predecessor was Paul II, a pope famous for banning the study of pagan works (McBrien 1997, 263–64). See *FH* I.23 for Machiavelli's assessment of the ascent of the Church's worldly influence.

67.   Machiavelli is perhaps overstating the damage wrought by the Borgias and is certainly overstating the ability of Julius (cf. *P* 25). Without Alexander's efforts to eliminate the factions of Rome, it seems unlikely that Julius would have long survived.

68.   For another aspect of the pope's ineffective rule, see chapter 6, below. See also Scott and Sullivan 1994 (895–96), which describes the tragicomic circumstances that purportedly led to Alexander VI's death and Cesare's illness. Compare the discussion in the text that follows with *Discourses* I.12, in which Machiavelli explicitly blames the Church for the divisions that wrack Italy. See also Machiavelli's critique of the indolent "gentlemen" (*D* I.55), who populate the Papal States in particularly large numbers and make "political life" impossible (Scott and Sullivan 1994, 890).

69.   Machiavelli alters this quote from Tacitus's *Annals* by redacting the qualifying phrase "of mortal things" from the historian's original. Machiavelli thus applies this judgment to the entire universe, rather than merely men. I am indebted to Harvey Mansfield (*P* 13, 57n9) for this observation. See also Tarcov 2013a (586), which notes that this is the only time Machiavelli defers to the opinion of "the wise" in *The Prince.*

The context of the quote may also be significant: Tacitus is criticizing Agrippina the Younger, who had been alienated from her son, Emperor Nero. The two had been engaged in an incestuous relationship and had, effectively, shared rule of the empire. Recently, however, Nero had begun isolating himself from his domineering mother. Enraged by Nero's affections for a freedwoman and recent association with her political rivals, she announced that her hopes lay with Britannicus, her adolescent stepson, who by the efforts of "the gods and she herself" remained alive as the "true and worthy heir" (*Annals* XIII.15). Nero responded by poisoning the young man and placing Agrippina in isolation. I am indebted to Alexander Orwin, who alerted me to the context of this quote and suggested that one might compare the fiendish Agrippina to the holy Mary, who also places her hopes in a son (Luke 1:46–55) who suffers an early death. Machiavelli links the subjection to women to support for Christianity throughout *The Prince* (see chapter 6, below).

70.   Matthew 26:47, 50–54. Cf. John 18:36.

71.   While "the four . . . named above" (*P* 13) could be the four princes named in chapter 13 (Hiero, David, Cesare Borgia, and Charles VII), the context suggests Machiavelli is referring to Moses, Romulus, Theseus, and Cyrus. Earlier, when reintroducing Hiero (also first mentioned in chapter 6), he uses the similar language: "he was one of those named above by me" (*P* 13). As Mansfield (1996, 266) notes, Machiavelli also submits himself to the orders of the mercenary captain Philip of Macedon.

72.   Strauss (1958, 172) thus comments: "In saying that the unarmed prophets have failed, he exaggerates in order to bring to light the difficulty with which he is faced." In the *Discourses* (II.13.1), Machiavelli suggests that unlike force, "fraud alone will be found to be quite enough . . . to come to great ranks." The men he names as supreme frauds (Agathocles, Cyrus, and Philip II of Macedon) possessed arms (*D* II.13.1) but are also constrained by a "necessity to deceive." I am indebted to Vickie Sullivan, who raised this point in response to a draft of this work.

73.   Cf. Strauss 1958 (171): "Machiavelli's critique of the old modes and orders therefore takes on the character of a war waged by an unarmed man, or a spiritual war. This war can be described, with the somewhat free use of Christian terms, as a war of the Anti-Christ or of the Devil who recruits his army while fighting or through fighting against the army led by God or Christ." Unlike Strauss (84), I judge that Machiavelli provides answers to the question of how he might "reasonably hope for the success of his enormous venture": his efforts to enflame the desire for worldly goods and glorify the possession of arms will help him overcome his unarmed state, if only posthumously. See Strauss 1958, 307–8n29 for a discussion of the chief implication of Italian weakness: Italy's redeeming army cannot be composed of Italian citizens.

74.   1 John 4:3 and 4:5. Cf. 1 John 2:15–17. See also Strauss 1958, 171.

75.   John 18:36.

Chapter Four

1.   Many scholars have treated this chapter in detail. See esp. Mansfield 1996, 266–70; de Alvarez 2008, 64–71; and Benner 2013, 169–75.

2.   Mark 15:16–20. See also Matthew 27:27–31 and 28:11–15; Luke 23:36–37 (contrast with Matthew 8:15, 27:48–49, and 27:54; Mark 15:39; and Luke 7:1–10 and 23:44–47); and John 19:2–3. In addition to the exceptions within the Gospels, Tarcov (2003, 119) notes that—despite the unreasonableness of

the arrangement—the rule of priests confirms that the armed sometimes do obey the unarmed.

3. Cf. John 14:27–28. See de Alvarez 2008, 65.

4. See esp. Mansfield 1979, 421–24; and 1996, 269; and Benner 2009, 121–24; and 2013, 171. In Machiavelli's curious presentation, this mental preparation eclipses even the importance of trained armies.

5. In chapter 14, Machiavelli reveals more fully the sinister implications of his own, superior, knowledge of Tuscany's natural sites—which "have a natural similarity to those of other provinces" (2008, 66). De Alvarez observes that Tuscany's landscape bears a strong resemblance to Rome's: Machiavelli's knowledge of nature can thus enable conquest of Lorenzo and his patron.

6. See *D* III.39.1. Cf. *P* 12; and *D* III.31.4; see Mansfield 1996, 268–69.

7. As head of the Achaean League, Philopoemen incidentally aids Roman interests by waging war against the Spartan tyrant Nabis (Livy XXXV.25–37) before the Achaeans ally themselves more formally with Rome in its war against the Syrian king Antiochus (XXXV.50). Due to his consummate skill and patriotic bent, Philopoemen earns the hostility of the jealous and self-aggrandizing Romans, who eventually betray the Achaeans (for the jealousy of the Romans, see XXXV.47; for the dissolution of the accord between the Romans and the Achaeans, see XXXVIII.31–33; for Rome's betrayal of Achaea over the issue of Sparta, see XXXIX.34–37; for the Roman Senate's imperial conduct toward its former ally, see XXXIX.48; and Plutarch, *Philopoemen* 17.1–3). Philopoemen eventually denounces their advances in Greece (*Philopoemen* 17.3), partly because as "last of the Greeks, . . . his lofty spirit [led] him to strive and contend against men in power" (1:4 and 17.4). I discuss his failed opposition to Rome below, in this chapter and in chapter 6. See Sullivan 2013 and Benner 2013 (41–49) for discussions of Rome's conduct in Greece. Publius Decius was a tribune of the soldiers under the consul Cornelius during an engagement against the Samnites. I discuss the significance of his efforts in this chapter, but see Mansfield 1979, 422–24.

8. *Opere*, 279. This passage closely resembles Livy's account (XXXV.28) of a battle against Nabis, but Livy does not record a conversation, and it is unclear whether he places Philopoemen on the plain. Cf. Plutarch (*Philopoemen* 4.6), who does not report this conversation, but criticizes Philopoemen's extreme devotion to "military science." Cf. Polybius, *Histories* XXI.32c.

9. Tarcov 2007, 141. See also Tarcov 2013a, 586; and forthcoming; Mansfield, 1996, 268; and Benner, 2013, 172–73.

10. Plutarch, *Philopoemen* 4.6.

11. As with Philopoemen's appearance, Machiavelli fabricates many of Decius's statements (see Livy VII.34). Machiavelli also names Decius as a man of exemplary virtue whose self-sacrifice was responsible for drawing Rome back to its beginning (*D* III.1.3 and II.16.1; cf. Livy VIII.8–9; and Coby 1999, 75). Publius Decius's son exhibits similar virtue (Livy X.28–29): the Decii appear to embody the republican virtue that Machiavelli praises but does not necessarily practice. Cf. Strauss 1958, 173.

Mansfield (1979, 424n24) suggests that in his discussion of Decius, Machiavelli uses Livy's language to allude to a passage from the Psalms, which

Mansfield misidentifies (as Psalm 18:62). Psalm 18:2 reads: "The LORD is my rock, my fortress and my deliverer; my God is my rock, in whom I take refuge, my shield and the horn of my salvation, my stronghold." Paul appears to imitate this language in 1 Thessalonians 5:2–9: the comparison of that passage with Decius's language yields even more pregnant results.

12.   *D* I.12, II.2.3, and II.2.2; *P* 26.

13.   *D* I.12–14. See Mansfield's (1979, 69–79), Coby's (1999, 66–77), and Najemy's (1999, 677) nuanced, but predominantly positive accounts of Roman religion; cf. Benner's (2009, 386–406) nuanced, but predominately negative account. Sullivan (1996, 104–17) most trenchantly elaborates the problematic consequences of this arrangement, which McCormick (2011a, 85) mentions only briefly in his critical account of Roman elites. See also Strauss 1958, 140–41.

14.   For Rome's use of prophecy before the battle with the Samnites, see *D* I.14.2; Mansfield 1979, 76–77; and Coby 1999, 71–73.

15.   See *D* II.2.2–4, discussed in chapter 1, above. Machiavelli explicitly laments the first two effects; see Sullivan 1996 (49–55), Mansfield 1996 (149–50), Coby 1999 (268–74), and Rahe 2009 (97–100) for succinct statements of the last position.

16.   For a description of Lorenzo's rule, see Tarcov 2007, 123–24. Philopoemen's first action against Sparta was directed against Cleomenes, whom Plutarch describes as a "king [*basileus*]" (Plutarch, *Philopoemen* 5.1), but his subsequent efforts were against Machanidas and Nabis, both of whom Plutarch identifies as "tyrants [*tyrannos*]" (*Philopoemen* 10.1 and 12.4). Both Livy (for example, XXXVII.3) and Plutarch (*Philopoemen* 16.1) describe Antiochus as a "king" (*rex* or *basileus*). Aside from Machiavelli's expressed preference for Italian unity (*P* 26), his remarkable praise of France (*P* 13) also suggests the superiority of unified states with proper military orders.

17.   See Strauss 1958, 171.

18.   Matthew 5:1.

19.   Matthew 24:3; Mark 13:3. Luke reports this as the site from which Jesus begins his kingly entrance into Jerusalem (19:28–31) and the place to which he returns each evening during his final days of preaching (21:37 and 22:39–46); John (12–14) reports that Jesus's secret conversations took place at Bethany, which lies on the slope of the Mount of Olives. Jesus also frequently meets with his disciples on mountains or mountainsides (see Matthew 28:16; and Mark 3:13).

20.   Matthew 17:1–9; see also Mark 9:1–9 and Luke 9:28–36.

21.   Matthew 27:33; Mark 15:22; Luke 23:33; John 19:17. The Gospels identify Golgotha as the site of Jesus's death; circumstantial evidence (Mark 15:40) suggests that it was on a hill—an opinion that tradition endorses. For Jesus's hostility toward the low places—and especially Jerusalem—see Matthew 24:2; see also Matthew 4:8. Cf. Luke 3:5, in which Mary identifies Christ's arrival with a profound leveling.

   Note that the Old Testament reminds us that God, too, is said to occupy a "mountain," to which believers turn for guidance and protection (see Exodus 19:20; for one of many examples within the Psalms, see Psalm 2:6).

Machiavelli's hostility toward the high places strengthens the proposition that his sustained critique of God's "one and only Son" (John 3:16) also betrays his hostility toward God (see esp. *P* 25–26; cf. esp. Nederman 2009 and Viroli 2010).

22. Matthew 24:39–31 and 24:36. Cf. *D* I.12.1 and I.56. In the latter passage, Machiavelli contemplates the possibility that some men might possess "knowledge of things natural and supernatural"; for a pithy and illuminating discussion of this passage, see Mansfield 1979, 164–65; cf. Wolin 1960, 211.

23. Matthew 21:21; see also Matthew 17:14–20; Mark 11:23; and Luke 23:30.

24. See, for example, Matthew 24–25.

25. John 14: 28–31; see also John 12:31 and 16:11 and Matthew 24:29. The word translated as "prince" is the word *archwn*; in the Vulgate, it appears as *princeps*. For Christ's promised redemption, see esp. Matthew 19:28–30 and 25:31–46; Mark 13:26–27; and Luke 21:28.

26. 2 Corinthians 10:3–6 (this passage is quoted from the New King James Version: the NIV misleadingly translates *sarki* or *carnem* as "world"). See also Romans 8:37, in which Paul announces that believers "are more than conquerors" through Christ's love.

27. 2 Corinthians 10:4 and 10:5.

28. John 14:30. Cf. John 16:6–11.

29. *P* 14. I ground the analysis that follows in the histories on which Machiavelli relied, but generally does not cite—especially Plutarch's and Livy's. See Tarcov forthcoming.

30. As Tarcov (forthcoming) explains persuasively, Machiavelli conflates the careers of Scipio Africanus Major (236–183 BC) and Scipio Africanus Minor (185–129 BC) in *The Prince*. Machiavelli's reference here is thus apparently to Scipio Africanus Minor, who, according to Cicero, "always had in his hands Xenophon, the disciple of Socrates" (*Tusculan Disputations* II.xxvi and II.131). In chapter 17, Machiavelli recounts details of Africanus Major's career, but in each instance, he refers to his subject only as "Scipio" (*P* 14 and 17). The preponderance of the evidence Tarcov (forthcoming) presents—including especially the historical events to which he refers in chapter 17—suggests that Machiavelli is primarily critical of Scipio Africanus Major, and intends for his reader to examine the history of his life. This informs my decision to examine his career in detail.

   Machiavelli perpetrates another confusion in this chapter by referring to Xenophon's work as the "life of Cyrus" (*P* 14 and 60n5); the work is actually titled *Cyropaedia*, or *The Education of Cyrus*. Christopher Nadon (2001, 14) observes that Machiavelli thus reminds the reader that more than one author offers a "life of Cyrus": Herodotus's *Histories* depicts Cyrus as a "savage king" who came to power in the way Machiavelli suggests in chapter 6 that founders must.

31. Many scholars offer treatments of this passage: see esp. Strauss 1958, 77–78; Mansfield 1996, 269–70; Palmer 2001, 84–85; Nadon 2001, 14–25; Tarcov 2003, 119–20; 2006, 87–88; and esp. forthcoming; de Alvarez 2008, 67–71; Benner 2013, 173–75; and Sullivan 2013, 530–32.

32. Plutarch, *Julius Caesar* 57.1.

33. See also Coby 1999, 50; cf. *D* I.10.6. McCormick (2015, 49–51) offers a subtle and equivocal judgment of Caesar.
34. Plutarch, *Alexander* 27.4.
35. Sullivan 2013, 536–37; *P* 4. See also *D* I.20. For the similarity of Christ's and Alexander's careers, see de Alvarez 2008 (20–21) and Sullivan 2013 (523–24 and 536; cf. *D* II.8.1).
36. Cf. *D* I.26.
37. Contrast Alexander's jealous ambition to learn with the generosity of Aristotle, Chiron, and Machiavelli.
38. Sullivan 2013, 536.
39. See also Statius, *Achilleid* I.573 and I.589.
40. For Chiron's skill in war, see Ovid, *Fasti* 5; for Chiron's medical skill, see Homer, *Iliad* 4.217–19 and 11.831; and Pindar, *Pythian Odes* 3.1–10. As Benner (2013, 216) pithily remarks, "Like Machiavelli's text, he looked more bestial than he was." Indeed, humanists commonly praised his gentleness, erudition, and artistry. According to Ingman (1982, 217), "The story of Chiron was well known" to Renaissance humanists, and Machiavelli's presentation, which emphasizes Chiron's beastly nature, "constitutes . . . almost a complete break with the traditional interpretation of the Chiron legend."
41. Little is known about Caesar's early education, although Suetonius reports that he received some education from Marcus Antonius Gnipho; a noted grammarian, Gnipho only devoted one day a week to instruction in rhetoric (Suetonius, *Lives* VII).
42. Palmer (2001, 88) follows Strauss's (1958, 78) suggestion; see also de Alvarez 2008, 86; cf. Benner 2009, 198–201; and Fontana 1999, 644. While the synoptic Gospels generally suggest that Jesus is the Son of God (Matthew 2:2–11 and 14:33; Mark 1:1), John famously identifies Christ as God (John 1:14 and 20:28); see also Colossians 2:9. For the commandment to imitate Christ, see esp. Matthew 16:24; Luke 9:23; 1 Corinthians 11:1–2; and Philippians 2:3–11.
43. Achilles dies young (*Odyssey* XI); Alexander dies of a fever, plagued by suspicion of his court (Plutarch, *Alexander* 75–76); Caesar is assassinated by Brutus (Plutarch, *Caesar* 68–69); for one account of Chiron's early demise, see Hyginus, *Astronomica* 2.38.
44. Mathew 16:24. See also Matthew 7:21; Mark 10:30; and Luke 18:30; in John (3:16, 6:50–58, 17:3), Christ promises eternal life even more explicitly. The rest of the New Testament conforms to John's language: see esp. Romans 2:5–7; 1 Corinthians 15:51–54; 2 Timothy 1:10; and 1 John 5:13–14.
45. Apollodorus, *Library* 2.5.4.
46. Apollodorus, *Library* 2.5.4. Accounts of Chiron's death vary. According to Apollodorus, his death gave Prometheus eternal life (see also Ovid, *Metamorphoses* 2.633–75). Lucian's (*Dialogi mortuorum* 26.1–2) report agrees with that of Apollodorus, but the former's interlocutor doubts the wisdom of Chiron's decision. For a different account of Chiron's death, see Ovid, *Fasti* 5.379–416. These accounts of Chiron, including Pindar's, were widely available during the Italian Renaissance (Ingman 1982, 217). Revard (2009, 2–3) recounts Pindar's currency among fifteenth-century Italian humanists but does not disclose whether Machiavelli was familiar with the poet. Pindaric-style odes were

nonetheless written for many of the figures Machiavelli discusses, including Francesco Sforza (18–20) and Ferdinand of Aragon (23).

47. Pindar, *Pythian Odes* 3.5. This ode is directed to Hiero I of Syracuse—not the Hiero of chapters 6 and 13 of *The Prince*.

48. Pindar, *Pythian Odes* 3.58–68. This quote appears in the context of Pindar's critique of Asclepius, who was a student of Chiron's and was killed by Zeus for attempting to raise the dead (Plato, *Republic* 408b). Asclepius's mother was Apollo's lover, and was killed for her subsequent infidelity. In the context of his rumination on her ill-fated love, Pindar remarks, "There is a worthless tribe among men which dishonors what is at home and looks far away, hunting down empty air with hopes that cannot be fulfilled" (*Pythian Odes* 3.20–24).

49. Pindar, *Pythian Odes* 3.58–68.

50. Machiavelli is perhaps playfully imitating Socrates, who also casts himself as a revised Achilles (*Apology* 28b–d). Machiavelli also appears to think himself superior to Asclepius, since the earthly glory he promises provides a balm for the infectious desire for immortality.

51. Plutarch, *Philopoemen* 4.4. Of course, many ambitious men of antiquity imitated Alexander. Machiavelli's treatment of Emperor Caracalla (*P* 19; Herodian, *History* IV.8) confirms that not all are worthy of praise.

52. Plutarch, *Philopoemen* 1.1. Cf. Polybius, *Histories* X.21–23. See also *Iliad* IX.441 and IX.492–97; and Apollodorus, *Library* 3.13.8.

53. Plutarch (*Philopoemen* 1.2–4) reports that these energetic philosopher-statesmen—who had orchestrated an assassination, expelled a tyrant, and calmed political confusion in a far-flung city—"beyond all men of their day had brought philosophy to bear upon political action and affairs of state. [Nonetheless, they] . . . counted the education of Philopoemen also among their many achievements, believing that their philosophical teachings had made him a common benefit to Greece."

54. Plutarch, *Philopoemen* 1.2.

55. Plutarch, *Philopoemen* 4.3–5. The "Tactics" of Evangelus does not survive (Aelian 1814, 3, "Notes"). Compare Philopoemen with Machiavelli, who intends to "write something useful," and thus seeks the "effectual truth" (*P* 15; see also *P* DL). See also Plutarch, *Philopoemen* 3.1.

56. Cf. Plutarch, *Philopoemen* 21.5. See esp. de Alvarez 2008, 66; and Benner 2013, 173. For the "Roman" character of Machiavellian wisdom, see Hulliung 1983, 132, 152–53.

57. Livy XXXIX.49; Plutarch, *Philopoemen* 18.4–8. Livy's and Plutarch's accounts of his death are very similar. Polybius (*Histories* XXIII.12) offers only a spare account of this event. According to Plutarch, Messene had been induced "to revolt from the Achaean league" (18.3) by Deinocrates, a man of suspect character who also harbored a grudge against Philopoemen.

58. Livy XXXIX.49.

59. Livy XXXIX.50; Plutarch (*Philopoemen* 19.3) does not report the existence of a pulley system.

60. Plutarch, *Philopoemen* 20.3.

61. Plutarch, *Philopoemen*, 20.3; Livy (XXXIX.50) reports that Philopoemen responded merely by saying, "It is well," before drinking the poison.

62. Livy XXXIX.50. Philopoemen's age and mode of death remind one of Socrates: might Machiavelli also seek to supplant him as a model for human life?

63. Plutarch, *Philopoemen* 21.2. Plutarch (*Philopoemen*, 21.2) reports that the chief conspirator, Deinocrates, escaped.

64. Livy XXXIX.50; Plutarch, *Philopoemen* 21.5.

65. Plutarch, *Philopoemen* 21.5.

66. In Matthew (26:27–29), Mark (14:22–26), and Luke (22:17–23), Christ is arrested after the Last Supper, during which he promises his disciples salvation by guaranteeing their place in "my Father's kingdom" (Matthew 27:29). John (17:20–26) reports that Jesus is arrested immediately after praying for the salvation of all believers.

67. For the popular accolades—and entrenched opposition—that greet Christ as he enters Jerusalem, see Matthew 21:1–11; Mark 11:1–11; Luke 19:28–44; and John 12:12–19.

68. Matthew 27:59–60; Mark 15:46; Luke 23:53 and 24:2; John 19:41 and 20:1.

69. Matthew (27:20–26), Mark (15:9–15), and John (19:6–16) each emphasize that the Jewish religious leaders are responsible for the crowd's bloodthirsty disposition toward Jesus; only Luke (23:13–24) attributes the crowd's disposition to naturally occurring malevolence, rather than manipulation by the chief priests.

70. Livy XXXIX.50. See esp. Benner 2013, 174–75.

71. Livy XXXIX.49.

72. Matthew 27:26–31; Mark 15:15–20; Luke 22:63–65; John 19:1–18.

73. Matthew (27.46–50) and Mark (15:34–37) emphasize Christ's mental anguish; Luke (23:39–46) and John (19:28–30) record that Christ exhibited sublime equanimity while on the cross.

74. For Jesus's miraculous disappearance from the tomb, see Matthew 28:1–10; Mark 16:1–8; Luke 24:1–12; and John 20:1–10. For his appearance before believers, see Matthew 28:16–20; Mark 16:9–20; Luke 24:13–53; and John 20:11–21:25. Matthew (28:4) reports that two dumbfounded guards witness Christ's resurrection, but are subsequently paid by the chief priests to report that Jesus's disciples stole the body (28:11–15). Cf. 1 Corinthians 15:6.

75. John 20:19. According to Matthew, when Christ is arrested "all the disciples deserted him and fled" (26:56; see also Mark 14:50). Peter's denial appears at Matthew 26:69–75; Mark 14:26–72; Luke 22:54–62; and John 18:13–27. Luke (22:54) and John (18:15) report, however, that Peter shows more mettle: according to them, he followed the detained Christ "at a distance" (Luke 22:54) before he is confronted and denies him. Luke and John also report that Peter and the unnamed "disciple whom Jesus loved," respectively, are not afraid when confronted with evidence of his disappearance (Luke 24:12; John 20:3–10). See Plutarch (*Philopoemen* 21.1) for an account of the military actions that Philopoemen's death prompts.

76. Matthew 28:19.

77. Luke 24:34; John 20:19, 21, and 26.

78. Rome formally adopted Christianity in 380. I discuss the importance of this fact in chapter 2. See also Strauss 1958 (84), which notes the significance of Constantine's adoption of Christianity.

79. Plutarch, *Philopoemen* 21.5. For an account of the relative insignificance of Christianity until the late third century and early fourth century, see Stark 1997, 6–13.

80. As I indicate above, despite some textual ambiguity, I conclude that Machiavelli is here referring to Scipio Africanus Major.

81. See also de Alvarez 2008, 69.

82. Matthew 5:17. See also Luke 24:44 for Jesus's relationship to the Mosaic law; see Matthew 17:3–4; Mark 9:4–5; and Luke 9:30–33 for the clearest evidence that Jesus intends to succeed Moses. See *Discourses* (I.11.2) for Machiavelli's praise of Numa, which he subsequently withdraws (1.19.1). Theseus (Plutarch, *Theseus* 35.4–5) did not have an obvious successor—except for perhaps Solon, who lived six hundred years later and refounded Athens. Machiavelli is critical of Solon's decision to found a popular state (I.2.6), but cites him as an effective religious pretender (I.9.3 and I.11.3; see also II.10.1 for Solon's praiseworthy view of the value of steel, rather than gold). Indeed, Jesus is the only successor of the founders whom Machiavelli does not identify explicitly as a religious pretender (cf., however, *D* I.12). Cf. de Alvarez 2008, 67.

83. While in the *Discourses* Machiavelli invites us to compare Christ's career to Numa's, in *The Prince* he invites us to compare it to Scipio's. For Numa's similarity to Christ, see esp. Strauss 1958, 225–32 and 337–38n122; Mansfield 1979, 69–79 and 88–90; Sullivan 1996, esp. 113–16; and Coby 1999, 56–68. Cf. Benner 2009, 386–93; and Viroli 2010, 176–77.

84. Cf. Strauss 1958, 59.

85. Much Machiavelli scholarship (Strauss 1958, 78, 139, 161–62; Mansfield 1996, 61; Palmer 2001, 85–86; Patapan 2006, 126; de Alvarez 2008; Newell 2013, 266; Tarcov 2013b, 112) notes the dubious authenticity of Xenophon's honorific account, but see esp. Nadon 2001 (17), which judges that Xenophon's Cyrus is "improved or sanitized." Nadon argues that Machiavelli is attuned to a "covert" (2001, 20) Xenophonic teaching that communicates the necessity of what would be considered vice. Cf. Benner 2009, 72–78; and 2013, 72–79 and 174–75.

86. *Opere*, 230, 163. See also Strauss 1958, 322n132. Cf. Hulliung 1983, 197.

87. Livy XXVI.19. Cicero informs us of the character of Scipio Africanus Minor's education (*Tusculan Disputations* II.26).

88. Cf. *D* III.20, where Machiavelli discreetly associates Scipio's humanity with Xenophon's work. Cf. also Benner 2013, 175.

89. Machiavelli elsewhere judges that while this "damaging quality" (*P* 17) may be necessary for a prince who cultivates a reputation for humanity, severity is to be preferred among republican captains (*D* III.22.4). His treatment of Scipio in the *Discourses* is complicated and ambivalent. Although he recommends imitating Scipio rather than Caesar (*D* I.10.2), since the former could be restrained by the Senate (*D* III.1.3; Livy XXIX.19–21; XXXVIII, 50–60) and was checked by the "voice of the people" (*D* I.58.3), Scipio also exhibits

many un-Machiavellian traits: for example, he "esteemed the power of God more than that of men" (*D* I.11.1, where Scipio relies also on "naked steel"; cf. Romulus's independence [I.11.2] and the cynical use of religion by the Senate [I.13]); always advocates for plans that conform to his audacious nature (I.53.4 and III.9.1; cf. II.12.1 and II.32.1, in which Scipio's assault on New Carthage appears to be a model for conquest); exhibits goodness and generosity that depend on the gratitude of others (*D* III.20; Livy XXVI.46 and 50); and relies on love to secure victory, which proves insufficient (*D* III.21 and III.22.3; Livy XXVIII.24–29). Perhaps Scipio's most notable quality is his ability to secure his "fame" and good reputation, which distinguishes him from the "hateful" Hannibal (*D* III.34.3), whom Machiavelli nonetheless praises. Ultimately, Hannibal's use of fear appears more worthy of imitation than Scipio's use of love, despite the latter's victory (III.21.2). Livy also reports that Hannibal seeks to imitate—and surpass—Alexander (XXXV.14).

90. Livy XXIX.19. Much scholarship (Strauss 1958, 192; Mansfield 1979, 376–79; Coby 1999, 191; Nadon 2001, 15–17; Sullivan 2006, 248; Benner 2009, 468–74; and 2013, 44, 198–202, and 210; McCormick 2015, 42–45) detects this critique of Scipio in Machiavelli's (and Livy's) writings, but see esp. de Alvarez 2008 (84), which observes that Scipio "corrupted the military orders of Rome, which is the corruption of the republic itself" and invites the reader to "think of other orders that show excessive pity or compassion for human beings but do not correct human injustice" (85). Cf. Viroli's (2014, 78) prosaic depiction of Scipio as "one of the finest republican heroes."

91. Livy XXVIII.24. This is not the first "mutiny" under Scipio's command (XXVI.48).

92. Livy XXVIII.25. Livy reports that the soldiers had cause to suspect that Scipio would show them "clemency" (*clementiae*) and "forgiveness" (*ignovisse*). Scipio's reputation for kindness and clemency was well known: he sought to hold allies with "bonds of kindness [*beneficio*] rather than by those of fear [*metu*]" (XXVI.49). For Scipio's scrupulously kind treatment of other men's wives and daughters, see XXVI.49–50. When Scipio departs from kindness, however, the consequences are especially grim (XXVIII.22–23).

93. The political events that precede this story, which resulted in Scipio being permitted to investigate the conquest of Africa, are recorded in Livy, XXVIII.39–42; cf. Diodorus Siculus, *Library of History* XXVII.4, which offers a slightly different account (cf. McCormick 2015, 45–46).

94. Livy XXIX.7.

95. Strauss 1958, 211. I am indebted to Nathan Tarcov, who directed me to this passage in Strauss's book. See also Hulliung 1983, 211. Compare the following discussion in the text with de Grazia 1994, 318–40.

96. *Opere*, 197.

97. Matthew 25:46.

98. John 8:1–12; Luke 23:41–43 and 19:1–10. A notable exception to Christ's mercy is his condemnation of lawyers, who will be "punished most severely" (Mark 12:40). Subsequent books of the New Testament (see, for example, 2 Thessalonians 1:6–10 or 2 Corinthians 10:6) invoke punishment more freely. A notable exception is 1 John 4:16–18.

99. Luke 6:35–36. Christ promises to reward the merciful in the Sermon on the Mount (Matthew 5:7), but his many miracles (Matthew 15:22–28, 17:14–20, and 20:29–34; Mark 5:18–19 and 10:46–52; Luke 10:25–37 and 18:35–43) constitute his chief acts of mercy. I discuss the implications of his merciful conduct below, in chapter 5. The word translated as "mercy" is the Greek *eleew* or *oiktirmos*, or the Latin *misericordia*.

100. Consider James 2:13: "Judgment without mercy will be shown to anyone who has not been merciful. Mercy triumphs over judgment." For the belief in the mercy of Christ and God among early Christians, see also Romans 11:30–32 and 15:9; 2 Corinthians 4:1; Ephesians 2:4–9; Titus 3:5; James 3:17 and 5:11; 1 Peter 1:3; 2 John 1:3; and Jude 1:21.

101. The harmful effects of Scipio's and Christ's mercy are exacerbated by their ambition, insofar as a glorious undertaking distracts each. Scipio is consumed with the thought of attacking Carthage, while Christ appears preoccupied with the divine reward that will attend his glorious return (Matthew 19:29 and 24:3–25:46).

102. For Moses's divinely ordained plundering of foreign peoples, see esp. Deuteronomy 1:26–46, 2:24–36, 7, and 20; and Numbers 31:1–7 and 35:50–55. I discuss this characteristic of his rule in chapter 2. As Mansfield explains, "The peoples who seized the Roman Empire" (*D* II.8.2) include "in some sense" (1979, 212) Moses himself (cf. Tarcov 2014, 202–3). Machiavelli quotes the Maurusians who fled from the Israelite invasion of Syria, only to displace populations living in Africa: "We are Maurusians, who fled before the face of Joshua the robber son of Nun" (II.8.2). Machiavelli renders the Greek source in Latin, rendering Joshua as "*Iesu*"—which is also the Latin word for Jesus (Mansfield and Tarcov 1996, 145n9). Thus are we reminded of Christianity's conquest of Rome, and the renaming of many sites and cities. Cf. de Grazia 1994, 85.

103. Exodus 33:19. See also Deuteronomy 13:12–18. More frequently, Moses promises that God will "redeem" the Israelites (see esp. Exodus 6:6; and Deuteronomy 7:8 and 15:15), albeit after much suffering. Luke teaches (24:21–27) that Jesus will redeem his people by his own suffering. Cf. Viroli, who conflates Moses and Christ (2010, 61–63 and 105–6) and omits discussion of the differences (2014, 110–11) between the redemption offered in the Pentateuch and that promised in the Gospels.

104. For the plagues on the Israelites' Egyptian masters, see Exodus 7–12. Exodus 14 records the drowning of the Pharaoh's army; divinely ordained natural disasters also consume wayward Israelites (Leviticus 10:1–2; Numbers 11:1–3 and 16:28–34, 35–45, and 46–50); violence and miracles continue to coincide under Moses's immediate successor, Joshua (see, for example, Joshua 3:14–17 and 10:12–14). Moses and Joshua also, however, produce miracles that sustain the Israelites (Exodus 15:23–25, 16:14–35, 17:5–7, and 20: 7–11). See Tarcov's (2014) revealing discussion of the status of miracles in Machiavelli's thought.

105. Leviticus 19:37; for the sanguinary nature of the penalties God prescribes, see, for example, Leviticus 20.

106. He calms a storm (Matthew 8:23–27; Mark 4:37–41; Luke 8:22–25); multiplies loaves and fishes (Matthew 16:8–10); feeds five thousand (Matthew 14:14–21;

Mark 6:30–44; Luke 9:10–17; John 6:1–14) and then four thousand (Matthew 15:32–39; Mark 8:1–9); calms the waters after walking on water (admittedly, this miracle has ambiguous aims: John [6:16–21] reports that his arrival hastens the ship's journey; Matthew [14:22–32] and Mark [6:47–52] suggest that his primary purpose was to persuade disciples of his miraculous powers); produces a coin from a fish (Matthew 17:24–27); produces a large catch of fish (Luke 5:4–11; John 21:1–11); and turns water into wine (John 2:1–11).

107. He heals five blind persons (Matthew 9:27–31 and 20:29–34, Mark 8:22–26 and 10:46–52; Luke 18:35–43; John 9:1–41); heals eleven of leprosy (Matthew 8:1–4; Mark 1:40–44; Luke 5:12–14 and 17:11–19); frees five of possession (Matthew 8:28–34 and 17:14–21; Mark 1:21–28, 5:1–15, and 9:17–29; and Luke 4:31–37, 8:27–39, and 9:38–43); and cures ten of various maladies (Matthew 8:5–13 and 14–15, 9:2–7 and 20–22, and 15:21–28; Mark 1:30–31, 2:3–12, 5:25–34, and 7:24–30; Luke 4:38–39, 5:18–26, 7:1–10, 8:43–48, 13:10–17, 14:1–4, and 22:50–51; John 4:46–54 and 5:1–15). Matthew 4:24 and 8:16 also report he healed others. For his resurrection of the dead, see Matthew 9:18–26; Mark 5:21–43; Luke 7:11–17 and 8:40–56; and John 11:1–44. In addition to specific miracles recounted in the Gospels, see Matthew 9:36 and 14:34–36. Jesus's immediate successors do not share his unblemished record of mercy (see esp. Acts 5:1–10, 12:21–23, and 13:6–11).

108. See, for example, Matthew 15:22, 17:15, and 20:30–31; Mark 10:47–48; and Luke 18:38–39. See also Matthew 5:7; Mark 5:19; and Luke 10:37 and 18:13–14. The wonders associated with his death and resurrection (Matthew 27:52–28:20; Mark 15:33–16:8; Luke 23:44–24:12; John 19:29–20:18) are the important exception to the rule that miracles tangibly benefit human beings—unless, of course, one views his death and resurrection as redemptive of humanity (see, for example, Luke 24:45–49).

109. Matthew 21:18–22; Mark 11:12–14 and 20–25. He also drives the money changers from the temple with a whip (John 2:15). I treat both of these passages in chapter 2.

110. Matthew 5:17. I discuss the importance of love to Christianity, and fear to Machiavelli, in chapter 1. I contrast Moses's and Christ's teachings in chapter 2.

111. His rescue of the adulteress is recorded in John 7:53–8:11; for his prohibition of divorce, see Matthew 5:31–32 and 19:1–11; Mark 10:1–12; and Luke 16:18; his disciples' alleged violation of the Sabbath is reported in Matthew 12:1–14; Mark 2:23–27; and Luke 6:1–11. In each instance, Jesus uses the teachings of the Old Testament to justify his position before the law. Both Leviticus 20:10 and Deuteronomy 22:22 stipulate that adulterers and adulteresses must be executed, so the fact that only the adulteress was targeted for execution might explain why Jesus's invitation "Let any one of you who is without sin be the first to throw a stone at her" so effectively disperses the mob that had assembled to stone her (John 8:8). When the Pharisees accuse his disciples of violating the Sabbath (Genesis 2:2–3; Exodus 16:23–30 and 20:8–11; Leviticus 23:3) by plucking and eating grain, Jesus responds by invoking necessity, reminding the Pharisees that even priests must bake bread on the Sabbath, comparing their act to one committed by David (1 Samuel 21:1–6), and

alluding to his authority of the Son of Man to revise the rules of the Sabbath (Matthew 12:8; Mark 2:28; Luke 6:5). Jesus's general prohibition of divorce contradicts Mosaic law more plainly (Deuteronomy 24:1–4; for Mosaic restrictions on divorce, see Deuteronomy 22:13–19 and 28–29), but Jesus cites earlier Old Testament passages that suggest the permanence of such unions (see Matthew 19:4–5; and Mark 10:5–9, citing Genesis 1:27 and 2:24) and attributes Moses's departure from this fundamental rule to the "hard" "hearts" of the Israelites (Matthew 19:8; Mark 10:5). The synoptic Gospels, in particular, feature many confrontations with the Pharisees, nearly all of which suggest that the Pharisees doubt the legality of Christ's activities and teachings; representative passages include Matthew 16:1–12 and 23:13–37. John (12:42) departs from these accounts by suggesting that many of the Pharisees secretly believed in Christ.

112. Matthew 12:7. The original passage appears in Hosea 6:6, which Jesus also cites in Matthew 9:13. Cf. the Pentateuch's repeated requirement that one must sacrifice (see esp. Deuteronomy 12:11 and 27–28). See also Mark 12:33–34.

113. Genesis 18:18. See also Genesis 12:7; 13:2, 14–17; 15:4–6, 18; 17:1–8, 15–16; 21:1–3; and 22:16–18. Cf. Luke 22:30 and Galatians 3:16.

114. Matthew 5:17. See also John 5:46, in which Christ maintains that Moses "wrote about me."

115. Cf. Sullivan's (1996, 156), claim that "a commentator must conclude that Machiavelli finds political utility in the example of Christ's death" (see also 155–71).

116. Strauss 1958, 211.

117. Jude 1:21 (the Vulgate differs significantly from the Greek, which writes of Christ's *eleos*, or "mercy"). See also Romans 11:32.

118. John 16:33.

119. Livy XXVI.19. Sullivan (1996, 105–6) has also noted Scipio's overreliance on religion in her analysis of I.11 of *Discourses*.

120. Livy XXVI.19. See also XXVI.41 and XXVI.48 for examples of Scipio's use of religious language. Polybius offers a similar account, but abandons Livy's vacillations by describing Scipio as an effective religious pretender who manipulated the "minds of the vulgar" for salutary ends (*Histories* X.2).

121. See esp. Mark 12:13–17; and Luke 2:39–52.

122. Matthew 4:11; Mark 1:13; Luke 3:21 and 22:43; John 12:28–30.

123. Luke 5:16. Jesus withdraws to pray before walking on water (Matthew 14:23; Mark 6:47; John 6:15); preaching throughout Galilee (Mark 1:35); and selecting his twelve apostles (Luke 6:12). Excepting the company of the devil and angels, Jesus is also alone during his time in the wilderness (Matthew 4:1–11; Mark 1:12–13; Luke 4:1–13). When he prays at Gethsemane before his arrest, he withdraws a short distance from his disciples (Matthew 26:38–39; Mark 14:34–35; Luke 22:40–41). See John 8:16 and 8:29 for Christ's insistence that he is not alone, but accompanied by God.

124. A similar story was circulated about Alexander's conception (Plutarch, *Alexander* 2.1–4).

125. Matthew 1:18–25; Luke 1:27–38.

126. Romans 1:1–4 and 8:3–4; Galatians 4:4.
127. As I discuss below, in this chapter, Christ explicitly confesses his heavenly paternity only once (Mark 14:62), and then, he does not address Mary's alleged virtue.
128. Luke 1:35; John 1:34; Nathanael confesses Christ at John 1:49; Martha does so later, at John 11:27; astonished disciples exclaim his divine parentage at Matthew 14:33; the faith of the centurion is reported in Matthew 27:54; for demons' ability to recognize Christ's true nature, see Matthew 8:28–30; Mark 3:11 and 5:6–8; and Luke 4:41 and 8:28; a voice from the clouds also identifies Jesus as his son (Mark 9:7; Luke 3:21–23 and 9:35). Jesus is sometimes identified as the "Son of David" (see, for example, Matthew 9:27, 12:33, 15:22, 20:31, and 21:9–15; and Mark 10:48), whom men believe to be the Messiah (Matthew 22:42).
129. Matthew 16:15–17. See also Mark 8:27–30; and Luke 9:18–21. Matthew 24 and Mark 13 contain numerous warnings against believing false messiahs.
130. Matthew 16:20. Later, he stipulates that the Messiah must be the Son of God (Matthew 22:41–46; Mark 12:35–37; Luke 20:41–44); thus, those who believe him to be the Messiah must also endorse his divine parentage.
131. Matthew, Luke, and John each contain numerous instances in which Christ refers to "my Father." For instances in which Christ suggests that he enjoys a special status as the Son of God, see esp. Matthew 11:27, 16:27, 20:23, and 26:53; Luke 2:49, 10:21–23, 22:28–30, and 24:49; and John 3:35, 5:17–44, 11:41; 17:1 and 21–25. Chapters 6, 8, 10, 12, 14, 15, and 16 of John are salted with this term (see esp. 8:58). In Mark, Christ uses this language only twice. The first instance (8:34–38) is more ambiguous than that found in the other Gospels. The second usage (14:60–62) is the most emphatic of any account. In the first and last verses of his account, Mark himself states (1:1) and implies (16:19–20; cf. John 20:31) that Jesus was the Son of God. As the earliest Gospel, might it—in contrast to Paul's letters—have been inoculated against a fabulous tradition that grew after Christ's death?
132. Matthew 11:27.
133. John 8:12 and 18–20. See also John 10:22–39, which features a sophistic explanation of the meaning of Christ's claim that he is "God's son." Compare his public reticence with his confidential discussions with his apostles (for example, John 14:9–10).
134. Mark 14:60–62.
135. Matthew 26:62–64; Luke 22:66–71. See also Mark 1:1. All accounts confirm that his exchange with Pilate is laconic and cryptic (Matthew 27:11; Mark 15:2–5; Luke 23:3; John 18:37; see Fontana's [1999, 650–52] intriguing discussion of this confrontation). Cf. 1 John 4:15, which establishes the importance of believing this claim.
136. Livy XXVI.19.
137. Matthew 27:42. Cf. Luke 22:69–71.
138. Livy XXVI.19.
139. John 16:33. For scriptural evidence of Christ's founding of the Christian Church, see esp. Ephesians 1:20–23 and 2:11–22.

140. Livy XXVI.19. Cf. Christ's mandate to his disciples (Matthew 28:16–20; Mark 16:15–20; Luke 24:45–49; John 20:21–22).

141. Livy XXVI.19; Luke 4:18–20. In this passage, Christ quotes from Isaiah 61:1–2.

142. Tarcov (2014, 196) suggests the following argument about Christ's authenticity with considerable delicacy. Cf. Mansfield 1979, 74. Neither de Grazia (1994, 101) nor Najemy (1999, 672) nor Viroli (2010, 182) detects the significance of this statement.

143. *Opere*, 95. See also Parel 1992, 47.

144. See Coby 1999, 191.

145. For Rome's growing inequality and its relationship to Christianity, see esp. Sullivan 1996, but also McCormick 2011a.

146. See esp. Ephesians 2. Savonarola observed a different connection between Roman ascendancy and Christianity (Brown 1988, 59).

Chapter Five

1. Machiavelli's teaching on virtues and vices—and the spirit required to apply his teaching—have earned more attention than any other aspect of his thought. Many scholars note the ways Machiavelli's teachings distort or contravene the classical virtues and herald a modern, morally obtuse, or scientific vision of virtue and vice: see Strauss 1958, esp. 232–52; but also 295 and 298; Wolin 1960, 224–28; Orwin 1978; Mansfield 1981 and 1996, 6–52; de Alvarez 2008, 75–100; and Tarcov forthcoming. Hulliung (1983, 172–74) exhorts the reader to "recognize that Machiavelli unified theory and practice by ideology rather than science" (166). Scholars have more rarely examined the tensions between Machiavelli's arguments and the requirements of Christian virtue. Especially influential to this book is Orwin's (1978) article, to which the title of this chapter alludes; but see also Palmer 2001, esp. 80; Tarcov 2013a, 2014, and esp. forthcoming; Sullivan 1996, esp. 36–55; Berlin 1979, 45–47; and Hulliung 1983, 66–67. Others, however, doubt that Machiavelli's teaching is novel or especially unchristian. Some judge that Machiavelli seeks to resuscitate pagan virtues (see Benner 2013, 179–224; but cf. Hulliung 1983, 201); Skinner (2001, 42; 2002, 180–83), who is aware of the gulf between Machiavelli's teaching and Christianity, nonetheless emphasizes the importance of Machiavelli's agreement with neopagan civic humanists, rather than his break with that religion; for a trenchant critique of Skinner's approach, see Tarcov 1982, 706–8; Parel 1992; and Pocock 1975a, esp. 193–94 and 213. Still others within this group think he promotes a variation of Christian virtue: see Nederman 1999; 2009, 37 and esp. 50–62; McCormick 2011b; Viroli 2010, 24–25, 47–49, 54–57, and 61; and Viroli 2014, 81–91 (cf. Mansfield 1981).

2. See Orwin 1978, 1217. Other universal teachings thus far include Machiavelli's teachings on acquisition (*P* 3) and the nature of obligation (*P* 10).

3. See also Tarcov forthcoming.

4.   My redaction omits Machiavelli's obscure discussion of the distinctions among liberality, meanness, giving, and rapacity—during which he introduces "avarice," which remains unopposed by a contrasting quality (de Alvarez 2008, 77). My interpretation of this list generally adheres to de Alvarez's (2008, 76–77) account, except that he identifies being "hard" as a vice and being "easy" as a virtue (76). See also Strauss 1958, 242; Tarcov 2013a, 573–74. By presenting these qualities as extremes, Machiavelli abandons the rule of moderation that informed Aristotle's famous account (Orwin 1978, 1220; de Alvarez 2008, 76–77). For a particularly helpful discussion of this list and the significance of Machiavelli's persistent use of the word "quality," see Tarcov forthcoming.

5.   See Benner 2013, liii.

6.   *Opere*, 280. See de Alvarez 2008, 77.

7.   Cf. Tarcov forthcoming; and Benner 2013, 180–82, 224.

8.   Matthew 22:36–38. See also Mark 12:28–31; and Luke 10:25–28. Jesus quotes from Deuteronomy 6:5.

9.   Matthew 6:1. Christ's extensive critique of the pretended virtue of hypocrites occurs in Matthew 6:1–18. See also Matthew 15:6–8. For the importance of the internal disposition of a believer's soul, see esp. Matthew 5:27–30; 7:5; and 10:28; Mark 7:5–14; Luke 6:42; and John 17:19–21. See also Acts 4:32; 1 Thessalonians 5:22–23; 2 Thessalonians 2:10–14; 1 Peter 2:10–12; and 2 Peter 2:8. Matthew 7:5 and Luke 6:42 remind believers to tend to the care of their own souls. For a general discussion of the importance of faith to Christianity, see esp. Matthew 6:30, 8:26, 14:31, and 16:8; Mark 11:21–23; Luke 12:28; and Romans 1:16–18.

10.   Matthew 23:5 and 23:27–28.

11.   Matthew 24:51.

12.   See, for example, Matthew 6:4. See chapter 3, above, for a fuller account of the importance of sacrifice to Christianity and Machiavelli's judgment of the calculative nature of the Christian's apparent self-forgetting virtue.

13.   Connell (2005, xii) suggests that a proper translation of "*andare dreto alla verità* effetuale della cosa" (*Opere*, 280) would be "to go after the effectual truth of the thing" (2005, 87); this would render Machiavelli more "rhetorically modest" (xii) than Mansfield's Machiavelli.

14.   See, for example, Matthew 18:3. Cf. Strauss 1958, 233–34; Mansfield 1996, 269–70 and 273; de Alvarez 2008, 75; and Korvela 2006, 87–92.

15.   Orwin (1978) notes both the conventional (1218) and revolutionary (1218–19) aspects of this judgment. This is the only appearance of the word *professione* in either *The Prince* or the *Discourses*. As a noun, it can mean an occupation or a public statement; in the context of Catholicism, men can be said to make a "profession of faith" (*professione di fede*); priests' vows are also considered *professioni*. It is perhaps significant that Machiavelli's lone use of this term suggests that professions lead to "ruin" (*P* 15). For the broad significance of Machiavelli's opposition to those who prize "a profession of good," and the connection between the life of Christ and the tradition of classical moral philosophy, see Mansfield 1996, 36. See also Tarcov forthcoming.

16.   For the requirements of war in Aristotle's regime, see esp. *Politics* VII.11; for the limits on war, see VII.14; for the existence of crime, see VII.12. Socrates announces the necessity of the throng of lies at 459c–d of the *Republic*; for the foreign policy of Kallipolis, see 420a–424c; see also 373d–e, for the unjust act that is required to found the city. See also Plato, *Laws* 626a–e.

17.   Cf. *Opere*, 280. For a trenchant summary of the ancients' skeptical view of political idealism, see Bloom's (1968, esp. 409–12) commentary on the *Republic*.

18.   Matthew 13:49; 23:13; Mark 10:23–24; Luke 18:17; and John 3:3. Cf. Matthew 3:12 and Revelation 20:11–15.

19.   Revelation 21; Augustine, *City of God* XXII.30. Indeed, the fundamental theme of the latter half of the *City of God* is the tension between the sinful City of the World and the heavenly City of God, which is resolved by the decisive triumph of the latter.

20.   He uses the phrase "kingdom of heaven" (*basileia twn ouranwn* or *regnum caelorum*) thirty times in Matthew. He refers to the "kingdom of God" (*basileia tou theou* or *regnum Dei*) thirteen times in Mark; twenty-eight times in Luke; and four times in Matthew. The term appears only twice in John, where Jesus nonetheless invokes "my kingdom," which is "not of this world" (John 18:36). Machiavelli criticizes "the Christian republic" in *D* I.12.2.

21.   For a representative sample of the first usage, see Matthew 4:17 or Luke 21:31; for the second, John 3:5 or Luke 6:20; for the third, see Matthew 13:1–52 or Luke 14:15–23.

22.   Matthew 25:34; 13:47–50.

23.   Revelation 21 offers a relatively concrete account of the "new Jerusalem" (21.2); Saint Augustine's book is primarily a work of theology, but his description of the City of God in the final book is nonetheless more specific than anything Christ adumbrates (see esp. XXII.13–22).

24.   Luke 21:26.

25.   Machiavelli confuses the subject of liberality further by introducing a new term to describe its opposite: parsimony. As Orwin (1978, 1221) notes, by replacing "meanness" with "parsimony," he may be attempting to offer a more positive account of tight-fistedness. Against this view, an anonymous reviewer suggested that Machiavelli's use of Latin titles might have compelled him to change the language, since the Latin equivalent of the Italian *misero* ("mean") is *miser* ("pitiable"). The possible qualities one might exhibit with regard to wealth are liberality, meanness, avarice, giving, rapacity, and parsimony. See Benner's insightful account (2013, 185–88) of Machiavelli's consonance with some ancient notions of liberality; Benner's dim account of the aggrandizing founders (2013, 69–87), however, leads her to view Machiavelli's ultimate recommendation to rapacity as ironic (2013, 192–93).

26.   Matthew 6:24; Luke 12:27–31. See also 1 Timothy 6:5–9.

27.   Luke 12:34.

28.   Luke 6:30. See also 1 Corinthians 4:8–21; 2 Corinthians 2:17; 1 Thessalonians 2:5; 1 Timothy 6:5–12; and James 1:9–11. Christ's first followers endorse his judgment of private property with alacrity (Acts 2:44–45, 4:32–35, and 5:1–11). The Christian's wary and instrumental view of wealth is roughly

compatible with ancient notions (see, for example, Aristotle, *Politics* I.9.1–18 and I.10.5), but ancients do not share Christ's belief that virtue and poverty easily coincide (see, for example, Aristotle, *Politics* 1.7.5). See esp. Orwin 1978, 1220–21; and Mansfield 1996, 21–22.

29. Luke 16:11. While the context supports the translation, provided above, the word translated as "worldly" is *adikw* or *iniquo*, which literally means "unjust."

30. Luke 14:12–14. See also the parable (14:15–23) that follows this passage. Cf., however, Matthew 26:6–13; Mark 14:3–9; Luke 7:36–50; and John 12:1–11.

31. 1 John 3:16–17. Cf. Luke 16:19–26. See also James 5:1–5, which promises wrath to the wealthy.

32. Luke 12:21.

33. Matthew 6:3–4.

34. Matthew 6:4.

35. *P* 11, 47n7.

36. *Converso* was the term applied to Jews and Muslims who converted to Christianity, and thus achieved some status within Spain's Christian society; Ferdinand targeted them with particular alacrity (Peters 1988, 86–87). I discuss this "pious cruelty" later in this chapter, and also in chapter 6. See Tarcov 2014, 210. Because he exercised rapacity against his own subjects, Ferdinand did not need to satisfy soldiers by liberally bestowing on them booty. All proceeds accrued to the state. Presumably, those like Machiavelli who viewed Ferdinand's religious justifications as mere pretense would find him "hateful" (*P* 16).

37. See, for example, Deuteronomy 20:10–16; see also *D* II.8.2. For a pithy statement of Romulus's and Theseus's rapacity, and the superiority of Romulus, see Plutarch's *Comparison of Romulus and Theseus* 6.1–4. For colorful evidence of Cyrus's hateful reputation among foreign powers that he pillaged, see Herodotus, *Histories* I.214. While his conquest was hateful to his enemies, the Persians later judged that "he saw to it that all good things would be theirs" (*Histories* III.89). See Orwin's (1978, 1222) assessment of "the scorpion's sting characteristic" of this argument. See also Strauss 1958, 239–40; and Tarcov 2007, 139–40.

38. Cf. *D* III.22.4. See also McCormick 2011a, 87–88.

39. Luke 21:8. See also Matthew 24:5; and Mark 13:6. See Sullivan 1996 (66–77) for a thorough account of liberality's damaging effect on Roman liberty, and the connections among acquisitive desires, grandiose promises, the rise of tyranny, and the strength of Christianity in Rome; for Machiavelli's solution to this problem, according to Sullivan, see 1996, 161–71. See also Benner 2013, 193–95.

40. *Opere*, 281. See Orwin 1978, 1222.

41. The word translated as "mercy" in most English versions of the New Testament is the Greek *eleew* or *oiktirmos*, or Latin and Italian *misericordia*. Cf. Orwin 1978, 1223.

42. *Opere*, 212. Compare, however, Machiavelli's account with Livy's (VI.20).

43. Orwin 1978, 1225. Cf. Benner 2013, 198.

44. *Opere*, 282.

45. Machiavelli's implicit judgment of Agathocles is not novel (see Polybius, *Histories* IX.23). Despite his invocation of the "utility for the subject," it is not clear whether the utility to which Machiavelli refers amounts to anything more than the pacification of the community and the abjuring of further cruelty.

46. Luke 6:36. See de Alvarez 2008, 83.

47. Luke 23:34.

48. 2 Corinthians 5:10; 2 Timothy 2:19; 1 John 2:3–7; and 3:5–10. Cf. Mansfield 1996, 25–26.

49. Acts 24:15–16. See also Mark 2:8; Romans 2:15; 1 Corinthians 11:28; 2 Corinthians 13:5; Galatians 6:4; Hebrews 10:12; and 1 John 1:9. The Old Testament also recommends self-examination (see, for example, Psalm 139:23–24; and Lamentations 3:4). The word translated as "conscience" is *syneidesin* or *conscientiam*. The Italian *conscienza* does not appear in *The Prince*, and appears only three times in the *Discourses*: it is not the cause of Giovampagolo Baglioni's reluctance to kill Julius II (I.27.1); it is the cause of the scrupulous virtue of the citizens of Germany (I.55.2), whose cities appear to be imaginary; and it frequently betrays conspirators (III.6.16; cf. Mansfield 1996, 26).

50. Cf. Hulliung 1983 (26), which offers a similar observation concerning empire.

51. Machiavelli says this of a "certain prince" who is unnamed, but appears to be Ferdinand. I discuss this ambiguous reference in more detail later in this chapter.

52. Indeed, the inquisition would last from 1483 until 1834 (Peters 1988, 90). I discuss the ghastly limits of Ferdinand's Christian politics in chapter 6.

53. Against the view that pious cruelties are rare, consider Edward I's edict of expulsion (Mundill 1998, 253). For a thorough documentary record of governmental persecution of Jews in the centuries before Machiavelli, see Chazan 1980, 277–319.

54. Romans 2:6–8. Christ quotes from either Psalm 62:12 or Proverbs 24:12. Christ generally speaks of his final judgment in parables (see esp. Matthew 7:13–23, 13:24–30, 13:36–43, and 25:31–46; and Luke 12:4–5, 12:9, and 13:23–28).

55. Compare Machiavelli's language here with Acts 24:15–16. See also Proverbs 3:4. Based on Machiavelli's use of this phrase, de Alvarez (2008, 82) observes, "Thus chapter XVII would seem to be Machiavelli's own faith or religion." As Orwin (1978, 1224) notes, Machiavelli's cruelty is tempered with "prudence and humanity" (*P* 17); Machiavelli's emphasis on humanity, rather than piety, confirms that his concerns are "this-worldly" (1978, 1224).

56. The passage is *Aeneid* I.563–64.

57. Machiavelli also quotes from an unnamed source in *P* 6; an unnamed "wise" man (Tacitus) in *P* 13; a Roman consul in *P* 21; and Petrarch in *P* 26.

58. Virgil, *Aeneid* I.353–70.

59. The word *miserere*—which is closely related to *misericordia*—is prominent throughout this account. Cruelty (*crudelis*) is also present.

60. Benner, who praises Aeneas (2013, 76), observes neither Aeneas's deception nor Dido's regrets (2013, 205–6); cf. Orwin 1978, 1223n36, which notes both; and de Alvarez 2008, 82–83.

61. *Opere*, 273.
62. Luke 14:12–14; Mark 12:31.
63. Citing a similar passage from Aristotle's *Rhetoric*, Benner (2013, 207) notes that Machiavelli's "view of human nature is neither a new nor a shockingly amoral one." Here, as elsewhere, Benner's strenuous effort to show Machiavelli's consonance with ancient thinkers obscures his—and their—disagreements with Christian thinkers. The classically virtuous man—and Machiavelli's virtuous prince—may view men as generally wicked, and prepare himself accordingly. A Christian commanded to brotherly love imperils his soul by doing the same.
64. Aeneas's initial concealment (I.410–14) and final deception (cf. IV.288–96 and IV.337–38) are the chief examples of his injustice toward Dido. Compare Dido's wrath with Strauss's comments (1958, 188–89) about the vengefulness of the "God of Love."
65. Aeneas cites the need to fulfill the divine will as his main reason for leaving Carthage (Virgil, *Aeneid* IV.265–78, 331, 345–47, and 356–61).
66. Cf. *D* II.31.
67. Tarcov (2013a, 581) persuasively argues that the temperance and humanity Machiavelli recommends will lead a prudent prince to "believe in, trust, or put his faith in some of his subjects." An anonymous reviewer strengthened Tarcov's interpretation by noting the ambiguity of the Italian in the above quoted passage from *The Prince* (*Opere*, 282), and recommending that it be translated as "nor should he make himself fear." Compare Tarcov's judgment with Benner's (2013, esp. 146–48 and 247–71) more optimistic account.
68. Thus, compare the tender mercy (I.569–74) Dido offers to the shipwrecked Trojans to her contemplation of their grisly destruction (IV.597–606).
69. Cf. esp. the parable of the Good Samaritan (Luke 10:25–37).
70. Compare this treatment of cruelty with Strauss 1958, 248.
71. Cf. Benner 2013, 222.
72. As in chapter 3, the Italian rendering of "faith" is generally *la fede*—which might also be translated as "the faith."
73. Benner (2013, liii) views *astuzia* as a "negative" code word; compare her judgment, however, with *P* 9, 19, and 20. In the *Discourses*, Machiavelli uses *astuzia* as a positive (II.12.2 and III.17) and negative (I.6.4, I.41, and II.5.2) adjective. Given the context of its appearances, it seems to be a quality necessary to princely rule (see esp. *P* 20), but harmful to the republican way of life (see esp. *D* I.41)—and a poor substitute for adequate arms (*D* I.6.4). Machiavelli suggests the definite limits of astuteness in *D* II.5.2.
74. Machiavelli does not note that God, too, engages in combat, nor does he recommend enlisting God's supernatural help (Genesis 19:24–25; Exodus 14:21–31; Joshua 6:6–20 and 10:12–14; 2 Kings 19:35; see also Luke 17:20–37). Cf. de Grazia 1994; Viroli 2010; and Nederman 1999 and 2009.
75. Since laws are sometimes sufficient for princely combat, Machiavelli's presentation does not constitute an absolute denigration of laws. As Tarcov (2006, 78) observes, "From Machiavelli's peculiar perspective, with its emphasis on the ineluctability of conflict, to say that laws are a means of combat is rather an elevation or appreciation of laws." See also Tarcov 2014, 213.

76. Ephesians 5:1–2. For evidence of Christ's hypostatic nature, see, for example, John 10:30–33 and 20:28.

77. I am indebted to Benner (2013, 217) for this observation.

78. *Opere*, 280. Benner (2013, 217) also notes this. Cf. de Alvarez 2008, 86–87. Mansfield translates this as "faithlessness."

79. John 1:29 and 1:36. See also Acts 8:26–35; 1 Corinthians 5:7; 1 Peter 1:19; and Revelation 7:10. The lion and the fox are paired in many stories of antiquity, but Cicero's *De Officiis* (see Hulliung 1983, xi and 213–14; and Benner 2013, 217n6) is the most likely ancient source for Machiavelli's imagery. Notwithstanding Benner's (2013, 213) claim that Machiavelli's teaching is largely ironic, Machiavelli's teaching on the fox and the lion plainly contradicts Cicero (see also Benner 2013, 218), whose condemnation of hypocrites (*De Officiis* I.41) resembles Christ's. For Machiavelli's general opposition to Cicero, see Mansfield 1996, 35–36; and Duff 2011. Other possible ancient sources include Aesop (see esp. "The Ass, the Lion, and the Fox" [1868, 20], which emphasizes both the strength and the limits of foxlike cunning), Plutarch (*Sulla* 28.3), and Talmudic fables (Ha-Nakdan 1967).

80. Matthew 9:36, 10:6, 15:23–24, 18:10–13, 25:31–46, and 26:31; Mark 6:34 and 14:27; Luke 12:32 and 15:1–7; John 10:1–27 and 21:15–19. See also Acts 20:28–29; Hebrews 13:20; 1 Peter 2:25; 5:1–3; and Revelation 7:17. See Matthew (12:11–12) for the superiority of human beings to sheep; for Christ's claim that he is a shepherd, see esp. Matthew 2:6, 9:36, and 26:31; Mark 6:34; and John 10:14.

81. Luke 10:3; Matthew 7:15. See also Luke 10:19, where Jesus promises his disciples' safety. Paul also describes false prophets as wolves in Acts 20:29. The identity of the wolf of John 10:12–13 is unclear.

82. Romans 8:36, quoted from Psalm 44:22.

83. The Old Testament contains dozens of references to lions, the majority of which are positive: leonine qualities are frequently ascribed to royalty or adorn royal trappings (2 Chronicles 9:18–19; 1 Kings 7:29, 7:36, and 10:19–20; Proverbs 19:12, 20:2, and 30:30); they are ascribed to favored people and individuals (Genesis 49:9 and 33:20–22; Numbers 23:24 and 24:9; 2 Samuel 17:10; 1 Chronicles 12:8); and Proverbs (28:1) describes the righteous as a lion.

For pejorative references, in which wicked men and Israel's internal and external enemies are described as lions, see Psalms 7:2, 10:9, 17:12, 22:13, 22:21, 34:10, 35:17, 57:4, 58:6; and 91:13; Proverbs 28:15; Jeremiah 2:15, 2:30, 4:2, 5:6, 12:8, and 51:38; Ezekiel 19:1–6, 22:25, and 32:2; Joel 1:6; Nahum 2:11–12; Zephaniah 3:3; and Zechariah 11:3. The lion's mixed reputation—and perhaps especially David's overwhelmingly pejorative use of the lion—might explain Christ's refusal to use it in his parables.

84. For God's leonine qualities, see esp. Job 10:16; Isaiah 31:4 and 38:13; Jeremiah 25:38, 49:19, and 50:44; Lamentations 3:10; Hosea 5:14, 11:10, and 13:7–8; and Amos 3:1–12. Lions are also frequently instruments in God's judgment: they make manifest divine punishment (1 Kings 13:11–26 and 20:36; 2 Kings 17:25–26; Proverbs 22:13 and 26:13; Isaiah 5:29 and 15:4; Jeremiah 2:15, 4:7, 5:6, and 50:17; Micah 5:8); and are featured in tests of

righteousness or signs of strength (Judges 14:5–9; 1 Samuel 17:34–37; 1 Chronicles 11:22; Daniel 6:1–27). Old Testament figures also claim that God will demonstrate his power by depriving the lion of his roar and teeth (Job 4:10–11) or changing the lion's nature at the end of times (Isaiah 11:6–7 and 65:25); Isaiah also claims (35:9) that the lion will be absent among the redeemed.

85. Aside from the pregnant reference in 1 Peter (5:8), discussed later in this chapter, the word "lion" (*lewn* or *leo*) appears only in two references to the story of Daniel in the lions' den (2 Timothy 4:7; Hebrews 11:33) and in the allegorical and obscure book of Revelation. Most of the references in Revelation describe physical characteristics of the various fabulous creatures contained therein. Exceptions are Revelation 5:5–6, in which John invokes "the Lion of the tribe of Judah," and 10:3. Cf. Isaiah 65:25.

86. 1 Peter 5:8. The word translated as devil is *diabolos*. Cf. Revelation 14:4.

87. John 8:44. For the devil's temptation of Christ, see Matthew 4:1–11 and Luke 4:1–13; for the devil's power to corrupt belief, see Luke 8:12; for his role in Judas's betrayal, see John 13:2.

88. The Hebrew word for "jackal" is frequently—but not always—translated as "fox" (*vulpes*) in the Vulgate (see, for example, Jeremiah 10:22 or Isaiah 35:7, where the word is translated as *draco*, or "dragon"). Modern English translations render the word as both jackal and fox. The word for fox in New Testament Greek is the unambiguous *alwpes*. Even with these mistranslations, the Old Testament contains very few references to the fox (or jackal); these are nonetheless generally pejorative. Samson uses foxes to destroy the Philistines' crops (Judges 15:3–5); the example of the fox is used in ridicule directed against the Israelites (Nehemiah 4:3); the Songs of Songs casts them as pests (2:15); Lamentations says they inhabit desolate places (5:18); and Ezekiel describes Israel's false prophets as "foxes among ruins" (13:4).

89. Matthew 8:20; see also Luke 9:58.

90. Luke 13:32. This passage refers to Herod Antipas, whose father sought the Christ-child's death (Matthew 2:1–19).

91. Luke 13:32.

92. For accounts of the role of Herod Antipas in John the Baptist's imprisonment and death, see Matthew 14:1–12; Mark 6:14–29; and Luke 3:20 and 9:9. For his efforts to conspire with Pharisees to ensnare Christ, see Matthew 22:16; and Mark 3:6, 8:14–15, and 12:13. Luke (23:12) reports the friendship of Herod and Pilate. For Pilate's relationship to Machiavelli's thought, see Fontana 1999, 649–50. For Herod's persecutions of early Christians, see Acts 12:1–19; he is the first ruler to order the execution of a disciple—James (Acts 12:1–2; cf. Acts 7:54–60, which records Stephen's stoning at the hands of religious authorities). According to Acts (12:22–23), the hubristic Herod is struck dead by an angel of the Lord.

93. *Opere*, 283. Cf. Revelation 13:4–7 and 19:20.

94. Luke 23:15. Cf., however, Acts 4:27. I am indebted to Jeffrey Metzger, who suggested this conclusion.

95. The word translated as spirit is *animo* (see, for example, *Opere*, 284); the word soul (*anima*) does not appear in either *The Prince* or the *Discourses* (de Alvarez

2008, 77–78). As Mansfield (*P* Glossary and 127) notes, Machiavelli refers obliquely to the soul only twice in *The Prince*, when he uses the verb *animare* twice (*Opere*, 272 and 292); see also Tarcov forthcoming. In each instance (*P* 9 and 21), he comments on the ability of a popular prince to "inspire" his people. Cf. *Discourses* (I.11.2), where Machiavelli describes religion's salutary ability to "animate the plebs" through deception, and *Discourses* (III.6.8), where Machiavelli praises Piso's ability to "inspire" a failed conspiracy (III.6.5) against Nero.

96. Benner (2013, 222), by contrast, judges this "a stunning turnaround." De Grazia (1994, 296), who diminishes the impiety of this advice, describes it as "rhetoric of imposture."

97. Mark 7:6–7; the quoted passage is from Isaiah 29:13. Cf. James 1:22–26.

98. Matthew 5:8. The word is *kardia* or *corde*. See also James 1:26–27.

99. Matthew 12:34. See also Matthew 5:28, 6:21, 9:4, 11:28–30, 13:15, 15:1–19, 18:35, 19:8, and 22:37; Mark 2:8, 3:5, 6:52, 7:6, 7:19–21, 8:21, 10:5, 11:23, and 12:30–33; Luke 2:35, 5:22, 6:45, 8:12–15, 10:27, 12:29–34; 16:15, and 24:32; and John 5:42, 12:40, and 14:1. Subsequent books emphasize repeatedly the importance of the "hearts" of believers; see esp. Acts 15:8–9; Romans 2:15; and 1 Corinthians 4:5. A notable exception is Philippians 1:15–18, in which Paul expresses indifference about the motives of Christ's evangelizers.

100. John 8:44; John 1:14. So, too, is goodness identified with truth telling, and wickedness with its opposite. For Christ's identification of godliness with truth telling, see esp. Matthew 22:16; Mark 12:14; Luke 20:21; John 3:33, 8:32, 14:6, 16:13, and 18:37; and Romans 2:2, 3:1–8, and 15:8; see also 1 Corinthians 13:6; 2 Corinthians 4:2, 6:7, and 13:8; Ephesians 4:15–25 and 6:14; Philippians 4:8; Titus 1:1–2; and Hebrews 6:18. For the New Testament's identification of lies with the devil, see Matthew 5:33–37 and 2 Corinthians 11:13–15; for the New Testament's identification of wickedness with dishonesty, see Matthew 22:18 and 26:59–60; Mark 14:56–57; Acts 20:30; Romans 1:18–32 and 2:8; 2 Thessalonians 2:9–12; 1 Timothy 6:5; 2 Timothy 3:8; 2 Peter 2:1; and 1 John 2:4 and 4:6.

101. Matthew 10:22 and 24:13; Mark 13:13; Luke 21:19. See also 1 Corinthians 15:58; 2 Corinthians 1:24; Ephesians 6:14; Philippians 1:27; 2 Thessalonians 2:15; and 1 Peter 5:9–10.

102. Luke 16:15. Christ discloses this in the context (16:1–15) of his critique of the Pharisees' attachment to money. See also Acts 15:8; 2 Corinthians 11:31; 2 Timothy 2:19; and 1 John 3:20.

103. Ephesians 4:22–25.

104. Luke 21:19.

105. Compare this discussion of men's brains with Strauss 1958, 269; Tarcov 2014, 209.

106. Matthew 6:13.

107. This is the third time Machiavelli has listed qualities that pertain to faithfulness in this chapter. The first stresses the necessity to appear (and be) "merciful, faithful, humane, honest, and religious" (*P* 18); the second stipulates that circumstances sometimes require that the prince act "against faith, against charity, against humanity, against religion"; the

third (quoted here) represents a return to the subject of appearances, and repeats the first list, while reversing the order of humanity and honesty. One can discern three judgments from these varied lists. First, Machiavelli does not think that the prince who "enter[s] into evil" (*P* 18) necessarily acts "against" mercy; second, the honesty of the prince must remain merely apparent; third, a prince does not need to appear charitable, except perhaps insofar as the appearance of charity is required to appear religious. Cf. de Alvarez 2008, 89.

108. See de Alvarez's (2008, 87–89) discussion of touching, seeing, and the implications of Machiavelli's argument for enlightenment. Cf. Mansfield 1996 (30), which connects the decisive power of "seeing" with Machiavelli's decision to turn to the effectual truth: "To be impressive, virtue must create a visible effect." Compare both with de Grazia 1994, 293–94.

109. Luke 16:15; John 5:22–23. Mansfield (1996, 48) emphasizes the worldliness of Machiavelli's virtue, which is "not in need of a blessing" from the next world.

110. See esp. Orwin's (1978, 1219) penetrating account of this feature of Machiavelli's presentation, to which I largely owe my understanding. Contrast this with Benner 2013, 224.

111. Cf. Matthew 25:31–46; see also Acts 17:31. For an especially illuminating analysis, see Orwin 1978, 1219. Cf. Mansfield 1996, 38.

112. 1 Corinthians 15:54; cf. Isaiah 25:8.

113. Cf. Matthew 5:33–37.

114. See de Alvarez 2008, 87.

115. *Opere*, 284. This is not Machiavelli's usual word for "subject": that word is *suddito*, and refers to someone who is under kingly rule and derives from the Latin *subditus* (see, for example, *P* 15 [*Opere*, 280]). While *subbieto* might simply mean a "subject for discussion" (see Machiavelli's usage in *P* DL [*Opere*, 257], *P* 9 [*Opere*, 272; Mansfield translates this instance as "circumstances"], and *P* 20 [*Opere*, 290]), it can also refer to persons under the influence or direction of some external power (see *P* 4 [*Opere*, 263]). This appears to be the sense of the word in this context. Machiavelli does not employ this form in the *Discourses*, where he utilizes the more modern form, *suggetto* (see, for example, *D* I.11.5 [*Opere*, 95]), a word that implies a more amorphous form of rule than is implied by *suddito*. Subjection to religious power thus appears less formal than subjection to conventional political power.

116. Cf. Benner 2013, 221.

117. *P* 18 and 71n6.

118. Mansfield (*P* 18 and 71n5) alerts the reader to an ambiguity in the manuscript: following most manuscripts, Mansfield records Machiavelli as writing "in the world there is no one but the vulgar; the few have a place there when the many have somewhere to lean on," yet one manuscript reads "the few have *no place* there" (*P* 18 and 71S). The latter reading makes more sense, given the context: since Machiavelli has just established that the few can be silenced by religious pretenders who deceive "men in general" and lend support to that mistaken judgment with the "majesty of the state" (*P* 18), one

can conceive how the place of the few in the world might be obliterated by this arrangement between a people and a prince.

119. See also Benner 2013 (224 and 255–57), which sketches Machiavelli's negative judgment of Ferdinand, as disclosed in the former's private correspondence. Both de Alvarez (2008, 90) and Tarcov (2014, 215n11) suggest discreetly that this "certain prince of present times" (*P* 18) might actually refer to Christ, whose teachings—as Machiavelli has suggested in *The Prince*—serve to undermine peace and corrupt faith. If true, Machiavelli resolves the puzzle suggested by his implied comparison of Scipio and Christ in chapters 14 and 17: Christ is unequivocally a religious pretender, who feigns both faith and pacifism. This may be Machiavelli's playful suggestion, but I conclude that Machiavelli generally seeks to preserve ambiguity about Christ's belief (cf., however, *D* I.12.2); this is evident especially in the suggested comparison of Savonarola and Christ, in chapter 6 of *The Prince*.

Chapter Six

1. When one considers the exemplary virtue of the prince discussed at the end of chapter 18, it is striking that few scholars have turned their attentions to chapter 19. The most notable exception is Strauss (1958, see esp. 46, 180, 187, 255, and 274; see also Strauss 1987, 302), who suggests that chapters 19 and 20 are crucially important to any effort to understand *The Prince* and that chapter 19, in particular, "reveals the truth about the founders . . . most fully," and is the "peak of *The Prince* as a whole" (1958, 60). See also Palmer 2001, 87–88. De Alvarez (2008, 90–100) and Benner (2013, 225–46) offer the most comprehensive accounts, but disagree about what Machiavelli intends (see also Sullivan 2013, 533–34).

2. Men appear to value their women more highly than their fathers, but only because the death of one's father often means enrichment. Cf. de Alvarez 2008, 96.

3. *Opere*, 284. *Ingegnarsi* might also be translated as "try one's best" or "make do." Compare this with the flexible spirit of the model prince of chapter 18.

4. For the details of the Canneschi conspiracy, see *FH* IV.9–10 (cf. de Alvarez 2008, 93); Livy (XXXV.36) offers the principal account of Nabis's assassination.

5. Machiavelli describes these partisans as followers, rather than friends. He reinforces this teaching in his subsequent discussion of Emperor Septimius Severus; he also offers a version of this teaching in chapter 20 of *The Prince*.

6. Cf. *D* II.P.2.

7. Livy XXXV.36. Nabis was felled by a foreign conspiracy while the people gaped at the bloody scene and his bodyguard, alone, tried to save him. The people rose to resist the assassins only after they began looting Sparta (XXXV.36; cf. *P* 19, 72n3), thus confirming that the people care more for their material goods than their prince's life (cf. *P* 10). Nabis was killed partly at the instigation of the Romans, who appear to work constantly to ensure

that "things outside" never remain "steady" (*P* 19; Livy XXXV.35). Cf. McCormick 2015, 51.

8.   I am indebted to de Alvarez (2008, 92), who makes this argument about chapter 19. For appraisals of Machiavelli's conspiratorial efforts, see Dietz 1986, 796; cf. Langton and Dietz 1987; and Tarcov 2013a, 581. See also de Alvarez 2008, 91, 93, 98; and Benner 2013, 225 (but also 229).

9.   By using the narrower term, "virtue of spirit" (*virtù d'animo*) (*Opere*, 286), Machiavelli suggests that these examples are not strictly comparable to the founders, who possess unqualified "virtue" (*P* 6). Benner (2013, 234), who judges that "*virtu* of *animo* is insufficient for good ordering, and often works against it" endorses a categorically dim view of these emperors.

10.   See esp. *P* 14; *P* 18; and *P* 25.

11.   Cf. *D* I.10 (Strauss 1958, 25–26; Mansfield 1979, 66–69).

12.   Herodian, *History of the Empire since the Time of Marcus Aurelius.* Other possible sources include the *Historia Augusta* and Cassius Dio's *Roman History.*

13.   Heliogabalus was a priest (Herodian, *History* V.3.5); Commodus and Caracalla were both sons of emperors.

14.   *Opere*, 286. For the decision that entrenched Praetorian authority, see Herodian, *History* I.8.1–2. For Machiavelli's previous discussion of the problem of avarice in one's arms, see esp. *P* 12; *P* 13; and *P* 16. See also Parel 1992, 119–20.

15.   For Pertinax's rise, see Herodian, *History* II.2.1—II.3.11; for his decency, moderation, and piety, see II.4.1–2; for the imperial bodyguard's dissatisfaction with these qualities, see II.4.4–5 and II.5.1–8. Alexander was governed by the women in his family, who created a beneficent closed aristocracy from a handful of respectable senators (Herodian, *History* VI.1); Herodian (VI.1.10) describes his subjection to his mother as the "one thing for which he can be faulted," and offers that "as far as his subjects were concerned, [his rule] was without fault or bloodshed" (VI.9.8). I discuss Alexander in more detail, later in this chapter.

16.   De Alvarez (2008, 97) also notes this.

17.   Machiavelli is able to discuss Severus as the central example, after Alexander, only because he alters the chronology: first, he refuses to discuss Heliogabalus, Macrinus, or Julianus, noting that they were so contemptible that they "were immediately eliminated" (*P* 19); second, he moves Commodus (son of Marcus) from his chronological position. Thus Severus becomes the central of seven emperors that Machiavelli discusses. The historical order is: Marcus, Commodus, Pertinax, Julianus, Severus, Caracalla, Macrinus, Heliogabalus, Alexander, and Maximinus; Machiavelli's revised order is: Marcus, Pertinax, Alexander, Severus, Caracalla, Commodus, and Maximinus. De Alvarez (2008, 96) also notes this alteration.

The fates of the contemptible emperors are perhaps more instructive than Machiavelli's dismissive tone indicates. For the pregnant features of Julianus's career, see Herodian, *History*, II.6.4–11, II.6.13–14, II.12.3, and II.12.6–7. For the same of Macrinus's career, see Herodian, *History* IV.13, IV.14.2, IV.15.7–9, V.1.1—V.2.1–5, and V.4.12. Contrary to Machiavelli's claim (*P* 19), Heliogabalus was not "immediately eliminated." For the significant features of his rule, see V.3.9–10, V.5.3–7, and V.6.3–4. After five years of religious excess under the dissolute Heliogabalus, the soldiers dispatched him in favor of his successor, Alexander (V.8.8).

18. *Opere*, 287.

19. Borgia's example remains a miniature: he enjoys the benefits of his well-used cruelty for "more than a month" (*P* 7, 32). See Orwin 2014; and 1978, 1223.

20. For Herodian's judgment of Severus's positive qualities, see *History* II.9.2, II.14.2, III.6.10, and III.8.10. For a pithy statement of his accomplishments in war, see III.7.7–8.

21. For Severus's outrage against the Praetorians, see II.9.8–10; for his claims to divine inspiration, see Herodian, *History* II.9.3–7, esp. II.9.3.

22. See also Severus's assault against Niger's mountain fortification (Herodian, *History* III.3.1–8), and cf. *P* DL and *P* 14.

23. Whittaker translates *philanthrwpia* as "generosity."

24. Cf. Polybius, *Histories* I.9, which also reports that Hiero nonetheless employed his own, more faithful, mercenaries after destroying the corrupted arms. I discuss the implications of this fact later in this chapter.

25. Livy XXIV.4; cf. Herodian, *History* II.9.9–10.

26. Herodian, *History* II.14.5; *P* 13, 57. Compare Severus's manipulative act of philanthropy with Machiavelli's identification of severity with healthy republican orders in *D* III.22.4.

27. Herodian, *History* II.14.1. For the terror that Severus regularly inspired in the people, see also III.8.2–3 and III.8.8.

28. An anonymous reviewer has noted that the Italian phrase "*avevano potuto concipere*" (*Opere*, 287) could be translated as "had been able to conceive"—thus suggesting that Severus's subjects hated him, but that Severus was able to defend himself.

29. For Severus's novel practice of indulging the avarice of soldiers, see Herodian, *History* III.8.5; he granted special license to his beloved subordinate Plautianus (III.10.5–7). For his own infamous avarice, see Herodian, *History* III.8.7–8. Machiavelli describes Severus as a criminal in the *Discourses* (I.10.4). I am indebted particularly to Michael Palmer's excellent lectures on this subject, which he reproduced partially in "Machiavelli's Inhuman Humanism" (2001).

30. Herodian, *History* II.9.13. For one of Severus's lies, see II.13.3–4. For the aptness of comparing Severus and Alexander VI, see the discussion later in the chapter.

31. I am indebted to Clifford Orwin's undergraduate lectures, in which he offered an approximation of this formulation. Palmer (2001, 88), following Strauss (1958, 46 and 255), describes Severus as a model for Machiavellian founders; de Alvarez observes the same, and suggests that chapter 19 reveals the founders' natures to be "criminal" (2008, 99). See also Mansfield 1996, 187.

32. Tarcov (forthcoming) describes this method as a "destructive analysis."

33. Herodian, *History* III.8.5. Importantly, he would only be confirming the corruption that Commodus had initiated. For evidence that Roman military orders were already corrupted, see Sullivan 1996, 66–80; cf. McCormick

2011a, 59; and 2015, 48–49. See also *D* III.16.2 (cf. Benner 2013, 237–38; and Mansfield 1979, 365–68).

34. Strauss 1958, 307–8n29. Hulliung's (1983, 35) scandalous account of Machiavelli does not extend to this scandalous judgment.

35. *P* 13, 57. For Philip's mercenary career, see *P* 12, 50; for David's mercenary origins, see 1 Samuel 17:25; for Philopoemen's career as a mercenary in Crete, see Plutarch, *Philopoemen* 7.1–2.

36. Agathocles selected these soldiers from the ranks of the civil military (Diodorus Siculus, *Library of History* XIX.6.1–3); to these he added a number of impoverished and envious citizens. For his subsequent employment of mercenaries, see XX.63.6–7.

37. See Deuteronomy 20; and Plutarch, *Romulus* 14. The evidence of Theseus's rapacity is less strong, as many of his exploits are overtly mythical, but see Plutarch, *Theseus* 2 and 24–30.

38. Polybius, *Histories* I.9.

39. For Christ's rejection of worldly treasure, see the discussion of acquisition in chapter 1 of this work. For Christ's concern that the law and the prophets be observed see esp., Matthew 5:17–19; see also my discussion in chapter 4 of Christ's defense against the charge that he violates certain Mosaic laws. For Christ's instruction to obey civil authority, which nonetheless often communicates passive hostility or practiced indifference to that power, see Luke 20:25; see also Romans 13:1–7; Titus 3:1; 1 Peter 2:13–17; and 1 John 3:4. For the teaching that earthly law can never contravene one's duty to preach about Christ, see Acts 5:27–42. For the ultimate insufficiency of law, see Romans 3:19–31; and Galatians 5:3–6; yet when Christ returns all authorities will nonetheless accede to his rule (Matthew 28:18). Christ's ambivalence toward the existing political and religious orders is the main theme of chapters 2 and 4, above.

40. See Strauss 1958, 286.

41. Cf. Benner 2013, 243. See also Sullivan 2013, 533.

42. *D* I.10.2.

43. Machiavelli pointedly omits discussion of the piety of these emperors (see de Alvarez 2008, 97; and Tarcov 2014, 205 and 209).

44. See de Alvarez 2008, 91–92, for the crucial importance of this section. Severus's dynasty, which includes several of the deficient emperors discussed in this chapter, does not last fifty years.

45. The conspiracy is more complicated than Machiavelli suggests here. See *P* 19; cf. Herodian, *History* IV.12.4–7 and 13.1–2; and *D* III.6.11.

46. For Caracalla's stunning capacity for violence, see Herodian, *History* IV.3.4, IV.6.4–5, and IV.9. For his devotion to oracles, see IV.12.3. Caracalla also lacked complete control of his own army (see IV.4.7–8; cf. II.13.2–12).

47. *D* I.10.4–5.

48. See Herodian, *History* I.15 and II.2.5. For evidence of his momentous decision to indulge soldiers, see I.8.1–2.

49. Cf. Herodian, *History* II.10.3, which reports a similar judgment in the mouth of Severus—who nonetheless excuses Commodus, while blaming his

"sycophants." Cf. Tarcov forthcoming. As evidence of the ascendancy of the Praetorian Guard after Commodus, see Herodian, *History* II.2.1.

50. This opinion was neither universal nor strictly orthodox. While Machiavelli does not mention this, one can safely consider this fact when analyzing chapter 19: recall that Machiavelli also neglects to note the prophetic qualities of Romulus, Theseus, and Cyrus. See the *Historia Augusta* ("The Life of Marcus Aurelius," 19.10–12) for evidence of the Romans' pious awe.

51. Another possible explanation of Marcus's success would be Rome's particularly bellicose foreign policy during his reign; the cruelty and the avarice of the army could thus be vented on foreigners rather than citizens (cf. *P* 16, 64). Cf. also Tarcov 2003, 111; and Orwin 1978, 1220–22.

52. See *D* I.10.4 for Machiavelli's critique of hereditary power in the Roman Empire.

53. De Alvarez (2008, 98) also suggests this.

54. For Maximinus's blunders and eventual demise, see Herodian, *History* VII.1.6, VII.3.6, and VIII.5.8–9.

55. Mansfield 1996, 263. Like most emperors, Severus is formally deified upon his death (Herodian, *History* IV.2.1–3.1), but consider Severus's reputation in light of Machiavelli's distinction between internal and external rapacity, which I discuss in chapter 5.

56. De Alvarez (2008, 113) suggests this about the book as a whole.

57. For evidence of the dangers posed to popes by the ecclesiastical order, see, for example, Scott and Sullivan 1994, 895–96.

58. See also *FH* I.23 (cf. Korvela 2006, 57); and Mansfield 1979, 226n10.

59. Leo X failed in his efforts to correct the injustice of the ecclesiastical order; during his reign, the Protestant Reformation blossomed. While one can easily imagine how priests could—and did—enrich themselves by exploiting the people, the Church's complicity in Ferdinand of Spain's "pious cruelty" (*P* 21) constitutes sufficient evidence of the ecclesiastical order's capacity for cruelty; see also the events that precipitated the War of the Eight Saints (*FH* III.7), to which Machiavelli apparently alludes in chapter 21 (cf. Chazan 1980, 277–319).

60. Matthew 16:18 and 28:16–20; Acts 1:6–8.

61. Cf. Benner 2013, 243–44; see also 2013, 77–84.

62. See also Scott and Sullivan 1994. Cf. Hulliung 1983, 207.

63. I can cite no dispositive evidence that Machiavelli consulted this collection of imperial biographies, but the editor of the *Historia Augusta* ("Introduction," 1:xxvii) notes that Petrarch probably consulted it and that "the general interest in the *Historia Augusta* in the fifteenth century is well attested by the number of manuscripts that were made in that period" (xxviii). Its comparatively greater attention to the fate of the Christians under the emperors reflects perhaps the time it was composed; some of the biographies—including that of Heliogabalus and Alexander—were even commissioned by Constantine ("Life of Elegabalus," 2.4; "Life of Severus Alexander," 65.1). Severus's biography is addressed to Diocletian, the last Roman emperor to persecute Christians with alacrity ("Life of Septimius Severus," 20.4). For an account of the growth of Christianity in its early centuries, see Stark 1997.

64.   *Historia Augusta*, "Life of Septimius Severus," 17.1–2.
65.   *Historia Augusta*, "Life of Elegabalus," 3.5.
66.   *Historia Augusta*, "Life of Severus Alexander," 22.6; see also 14.5 and 45.7.
67.   Despite its negative formulation, Alexander's maxim appears to refer to Matthew 12:7. See Warfield's (1886, 142–43) discussion of the text's differences with Matthew's.
68.   *D* I.12.1.
69.   See, for example, Exodus 34:14; Matthew 28:16–20; and 1 Timothy 2:5.
70.   For an account of his religious eccentricities, see Herodian, *History* V.5–6; the soldiers nonetheless eventually slew him and threw his body into a sewer (V.8.8–9).
71.   Severus ruled for eighteen years; Marcus ruled for nineteen.
72.   Herodian, *History* VI.5.8.
73.   *Opere*, 287; for Machiavelli's only other use of "goodness" (*bontà*) in *The Prince*, see *P* 11 (*Opere*, 274). For Herodian's praise of the positive influence of Alexander's grandmother, see *History* VI.1.1–5.
74.   Matthew 7:12.
75.   See also Luke 13:32 and 1 Peter 5:8; cf. also Machiavelli's discussion of the fox and the lion in chapter 18, which is treated in chapter 5.
76.   Cf. de Alvarez 2008, 113.
77.   See esp. *P* 3 and *P* 11.
78.   See esp. *P* 6, *P* 7, *P* 12, *P* 13, *P* 14, and *P* 19.
79.   Indeed, in chapter 20, Machiavelli directs the reader to that critique (*P* 12), in which the Church emerges as responsible for the ascendancy of mercenary arms in Italy.
80.   *Opere*, 289. Benner (2013, 248–50) offers a similar judgment of this passage.
81.   Chapter 20 contains only Italian examples. Of course, much of Machiavelli's advice in *The Prince* might be used against the fragmented political communities of Italy.
82.   Machiavelli notes that the Venetians—whose military practices he criticizes in chapter 12—also employ this failed strategy. See de Alvarez 2008, 104–5, 108. See also Benner 2013, 249–50.
83.   He overstates the security of this course: cf. *P* 9 and *P* 18. For the significance of Machiavelli's example of Pandolfo Petrucci, see *D* III.6.19. See also Benner 2013, 267–68. Both de Alvarez (2008, 106) and Benner (2013, 251) note the self-referential quality of this argument.
84.   Cf. Mansfield 1979, 266–71.
85.   This prince would appear to be in desperate straits, yet one ought to doubt Machiavelli's pronouncement that "the best fortress is not to be hated by the people" (*P* 20)—a teaching that he offers in chapter 9, but revises radically in chapter 19. Cf. Benner 2013, 253.
86.   *D* III.6.18 and *FH* VIII.34. According to Hairston (2000, 687), Machiavelli's version departs significantly from the historical record, and is the origin of all similar subsequent versions. Cf. Viroli 2014, 70–72. Compare the discussion that follows with Clarke 2005.

87.   *Opere*, 208. See Mansfield 1979, 338–39. In *FH* VIII.34, Machiavelli writes that the conspirators "begged" or "prayed" (*pregorono*) (*Opere*, 842) for the countess's help.

88.   Cf. *FH* IV.9–10.

89.   Mansfield 1979, 338–39.

90.   The last point especially is Mansfield's (1979, 339).

91.   See also Mansfield 1979, 338–39.

92.   Psalm 18:2. On the preponderance of references to the Psalms in the New Testament, see Daly-Denton 2008. The Psalms frequently describe God as a "fortress" in whom believers can take refuge against external enemies (see also 28:8, 31:2–3, 46:7, 46:11, 48:3, 59:1, 59:9, 59:16–17, 62:2–6, 71:3, 91:2, 94:22, and 144:2; Proverbs 14:26; Isaiah 17:10; and Jeremiah 16:19).

93.   McBrien 1997, 267.

94.   It is strange that Machiavelli does not mention the Inquisition by name. One is tempted to conclude that he refrains from doing so precisely because it represents the most immediate danger to him and his intellectual kin; certainly, it is most clearly representative of "the malignity of the times" (*D* I.P.2) that tends to distort the study of history and the knowledge of human affairs.

95.   Peters 1988, 85–87.

96.   For evidence of the weak moral constraints imposed on papal rule, note that Sixtus IV's confirmation of Tomás de Torquemada as Grand Inquisitor of Spain was followed shortly by a failed protest to Ferdinand that the Inquisition was being improperly conducted (Peters 1988, 86).

97.   The similarity of this passage to the final four sections of Xenophon's *Hiero* (8–11) is unmistakable. There, Simonides exhorts Hiero to moderate his tyranny by enacting the proposals described in chapter 21 of *The Prince*. Cf. Benner 2013, 233; contrast with Connell 2005, 30.

98.   See esp. *D* II.2.3; cf. *P* 21 and *P* 5.

99.   See Sullivan 1996, 42–49, de Alvarez 2008, 112–13, and Benner 2013, 264–66, none of which relates this critique of Ferdinand so explicitly to the argument of chapter 19. See also Benner 2013 (256), which notes that Machiavelli's letters to Vettori are critical of Ferdinand (see, for example, Machiavelli 1988b, "Niccolò Machiavelli to Francesco Vettori," April 29, 1514, 107–17). Cf. Viroli's (2014, 34–35) and Colish's (1999, 607–8) qualified praise of Ferdinand.

100. See esp. *P* 3.

101. For Machiavelli's various brief accounts of Bernabò's death, see *D* II.13.1; and *FH* I.27, I.33, and III.25. The nephew, Giovan Galeazzo, was known as the "Count of Virtue"; his ambition was to become "king of Italy" (*FH* III.25), and his ability to deceive Bernabò suggests that the latter did not always reward and punish those under his supervision with consummate skill.

102. Cf. John 21:15–17.

103. During this war, Gregory returned the Church's court to Rome from Avignon (*FH* I.32 and III.7). For the Eight Saints' authority to tax, see Baron 1966, 469n12b; for a brief account of this war and its implications, see Baron 1966, 23–25.

104. Cf. Machiavelli 1988b, "Niccolò Machiavelli to Francesco Vettori," April 16, 1527, 249. Cf. de Grazia 1994, 352.

105. See Strauss 1958, 102.

106. For the significance of these events, see esp. Sullivan 2013, according to which the Aetolians formerly had been "Rome's first ally outside Italy" (527).

107. Livy XXXV.48; for an account of Roman-Achaean cooperation against Nabis, see XXXV.25–37; and Plutarch, *Philopoemen* 14. Compare the discussion that follows with de Alvarez 2008, 110.

108. Machiavelli quotes accurately from Livy XXXV.49. This Quinctius appears to be the consul whom Livy reports as jealous of Philopoemen (XXXV.47). Machiavelli refers to him as a legate (*legato*) (*Opere*, 292).

109. Livy XXXV.49.

110. *Opere*, 292. This is the second appearance of the word "justice" (*giustizia*) in *The Prince*.

111. Livy XXXVIII.31–33.

112. Livy XXXVIII.32. Livy reports that Philopoemen was "the prime mover" in these events, while the Achaean representative Lycortas was "acting on instructions from Philopoemen" (XXXIX.36). Lycortas and Philopoemen were friends: see Plutarch, *Philopoemen* 20.2 and 21.1.

113. Livy XXXVIII.33–34.

114. Livy XXXIX.33. At around the same time, the Achaeans convened an assembly, at which Lycortas complained that while in the previous war the "Achaeans had found the Romans useful allies; now these very Romans were more partial to the Lacedaemonians than to the Achaeans" (XXXIX.35). According to Plutarch, it is also around this time that Philopoemen, who was suffering in "silent indignation," through a speech that encouraged deference to Rome "at last, overcome by anger, said to [the speaker]: 'My man, why art thou eager to behold the fated end of Greece?'" (*Philopoemen* 17.3).

115. Livy XXXIX.37. Machiavelli's reasoning (*P* 21, 90) vindicates Rome's strategy. Contrast this judgment with Benner 2013, 258–61; cf. Sullivan 2013, 530.

116. Livy XXXIX.49–50. According to Machiavelli, the victory over Antiochus also established the preconditions for the corruption of the Roman military that would deepen during Commodus's reign (*D* III.16.2; Benner 2013, 237–38).

117. In this regard, Achaean acquiescence to Rome ought to be compared to Florence's acquiescence to Spain and the Church, which Machiavelli excuses (*P* 21).

118. For Machiavelli's departure from Aristotelian notions of prudence, see de Alvarez 2008, 112.

119. Plutarch, *Philopoemen* 17.2. Plutarch notes that "when the Romans went to war with Antiochus in Greece, Philopoemen was without command" (17.1). Reputed to be a "malevolent enemy of the Romans" (21.5), might he have doubted the wisdom of allying with Rome? For Philopoemen's opposition to tyranny, see Livy XXXIX.37 and XXXVIII.31. For his problematic refusal to ally with Philip V of Macedon, see chapter 7, below.

120. Sullivan 2013, 536. Benner (2013, 259) identifies Italy's "Roman" adversary as France.

121. The comparison of ancient Sparta and the Church may be more apt than is suggested by the current scholarship's silence on the subject. Each enjoyed a sterling reputation for virtue that was nonetheless doubted by its most informed observers; each is noted to have indulged the criminal conduct of its citizens; each maintained its position by exploiting those who lived outside its orders; and finally, the triumph of each signaled the dawn of servitude for their respective regions.

122. De Alvarez's (2008, 111) incisive treatment of this passage helped clarify for me Machiavelli's use of "*contratto l'amore*" (*Opere*, 292). Note, however, that Machiavelli's word for "love" (*amore*) here is less pregnant than his use of *carità* in chapters 10 and 18 of *The Prince* (*Opere*, 273 and 284).

123. Plutarch, *Philopoemen* 1.4.

124. Plutarch, *Philopoemen*, 17.2.

125. De Alvarez (2008, 117) observes that the "lack of prudence brought about by the times" constitutes an opportunity for a prudent captain at the head of a mercenary force. See also Strauss 1958 (307–8n29), which intimates the necessity of an absolute prince at the head of a personal mercenary army composed of non-Italians.

126. One ought to subject Machiavelli's discussion of the great in chapter 9 to a similar analysis. Cf. Machiavelli's earlier advice concerning the apparently pusillanimous and dependent (*P* 9, 18, and 20). For Machiavelli's irony see de Alvarez 2008, 114–15.

127. The man is Luca Rinaldi, a bishop who served as an ambassador for Maximilian (*P* 23, 942). It is not clear that Machiavelli learned this information directly from Father Luca; unlike in his reported conversations with the cardinal of Rouen (*P* 3 [*Opere*, 262]) and Cesare Borgia (*P* 7 [*Opere*, 268]), Machiavelli does not employ the first person. Francesco Vettori, who also served as an ambassador to Maximilian, is the likely source. For evidence of Vettori's leading role in this embassy, see Jones 1968, 102 and 110. Cf. de Alvarez 2008, 116.

128. Cf. Strauss 1958, 84.

Chapter Seven

1. Only the first lines of chapter 12 betray a similar structure (cf. *P* 19); indeed, insofar as chapter 12 commences Machiavelli's explicit teaching on arms that culminates in chapter 14, it also commences an elaborated recapitulation of the teaching in chapters 1 through 11—or the conclusion to the first half of the book.

2. Machiavelli does not use this phrase in chapter 2. For a discussion of the Eucharist, see chapter 1, above; Matthew 26:28; Mark 14:24; and Luke 22:20.

3. Matthew 26:28 and 26:29.

4. Luke 22:19.

5. This is consistent with his teaching on obligation in chapter 10, which emphasized the precariousness of men's attachment to the unarmed prince.

See the discussion of this passage in chapter 3 of this work, and compare it with the obligation engendered by arming one's people (*P* 20) discussed in chapter 6.

6. In addition to the countless individual examples of hope-born efforts to acquire principalities, see esp. Machiavelli's more general statements (*P* 3; *P* 17): the intertwined desires to acquire and to remain secure seem to be men's principal motivations.

7. Cf. de Alvarez 2008, 118.

8. For the necessity of arms see, for example, *P* 1, 6; *P* 6, 24; *P* 13, 57; *P* 14; *P* 16; *P* 19; and *P* 20. For Machiavelli's statement that good arms produce good laws, see *P* 12 (discussed in chapter 3); for the requirements of good friends, see *P* 19 (discussed in chapter 6).

9. *P* Glossary.

10. See, for example, Machiavelli's introduction of Rome's conduct in Greece as an "example" of the conduct of a "wise" prince (*P* 3).

11. The preponderance of examples in chapter 21 conforms to the title.

12. Arms might nonetheless be necessary eventually to compel belief among his lukewarm supporters (*P* 6; *P* 26).

13. John 18:36. For Machiavelli's critique of Christ's lack of arms, see chapters 2 and 3 of this work; for his critique of Christ's indifference to worldly goods, see esp. chapters 1 and 4.

14. For Christ's reliance on miracles, see John 10:24–39; see also chapter 2, above. See Fischer 1997 (828–29) for the limits of glory.

15. Machiavelli discussed Alexander's plot in detail in chapters 3 and 7 of *The Prince*. Alexander's negotiations with Louis XII led the latter to attack the younger Sforza's city (*P* "Chronology," xxix–xxx); the king of Naples lost his state when Louis thereafter allied with Spain, which seized sole control over Naples when Julius II's Holy League expelled Louis XII from Italy (*P* 3; *P* "Chronology," xxx). Machiavelli contrasts the elder Sforza with the king of Naples in chapter 1 of *The Prince*.

16. See Strauss 1958, 61. Compare the discussion that follows with Benner 2013, 286–88.

17. See also *D* II.4.2. I am indebted to Mansfield and Tarcov's footnotes to the *Discourses*, which directed me to these passages in Livy.

18. Livy XXXII.32. See de Alvarez's (2008, 120) and Strauss's (1958, 161) claims regarding the significance of the Roman consul who subdued Philip, Titus Quinctius Flaminius.

19. Machiavelli vindicates Philip's judgment in *P* 3. Compare Philip's circumspection with Machiavelli's discussion of the Achaeans' decision to ally with Rome against Antiochus (*P* 21), discussed in chapter 6.

20. Livy XXXII.33; cf. *P* 21; and Livy XXX.49. In certain ways, Philip's character resembles Machiavelli's. After reporting a humorous exchange between Philip and an Aetolian, Livy reports, "He was by nature more given to jesting than a king ought to be, and even in the midst of serious business did not sufficiently restrain his laughter" (XXXII.34).

21. Machiavelli discusses this military strategy in *D* III.10.2–3, where against the advancing Romans, Philip employed a cunctative strategy after he learned

that it "was not enough to stay on top of mountains" (III.10.3). (Compare this evalution of Philip's strategy with Machiavelli's general denigration of the security afforded by the high places, discussed in chapter 4 of this work.) This strategy did not work, and Philip was eventually defeated by Rome— although he was never subjugated entirely. His defeat was among the first causes of Rome's influence in the region (Livy XXXIII.31–32).

22. Livy XXXII.13.
23. *D* III.37.2.
24. Livy XXXI.14. The Latin translation is mine: Roberts's less literal translation reads "horrible crime."
25. Livy XXXI.26. Cf. Polybius, *Histories* IX.30, V.9, and XI.7.
26. Polybius, *Histories* XXIV.13–15.
27. Polybius, *Histories*, XVI.37–38.
28. For an account of these events, see chapter 6. See also Sullivan 2013. Cf. de Alvarez 2008, 120.
29. Polybius (*Histories* VII.12–13), who is critical of Philip, attributes this transformation to a change in advisers.
30. See Polybius, *Histories* VII.9–13 and XXIII.10.
31. Polybius XXIII.7–8. Livy (XL.24), who actually reports the death, also reports that Philip regretted this decision. Compare Philip's action with Hiero's (XXIII.30).
32. *Opere*, 295. See Tarcov 2014, 211. Compare Machiavelli's admonition to prepare assiduously for the storm with Christ's ability to calm storms miraculously (Matthew 8:23–27; Mark 4:35–41).
33. Psalm 37:23–24; cf. also Psalm 145:14, which promises, "The LORD upholds all who fall and lifts up all who are bowed down." Cf. Psalm 36:12. Machiavelli's teaching here appears to allude to the general teaching of the Psalms, but its form and language (while Machiavelli uses *cadere*, the Latin features *ceciderit*) resembles Psalm 37:24 most closely.
34. On the preponderance of references to the Psalms in the New Testament, see Daly-Denton 2008.
35. Matthew 27:46; Mark 15:34; Christ's exclamation is from Psalm 22:1. Christ also quotes from the Psalms (69:4) in John 15:25. The appeal for support occurs in Psalm 22:19–21. See also the discussion of Christ's crucifixion in chapter 2 of this work. For the Gospels' general judgment of God's capacity to protect believers, see: Matthew 5:45; 6:13; and 18:10; Luke 1:51–53 and 1:68–74; and John 17:15.
36. Matthew 10:29–31; see also Luke 12:6–7.
37. Luke 12:27. For the full metaphor, see Luke 12:27–31.
38. Jude 1:24. See Acts 14:17 and 18:10; Romans 8:29; 9:23; and 11:36; 2 Corinthians 1:10; Ephesians 67:11–12; Philippians 4:7; 2 Thessalonians 3:3; Hebrews 1:3 and 1:14; and 1 John 4:4.
39. Psalm 145:14.
40. Matthew 10:30.
41. Matthew 8:23–27; Mark 4:35–41.
42. Romans 8:38–39; Hebrews 7:25.
43. Cf. Jeremiah 18:7–10; and Daniel 5:26.

44. See Brown 2010b, 51 and 71–75, which attribute Machiavelli's opinions in this chapter to the influence of Adriani and Lucretius, respectively.

45. The word is *humanis* in chapter 25 (*Opere*, 295); in chapter 15, Machiavelli addressed "men," or *homines* (*Opere*, 280).

46. Cf. Fontana 1999, 652–54.

47. *Opere*, 295. *Sorte* connotes more than mere luck: it is linked with notions of prophecy, destiny, or fate.

48. For God's power see Nehemiah 9:6; Job 5:9–10; Psalms 104:27–28 and 145:15–16; Isaiah 40:26; and Habakkuk 1:12; see also Acts 14:17; Romans 8:28; and 1 Timothy 6:13–17. For God's alleged sovereignty see: Job 42:2; Psalm 135:6; Daniel 4:35; Matthew 19:26; Romans 9:19–21; and Ephesians 3:20. For the glory that attends that power, see Psalm 46:10; Romans 9:23 and 11:36; and Ephesians 1:4–6 and 1:11–12.

49. Compare the discussion that follows with Nederman 1999 and 2009, 34–39; see also Brown 2010b, 85; and 2010a, 161–63.

50. Contrast the discussion that follows with de Grazia's (1994, 31) argument that "the references to the divine in *The Prince* comprise significant metaphysical and theological statements, with political bearings just as significant."

51. *The Prince* thus conforms to Machiavelli's pithy marginal note on his copy of Lucretius's *On the Nature of Things* (646–51): "the gods don't care about the affairs of mortals" (quoted and translated in Brown 2010b, 75; see also Palmer 2014, 82–83).

52. For another of Machiavelli's references to a flood, see Niccoli 1990, 142.

53. Matthew (27:45–53) reports the first two events, and also asserts that the saints left their tombs to appear among the people. Mark (15:38) reports the first event only; Luke (23:45–48) reports the first and third. The synoptic Gospels also agree that the skies darkened. Matthew (27:54), Luke (23:43), and Mark (15:39) report that at least one centurion comes to believe as a result of these events. John's account (19:28–30) of Jesus's death is very spare.

54. Job 5:9–12. For other accounts of God's control of the weather (and especially rain), see Genesis 6–7; 8:22; and 9:14–16; Deuteronomy 33:13–14; Job 5:8–16; 28:25–27; and 38:34; Psalms 68:7–9 and 135:7; Isaiah 8:7 and 30:23; Jeremiah 10:13; Joel 2:23; Jonah 1:4 and 4:8; and Zechariah 10:1; in the New Testament, see Matthew 5:45; 8:26–27; and 24:39; Mark 4:39–41; Luke 8:24–25; John 3:8; Acts 14:17; James 5:17–18; and 2 Peter 2:5.

55. Acts 1:8.

56. Machiavelli describes Italy as "*la sedia di queste variazioni*" (*Opere*, 295).

57. Cf. *D* I.12. Dams and dikes do not, of course, accomplish the same things. Machiavelli has provided models of dam-builders and dike-builders that Italians might imitate: Philopoemon sought to build dikes to make the best of ascendant Roman power in Greece; the tyrannical Philip V built a dam.

58. See chapter 1 of this work for a discussion of Christ's judgment of these "ends." Cf. Proverbs 8:18; and Philippians 4:19. See also Fischer 1997, which notes the rarity of true glory: most men seek gain in a variety of ways (816–18).

59. *Opere*, 296. See chapter 5 of this work. Cf. Machiavelli 1988b, "Niccolò Machiavelli to Piero Soderini," January 1513, 99 (see, however, Gaeta's version of *Lettere* [Machiavelli 1984, 239–45], in which he corrects the true addressee and date of this letter; it is now believed to have been sent to Soderini's nephew in September 1506; see also Skinner and Price 1988, 95–96). This letter contains early versions of Machiavelli's arguments in *The Prince*, which nonetheless differ in important ways—especially on the ultimate effect of human agency.

60. Matthew 10:28 and 10:33; John 3:36, 11:25–26, and 17:3. See also Acts 4:12 and 16:30–31; 1 Peter 1:15–25 and 5:4–10; Romans 1:16 and 10:9–10; 2 Corinthians 4:17; and 2 Timothy 2:10. For Christ's muddling of earthly and heavenly goods, see Matthew 19:29; Mark 10:30; and Luke 18:30. Cf. *Art of War* I.2.

61. John 14:6; Matthew 19:16–17.

62. John 3:36.

63. *Opere*, 296.

64. Cf. Benner 2013, 298–301.

65. Polybius, *Histories* XXV.3.

66. Cf. *D* III.9 and III.44.

67. John 3:16.

68. Clarke (2005, 232) notes that women perhaps excel particularly as partners in conspiracies.

69. For evidence of the other defects, see *D* III.10.1; *P* 15; *P* 19; and *Historia Augusta*, "Life of Elegabalus," II.1; and "Life of Severus Alexander," 60.2. Hulliung (1983, 29) makes a similar argument concerning Machiavelli's preference for impetuosity.

70. Matthew 5:27–28. See also Matthew 26:7–10, 27:60–61, and 28:1–10; Mark 16:1–11; Luke 1:28–56, 2:36–38, 7:37–50, and 24:1–11; and John 19:25 and 20:1–11. See also Acts 1:14. Consider also that daring manliness might aid efforts to change one's nature.

71. John 3:23–36 and 8:1–11. Cf. Mark 14:51–52.

72. Compare the discussion that follows with Viroli 2014, 23–65; Jaeckel 1995; and Strauss 1957, 19—32.

73. Benner 2013, 312; McBrien 1997, 247–74.

74. Luke 1:68–75; for the spiritual redemption that Christ offers, see Acts 26:28; Romans 3:23–24 and 6:18; Galatians 1:4 and 4:3; Ephesians 1:7–14; Colossians 1:13–14, 1:30, and 2:20; Titus 2:14 and 3:3–5; Hebrews 9:14–15; 1 Peter 1:18 and 3:18; and 1 John 1:7. Wolin (1960, 204) observes a parallel between Italy's degradation and suffering of "the *corpus Christi*," since both Italy and Christ could "escape disintegration" only by recourse to a "revivifying principle" (205). According to Wolin, Machiavelli could convey the "national inspiration" evident in the exhortation only "through the older language of religious emotion and thought" (205) to which Machiavelli recurred when endorsing his "unexamined preferences" (206).

75. Romans 6:22. Cf. 1 Corinthians 7:23.

76. Matthew 20:28; Mark 10:45; Romans 5:9 and 8:1–2; 1 Thessalonians 1:10; Hebrews 2:14–15.

77. Luke 21:23; 21:5–28.

78. See Tarcov forthcoming. Cf. de Grazia 1994, 53, which attributes Romulus's absence to his alleged secular character; cf., however, Mansfield's (1979, 71) more careful reading of the *Discourses*: he notes that Romulus's successor found Rome "full of religion" (*D* I.11.3; see also Livy I.7–8).

79. See also *D* I.16–18. De Grazia (1994, 235–36) notes this teaching, but does not identify Italian corruption with the ascendancy of Christianity.

80. *P* 7 and *P* 11. Benner (2013, 307) offers that Machiavelli might also be referring to Savonarola.

81. Cf. de Grazia 1994, 49; cf. Germino 1972, 33–36.

82. Cf. *P* 6. Italy's redeemer may not be the red-blooded Italian some scholars (see esp. Viroli 2014 and Nederman 2009) imagine him to be: Moses, although an Israelite, was nonetheless raised by Egyptians—and thus (perhaps crucially) remained uncorrupted by their servility. On God's choosiness, compare Machiavelli's account with Exodus 3:15 and 1 Corinthians 8:6.

83. Romans 8:33.

84. Machiavelli quotes from Livy IX.1.

85. They do not, although an early success promises a great victory. After notable vacillation by the Samnites, the virtue of the Romans (and especially Papirius Cursor) overcomes the Samnites—and their divine support (Livy IX.2–15).

86. For a contextual understanding of Machiavelli's casual use of prophecy, see Niccoli 1990.

87. Exodus 3:1–10.

88. Exodus 4:12 and 4:11–15.

89. Aaron's assistance is not unequivocally helpful (see, for example, Exodus 32:2–24), and eventually Moses persists (Numbers 20:22–29) without him. This vindicates God's original inclination to empower Moses alone. Cf. *D* I.9.

90. See *D* I.P.1; cf. Exodus 3:8.

91. *P* 26, 103n7; Lynch 2006, 183–84. Lynch (2006, 183n69) credits Jackel (1995) with this observation. Jackel's interpretation nonetheless differs: he judges (1995, 60–61) that this list of miracles refers to a French invasion (61–65), which enflamed Machiavelli's hopes for Italy, notwithstanding papal blunders (78–84).

92. Cf. Viroli 2014, 53. Machiavelli does not mention that the cloud turned into a "pillar of fire" (Exodus 13:22), nor the miraculous "sweetening" of the waters at Marah (Exodus 15:23–25).

93. Matthew 25:31. Cf. Geerken 1999, 593.

94. Cf. *D* III.30.1.

95. Psalm 78:8 and 32–35. My analysis of this passage follows Lynch's account (2006, 183–84) very closely.

96. Psalm 78:31.

97. Psalm 78:9–10; cf. Judges 12:2–6.

98. Judges 12:6.

99. Psalm 78:2. See Lynch 2006, 183n70.

100. Psalm 78:10. The only other event in Psalm 78 that occurs outside the Pentateuch is the last reported in the psalm: the abandonment of the tabernacle of Shiloh (59–61), during which the Philistines defeated the Israelites and

seized the Ark of the Covenant (1 Samuel 4:10–11). David's kingship (78:65–72) thus represents God's return to his people.

101. Matthew 3:6; Mark 1:9; Luke 3:21. See also Acts 22:14–15.

102. 1 John 1:7; Romans 8:36. See also 1 Peter 1:18–20.

103. Psalm 78:71–72.

104. John 10:11; *P* 13, 55–56.

105. Psalm 78:71; Titus 2:13–14.

106. Romans 13; 1 Peter 2:13.

107. Hebrews 5:8–9.

108. *Opere*, 297.

109. *P* 7 (*Opere*, 268: Mansfield translates *antiqui* as "old"); *P* 11 (*Opere*, 273: Mansfield translates *antiquati* as "old"); *P* 19 (*Opere*, 288).

110. *Opere*, 264.

111. *Opere*, 297. Compare Machiavelli's assessment of Italy's "matter" with the "matter" available to founders (*P* 6, 23). Compare the discussion that follows with Viroli 2014.

112. The translation is mine; Mansfield (*P* 26) translates *capi* (*Opere*, 297) as a singular, rather than plural, noun.

113. 1 Corinthians 11:3; the word here translated as "head" is *kephale* or *caput*. Cf. Ephesians 4:14–16.

114. Ephesians 1:19–23; see also Ephesians 5:23; and Colossians 1:18 and 2:10–19. Savonarola relied on Ephesians in a December 1494 sermon, in which he exhorted Florentines seeking a "head" to "take Christ for your king and stay under his law and with it he will govern you. . . . Let Christ be your Captain . . . be with Christ and don't seek another head" (quoted from Brown 1988, 58–59). Brown's literal translation captures Savonarola's use of Ephesians, but she does not, however, note the connection to Ephesians or chapter 26 of *The Prince*. Brown (1988, 58) indicates that the sermon was delivered on December 27, but Borelli and Passaro (Savonarola 2006, 163) record it as occurring on December 28.

115. 1 Corinthians 11:3.

116. In this context, Machiavelli's invocation of a "third order" reminds the reader of the third mode of securing oneself that Machiavelli discloses in chapter 19: venting the "avarice and cruelty" of the soldiers. See Exodus 32:25–29 and Deuteronomy 33:8–11.

117. Machiavelli hopes that Italy will actually "see her redeemer," rather than merely observe his good works; cf. esp. Job 19:24–26.

118. Matthew 5:44 and 6:14–15. For God's ability to satisfy the desire for revenge as a redeemer, see, for example, Psalms 18:47 and 107:41–42; and Isaiah 49:25–26. For the Christian God's punishment of deliberate sinners, see Romans 12:17–21 and Hebrews 10:26–31; cf. Proverbs 20:22.

119. Genesis 2:7.

120. I rely generally on Musa's translation of *Italia Mia* by Petrarch (1996, 204–10), but for consistency, I leave *pietà* in the original Italian. Compare Machiavelli's exhortation to form an army to Petrarch's more skeptical view of arms: "He with more followers is surrounded by his enemies" (*Italia Mia*, 26–27).

121. *Italia Mia*, 7–9.

122. *Italia Mia*, 40. Cf. Matthew 7:15 and Luke 10:3 and 10:19. See chapter 5, above.
123. *Italia Mia*, 87–96.
124. This translation of Petrarch (*Italia Mia*, 27) is mine; Musa translates *del ciel* as "the heavens" (1996, 208).
125. *Italia Mia*, 113–22.

Conclusion

Epigraph. Machiavelli 1988b, "Niccolò Machiavelli to Franscesco Vettori," April 16, 1527, 249.

1. For the possible ends of Machiavelli's project, compare *D* I.25 with *D* I.26.
2. Cf. *D* I.P.2 and *D* II.5.1.
3. See *D* 1.26; cf. *D* II.8.2 and *D* III.30.1.
4. As McBrayer (2013) notes, one might also consider the structural similarities of the New Testament and *The Prince.* Each consists of twenty-six parts, and each ends with a destructive apocalyptic vision of the future. One might add that the lone quote of the New Testament in either work occurs in the twenty-sixth chapter of the *Discourses.* Cf. Strauss 1958, 48; and Mansfield 1996, xvi.
5. This phrase is Tarcov's (forthcoming), who uses it in a different context.
6. Mansfield (1979, 101) used this phrase in a different context; Livy XXXII.32.
7. Matthew 24:30.
8. Cf. *P* 6; see also *D* I.9.5 and *D* III.30.
9. Diodorus Siculus, *Library of History* XL.2–3; Plutarch, *Romulus* 9.4–7, 10.1; Plutarch, *Theseus* 24.3; Herodotus, I.209.
10. John 15:19.
11. *Opere*, 273.
12. For Reformation views on wealth, see Calvin, *Institutes of the Christian Religion*, 10 and 18; and Luther, *Freedom of the Christian.* For their changing views on civil government, see *Institutes of the Christian Religion*, 20; and Luther, *Secular Authority*, esp. I.VI, and II. Importantly, both seek to ground their views in New Testament texts. For an account of Machiavelli's "secular reformation," see Maddox 2002, 539.
13. For these thinkers' problematic appropriation of Christianity, which is nonetheless debated in the scholarship, see, for example, Weinberger 1985; Curley 1994; and Pangle 1988.
14. Machiavelli 1988b, "Niccolò Machiavelli to Franscesco Vettori," April 16, 1527, 249.

WORKS CITED

Aelian. 1814. *The Tactics of Aelian, Comprising the Military System of the Grecians.* Translated by Henry Augustus. London: Cox and Baylis.

Aesop. 1868. *A Selection of Aesop's Fables.* Cambridge: Foister and Jagg.

Ágoston, Gábor, and Bruce Masters. 2009. *Encyclopedia of the Ottoman Empire.* New York: Facts on File.

Apollodorus. 1921. *Library.* Edited and Translated by Sir James George Frazer. Cambridge, MA: Harvard University Press.

Aristotle. 1984. *Politics.* Translated by Carnes Lord. Chicago: University of Chicago Press.

———. 2012. *Nicomachean Ethics.* Translated by Robert Bartlett and Susan Collins. Chicago: University of Chicago Press.

Augustine. 2003. *City of God.* Translated by Henry Bettenson. London: Penguin Books.

Bacon, Francis. 2000. *The Advancement of Learning.* Edited by Michael Kieman. Oxford: Oxford University Press.

Baron, Hans. 1966. *The Crisis of the Early Italian Renaissance.* Princeton, NJ: Princeton University Press.

Beiner, Ronald. 2011. *Civil Religion: A Dialogue in the History of Political Philosophy.* Cambridge: Cambridge University Press.

Benner, Erica. 2009. *Machiavelli's Ethics.* Princeton, NJ: Princeton University Press.

———. 2013. *Machiavelli's Prince: A New Reading.* Oxford: Oxford University Press.

Berlin, Isaiah. 1979. "The Originality of Machiavelli." In *Against the Current: Essays in the History of Ideas,* edited by Henry Hardy and with an introduction by Roger Hausheer, 25–79. New York: Viking Press.

Brown, Alison. 1988. "Savonarola, Machiavelli, and Moses: A Changing Model." In *Florence and Italy: Renaissance Studies in Honour of Nicolai Rubinstein,* edited by Peter Denley and Caroline Elam, 57–72. London: Westfield College and University of London, Committee for Medieval Studies.

———. 2010a. "Philosophy and Religion in Machiavelli." In *The Cambridge Companion to Machiavelli,* edited by John M. Najemy, 157–72. Cambridge: Cambridge University Press.

———. 2010b. *The Return of Lucretius to Renaissance Florence.* Cambridge, MA: Harvard University Press.

Calvin, John. 1960. *Institutes of the Christian Religion.* 2 vols. Edited by John Thomas McNeill and translated by Ford Lewis Battles. Philadelphia: John Knox Press.

Cassidy, Richard J. 2001. *Christians and Roman Rule in the New Testament: New Perspectives.* New York: Crossroads Publishing.

Chazan, Robert. 1980. *Church, State and Jew in the Middle Ages.* Springfield, NJ: Behrman House.

Cicero. 1886. *Tusculan Disputations.* Translated by Andrew P. Peabody. Boston: Little, Brown.

———. 1913. *De Officiis.* Translated by Walter Miller. Cambridge, MA: Harvard University Press.

Clarke, Michelle Tolman. 2005. "On the Woman Question in Machiavelli." *Review of Politics* 67, no. 2: 229–55.

Coby, Patrick. 1999. *Machiavelli's Romans: Liberty and Greatness in the "Discourses on Livy."* Lanham, MD: Lexington Books.

Colish, Marcia L. 1999. "Republicanism, Religion, and Machiavelli's Savonarolan Moment." *Journal of the History of Ideas* 60, no. 4 (October): 597–616.

Connell, William J. 2005. *"The Prince," by Niccolò Machiavelli, with Related Documents.* Translated, edited, and with an introduction. Boston: Bedford/St. Martin's Press.

Curley, Edwin. 1994. "Introduction to Hobbes' *Leviathan.*" In *"Leviathan": With Selected Variants from the Latin Edition of 1668.* By Thomas Hobbes. Edited by Edwin Curley. Indianapolis: Hackett.

Daly-Denton, Margaret. 2008. "Early Christian Writers as Jewish Readers: The New Testament Reception of the Psalms." *Review of Rabbinic Judaism* 11, no. 2: 181–99.

de Alvarez, Leo Paul. 2008. *The Machiavellian Enterprise: A Commentary on "The Prince."* DeKalb: Northern Illinois University Press.

de Grazia, Sebastian. 1994. *Machiavelli in Hell.* 2nd ed. New York: Vintage Books.

Dietz, Mary G. 1986. "Trapping the Prince: Machiavelli and the Politics of Deception." *American Political Science Review* 80, no. 3: 777–99.

Diodorus Siculus. 1933. *Library of History.* 12 vols. Translated by Francis Walton. Loeb Classical Library. Cambridge: Harvard University Press.

Duff, Alexander. 2011. "Republicanism and the Problem of Ambition: The Critique of Cicero in Machiavelli's Discourses." *Journal of Politics* 73, no. 4 (October): 980–92.

Encyclopedia of World Biography. 2004. "Henry VIII." The Gale Group. Encyclopedia. com. http://www.encyclopedia.com/topic/Henry_VIII.aspx.

———. 2004. "Louis XII." The Gale Group. Encyclopedia.com. http://www.encyclopedia.com/topic/Louis_XII.aspx.

Erasmus, Desiderius. 1688. *In Praise of Folly.* Translated by John Wilson. Grand Rapids, MI: Christian Classics Ethereal Library. http://www.ccel.org/ccel/erasmus/folly.pdf.

Fischer, Markus. 1997. "Machiavelli's Political Psychology." *Review of Politics* 59, no. 4 (Autumn): 789–829.

Fontana, Benedetto. 1999. "Love of Country and Love of God: The Political Uses of Religion in Machiavelli." *Journal of the History of Ideas* 60, no. 4 (October): 639–58.

Forde, Steven. 1992. "Varieties of Realism: Thucydides and Machiavelli." *Journal of Politics* 54, no. 2: 372–93.

———. 1995. "International Realism and the Science of Politics." *International Studies Quarterly* 39, no. 2: 141–60.

Geerken, John H. 1999. "Machiavelli's Moses and Renaissance Politics." *Journal of the History of Ideas* 60, no. 4 (October): 579–95.

Germino, Dante. 1972. *Machiavelli to Marx: Modern Western Political Thought.* Chicago: University of Chicago Press.

Gilbert, Allan H. 1938. *Machiavelli's "Prince" and Its Forerunners: "The Prince" as a Typical Book* de Regime Principum. Durham, NC: Duke University Press.

Gilbert, Felix. 1939. "The Humanist Concept of the Prince and *The Prince* of Machiavelli." *Journal of Modern History* 11 (December): 449–83.

Hairston, Julia L. 2000. "Skirting the Issue: Machiavelli's Caterina Sforza." *Renaissance Quarterly* 53, no. 3 (Autumn): 687–712.

Hale, J. R. 1961. *Machiavelli and Renaissance Italy.* London: English Universities Press.

Ha-Nakdan, Berekiah. 1967. *Fables of a Jewish Aesop.* Translated by Moses Hadas. New York: Columbia University Press.

Hancock, Ralph C. 2000. "Necessity, Morality, and Christianity." In *Educating the Prince: Essays in Honor of Harvey Mansfield,* edited by Mark Blitz and William Kristol, 45–61. Lanham, MD: Rowman and Littlefield.

Hariman, Robert. 1989. "Composing Modernity in Machiavelli's *Prince.*" *Journal of the History of Ideas* 50, no. 1 (January–March): 3–29.

Herodian. 1969. *History of the Empire since the Time of Marcus Aurelius.* 2 vols. Translated by C. R. Whittaker. Loeb Classical Library. Cambridge, MA: Harvard University Press.

Herodotus. 2007. *Histories.* Edited by Robert Strassler and translated by Andrea L. Purvis. New York: Anchor Books.

Hesiod. 2007. *Theogony, Works and Days, Testimonia.* Edited and Translated by Glenn W. Most. Loeb Classical Library 57. Cambridge, MA: Harvard University Press.

Historia Augusta. 1921. 3 vols. Translated by David Magie. Loeb Classical Library. Cambridge, MA: Harvard University Press.

Hyginus. 1960. *The Myths of Hyginus, Including the Fabulae and the Second Book of the Poetica Astronomica.* Translated and edited by Mary Grant. Lawrence: University Press of Kansas.

Homer. 1951. *The Iliad.* Translated by Richmond Lattimore. Chicago: University of Chicago Press.

———. 1965. *The Odyssey of Homer.* Translated by Richmond Lattimore. New York: Harper and Row.

Hulliung, Mark. 1983. *Citizen Machiavelli.* Princeton, NJ: Princeton University Press.

Ingman, Heather. 1982. "Machiavelli and the Interpretation of the Chiron Myth in France." *Journal of Warburg and Courtauld Institutes* 45: 217–25.

Jaeckel, Hugo. 1995. "What Is Machiavelli Exhorting in his *Exhortatio?*" In *Niccolò Machiavelli: Politico Storico Letterato,* edited by Jean-Jacques Marchand, 59–84. Rome: Salerno Editrice.

Jones, Rosemary Devonshire. 1968. "Some Observations on the Relations between Francesco Vettori and Niccolò Machiavelli during the Embassy to Maximilian I." *Italian Studies* 23: 93–113.

Josephus, Flavius. 1998. *The Antiquities of the Jews.* In *Josephus: The Complete Works.* Translated by William Whiston. Nashville: Thomas Nelson Publishers.

Justin. 1853. *Epitome of the Philippic History of Pompeius Trogus.* Translated, with notes, by John Selby Watson. London: Henry G. Bohn.

Korvela, Paul-Erik. 2006. *The Machiavellian Reformation: An Essay in Political Theory.* Jyväskylä, Fin.: University of Jyväskylä Press.

Kyle, Melvin Grove, ed. 1986. *The International Standard Bible Encyclopedia.* Vol. 1. Grand Rapids, MI: Wm. B. Eerdmans Publishing.

Langton, John, and Mary G. Dietz. 1987. "Machiavelli's Paradox: Trapping or Teaching the Prince." *American Political Science Review* 81, no. 4: 1277–88.

Livy. 1905. *The History of Rome.* 6 vols. Edited by Ernest Rhys and translated by Canon Roberts. London: J. M. Dent & Sons.

———. 1911. *Ab Urbe Condita Libri.* Edited by William Weissenborn and H. J. Muller. Leipzig: Teubner. Perseus Digital Library. http://www.perseus.tufts.edu/hopper.

Lucian. 1896. *Dialogi mortuorum.* Edited by Karl Jacobitz. Leipzig. Perseus Digital Library. http://data.perseus.org/citations/urn:cts:greekLit:tlg 0062.tlg066.perseus-grc1:1.1.

Luther, Martin. 1962. *The Freedom of a Christian.* In *Selections from His Writings,* edited by John Dillenberger, 42–85. New York: Anchor Books.

———. 1962. *Secular Authority: To What Extent It Should Be Obeyed.* In *Selections from His Writings,* edited by John Dillenberger, 363–402. New York: Anchor Books.

Lynch, Christopher. 2003. "Interpretive Essay." In *Art of War,* edited by Christopher Lynch. Chicago: University of Chicago Press.

———. 2006. "Machiavelli on Reading the Bible Judiciously." *Hebraic Political Studies* 1, no. 2: 162–85.

———. 2012. "War and Foreign Affairs in Machiavelli's *Florentine Histories.*" *Review of Politics* 74: 1–26.

Machiavelli, Niccolò. 1984. *Lettere.* Edited by Franco Gaeta. Turin: UTET. First published in 1961.

———. 1988a. *Florentine Histories.* Translated by Harvey C. Mansfield and Laura Banfield. Princeton, NJ: Princeton University Press.

———. 1988b. *The Letters of Machiavelli.* Edited and Translated by Allan Gilbert. Chicago: University of Chicago Press.

———. 1989. *The Chief Works and Others.* 3 vols. Edited by Allan Gilbert. Durham, NC: Duke University Press.

———. 1992. *Tutte Le Opere.* Edited by Mario Martelli. Florence: Sansoni.

———. 1996. *Discourses on Livy.* Edited and translated by Harvey C. Mansfield and Nathan Tarcov. Chicago: University of Chicago Press.

———. 1998. *The Prince.* Translated by Harvey C. Mansfield. Chicago: University of Chicago Press.

———. 2003. *Art of War.* Translated by Christopher Lynch. Chicago: University of Chicago Press.

Maddox, Graham. 2002. "The Secular Reformation and the Influence of Machiavelli." *Journal of Religion* 84, no. 4 (October): 539–62.

Major, Rafael. 2007. "A New Argument for Morality: Machiavelli and the Ancients." *Political Research Quarterly* 60, no. 2: 171–79.

Mansfield, Harvey. 1975a. "Reply to Pocock." *Political Theory* 3, no. 4: 402–5.

———. 1975b. "Strauss's Machiavelli." *Political Theory* 3, no. 4: 372–84.

———. 1979. *Machiavelli's New Modes and Orders: A Study of the "Discourses on Livy."* Ithaca, NY: Cornell University Press.

———. 1981. "Machiavelli's Political Science." *American Political Science Review* 75, no. 2: 293–305.

———. 1996. *Machiavelli's Virtue.* Chicago: University of Chicago Press.

Mayhew, Jonathan. 2007. "A Discourse Concerning Unlimited Submission and Non-Resistance to the Higher Powers" (1750). In *Classics of American Political and Constitutional Thought.* Vol. 1. Edited, with introductions, by Scott J. Hammond, Kevin R. Hardwick, and Howard L. Lubert, 134–37. Indianapolis: Hackett.

McBrayer, Gregory Alan. 2013. "The New Testament of Niccolò Machiavelli: A Revelation for Human Happiness in the Modern World." Paper presented at the annual meeting of the Midwest Political Science Association, Chicago, April, 11–14.

McBrien, Richard P. 1997. *The Lives of the Popes: The Pontiffs from Peter to John Paul II.* New York: Harper Collins.

McCormick, John. 2003. "Machiavelli against Republicanism: On the Cambridge School's 'Gucciardinian Moment.'" *Political Theory* 31, no. 5: 615–43.

———. 2011a. *Machiavellian Democracy.* Cambridge: Cambridge University Press.

———. 2011b. "Prophetic Statebuilding: Machiavelli and the Passion of the Duke." *Reflections* 115, no. 1 (Summer): 1–19.

———. 2014. "The Enduring Ambiguity of Machiavellian Virtue: Cruelty, Crime, and Christianity in *The Prince.*" *Social Research* 81, no. 1 (Spring): 153–64.

———. 2015. "Machiavelli's Inglorious Tyrants: On Agathocles, Scipio, and Unmerited Glory." *History of Political Thought* 36, no. 1 (Spring): 29–52.

Mcintosh, Donald. 1984. "The Modernity of Machiavelli." *Political Theory* 12, no. 2: 184–203.

Mundill, Robert R. 1998. *England's Jewish Solution: Experiment and Expulsion, 1262–1290.* Cambridge: Cambridge University Press.

Nadon, Christopher. 2001. *Xenophon's Prince.* Berkeley: University of California Press.

Najemy, John. 1993. *Between Friends: Discourses of Power and Desire in the Machiavelli-Vettori Letters of 1513–1515.* Princeton, NJ: Princeton University Press.

———. 1999. "Papirius and the Chickens: Or Machiavelli on the Necessity of Interpreting Religion." *Journal of the History of Ideas* 60, no. 4 (October): 659–81.

Nederman, Cary J. 1999. "Amazing Grace: Fortune, God, and Free Will in Machiavelli's Thought." *Journal of the History of Ideas* 62, no. 4 (October): 617–38.

———. 2009. *Machiavelli: A Beginner's Guide.* Oxford: Oneworld Publications.

Newell, W. R. 2013. *Tyranny: A New Interpretation.* Cambridge: Cambridge University Press.

Niccoli, Ottavia. 1990. *Prophecy and People in Renaissance Italy.* Translated by Lydia G. Cochrane. Princeton, NJ: Princeton University Press.

Nicholas, David. 2014. *The Growth of the Medieval City: From Late Antiquity to the Early Fourteenth Century.* New York: Routledge.

Orwin, Clifford. 1978. "Machiavelli's Unchristian Charity." *American Political Science Review* 72, no. 4: 1217–28.

———. 2014. "The Riddle of Cesare Borgia." Paper presented at "Between Past and Future: Reflections on the 500th Anniversary of *The Prince* and the State of Machiavelli Scholarship." College Station: Texas A&M University, February 9.

Ovid. 1922. *Metamorphoses.* Translated and edited by Brookes More. Boston: Corn-hill Publishing.

———. 1931. *Fasti.* Translated by Jamed G. Frazer. Loeb Classical Library. Cambridge, MA: Harvard University Press.

Palmer, Ada. 2014. *Reading Lucretius in the Renaissance.* Cambridge, MA: Harvard University Press.

Palmer, Michael. 2001. "Machiavelli's Inhuman Humanism in *The Prince.*" In *Masters and Slaves: Revisioned Essays in Political Philosophy,* edited by Michael Palmer, 79–98. Lanham, MD: Lexington Books.

Pangle, Thomas L. 1988. *The Spirit of Modern Republicanism.* Chicago: University of Chicago Press.

Parel, Anthony J. 1992. *The Machiavellian Cosmos.* New Haven, CT: Yale University Press.

Patapan, Haig. 2006. *Machiavelli in Love: The Modern Politics of Love and Fear.* Lanham, MD: Lexington Books.

Peters, Edward. 1988. *Inquisition.* Berkeley: University of California Press.

Petrarch. 1996. *Petrarch: The Canzoniere, or Rerum Vulgarium Fragmenta.* Edited and translated by Mark Musa. Bloomington: University of Indiana Press.

Pindar. 1990. *Pythian Odes.* Translated by Diane Arnson Svarlein. Perseus Digital Library. http://data.perseus.org/citations/urn:cts:greekLit:tlg0033.tlg002.perseus-eng1:1.

Plato. 1980. *The Laws.* Translated by Thomas L. Pangle. Chicago: University of Chicago Press.

———. 1991. *The Republic.* Translated by Allan Bloom. New York: Basic Books.

———. 1998. *Apology of Socrates.* In *Four Texts on Socrates: Plato's "Euthyphro," "Apology," and "Crito" and Aristohanes' "Clouds."* Translated with notes by Thomas G. West and Grace Starry West. Ithaca: Cornell University Press.

Plutarch. 1921. *Plutarch's Lives.* 11 vols. With a Translation by Bernadotte Perrin. Cambridge, MA: Harvard University Press.

Pocock, J. G. A. 1975a. *The Machiavellian Moment: Florentine Political Thought and the Atlantic Republican Tradition.* Princeton, NJ: Princeton University Press.

———. 1975b. "Prophet and Inquisitor; or, a Church Built on Bayonets Cannot Stand: A Comment on Mansfield's 'Strauss' Machiavelli.'" *Political Theory* 3, no. 4: 385–401.

Polybius. 1889. Reprint, 1962. *Histories.* Edited by Friedrich Otto Hutsch and translated by Evelyn S. Shuckburgh. Bloomington: Indiana University Press.

Rahe, Paul A. 2009. *Against Throne and Altar: Machiavelli and Political Theory under the English Republic.* New York: Cambridge University Press.

Revard, Stella P. 2009. *Politics, Poetics, and the Pindaric Ode: 1450–1700.* Tempe: Arizona Center for Medieval and Renaissance Studies.

Ridolfi, Roberto. 1963. *The Life of Niccolò Machiavelli.* Chicago: University of Chicago Press.

Savonarola, Girolamo. 2006. *Selected Writings of Girolamo Savonarola: Religion and Politics, 1490–1494.* Translated and edited by Anne Borelli and Maria Pastore Passaro. New Haven, CT: Yale University Press.

Scott, John T., and Vickie B. Sullivan. 1994. "Patricide and the Plot of *The Prince*: Cesare Borgia and Machiavelli's Italy." *American Political Science Review* 88, no. 4: 887–900.

Shell, Susan Meld. 2000. "Machiavelli's Discourse on Language." In *The Comedy and Tragedy of Machiavelli: Essays on the Literary Works*, edited by Vickie B. Sullivan, 78–101. New Haven, CT: Yale University Press.

Skinner, Quentin. 2000. *Machiavelli*. New York: Hill and Wang.

———. 2002. "Machiavelli on Virtue and the Maintenance of Liberty." In *Visions of Politics*. Vol. 2. Edited by Quentin Skinner. Cambridge: Cambridge University Press.

Skinner, Quentin, and Russell Price, ed. and trans. 1988. *Machiavelli: "The Prince."* Cambridge: Cambridge University Press.

Stark, Rodney. 1997. *The Rise of Christianity: How the Obscure, Marginal Jesus Movement Became the Dominant Religious Force in the Western World in a Few Centuries.* New York: Harper Collins.

Statius, Publius Papinius. 1928. *Achilleid*. In *Statius*. Vol. 2. Translated by J. H. Mozley. New York: G. P. Putnam's Sons.

Strauss, Leo. 1957. "Machiavelli's Intention: *The Prince*." *American Political Science Review* 51, no. 1: 13–40.

———. 1958. *Thoughts on Machiavelli*. Chicago: University of Chicago Press.

———. 1987. "Niccolo Machiavelli." In *History of Political Philosophy*, edited by Leo Strauss and Joseph Cropsey, 296–317. Chicago: University of Chicago Press.

Suetonius. 1914. *Lives of Illustrious Men: Grammarians and Rhetoricians*. In *Lives of the Caesars*. Vol. 2. Translated by J. C. Rolfe. Loeb Classical Library. Cambridge, MA: Harvard University Press.

Sullivan, Vickie B. 1996. *Machiavelli's Three Romes: Religion, Human Liberty, and Politics Reformed*. DeKalb: Northern Illinois University Press.

———. 2006. *Machiavelli, Hobbes, and the Formation of a Liberal Republicanism in England*. Cambridge: Cambridge University Press.

———. 2013. "Alexander the Great as 'Lord of Asia' and Rome as His Successor in Machiavelli's *Prince*." *Review of Politics* 75, no. 4 (Fall): 515–37.

Tacitus. 1942. *Annals*. Translated by Alfred John Church. Edited by William Jackson Brondribb. Reprint, New York: Random House.

Tarcov, Nathan. 1982. "Quentin Skinner's Method and Machiavelli's *Prince*." *Ethics* 92: 692–709.

———. 2000. "Machiavelli and the Foundations of Modernity: A Reading of Chapter 3 of *The Prince*." In *Educating the Prince: Essays in Honor of Harvey Mansfield*. Edited by Mark Blitz and William Kristol, 30–44. Lanham, MD: Rowman and Littlefield.

———. 2003. "Arms and Politics in Machiavelli's *Prince*." In *Entre Kant et Kosovo: Études offertes à Pierre Hassner*, edited by Anne-Marie Le Gloannec and Aleksander Smolar, 109–21. Paris: Presses de Sciences PO.

———. 2006. "Law and Innovation in Machiavelli's *Prince*." In *Enlightening Revolutions: Essays in Honor of Ralph Lerner*, edited by Svetozar Minkov, assisted by Stéphane Douard, 77–90. Lanham, MD: Lexington Books.

———. 2007. "Freedom, Republics, and Peoples in Machiavelli's *Prince*." In *Freedom and the Human Person*, edited by Richard Velkley, 122–42. Washington, DC: Catholic University Press of America.

———. 2013a. "Belief and Opinion in Machiavelli's *Prince*." *Review of Politics* 75: 573–86.

———. 2013b. "Machiavelli in *The Prince*: His Way of Life in Question." In *Political Philosophy Cross-Examined*, edited by Thomas Pangle and J. Harvey Lomax, 101–18. New York: Palgrave Macmillan.

———. 2014. "Machiavelli's Critique of Religion." *Social Research* 81, no. 1 (Spring): 193–216.

———. Forthcoming. "Machiavelli's Modern Turn." In *The Modern Turn*, edited by Michael Rohlf. Catholic University of America Press,

Thucydides. 1998. *History of the Peloponnesian War*. Translated by Robert Strassler. New York: Touchstone.

Varotti, Carlo. 2011. "A '*cavalier pensoso*' between Machiavelli and Petrarch." *Humanist Studies in the Digital Age* 1, no. 1: 194–200.

Virgil. 1930. *Aeneid: Books I–VI*. Translated by H. Rushton Fairclough. New York: Loeb Classical Library.

Viroli, Maurizio. 1990. "Machiavelli and the Republican Idea of Politics." *Machiavelli and Republicanism*. Edited by Gisela Bock, Quentin Skinner, and Maurizio Viroli, 143–71. New York: Cambridge University Press.

———. 1998. *Niccolò's Smile: A Biography of Machiavelli*. Translated by Anthony Shugaar. New York: Hill and Wang.

———. 2010. *Machiavelli's God*. Translated by Anthony Shugaar. Princeton, NJ: Princeton University Press.

———. 2014. *Redeeming "The Prince."* Princeton, NJ: Princeton University Press.

Von Vacano, Diego. 2007. *The Art of Power: Machiavelli, Nietzsche, and the Making of Aesthetic Political Theory*. Lanham, MD: Lexington Books.

Warfield, Benjamin B. 1886. "Texts, Sources, and Contents of 'The Two Ways,' or First Section of the Didache." *Bibliotheca Sacra* 43, no. 169 (January): 100–161.

Warner, John M., and John T. Scott. 2011. "Sin City: Augustine and Machiavelli's Reordering of Rome." *Journal of Politics* 73, no. 3: 857–71.

Weinberger, Jerry. 1985. *Science, Faith, and Politics: Francis Bacon and the Utopian Roots of the Modern Age*. Ithaca, NY: Cornell University Press.

Weinstein, Donald. 2011. *Savonarola: The Rise and Fall of a Renaissance Prophet*. New Haven, CT: Yale University Press.

Whitfield, J. H. 1947. *Machiavelli*. Oxford: Basil Blackwell.

Wolin, Sheldon. 1960. "Machiavelli: Politics and the Economy of Violence." In *Politics and Vision: Continuity and Innovation in Western Political Thought*, 195–238. Boston: Little, Brown.

Wood, Neal. 1990. Introduction to *The Art of War*. Translated by Ellis Farneworth, ix–lxxix. Cambridge, MA: Da Capo Press.

Xenophon. 1914. *Cyropaedia*. Vols. 5–6 of *Xenophon in Seven Volumes*. Translated by Walter Miller. Cambridge, MA: Harvard University Press.

———. 1968. *Hiero, or Tyrannicus*. Translated by Marvin Kendrick. In *On Tyranny*, edited by Leo Strauss, 1–20. Ithaca, NY: Cornell University Press.

INDEX